PRIMROSE HILL

Isaac Cruikshank, *Pastimes of Primrose Hill*, wood engraving, September 1791.
A steady stream of Londoners make their was across Marylebone Park to the
hill, already a popular place for an excursion. (*British Museum*)

Primrose Hill

A History

MARTIN SHEPPARD

Primrose Hill: A History

Copyright © Martin Sheppard

The moral rights of the author have been asserted by him
in accordance with the Copyright, Designs and Patents Act 1988

First edition

First published in 2013 by
Carnegie Publishing Ltd
Chatsworth Road
Lancaster LA1 4SL
www.carnegiepublishing.com

British Library Cataloguing-in-Publication data
A catalogue record for this book is available from the British Library

ISBN 978-1-85936-222-8 (*hardback*)

Designed, typeset and originated by Carnegie Publishing
Printed and bound by Jellyfish Solutions

Cover illustration: 'The Perambulator or Matilda's Young Guard', sung by the Music Hall star 'The Great Vance' (1839–88), was a hit in 1865. Its opening lines were 'I've fallen in love with a pretty young girl, My wife I think I'll make her. I met her first up Primrose Hill, As she drove a perambulator'. The original cover illustration to the song, by Alfred Concanen (1839–88), shows a Life Guard, with gloves, spurs and riding crop, about to follow Matilda Baker up a Primrose Hill still without trees. Alfred Vance's 1867 song 'Walking in the Zoo', with its opening 'The Stilton, Sir, the Cheese, the O.K. thing to do, On Sunday afternoon is to toddle in the Zoo', contains a very early use of the Americanism 'O.K.' and of the abbreviation 'Zoo'. (*Camden Local Studies and Archives Centre*)

Contents

Illustrations

Text illustrations

Acknowledgements

The author and publisher are grateful to the following for permission to reproduce images. The British Museum p. ii; Camden Local Studies and Archives Centre (CLSAC), colour plates 1–3, plates 1, 2, 11, pages 84, 90, 103, 144, 165; the Provost and Fellows of Eton College, plates 3 and 4; the Freud Museum, plate 30; the Imperial War Museum, plates 25–29; Alan Jones, colour plate 12; Sandra Lousada, plate 27; the National Archives, colour plate 5; the Royal Artillery Historical Trust, pages 200 and 201; the Royal Photographic Society, plate 10; the Société Française de Photographie, plate 12; the Southampton Estate, pages 114, 121, 122, 123; Westminster City Archives, colour plates 6–8. They are particularly grateful to Roger Cline for allowing them to photograph items from his remarkable collection of material on the history of London.

The author is grateful to the following for permission to reproduce quotations: the Friends of Chalk Farm Library for the reminiscences of Maureen Hawes and Sylvia Ballerini (pp. 202–3); the London Metropolitan Archives for the diary of Anthony Heap (pp. 194, 197, 219, 222); the Royal Artillery Historical Trust for the diary of Harold Danks (pp. 198–201); and Taylor and Francis for F.M.L. Thompson, *English Landed Society in the Nineteenth Century* (pp. 129–30) and *Hampstead* (p. 147).

To Lucy

Preface

THE history of Primrose Hill is a unique reflection of the history of London. Long before it became a public park in 1842, the hill attracted duellists, poets, revolutionaries, soldiers and sportsmen, as well as prospective developers and large numbers of ordinary Londoners. The site of William Blake's vision of the sun, and the subject of one of W.H. Auden's earliest poems, Primrose Hill exercises a hold upon the imagination of everyone who climbs it. A green sanctuary above the city, the hill has given pleasure to millions of people.

Like many other people, I used to wonder how Primrose Hill had survived the tide of building which first surrounded and then swept past it in the nineteenth century. Some years ago I started reading about the growth of London and about the areas around the hill: Belsize Park, Camden Town, Chalk Farm, the Eton Estate, Hampstead, Highgate, Kentish Town, Kilburn, Primrose Hill Village, St John's Wood, St Marylebone, St Pancras and Swiss Cottage. In particular, I investigated the history of Regent's Park, and its predecessor Marylebone Park, and Primrose Hill itself. The result was a book about Regent's Park, published in 2010, which has a short chapter on Primrose Hill. This led me on to the writing of this more ambitious book.

Because of John Nash, and his importance in architectural history, the history of Regent's Park has been written about extensively. In complete contrast, almost no one has written about Primrose Hill. This has meant that, while sometimes having to piece elements of Primrose Hill's history together almost from scratch, I have also often had the pleasure of discovering things for the first time, in original handwritten letters, estate records, official documents, leases, maps, old photographs and long unread books.

I am grateful to everyone who has helped make researching and writing this book so enjoyable. The fruitful suggestion that I should write about Primrose Hill came from Tony Morris. The staff of the British Library, the Camden Local Studies and Archives Centre, Eton College Archives, the Imperial War Museum, Lambeth Palace Library, the London Metropolitan Archives, the National Archives, the National Art Library, the Royal Artillery Museum Library, Warwickshire Record

Office and Westminster City Archives have been uniformly patient, polite and helpful. I am also grateful to these and other archives for permission to reproduce illustrations, as I am to Hilary Bach, Roger Cline, Steve and Siobhan Frost, Sandra Lousada and Juliet Woollcombe. The short biographies available in the *Oxford Dictionary of National Biography* provided a wealth of useful and entertaining information; as, in a darker focus, did the searchable database of *The Proceedings of the Old Bailey, 1674–1913*. The identification of relevant newspaper articles has become far easier due to searchable databases of contemporary newspapers. The very different archives created by Ambrose Heal, now at Camden Local Studies and Archives Centre, and by John Black, on the internet, have both been invaluable. Fortunately from my viewpoint, and also for the residents of the borough, the Camden History Society is the most active and scholarly history society in London. Its annual reviews and other publications have been illuminating and stimulating on a wide range of subjects.

I have profited from discussions with too many people to list them all. I am, however, most grateful to everyone who has helped me in any way. I am indebted, in particular, to those who have read chapters of this book in draft and saved me from mistakes and infelicities: Caroline Barron, Joe Mordaunt Crook, Arnold Harvey, Judy Hillman, Ronald Hutton, Leslie Mitchell, Eva Osborne, Audrey Sheppard, Bob Shoemaker, Michael Thompson, John Tosh and Robin Woolven. Diana Eyre allowed me to see her excellent Architectural Association thesis on Primrose Hill and Caroline Cooper gave me her collection of modern cuttings about the hill. Dee Devine and Vinota Karunasaagarar of the University of Central Lancashire made timely suggestions on how to improve the book. My brother, Peter Sheppard, helped me check the index. Any remaining errors are entirely my own responsibility.

I thank my wife, Lucy, and my daughters, Catherine, Eleanor and Matilda, for their love, support and tolerance. Alistair Hodge of Carnegie Publishing is an exemplary publisher with whom it has been a great pleasure to work. Rachel Clarke, also at Carnegie, has dealt with all questions about the text and illustrations of the book with supreme confidence and professionalism. Anna Goddard has overseen the completion of the book and the design of its stunning dust-wrapper.

My interest in history was originally kindled near Primrose Hill, by an exceptional teacher at the Hall School, Mr R.G. Bathurst. I have shared the completion of this book with my dog, Anna, who has accompanied me on daily walks on Primrose Hill. She and I have also recently completed two walking circuits around London, the Capital Ring and the London Loop, in all a distance of 228 miles. Together, we discovered how much delightful countryside still remains within easy range of London. Many of the most attractive places on these walks were saved from being built over by a mixture of historical accident, local effort and good fortune, as was Primrose Hill.

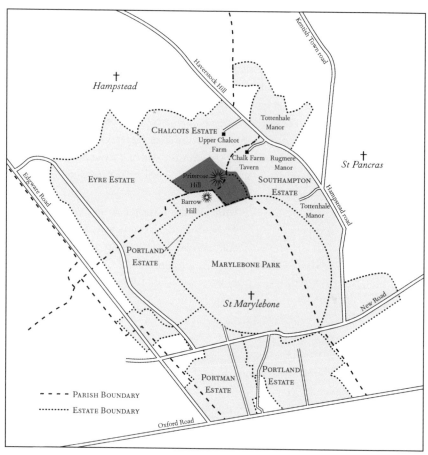

In 1800 Primrose Hill, and its neighbour, Barrow Hill, stood amongst fields. The only nearby building was the Chalk Farm Tavern, reached by a lane off the Hampstead road. To the south was Marylebone Park, established by Henry VIII for hunting in the 1530s. After the Restoration, it was divided into farms and used to fatten cattle. Other than scattered housing along the main roads, the built-up area of London was still almost all to the south of the New Road.

Primrose Hill, which became a popular place of excursion in the eighteenth century, was divided between three parishes, Hampstead, St Marylebone and St Pancras, marked by boundary stones on the hill. The parishes reflected the boundaries of earlier manors.

Stella, my Muse! whose beauty prompts the song,
To whom the poet and the lays belong ...
To Primrose Hill lead on the flow'ry way,
And thence the matchless scenes around survey.
Mean while the Muse shall sing, with fond surprise,
The various prospects, as by turns they rise ...

Anon., 'The Prospect from Primrose Hill',
Gentleman's Magazine, June 1749

1

The Hill without Primroses

ONE DAY in 1855, a six-year-old boy living in Islington demanded to be taken to the countryside. In response, 'My Father, after a little reflection, proposed to take me to Primrose Hill. I had never heard of the place, and names have always appealed directly to my imagination. I was in the highest degree delighted, and could hardly restrain my impatience. ... I expected to see a mountain absolutely carpeted with primroses ...' The boy was the future author and critic Edmund Gosse. He is best known today for his autobiographical *Father and Son* (1907), a sustained denunciation of his father, Philip Gosse, one of the leading naturalists of the Victorian Age. Not surprisingly, the expedition turned out to be a disaster:

> But at length, as we walked from the Chalk Farm direction, a miserable acclivity stole into view – surrounded, even in those days, on most sides by houses, with its grass worn to the buff by millions of boots, and resembling what I meant by 'the country' about as much as Poplar resembles Paradise. We sat down on a bench at its inglorious summit, whereupon I burst into tears, and in a heart-rending whisper sobbed, 'Oh! Papa, let us go home!' [1]

Although determined not to enjoy the expedition on which his father was taking him, Edmund Gosse's disappointment at the absence of primroses on Primrose Hill was more understandable. That primroses once bloomed there is beyond doubt. According to A.D. Webster, for many years Superintendent of Regent's Park and Primrose Hill:

> The name Primrose Hill obviously arose from the growth of primroses there, and in an old list of wild plants in the Hampstead district the *Primula vulgaris*, or primrose, is included. But other evidence is not wanting that the primrose was at one time abundant on the hill, as in 1907 I had a letter from a lady, eighty years old, who remembers filling a basket with primroses, gathered between Primrose Hill and the adjoining Zoo boundary, prior to 1838. From this it may be inferred

that up to about sixty years ago primroses were abundant on the hill, and the connection between these and the name of the place will be obvious.*

The likely explanation for their disappearance is that primroses flourished in the hedgerows and ditches which had once divided the hill into fields. When, in the 1830s and 1840s, these hedges were cut down and the hill became a single piece of grassland, the primroses quickly disappeared without their damp and shady habitat. The large numbers of visitors to the hill, and the Victorian passion for picking and pressing flowers, cannot have helped.†

This, however, was not the last to be heard of primroses on the hill. A correspondent writing to the local newspaper in 1972 was by no means the only person to advocate their reintroduction:

> May I suggest something innocent and humble, non-controversial, above all, quite cheap, but which would bring glory to us all? It is simply this: to plant primroses now and lavishly on Primrose Hill. I suggest that all gardeners should plant primroses on the hill forthwith. They will then flower next spring. (They must be planted under the trees since they require some shade.) Too many things today have false names. Would we like it if some of our thousands of visitors were to bring an action under the Trade Descriptions Act? Let us make an honest hill of Primrose Hill.[2]

In May 1981 the London Wildlife Trust asked permission for Lord Melchett, the Opposition spokesman in the House of Lords, and Richard Mabey, the conservationist and author, to plant a primrose on the hill to mark the trust's own inauguration. Strangely, the Department of the Environment refused permission, on the curious grounds that it classified a primrose as a tree. Even when informed that a primrose was only three or four inches tall, the department refused to change its mind, viewing the proposed event as a publicity stunt. This led to an article, entitled 'The Hill with No Primrose', on the front page of the *Observer* and to considerable publicity elsewhere.[3] The London Wildlife Trust, forced to

---

* A.D. Webster, *The Regent's Park and Primrose Hill: History and Antiquities* (London, 1911), p. 84. Webster, however, admits that a few primroses were still to be seen: 'Primrose Hill was at one time famous for the primroses which flourished on the shady banks of its hedges and ditches, but today, except a few clumps which were reintroduced some years ago by way of experiment, not a specimen can be found.' Ibid., p. 99. In contrast, James Leigh Hunt in 1837 already referred to the hill as 'a place that once had primroses', in 'Primrose Hill', *The Idler and Breakfast-Table Companion*, 27 May 1837, p. 23.

† Since then, several attempts have been made to reintroduce primroses on Primrose Hill – and indeed a few primroses may be found by those who look carefully in the hedgerow near Barrow Hill Reservoir. The deputy manager of Regent's Park used to plant two hundred primroses a year in the early 1990s. Information from Francis Duncan.

look at another way of promoting its work, toyed 'with the idea of introducing a nightingale into Berkeley Square'.[*]

While Primrose Hill survived the loss of its eponymous flowers, how early it acquired its name is uncertain.[4] It was of course not the only hill to be given the name, as many other Primrose Hills are to be found throughout England. The distinction of being the nearest hill to the centre of the country's capital city has, however, long made London's Primrose Hill – with or without its primroses – by far the best known of all of them.

Few people, fortunately, have had so negative a view of the hill as the young Edmund Gosse. A more typical reaction was that of an Italian visitor in 1875:

> From its summit the eye ranges over the immense mass of houses, public buildings, and churches. ... The rising of the sun from Primrose Hill, with all the interesting associations, is not to be described; it must be seen to have an idea of its interest and grandeur.[5]

It has also appealed to those with a literary taste. According to Edmund Clerihew Bentley:

> Miss Dorothy Sayers
> Never cared about the Himalayas.
> The height that gave her a thrill
> Was Primrose Hill.

With no conspicuous features other than its own summit, Primrose Hill is nevertheless memorable. Its history, in its own right and as part of the history of London, is also a remarkable one.

---

[*] The *Primula vulgaris*, the common or English primrose (though found across Europe), flowers early in the spring, its appearance heralding the end of winter. Its English name derives from the Latin *prima rosa* or the French *primerose*, meaning 'first rose'. It was widely held to be a magical flower and to have healing powers. It is also remarkable for having two types of flowers, one called 'pin-eyed' and the other 'thrum-eyed', on separate plants. Picking or removing primroses from the wild is illegal under the Wildlife and Countryside Act (1981).

2

Above the City

L O N D O N was founded by the Romans. They built their first fort and settlement upon two small hills, later known as Cornhill and Ludgate Hill, on either side of the Walbrook stream, and on the north bank of the Thames.[1] Following the Roman withdrawal from Britain, and the reintroduction of Christianity to Kent by St Augustine in 597, Mellitus, the first bishop of London, established a church on Ludgate Hill in 604.[2] Rebuilt several times over the following thousand years, this was dedicated to St Paul. It was to be the site of the great medieval cathedral of St Paul's, constructed between 1087 and 1314. Old St Paul's was 585 feet long, the third longest church in Europe; and, with a spire 489 feet high, it was at one time the second tallest building in the world. While the medieval cathedral was destroyed in the Great Fire of 1666, its successor, designed by Sir Christopher Wren and built between 1675 and 1710, was at 365 feet high the tallest building in London until the second half of the twentieth century. From the hills around London, it was easily the city's most conspicuous landmark.[*]

Unlike Rome, London is not a city built on hills: the two little mounds of Londinium hardly bear comparison with the Capitoline or the Palatine. The ground rises slowly rather than precipitously north and south of the Thames, where it is interspersed by shallow valleys through which the rivers and streams of London once flowed. The waters of the Fleet, the Tyburn, the Walbrook and the Westbourne have long since disappeared underground, although the Ravensbourne and Wandle are still visible to the south of the Thames, as are the Brent and the Lea to the west and east of London.[†] As well as Cornhill and Ludgate Hill,

---

[*] Old St Paul's was the world's second tallest building for twelve years between the destruction by fire of the spire of Lincoln Cathedral, reputedly 525 feet high, in 1549 and the loss of its own spire to lightning in 1561. (The world's tallest building during these years was the church of St Olaf, Tallinn, which was 521 feet high.) Between 1561 and 1666 Old St Paul's is familiar in images of London with its tower but not its spire. Nothing survives of Mellitus's church, so its siting on Ludgate Hill, though likely, is not certain.

[†] Other London rivers, mostly now invisible, include the Beverley Brook, the Effra, the Falcon, the Neckinger and the Peck Pyl Brook. The Beck, the Pool and the Quaggy (also known as the

which are no more than sixty feet above the river, London has a variety of other minor hills, now mostly covered in housing. Three miles north of Westminster Abbey, and three miles north-west of St Paul's, is Primrose Hill, 219 feet high.[3] While behind it the land sloping up to Hampstead and Highgate soon rises higher, Primrose Hill has the finest view over the heart of London from any vantage point close to the city.

In the form 'Prymrose Hill', the name of the hill was recorded in 1586. In that year the title of a ballad, 'A Sweete and Courtly Songe of the Flowers that Grow on Prymrose Hill', was entered in the register of the Stationers Company, but no copy of the ballad itself has survived.[4] Its second literary appearance is in one of the Roxburghe Ballads. Not inappropriately, it made its first appearance as a venue for courtship:

> In the pleasant month of May, a young man met a maid
> On Primrose Hill so gay, and thus to her he said:
> 'Fair maid, sit down by me upon this flowerie place,
> Fine pastime thou shalt see within a little space.'

Over the following verses, matters progress swiftly, with a not unexpected result by the end of the ballad:

> Yet she did not forget the sport at Primrose Hill;
> He plai'd her such a fit, makes her to love him still.
> 'If I might have my will, if that it proves a boy,
> His name is Primrose Hill, his mother's only joy.'
>
> Fair maidens, now be wise, for fear this be your lot:
> If men do you intice, say this – 'I know you not!'[5]

Primrose Hill was originally one of a pair of hills, with Barrow Hill standing next to it at 175 feet high. Also known as Little Primrose Hill, Barrow Hill effectively disappeared when its top was levelled in the first half of the nineteenth century to make way for a reservoir. Primrose Hill itself was sometimes referred to as Barrow Hill by mistake and was also known as Greenberry Hill, while Barrow Hill was also occasionally referred to as Battle Hill.[6] Because of Primrose Hill's dramatic rise above the level of the surrounding land, many people have wondered

---

Kyd Brook) are tributaries of the Ravensbourne. The Brent, also known as the Dollis Brook, with its tributary the Mutton Brook, now flows into the Welsh Harp. After leaving the Welsh Harp, it reaches the Grand Union Canal near Hanwell and the Thames at Brentford. Stephen Inwood, *Historic London: An Explorer's Companion* (London, 2008), pp. 375–95.

whether it was raised by human hand, something reinforced by Barrow Hill's name, which conjures up a place of ancient burial. Others have believed that Primrose Hill is very recent, made from the spoil taken from the Regent's Canal or from the London and Birmingham Railway, both constructed nearby in the first half of the nineteenth century. In reality, both Primrose Hill and Barrow Hill are the result of natural forces.

About fifty million years ago, the area of the London Basin was covered by warm seas, supporting subtropical plants, fish and reptiles.[7] These seas laid down a thick layer of clay, up to two hundred feet deep, on the older limestone and sandstone beds beneath.[*] Clay, a mixture of tiny particles made by the wearing and erosion of rocks, has a variety of forms and types, depending on how it was formed and what materials went into its making. London clay, which has a bluish colour but turns brown when exposed to the air, is stiff rather than solid.[†]

The creation of Primrose Hill itself is the result of comparatively recent geological history, only dating back between 450,000 and 100,000 years. The glaciers of the Ice Age reached their southernmost point north of London, near Finchley and Alexandra Palace. Subsequent thawing released huge volumes of meltwater, which carved valleys through the Northern Heights. Great rivers ran towards the Thames, the course of which had itself been pushed further south by the glaciers.[‡] Two of these rivers created the valleys of the Fleet and the Tyburn. Areas between their valleys, which had offered greater resistance to the flow of water, were left behind as hills.

Primrose Hill itself was once capped by a top layer similar to Hampstead Heath, where Claygate beds and Bagshot sands still remain. Although Primrose Hill's own capping has long since disappeared, its one-time existence is the likely explanation of the survival of the hill. The Tyburn, or its early version, cut a course through St John's Wood and a branch of it separated Primrose Hill from

---

[*] Although the London clay holds palaeontological records of the flora and fauna of the ages before the seas receded, nothing has as yet been recovered from Primrose Hill itself which allows the date of its formation to be calculated more precisely than that of the general formation of the clay as a whole. The top of Barrow Hill was removed in the making of a reservoir on it in 1825 without any archaeological finds being recorded.

[†] Nearer to the Thames, brickearth overlies the youngest of the Thames gravels. This brickearth originated as a wind-blown loess or 'rock flour' of fine particles of clay, sand and chalk, blown from further north towards London as the most recent Ice Age began to retreat about twenty thousand years ago. It is ideal for making bricks and provided the main building material for much of London, a city without its own building stone and to which stone therefore had to be brought from a distance, usually by river. London clay itself can only be used to make bricks if sand and chalk, together with domestic ash and cinder, are added to it.

[‡] The early Thames, much wider than it is now, ran north-east along what is now the Colne Valley.

its neighbour, Barrow Hill. The south of the hill was given its distinctive slope by another watercourse, the now-vanished St John's Wood Stream, flowing east from the Tyburn towards the Fleet.

If a borehole were to be dug directly down from the summit of Primrose Hill, under the shallow soil on the surface it would very soon reach horizontal layers of London clay, occasionally interbedded with silt (where the clay is mixed with sand), 140 feet thick. Beneath that, and well below the surface of the lowest part of the park, would be found a sixty-foot layer of mixed clays, silts and sands. Below this lies a 400-foot thick layer of the white chalk which forms the floor of the London Basin.[8]

As clay does not absorb water, surface rainwater runs off it down the nearest slope. In wet weather, Primrose Hill is slippery on its slopes and boggy at its bottom. The flow of water is uneven, due to the springs which flow from the silts and sands interbedded with the impervious clay. This keeps the slopes moist and makes them prone to slippage. In botanical terms, the damp typical of clay encourages both mosses and buttercups, including primroses. In dry weather, the clay dries out and shrinks, causing deep cracks. Unlike land nearer the modern Thames, the area around Primrose Hill does not have a layer of gravel above the clay. This made it unsuitable for early habitation.

After the end of the last Ice Age, around ten thousand years ago, much of the landscape was wooded. Primrose Hill was part of the Middlesex Forest, but many of the trees in the area to the north of London, including those on the hill, were cut down during the Anglo-Saxon period or in the two hundred years following the Norman Conquest.[9] By 1300 the land was no longer covered by dense woodland. This had been replaced by a mixture of trees and shrubs interspersed with grassland and fields. Although only the owners had the right to fell timber, local inhabitants, as 'commoners', had the right to collect brushwood by coppicing and to feed their pigs on the edible seeds and fruit known collectively as mast. One indication that the area was not heavily wooded is that the number of pigs recorded for the area in Domesday Book (1086) is low.[10] Primrose Hill itself, however, may have had more trees than the areas to the south and east of it. To its west, the woodland in the sixteenth century remained thick enough to hide Anthony Babington after the failure of his conspiracy in 1586 to kill Queen Elizabeth I, and to have given reality to the name St John's Wood into the following century.

There were no roads, other than rough tracks, near Primrose Hill. The main roads north from London were all at a distance from the hill. The Roman road of Watling Street, which became the Edgware Road, was over a mile to its west, while Ermine Street, the Roman road to York, was well to its east.[11] The nearest road, probably little more than a track, was the one running up Haverstock Hill towards Hampstead. The River Fleet, rising near Hampstead, was also a considerable distance to the east of the hill. The small River Tyburn, now flowing around the west of Barrow Hill, and with two of its branches rising to the south and north of Primrose Hill, ran down to the Thames near Thorney Island at Westminster. Along its course were a number of ponds.

There were early settlements along the main roads leading north and west from London at Islington and Tyburn, while Hampstead dates from before the millennium.[12] Later villages grew up at Kentish Town and St Marylebone. It is possible, but by no means certain, that a village called Rugmore existed during the Middle Ages on the future site of the Zoo. It is mentioned in Domesday Book, and in a document of 1251, but any settlement had disappeared by 1535. It is most likely that it was abandoned after the Black Death of the mid-fourteenth century. Although the village itself has left no archaeological traces, its inhabitants may have been responsible for the lynchets, a sign of medieval cultivation, which have been detected on the south-west slopes of Primrose Hill.[*]

If the early records of human activity on or near Primrose Hill are sparse, this does not mean that the hill's existence was unaccounted for. Ownership of the land around London dates back to long before the Norman Conquest, with land being held from the king in units known as hundreds and manors. Much of London north of the Thames was in the hundred of Ossulstone, a name derived from Oswald's Stone, one of the divisions of Middlesex.[†] Ossulstone was divided into manors, some of which were also subdivided into other manors. Primrose Hill itself was split between three manors. Most of it was part of the manor of Hampstead, held by the Abbot of Westminster.[13] The south-west of the hill was in the manor of Tyburn, held by the Abbess of Barking, while the south-east was in the manor of Rugmere, held by the canons of St Paul's and forming one part of the larger manor of St Pancras.[14] These divisions were later reflected in parochial boundaries, evidence of which can still be seen on the hill in the form of stone and iron boundary markers indicating the parishes of Hampstead, St Marylebone and St Pancras.

---

[*] According to the Greater London Historic Buildings, Sites and Monuments Record, 'Fragments of two or three possible lynchets survive as earthworks on the SW slopes of Primrose Hill up to a maximum height of 0.3m. However the area has been heavily disturbed by WWII military activity and the RCHME level 1 survey was inconclusive', ML066399. For Rugmore, 'There is no evidence from aerial photographs or on the ground to confirm or deny the site of the village conclusively', ML09205. Prehistoric burnt flint has been found just to the west of the hill, MLO74880. A branch of the Tyburn, which would have made habitation possible, rises on the site of the Zoo.

[†] Or possibly Oswulf's Stone. The stone itself, an unmarked, pre-Roman monolith at Tyburn, disappeared in 1869 and has not been seen since. The other Middlesex hundreds were Edmonton, Elthorne, Gore, Isleworth and Spelthorne. Victoria County History, *A History of the County of Middlesex*, vi (London, 1989), pp. 1–5.

While the land was formally held by ecclesiastical institutions, it was in practice leased out to tenants, often for long terms. Once leased out, sometimes at low annual rents which changed little over the centuries, landholdings proved difficult to recover and became, in effect, independent of their original owners. The Abbess of Barking had lost control of the manor of Tyburn to tenants, the de Sanford family, by 1150. The effective ownership of Hampstead also passed from the Abbot of Westminster to Henry II's butler, Alexander de Barentin, in the last quarter of the twelfth century. When he died in 1191, de Barentin left the south-east part of the manor, known as Chalcots, as a charitable bequest to the hospital of St James near Westminster. In 1258 Chalcots, which contained most of Primrose Hill, was described as having a house, some arable land and forty acres of woodland.[15]

We know the names of the holders of the manor of Rugmere, all canons of St Paul's. At Domesday in 1086, Rugmere consisted of two hides of land, supporting one and a half ploughs, plus woodland worth four shillings. With a total value of 35 shillings, the manor was held by Canon Ralph.[16] Even during the Middle Ages, the area was used for feeding cattle. In 1377 the reeve of the manor, John atte Forde, was paid £7 for the 'pasturage of divers cattle'. He also accounted for a much lower sum for paying men to mow and spread grass.[17]

The main owner of Primrose Hill for over three hundred years was the hospital of St James, which stood on the site of the future St James's Palace. According to John Stow, the Tudor historian of London, 'The citizens of London, time out of mind, founded an hospitall of Saint James in the fieldes for leprous women of their citie'.[18] Leprosy, which had been brought to England from the Middle East during the Crusades, caused an epidemic that reached its height in the thirteenth century but then declined. The sick of St James's Hospital (to a maximum of sixteen) were restricted to 'leprous girls or virgins and no others'.[19] In addition, there were to be up to eight brothers, from whose number a master was elected. Brothers and sisters were to wear one colour, russet or black, and to say the *Ave Maria* and *Pater Noster* sixty times a day.

Over the years, as the incidence of leprosy declined, high standards of religious observance proved hard to sustain. The hospital was under the ecclesiastical supervision of Westminster Abbey. A series of visitations by abbey officials in the years after 1317 discovered the master enjoying special beer and the brothers frequenting taverns and visiting the sisters' rooms. Later accusations included sexual incontinence by both brothers and sisters, and even the murder of a woman by the master. All the brothers and sisters except one, however, succumbed to the Black Death, and by the late fourteenth century the almost empty hospital was being rented out to a wealthy widow. By this time, after considerable wrangling, the kings had established rights of visitation and presentation at the expense of the abbots of Westminster. It was the latter right that Henry VI exercised in 1449 to give perpetual custody of the hospital and its lands to his new foundation of Eton.[20] The master's residence became the Provost of Eton's town house. This began Eton's long connection with Primrose Hill.

At the Reformation, Henry VIII confiscated the lands belonging to the monasteries. In 1531, even before the more general dissolution, he forced Eton to exchange the hospital of St James and most of its land in Westminster for land in Kent and Sussex, although he allowed the college to keep the Chalcots Estate. As the land in Westminster amounted to 185 acres in what later became the most fashionable part of London, there is good reason behind the Eton rhyme: 'Henry Octavus took more than he gave us.'[21] According to Stow, on the site of the hospital itself, 'the king builded there a goodly mannor, annexing thereunto a parke, closed about with a wall of bricke, now called Saint James Parke, serving indifferently to the said mannor, and to the mannor or palace of White Hall'.[22] Later in the 1530s, to the north of the village of St Marylebone, Henry created Marylebone Park, stocking it with deer for hunting. Its 554 acres did not conform to existing manorial boundaries, and the land used to make it up was taken from a number of ecclesiastical and lay owners, some of whom were compensated. Eton now lost six acres of meadow, 'lying on Chawkehill', and fourteen acres of wood from its Chalcots Estate to the new park, which now became Primrose Hill's immediate neighbour to the south.*

The park, soon enclosed by banks and fences to keep in the deer, was used for hunting for the next 120 years. During the English Civil War, Charles I leased the park to two of his supporters in return for gunpowder. Their claims were, unsurprisingly, ignored by the republican government which abolished the monarchy immediately after the execution of Charles in January 1649. Desperate for money to pay the arrears of its army, the Rump Parliament put all royal property, including the crown lands, up for sale. Marylebone Park, which at this point included three lodges, a hunting stand, stables and orchards, 124 deer and 16,297 trees, fetched £13,215 6s. 8d. Its new owners, mostly officers in the parliamentary

---

* In an account of the land taken to make up Marylebone Park, the land acquired from the Provost and Fellows of Eton College is listed as six acres of meadow, valued at four shillings an acre, and fourteen acres of woodland, valued at twenty pence per acre annually, giving together an annual value of 47s. 4d. The land taken from the Master of the Prebend of Rugmere comprised twenty-three acres of mixed arable and pasture, forty acres of meadow, sixty-six acres of pasture and sixteen acres of woodland, together worth £24 13s. 6d. annually. The Master of the Prebend of Tottenhale or Tottenham lost fifty-five acres worth £11 0s. 0d. annually. National Archives, SC1 23/65, translated in Ann Saunders, *Regent's Park: From 1086 to the Present* (2nd edn, London, 1981), pp. 177–80; see also, ibid., p. 21. Eton's estate and hill appear in the list of place-names in John Norden, *Speculum Britanniae, the First Part: An Historicall and Chorographicall Discription of Middlesex* (London, 1593), p. 17, as 'Chalcot or Chalkhill'. On the accompanying map it is shown as 'Chalcote' and marked as being a 'house of knightes, gents etc.', ibid., map 1.

army, uncertain as to how long their tenure would last, let much of the land on short leases and made sure of a speedy profit by carrying out, or allowing, the wholesale felling of timber in the park.[23]

On the restoration of Charles II in 1660, once the recent owners of the park had been ejected, the lease of the park was granted, on easy terms, to Sir Henry Bennet, later first Earl of Arlington, one of Charles's closest advisers. Arlington was also granted advantageous leases in St John's Wood, as well the lease of the manor of Tottenhale to the east of the park. Disparked in 1668, Marylebone Park became farmland for the next century and a half. The lease of the park passed from Arlington through various hands and was split between several holders before coming together in 1789 into the hands of the dukes of Portland.

The dukes were also the leading landowners in the parish of St Marylebone. Still predominantly fields in 1700, and best known for Marylebone Gardens, a place of entertainment, what had until then been a small village around a church grew rapidly during the eighteenth century. Its principal developer was Edward Harley, the second Earl of Oxford, whose daughter and heir, Margaret, married William Bentinck, the second Duke of Portland, in 1734.[24] The duke's new London estate, essentially the ancient manor of Tyburn less Marylebone Park, included not only the extremely valuable land between Oxford Street and the park but also Barrow Hill Farm, to the north of the park.[25]

The most sensational event in the history of Primrose Hill took place in the final years of Charles II's reign. On Thursday 17 October 1678, two men, William Bromwell, a baker, and John Walters, a farrier, were walking from St Marylebone towards Primrose Hill when they saw 'a sword and belt, and a stick and a pair of gloves lying together hard by the hedge side, but they went not near to medle with them, supposing they had belong'd to some person that was gone into the ditch to ease himself'.[26] Reaching their destination, a nearby tavern called the White House, they told its landlord, John Rawson, what they had seen. Rawson was puzzled but told them that 'there had been several soldiers thereabout this week a hedgehog hunting'. He thought it possible that 'some of them may have left them behind them'.[27]

When the three men went to investigate, they found all the items except the sword (which they saw now was only a scabbard). As Rawson stooped to pick them up, 'he thought he saw some thing like a man in a ditch hard by, and so going to the ditch, there they saw a man lying, as they suppos'd upon his belly, with a sword run thorow him, and the point appearing about seven or eight inches above his back'.[28] The men immediately went to fetch a constable, who came quickly, accompanied by several neighbours. The body was lying in what was a remote place:

As to the place, it was in a ditch on the south side of Primrose Hill, surrounded with divers closes, fenced in with high mounds and ditches; no road near, only some deep dirty lanes, made only for the conveniency of driving cows and such like cattle in and out of the grounds; and those very lanes not coming near 500 yards of the place ...[29]

The man was soon identified as Sir Edmund Berry Godfrey, a Protestant magistrate and timber merchant, who had been knighted for his heroic conduct during the Great Plague of 1665 and who had been missing since Saturday 12 October, five days earlier. That morning Godfrey had gone out of his house in Greens Lane in the Strand. He was seen not long afterwards near St Marylebone and had met one of churchwardens of the parish of St Martin-in-the-Fields about some business at twelve the same day.[30]

An inquest held at the White House established that Godfrey had not been killed by his sword. Two surgeons, Nicholas Cambridge and Zachary Skillarne, who viewed the body at the inquest, were sure that he had been killed elsewhere and that

the wounds they found about him, were not the cause of his death, but that he was suffocated before the wounds were made. And that which may fully perswade any person of the truth thereof is, that there was not one drop of blood to be found in the place where he lay, not the least appearance of any such thing: though the ditch was dry, and it might have been easily seen, if there had been any. Another thing was, that the very bottom of the soles of his shoes were as clean as if he had just come out of his own chamber; which was an evident sign that he was carried thither.[31]

They also claimed that 'his face was of a fresh colour, though in his life time very pale, somewhat swell'd, and a green circle about his neck, as if he had been strangled, his blood settled about his neck, throat, and the upper part of his brest'.[32]

Nor was robbery the motive:

The constable having caus'd the body to be removed to the White House, and knowing it to be the body of Sir Edmondberry Godfrey, he caused his pockets to be searched, and found in one of them in one paper six guineys, and in another paper four broad pieces of gold, and a half crown; and in the other pocket two rings, whereof one was a diamond, one guiney, and four pound in silver, and two small pieces of gold, and one ring he had upon one of his fingers: his pocket book (in which he used to take notes of examinations) being only missing.[33]

That the body had only recently arrived on Primrose Hill was confirmed by evidence given by one of the coroner's jury. He claimed 'that a servant of his mother's (who is the owner of the ground where the body lay) with a butcher and two boys, made a very strict and narrow search in all parts of that ground for a calf that was missing, upon Monday and Tuesday last, and at that time there lay no dead body, belt, gloves, stick, or other things there'.[34] A man called Thomas Morgan had been at Primrose Hill on the Monday 'to dresse a horse and washed his hands in a pond, and saw nothing'.[35] Robert Fawcet later claimed that he had been hunting there, with his pack of hounds, on Tuesday and Wednesday, when he had beaten the area where the body was found in search of quarry, without finding Godfrey.[36] How the body had been brought there remained unclear. It was claimed that it was 'impossible for any man on horseback, with a dead corpse before him, at midnight to approach, unless gaps were made in the mounds, as the constable and his assistants found from experience when they came on horseback thither'.[37]

The discovery of the body provoked a national crisis. The fact that Sir Edmund's notebook, in which he had been accustomed to take down depositions made before him as a magistrate, was missing allowed room for wild speculation. An informer, Titus Oates, had recently claimed that he had evidence of a plot by Catholics to kill the king and leading Protestants. Oates and his associate, Israel Tonge, had a month before the magistrate's disappearance made a deposition before Godfrey about this, as well as bringing it to the attention of Charles II and his council. Although the king and the council had been sceptical about Oates's claims, the discovery of Godfrey's body quickly provoked public alarm and then widespread paranoia. Oates now claimed that Godfrey had been murdered because he had been about to disclose details of the plot. These sensational claims were highly sensitive at a time when feelings were running high at the prospect of a Roman Catholic – the king's brother, James, Duke of York – succeeding to the throne. Charles II, although he had many illegitimate children, for whom he made generous provision, had no legitimate son or daughter. In an atmosphere of increasing hysteria, and ever wilder claims by Oates, numerous Catholics were tried for treason and condemned to death.[38]

Another informer, the Catholic Miles Prance, then accused three of his co-religionists of the murder: Henry Berry, porter at Somerset House; Robert Green, cushionman of the queen's chapel there; and Lawrence Hill, servant to Dr Godden, the treasurer of the chapel.[39] Somerset House, the occasional residence of the wife of Charles II, Catherine of Braganza, and once the residence of Charles I's wife, Henrietta Maria, both of whom were Catholic, was widely seen as a hotbed of popery. Prance, whose testimony was almost certainly forced out of him in the Tower of London, claimed that Godfrey had been lured into Somerset House by the trio and strangled there. After carrying the body from room to room there during the following days, they had moved it by sedan chair and then horseback to Primrose Hill. Tried and convicted, the three men were executed at Tyburn. Their names, put together, made Greenberry Hill, an alternative name for Primrose Hill.[40] Gradually, however, the hysteria declined and the spate of treason trials came to an end. When James II came to the throne in 1685, Oates was tried for perjury. Sentenced to a whipping intended to kill him, he survived.[41] Prance, who had by this time withdrawn his evidence, was pilloried.

What had actually happened to Sir Edmund Berry Godfrey was never solved at the time and is unlikely to be solved now. Like the murders of Jack the Ripper, it has generated a wide range of possible suspects, from those closely involved with Godfrey, including Oates himself, to those with no obvious connection with him. The circle of suspicion extends to the leading politician of the day, the Earl of Osborne; to a homicidal maniac, the Earl of Pembroke; and to Colonel Blood, the man responsible for attempting to steal the Crown Jewels from the Tower of London in 1671.[42] Some have believed it was indeed carried out by Catholics, with the Jesuits as the prime suspects, or perhaps by Miles Prance himself, while others claim it was simply the work of a footpad with an unusual and notable disregard for money. Another possibility, although it would have involved Godfrey strangling rather than hanging himself, is that it was suicide. He was known to have been in a state of great anxiety before his death. If it was suicide, his brothers would have had a motive for making his death appear as murder, as the property of a suicide was forfeit to the crown. The very substantial sum of money found in his pockets (more than a labourer's yearly wage) may have been intended to show that the murder was *not* the result of a robbery.

Whatever the truth of Godfrey's death, the incidental details disclosed in the accounts of the case provide valuable evidence about Primrose Hill in 1678. The White House, the tavern to which Godfrey's body was taken, has usually been described as a predecessor of the Chalk Farm Tavern, on the eastern side of the hill towards the Hampstead road. It is far more likely that the body, having been discovered to the south of Primrose Hill, was carried to its west. An early eighteenth-century map of St Marylebone shows the fields to the north of Marylebone Park.[43] Here Thomas Baker, who also held three fields and a hay-yard in St Marylebone, itself still consisting overwhelmingly of fields, leased 63 acres divided into five fields: Upper Primrose Hill, Primrose Hill, White House Mead, White House Field and Wheat Field. (Neither of the first two of these was on what is now known as Primrose Hill, though Baker also farmed that in 1708.) Just north of White House Mead on the same map is a building marked 'The White House'. This is almost certainly the White House Tavern to which Godfrey's body was taken.[44] As the body was found 'in a dry ditch upon the south side of Primrose Hill, about two fields distant from the White House',[45] it was therefore found in either 'Primrose Hill' or 'Upper Primrose Hill', the fields which lay on the obvious route from the centre of London.[46]

The White House was clearly not much of an establishment, being described as no more than an alehouse, 'with no accommodation, nor hangings, nor scarce a window'.[47] It was large enough, however, to accommodate the inquest, with a jury of eighteen, as well as many other Londoners, including the historian Gilbert Burnet, who came to see Godfrey's body. He reported:

> There were many drops of white wax lights on his breeches; which he never used himself. And since only persons of quality, or priests, use those lights, this made all people conclude in whose hands he must have been. ... The body lay two days exposed, many going to see it, who went away much moved with the sight.[48]

Curiously, the White House was well known to the principal witness in the trial of Green, Berry and Hill, Miles Prance, who had attended meetings of fellow Catholics there. The area was clearly used principally as pasture, with the lanes suitable for cattle but not carts. The difficulties of getting there other than on foot complicated the claims that Godfrey's body had been brought there by sedan chair or on horseback. The landlord of the White House, John Rawson, thought initially that the sword seen by Bromwell and Walters had belonged to soldiers who had been hunting for hedgehogs. While this may have been for culinary or medicinal purposes, it is also possible that the soldiers were hoping for the bounty of threepence put on the head of hedgehogs in 1566 by the Elizabethan Parliament, as they were thought to steal milk from cows at night.[49]

From the mid-eighteenth century, with the publication of a number of maps, notably those by John Rocque in 1746, it is possible to get a more accurate view of Marylebone Park and its surroundings. These all show that the southern edge of the park was, for a long time, the northern limit of London. This boundary was reaffirmed by the construction of the New Road in 1756–57. The growth of the West End had brought with it a problem in the delivery of cattle, pigs and geese to the market at Smithfield. The passage of herds of cattle along Oxford Street, and through the narrow streets of London, caused traffic delays and other nuisances. This was addressed by the laying out of a wide new road from Paddington, running north of St Marylebone to Battle Bridge (the later site of King's Cross), to Islington and then down to the City. Its opponents, however, rumoured that its main aim was to expedite the movement of government troops to crush the liberties of free-born Englishmen. It was laid out easily enough, as the new road ran almost entirely through what was then countryside.[50]

Once in existence, the New Road quickly proved popular with many users other than drovers, while its tolls provided a valuable income to the parishes through which it ran. In the longer term, it also drew an important external link to London

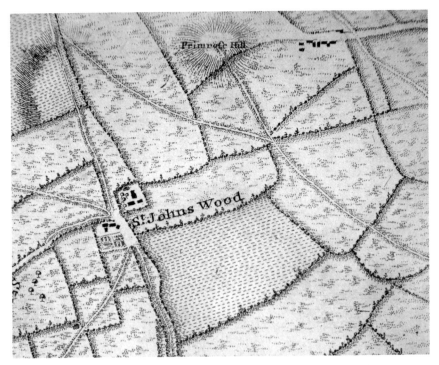

The first map of London in its wider surroundings, Roque's *Map of London*
(1746), shows a track leading across Marylebone Park to Primrose Hill.
Lisson Grove leads to St John's Wood Farm, seventy-five years before the
Finchley Road was built. (*Private Collection*)

to its western end. The Grand Junction Canal, built between 1793 and 1805 as part
of the great boom in canal construction in the second half of the eighteenth century,
had its terminus at Paddington, where the canal basins to be seen today were dug.
Any continuation of the canal through London, however, proved problematical,
due to the cost of buying up land already built upon and the fears of landowners
along the route that the canal would adversely affect the value of their property.[51]

Throughout the eighteenth century, Marylebone Park and the land to its north
was farmland. Because of the proximity to London, the farms were profitable,
supplying the city's inexhaustible appetite for milk and other dairy products. Its
fields supported large numbers of cattle, many of which had been driven from
further afield to London and were fattened close to the city before being sold at
Smithfield. There were three main farms, all in the south of the park, Willan's
Farm, White House Farm and Coneyburrow Farm. In the course of the eighteenth
century, John Willan, the largest farmer in Middlesex, added White House Farm
to his own.[52] The farmhouse itself was turned into the Jew's Harp, one of two

teahouses in the park.[53] William Blake gave Willan a small measure of immortality by mentioning him in *Jerusalem*:

> The Jew's Harp house and the Green Man,
> The ponds where boys to bathe delight,
> The fields of cows by Willan's farm,
> Shine in Jerusalem's pleasant sight.[54]

The architect John Nash, in contrast, complained of 'the very offensive stench from Mr Willan's property' and thought that 'his business as cowkeeper is undesirable'.[55]

To the north of the park, there was a similar pattern of farming. On what became the Eyre Estate in St John's Wood in 1732, when it was acquired by the wealthy wine importer, Henry Samuel Eyre, there were two farms, St John's Wood Farm and Bumper's Farm. These, and the neighbouring Barrow Hill Farm, were also farmed by the Willan family for much of the eighteenth century. On Eton's Chalcots Estate, the farmhouse of Upper Chalcot Farm was at the end of a track leading from Haverstock Hill. During the eighteenth century, the estate was leased to the Earle family, who in turn rented it out to the Rhodes family, who had a large dairy farm near the future site of Euston Station.[56] Farther north, reached by a turning off the road to Hampstead, Belsize House became a famous, and then notorious, pleasure resort.[57]

During the eighteenth century, Primrose Hill, due to its proximity to the rapidly growing West End and to St Marylebone, became a well-known place of excursion.[58] It was also part of a well-trodden route between St Marylebone and Hampstead. The hill's popularity, and its association with pleasure, is reflected in a rhyme, first recorded in 1780.

> As I was going up Primrose Hill,
> Primrose Hill was dirty;
> There I met a pretty Miss,
> And she dropped me a curtsey.
> Little Miss, pretty Miss,
> Blessings light upon you;
> If I had a half-a-crown a day,
> I'd spend it all upon you.[59]

A caricature by Isaac Cruikshank from 1791 shows a stream of people crossing Marylebone Park towards the hill, whose summit is crowded by sightseers.[60] A father, whose wigless brow is being mopped by his wife, is pulling four children up the hill in an early perambulator, while an officer passes to a girl a hip flask or wallet, which he may have removed from the pocket of a man intent on looking west through a telescope. In the foreground are two women, one of whom is smoking a pipe while the other has a basket of provisions for sale. A dog, the first whose image on the hill is preserved, is scratching itself.* In the description accompanying his caricature, Cruikshank tells us who the main figures are. They are two 'cits' or citizens, Tom Cheshire, a cheesemonger whose 'hobbyhorse is perspective', and Zachary Saveall, a tallow-chandler, who is pulling his children up the hill hoping to slim himself by the exercise: 'to reduce a corporal magnitude which ... is inconvenient in the duties of his counter'.[61]

Those who made the excursion to Primrose Hill may well have refreshed themselves at either the White House or at the Chalk Farm Tavern, the first non-agricultural building to the east of the hill. The early history of the Chalk Farm Tavern is obscure.[62] Although 'allowed by tradition to have been the country residence of Ben Jonson' and suggested as the site of the manor house of the manor of Rugmere, neither claim can be substantiated.† It is far more likely that the tavern was originally a farmhouse or other farm building, being sometimes indeed referred to as Chalk House Farm. (The name had nothing to do with chalk but was derived, like Chalcots itself, from an Old English word for cold hut.)

The first record of a licence for the tavern was in 1732, issued to Joshua Deane at Chalk House Farm. That it was not a completely respectable establishment is indicated by an early link with crime. Two men, both Catholics originally from Ireland and wanted for the serious crime of clipping coins, were arrested in the tavern in October 1748: 'On Sunday Usher Gahagan and Terence Conner, who

---

*   Not all dogs were safe on the hill. A case was heard at Bow Street in October 1789 of a spaniel stolen for its skin. John Burkett had been arrested after being seen dipping a bundle, in which was a warm dog's skin, a halter, a bloody knife and a piece of liver, in a pond near Chalk Farm. Burkett 'owned that he gained his living by dog-stealing, the skins of which he disposed of to a tanner in Long Lane, who gave him the money for them without asking him by what means he came by them; and that for the largest Newfoundland dog he could not get more than three shillings and sixpence'. *Whitehall Evening Post*, 13 October 1789; *World*, 14 October 1789.

†   Most of the ancient manor of Rugmere, once held by the canons of St Paul's Cathedral, had become part of Marylebone Park in the 1530s. Thomas Bennett, its holder at the time, was compensated by being given the rectory of Throwleigh in Kent. John Palmer, who farmed the manor as a tenant, was granted the freehold of the part of Rugmere not taken for the park. The freehold passed through various hands before being bought in 1786 by Charles Fitzroy, first Lord Southampton, from the executors of John Badcock. The younger brother of the third Duke of Grafton, Southampton had already acquired the freehold of the neighbouring manor of Tottenhale in 1768 from the canons for a payment of £300 a year. Survey of London, xix, *Old St Pancras and Kentish Town*, pp. 1–9; 'Charles, First Baron Southampton (1737–97)', *Oxford Dictionary of National Biography*.

have been concerned in filing guineas, etc., and the former several times advertised, were taken at Chalk Farm, Primrose Hill, near Hampstead, and taken to New Prison for farther examination.'[63] Accused that they 'with certain tools, called files and sheers, and other instruments, did diminish the current coin of Great Britain', they were tried for high treason in January 1749 and sentenced to death, after a former associate turned king's evidence. Both were hanged at Tyburn on 20 February.[64]

Two years later, in 1751, Edward Hipwood was the licensee of the Crown at Chalk House tile kilns. These tile kilns, close to the tavern, were demolished in 1756. From 1760 the tavern was known as the Stag and Hounds. It was sold, with three large barns, as part of the 120-acre Chalk House Farm in 1786. At this point, eighty of its acres were tenanted by Thomas and Samuel Rhodes, who also rented land on the Chalcots Estate.[65] In 1787 the tavern was still advertised as the Stag and Hounds, 'situated near that well-known prospect, called Primrose Hill, one mile and a half from Tottenham Court turnpike, on the road to Hampstead':

> James Rossiter, being so much indebted to his friends and the public in general, for former favors, thinks it his duty to acquaint them, that the house is fitted up, and the garden improved at a considerable expence, as to render them every way worthy the patronage of genteel company; having laid in real wines, and spirits, equally valuable for their goodness; being determined that such powerful supporters shall have the best of imported liquors, as well as teas, for the ladies, who will find his balloon rolls an improvement on other tea-houses.
>
> Dinners dressed for any number of people on the shortest notice; and a genteel ordinary, on Sundays, at two o'clock precisely. Independent of the coach-road, there are many pleasant walks across the fields, from any part of town.[66]

In 1790 the tavern was licensed to Thomas Rutherford as the Chalk Farm Tea Gardens. Rutherford ran the tavern until 1810. During his time as landlord, the tavern was well patronised but established a reputation for rowdiness and rough behaviour. Although calling itself a tea garden, it remained essentially a tavern. Without baths or much in the way of cultural pretensions, it was never a spa. An advertisement from 1793–94 set out what was on offer: 'T. Rutherford solicits the patronage of the public in general – his wines being real and his other liquors of a superior kind. Tea and hot rolls as usual.'[67] The tavern went through a number of alterations and extensions over the years. With grounds entered through an arch, it had a Long Room on the first floor.

In 1794 the Chalk Farm Tavern was the venue for a notable meeting of the London Corresponding Society.[68] The society had been founded, in 1792, by the shoemaker

Thomas Hardy and an attorney, John Frost, to campaign for parliamentary reform.[69] It established a network of links with other Radical societies and was opposed to the war with Revolutionary France, which broke out following the execution of Louis XVI in 1793. It had sent delegates to the French Convention before the outbreak of hostilities. Two of its members also attended the latter session of a British Convention, which brought together over 150 Radicals, the great majority from Scotland, and met in Edinburgh between 29 October and 1 November and again between 19 November and 4 December 1793. The members of the convention, who demanded annual parliaments and universal manhood suffrage, also passed a resolution which would bring into being an executive body as the focus of opposition, should Habeas Corpus be suspended, if foreign troops were brought by the government into Great Britain or Ireland, or in the case of invasion. It was left unclear whether this executive body would support the invaders, who would certainly have been French.[70]

For all these reasons, the British Convention and the societies who supported it were regarded with abhorrence by the authorities, who suspected the London Corresponding Society of fomenting opposition and of plotting to overthrow the government. The authorities in Scotland reacted vigorously, arresting the leading members of the convention, including two London Corresponding Society delegates, Maurice Margarot and Joseph Gerrald. Tried in January 1794 for sedition, before a notoriously biased judge, Lord Braxfield, Margarot and Gerrald were convicted and sentenced to transportation to Australia for fourteen years.

On Monday 14 April 1794, members of the society were due to meet in a dance hall in Store Street, off Tottenham Court Road. The threat by a magistrate to break up the meeting resulted in a move to the Chalk Farm Tavern, to which those gathered at Store Street walked, and where they were joined by other supporters. The numbers at the tavern were variously estimated as between 500 and 3,000, including several government spies.

> The peace officers having on Monday last taken possession of the room in Store Street, the London Corresponding Society found themselves under the necessity of adjourning to Chalk Farm. ... The Citizens assembled in the garden, for they were refused admittance to the house, and the chairman and committee ascended a few steps of an outer stair, and proposed a string of resolutions which were carried *par acclamation*.[71]

According to the *Morning Post*, the meeting had gone off peaceably: 'We cannot close this account without saying that their manner of conducting themselves deserves the admiration of all parties; for never was there so large an assemblage, and such regularity.'[72]

The meeting voted to send a message of support to Joseph Gerrald, who was awaiting transportation to Botany Bay. Addressed by the leading Radical John Thelwall, it also passed a series of resolutions.[73] Among other things, these claimed that political power was held in trust 'for the benefit of the community; yet the rights themselves are reserved by the People, and cannot be absolutely parted with by the People to those who are employed to conduct the business of the state'.[74] The office of king 'was not instituted by the People merely as an office of profit and honour to the king, but he was so appointed as chief trustee and guardian of the constitution and rights of the people'.[75] Two hundred thousand copies of the resolutions were to be printed and distributed.[76]

The Radical meeting at Chalk Farm was a conventional one in many ways, following others at the Globe and the Crown and Anchor, both in the Strand. What marked it out from previous meetings of the same sort was the extreme reaction of the government, although the meeting was by no means the only cause of this.[77] Determined to stamp out opposition at a time of war, and to prevent the growth of internal support for the French Revolution, the Tory government of Pitt the Younger suspended Habeas Corpus with reference to treason in May and arrested over twenty Radicals, including the leaders of the society.[78] Thomas Hardy, John Thelwall, John Horne Tooke and others were held in the Tower without trial from May to October 1794. A secret committee of Parliament was established to examine the evidence against them. In the autumn two Scots, Robert Watt and David Downie, arrested in May, were tried for treason in Edinburgh. The case against Watt, an ex-government spy who was shown to have been plotting armed rebellion, was strong. Both were sentenced to be hanged, drawn and quartered. Downie was reprieved but Watt was executed, though spared the barbarities of drawing and quartering.[79]

In late October Thomas Hardy finally stood trial at the Old Bailey for high treason, accused of 'compassing and imagining the king's death'.[80] Much of the trial focused on what had been said at the Chalk Farm Tavern in April and what had been meant by what had been said. Although some sensational, but dubious evidence was brought about members of the society having a sinister French knife, called a *couteau secret*, and of Thelwall blowing the froth off a pint of porter, saying 'This is the way I would serve all kings', it was not alleged that Hardy had a specific plan to kill the king.[81] The government's case was that a 'traitorous and detestable conspiracy' sought to undermine the constitution and introduce anarchy on the French model.[82] Sir John Scott, for the prosecution, in a nine-hour opening address – which must have tried the jury's patience – alleged that the society's plans to summon a national convention and impose electoral reform was a direct challenge to Parliament and, by extension, threatened the king's life.

Fortunately for Hardy, he was defended by the leading barrister of the day, the brilliant Thomas Erskine, who categorically denied the prosecution's doctrine of constructive treason.* Erskine, who was also a prominent Whig politician, argued that the London Corresponding Society simply aimed to achieve reform by constitutional and peaceful means. He even quoted Pitt's own reforming efforts, before the outbreak of the French Revolution, to show that suggesting constitutional reform was not necessarily treasonable. He also played on the sympathies of the jury by reminding them that Hardy's pregnant wife had died, losing their unborn baby, after his house was invaded by a loyalist mob celebrating the naval victory of the Glorious First of June.

After an eight-day trial, and despite a hostile summing-up by Chief Justice Eyre, Hardy was acquitted to scenes of popular rejoicing. The verdict was greeted with shouts of applause inside the Old Bailey, echoed by the crowd outside: 'like an electric shock, or the rapidity of lightning, the glad tidings spread through the whole town, and were conveyed much quicker than the regular post could travel, to the most distant parts of the island, where all ranks of people were anxiously awaiting the result of the trial'.[83] The horses were taken from Hardy's coach, which was drawn by supporters around the centre of London. The subsequent trials of John Horne Tooke, a leading Radical who had not been at Chalk Farm, and of John Thelwall also ended in acquittal, following which the government abandoned the trials of the other men arrested.[84] In the year following the acquittals, the London Corresponding Society held a series of large meetings, culminating in one in Copenhagen Fields, Islington, on 26 October 1795. This, however, proved to be the high-water mark of popular Radicalism during the war, as a series of Acts clamped down on political meetings.[85]

The trials, which were reported in great detail in the newspapers of the day, brought the Chalk Farm Tavern a notable place in Radical mythology and in the history of British liberty. It also brought the area a notoriety that was increased in the forty years after the London Corresponding Society's meeting for a different reason. Primrose Hill, and the tavern to the east of it, offered men who had quarrelled, and who were intent on fighting, a convenient place to meet.

---

* Erskine specialised in winning seemingly impossible cases. In 1781 he had secured Lord George Gordon's acquittal after the Gordon Riots of June 1780; and in 1800 he successfully defended James Hadfield, who, on the grounds of insanity, was acquitted of high treason after firing a pistol at George III at Drury Lane. 'Thomas Erskine, First Lord Erskine (1750–1823)', *Oxford Dictionary of National Biography*.

3

A Question of Honour

Towards the end of the eighteenth century Primrose Hill acquired a new but dubious distinction, as a place for duels. Most early duels had been fought nearer to the centre of London, with Hyde Park a favourite venue in the late seventeenth and early eighteenth centuries.* As London grew, the venues for duelling moved towards the periphery of the city. Primrose Hill, easily reached by carriage from the West End, was by no means the only location used for the purpose, but nevertheless established a reputation for it.† Indeed, it was described in 1806 as 'a place not less famous for duels than Parnassus for poetry'.[1]

Paradoxically, for a practice designed to lead to injury or death, the duel was in some ways a means of saving life in a quarrelsome society. By providing a system for the resolution of disputes, it discouraged vendettas and the lawless enforcement of revenge by ambush or affray.[2] The formal rules of the duel, established during the eighteenth century, with seconds negotiating for the principals, allowed time for the anger caused by an affront to cool – and where necessary for participants in a quarrel to sober up. By negotiating an apology, seconds might be able to avoid a fight. The replacement of swords by duelling pistols, following a general decline in expertise in fencing among the gentry, may also have saved lives.‡ In a sword

---

* From the City, Covent Garden or Lincoln's Inn Fields, duels moved first to Hyde Park and then to the peripheries of London. Of course, not all duels were fought in or near London. See Robert Shoemaker, *The London Mob: Violence and Disorder in Eighteenth-Century England* (London and New York, 2004), p. 93.
† Other established sites for duels, including those with a higher profile than any fought on Primrose Hill, were Wimbledon Common, where the Duke of York fought Colonel Lennox in 1789; Putney Heath, where William Pitt the Younger fought George Tierney in 1798 and George Canning fought Viscount Castlereagh in 1809; and Battersea, where the Duke of Wellington fought the Earl of Winchilsea in 1829. Edward Walford, *Old and New London* (London, c. 1880), v, pp. 292–3.
‡ Until the middle of the eighteenth century, gentlemen often wore swords in public, giving them an immediate opportunity to escalate a quarrel. No one, however, carried duelling pistols with them. A duel involving pistols therefore required an interval between a quarrel and its resolution. For an account of the changes in the practice of duelling, see Shoemaker, *The London*

fight, there was often no obvious moment to stop before a serious injury, or at least a wound, was inflicted. The sword also favoured the skilled swordsman over an unskilled opponent, an advantage much less marked in an exchange of pistol shots. Once one exchange of fire had been completed, it was open to the parties involved to declare their honour satisfied, although either of the parties could insist on further exchanges. Sometimes injury was avoided by the seconds colluding in agreeing a large number of paces between their principals, or even in not loading the pistols properly. This did much to counter the increased accuracy of duelling pistols achieved by the end of the eighteenth century. By this time the rules of duelling, which were largely obeyed by participants, also aided the chances of survival. Practising shooting before a duel was considered improper. Opponents receiving the signal to fire were expected to raise their pistols and fire at once, with a delay to take careful aim being frowned on, as was the use of pistols with rifled barrels. Nevertheless, duelling remained a deadly business.

Although in the eyes of the law any death caused by duelling was a culpable homicide, the defence of upholding honour under provocation made juries unwilling to convict, especially if the charge was one of murder.* The general reluctance of juries, made up largely of small householders and shopkeepers, to convict mainly upper-class duellists may reflect a wider, and longer lasting, acceptance of the legitimacy of duelling than is often assumed to be the case. It was also common for even mortally wounded combatants to exonerate their opponents from blame, seeking to keep their affairs private.

In the eyes of its protagonists, the duel offered a way of settling disputes for which the law had no remedy. In a narrow sense this might well apply to gambling debts, payment of which was unenforceable in court. In a wider sense, slights regarding honour, in a society where a man's reputation was of critical importance, could also not be satisfied by legal redress.[3] While most gentlemen avoided duelling, few can have been unaware of the risk of provoking a duel. This, in itself, may have encouraged the less hot-blooded members of society to settle by compromise disputes that might otherwise have led to a challenge.[4]

Mob, pp. 177–94. For a sceptical review of Shoemaker's arguments, see Stephen Banks, *A Polite Exchange of Bullets: The Duel and the English Gentleman, 1750–1850* (Woodbridge, 2010), pp. 126–31.

* Only four duellists were convicted of murder in the entire history of duelling in Britain after 1700. Until 1822 conviction for manslaughter attracted a maximum sentence of twelve months imprisonment; but often a lesser sentence was imposed on those duellists who, against the odds, were convicted of causing death. Antony Simpson, 'Dandelions on the Field of Honour': Duelling the Middle Classes and the Law in Nineteenth-Century England', *Criminal Justice History*, 9 (1988), p. 125; Banks, *A Polite Exchange of Bullets*, pp. 153, 155.

All the recorded duels on or near Primrose Hill were fought with pistols rather than swords. It is impossible to put an exact number on them, as duels which ended with no one being injured may well have escaped the notice of the newspapers and the courts. The authorities also stepped in to stop duels taking place, sometimes at an early stage and sometimes at the last minute. In such cases, the principals and their seconds would be bound over to keep the peace.[5] In 1807, for instance, 'two young gentlemen, who disagreed in the lobby of Drury Lane Theatre' were due to fight a duel at Chalk Farm the next day but 'were interrupted by the police officers, conveyed to Marlborough Street, and held in sureties to keep the peace'.[6] Sometimes, also, the parties settled their disputes themselves, instead of fighting. In 1824 two merchants who had disagreed 'on some point connected to the New Docks at St Katharine's', met in the fields leading to Chalk Farm. 'The seconds had just measured the ground, and delivered the pistols to the two disputants, when some friends of one of the antagonists appeared on the ground and by their intervention the dispute was adjusted.'[7] On the other hand, when in 1826 the police approached an ex-army officer and a naval officer who had just exchanged fire, and who were preparing for a second exchange, 'the parties precipitately took to their carriages and drove off, pledging themselves to conclude the matter elsewhere'.[8]

While highly sensational, at the time and in retrospect, duels were actually quite rare, with forty-two known challenges to duels at Primrose Hill spread over forty-eight years between 1790 and 1837.[*] Of these, seventeen were stopped either before the protagonists reached the duelling ground or before an actual exchange of fire. The rate of challenges was therefore less than one a year and the rate of duels fought out just over one every two years. While there were twenty-six years in this period without a challenge or duel, there was a cluster of seventeen challenges or duels between 1803 and 1810, with six in the single year of 1806. Four challenges or duels in the 1790s contrasted with sixteen between 1800 and 1809, ten between 1810 and 1819, and nine between 1820 and 1829. Of the two duels fought in the 1830s, one was a foreign affair between two Russian diplomats. In the farcical circumstances of the unfought challenge of April 1830, the two protagonists, bereft of any weapons due to the disappearance of a mutual friend supposed to have been bringing the pistols, ended up drinking brandy and milk together at the Chalk Farm Tavern.[9]

The reasons why the duels were fought varied. By the time that Primrose Hill became a well-known duelling site, from being bitter disputes of honour which

---

[*]   They may, however, have been part of an renewed outbreak of duelling. A newspaper in 1789 noted that 'the practice of duelling has returned to a pitch of frequency, and deadly intention, that has not been known for at least half a century', *Morning Post*, 18 July 1789. The war between 1793 and 1815 also greatly increased the numbers of officers, from whose ranks the majority of duellists were drawn.

could only be resolved by the infliction of death or the spilling of blood, duels had more often become occasions for those involved to prove their courage in defence of their honour. Nevertheless, duels remained lethal, however politely they were fought. Three categories of men, all jealous of preserving the honour of their castes, were prominent as duellists, on Primrose Hill as elsewhere: officers in the army and navy; members of high society; and Irish gentlemen.[10] Gamblers disputing over debts formed another distinct group of duellists. Also at risk were politicians and the editors of papers, with an adverse review sometimes provoking a challenge. Many of the quarrels arose in the West End, often on trivial points which were escalated to the point of challenge only by an exalted sense of honour.

The first duel recorded on or near Primrose Hill was between Captain Hervey Aston and Captain Fitzgerald in June 1790. The last was in May 1837.* The forty-two known challenges led to twenty-five duels in which fire was exchanged. In these twenty-five duels seven men were killed, a higher than usual fatality rate. Fourteen men, in addition, were wounded. In only six of the duels was neither principal wounded; and one of these was the occasion when the principals were interrupted by the police after one exchange and left hurriedly to finish their business elsewhere. The chance of being wounded in an exchange of shots on Primrose Hill shots was therefore 42 per cent; that of being killed was exactly 14 per cent.[11]

All the duels except one were fought at a fixed distance, agreed by the seconds. Contrary to the commonly received notion of how such matters were discharged, none of the duels involved the principals starting back to back, walking apart and then turning immediately to fire.[12] Nor, with a single exception, were any of the duels fought *à la barrière*, a method common on the Continent whereby opponents advanced in towards two parallel lines until one of them fired. The first to fire was then obliged to stand still to receive fire from his adversary, assuming the latter had survived the first shot, who was allowed to narrow the distance by walking in to his own line.[13]

Exactly where the duels were conducted is difficult to pinpoint.[14] Most, however, were fought not far from the Chalk Farm Tavern, which could be reached conveniently by carriage. Colonel Montgomery and Captain Macnamara in 1803, having arrived at the tavern in separate coaches, 'walked across Primrose Hill to the opposite side from Chalk Farm, and chose their ground in the most private spot'.[15] While few were sited as vaguely as the duel between Colonel M. and Mr W., fought in 1813 'between Paddington and Primrose Hill', most descriptions

---

*   The first duel, between Captain Hervey Aston and Captain Fitzgerald, was on 29 June 1792; the last, between J.P. J-s-n and R. T-k-r, was on 28 May 1837.

Duels on or near Primrose Hill

Year	Date	Protagonist	Protagonist	Cause	Location	Result	Source
1790	25 June	Captain Hervey Aston	Captain Fitzgerald	A slight at Ranelagh	A field belonging to Chalk Farm Lodge	Aston wounded	See below, pp. 31–2, 248–9
1790	August	Mr R–g–rs, a shoemaker	Slipperman, a Jew	Unknown	Near Primrose Hill	Abandoned without exchange	*English Chronicle*, 26 August 1790
1792	15 July	Mr A–r	Irish Student	Remarks by A–r on the Irish	A field westward of Primrose Hill	Two exchanges without injury	See below, pp. 44, 252
1796	18 July	V. Leander	Captain Compton	A lady	A field adjoining Chalk Farm	Compton killed	See below, pp. 45, 251
1803	6 April	Captain James Macnamara RN	Colonel Robert Montgomery	Fight between dogs in Hyde Park	Near the top of Primrose Hill	Montgomery killed	See below, pp. 33–7, 249
1804	16 May	Humphry Hobart	Thomas O'Reilly	Insult in ballroom	In a field on north side of Chalk Farm	O'Reilly killed	See below, pp. 44–5, 251
1805	2 April	Mr W–r, a military officer	Another military officer	Unknown	Near Chalk Farm	Bound over before exchange	Heal Collection, A IX, 14*
1806	11 August	Thomas Moore	Francis Jeffrey	Review of Moore's poetry	Primrose Hill	Bound over before exchange	See below, pp. 41–3, 250–1
1806	October	Major John Godfrey	Marshal (gave name as Parker)	Unknown	Chalk Farm	Bound over before exchange	Heal Collection, A IX, 16
1806	5 December	Mr S–y	Mr C–y	C–y struck S–y; both lawyers	On Primrose Hill	Adjusted amicably without exchange	*Morning Post*, 5 December 1806

* The Heal Collection is in the Camden Local Studies and Archives Centre.

Year	Date	Protagonist	Protagonist	Cause	Location	Result	Source
1806		French wine merchant	French officer in British service	Unknown	Near Primrose Hill	Bound over before exchange	Heal Collection, A IX, 14
1806		Captain E-n	Mr J-n	Private misunderstanding	Chalk Farm	Mr J-n wounded on second shot	Heal Collection, A IX, 16
1806		John Hutchinson	John Weir	Failure to keep meeting at a club	Chalk Farm	Weir bound over	Heal Collection, A IX, 16
1807	9 July	Son of an earl	Captain B.	Quarrel leaving the opera	Fields near Primrose Hill	Son of an earl wounded	Morning Chronicle, 10 July 1807
1807		A young gentleman	A young gentleman	Disagreement at Drury Lane Theatre	Chalk Farm	Bound over before exchange	Heal Collection, A IX, 14
1808	7 September	Captain M-n	Mr P-e	Being pushed off the pavement	A field near Primrose Hill	Mr P-e wounded on second shot	Johnson's, 11 September 1808
1808		Macrae	Mackintosh	Dispute in a public house	Chalk Farm	Settled without meeting	Heal Collection, A IX, 14
1808	July	Sandoz	Dubois	Unknown	Chalk Farm	Sandoz bound over	Morning Chronicle, 30 July 1808
1809	28 February	Viscount Falkland	Mr Powell	Use of an insulting nickname	Chalk Farm	Falkland killed	See below, pp. 37–40, 249–50
1809	3 October	Broadwood journeyman	Broadwood journeyman	Dispute on tuning	Bottom of Primrose Hill	Two exchanges without injury	Heal Collection, A IX, 14
1810		Hubbard	Wrathen	Dispute between two lawyers	Chalk Farm	Bound over before exchange	Heal Collection, A IX, 16

Year	Date	Protagonist	Protagonist	Cause	Location	Result	Source
1813	April	Colonel M.	Mr W.	Challenge by Mr W.	Between Paddington and Primrose Hill	Colonel M. wounded	*Morning Post*, 29 April 1813
1813	September	A stripling	A stripling	An affair of honour	Chalk Farm	One wounded	Heal Collection, A IX, 14
1817	May	Lt Br-ke	Lt Sh-rd-n	Dispute at the Cavendish Rooms	Chalk Farm	Br-ke mortally wounded	Heal Collection, A IX, 16
1818	12 January	Lieutenant Edmund Bailey	Theodore O'Callaghan	Fighting on behalf of others	A field near Chalk Farm	Bailey killed	See below, pp. 45, 251
1818	2 April	Captain N., RN	Lieutenant L.	A lady at Covent Garden Theatre	Chalk Farm	Captain N. wounded	Gilchrist, *A Brief Display*, pp. 270–71*
1818	21 June	Lieutenant Williams RN	Mr Walcot	Argument at Vauxhall	Chalk Farm	Walcot wounded on second exchange	Gilchrist, *A Brief Display*, p. 277
1818	9 August	Lieutenant Radwell RN	Mr Frame	Unknown	Chalk Farm	Frame wounded	Gilchrist, *A Brief Display*, p. 281
1818	25 November	Earl of H.	Lord W.	Gambling dispute	Chalk Farm	Reconciliation after exchange	*Morning Chronicle*, 27 November 1818
1819	3 February	James Good	George Smith	Dispute over bet of five shillings	Chalk Farm	Bound over before exchange	Heal Collection, A IX, 14
1821	23 February	John Scott	Jonathan Christie	Articles by Scott	On Primrose Hill	Scott killed	*Times*, 19 February 1821

* James Gilchrist, *A Brief Display of the Origin and History of Duels* (London, 1821).

Year	Date	Protagonist	Protagonist	Cause	Location	Result	Source
1821	17 October	John Duggin	Mr Gibling	Dispute about debt	Primrose Hill	Settled before meeting	*Morning Chronicle*, 17 October 1821
1821	November	Lieutenant W.	Army officer	Unknown	Chalk Farm	Interrupted by constable	Heal Collection, A IX, 15
1822	May	Military gentleman	Military gentleman	Quarrel over loss of £3,000 at one throw	Chalk Farm	Both wounded	Heal Collection, A IX, 16
1823	26 November	Ugo Foscolo	Samuel Carter Hall	Letter by Foscolo	Barrow Hill	Exchange without injury	See below, pp. 43, 251
1824	14 October	Littleton	Rogers	Disputed bet on St Leger	A field west of Primrose Hill	Littleton wounded	*Caledonian Mercury*, 14 October 1824
1824		A merchant	A merchant	Dispute over new docks	Fields leading to Chalk Farm	Settled before exchange	Heal Collection, A IX, 16
1826	February	John Murray or John Barrow	Dr Robert Lyall	Review by John Barrow	Fields near Chalk Farm	Challenge rejected by Lyall	*Examiner*, 19 February 1826
1826		Mr J.V., ex-army officer	Mr O'B., RN	Unknown	Chalk Farm	Left to fight elsewhere	Heal Collection, A IX, 16
1830	6 April	Lieutenant of the Coast Blockade	Veteran army captain on half pay	Disparagement of the navy	Chalk Farm	Pistols removed by third party	*Standard*, 7 April 1830
1832	25 August	Count Tolstoy	Prince Troubetskoy	Slur by Tolstoy on Troubetskoy	A field at the foot of Primrose Hill	Exchange without injury	*Jackson's*, 25 August 1832
1837	27 May	J.P. J-s-n	R T-k-r	Elopement by T-k-r with J-s-n's sister	Near Primrose Hill	Fought *à la barrière*; Mr T-k-r wounded	*Examiner*, 28 May 1837

go no further than stating that the duel was fought 'on Primrose Hill', 'in a field to the westward of Primrose Hill', 'in a field between Chalk Farm and Primrose Hill', or 'at Chalk Farm'.[16] At least two of the duels were fought at the top of the hill or nearby. The vintner James Harding, one of the witnesses at the trial of Captain Macnamara in 1803, reported seeing 'the parties, Colonel Montgomery and Captain Macnamara, and other gentlemen ascend Primrose Hill'. Thomas Pettigrew, a surgeon who attended the duel between John Scott and Jonathan Christie in 1821, testified that, 'I reached the top of the hill, and saw four gentlemen in the neighbouring field'.[17]

The first duel recorded on Primrose Hill, on 25 June 1790, was fought by two officers over a real or imaginary slight:

> A duel was fought between Harvey Aston Esq. and Captain Fitzgerald.* The quarrel originated at Ranelagh, where Mr Fitzgerald conceived himself to be affronted by Mr Aston, at that time a perfect stranger. Mr Fitzgerald remonstrated, and being told that *he might make the most of it*, and the expression being accompanied by a push, blows immediately ensued. Mr Aston in pugilistic science was evidently the superior, and after a sharp contest, he, in the boxing phrase, *sealed up the eyes* of his adversary, and was so far victorious.
>
> As soon as Mr Fitzgerald was sufficiently recovered, he requested Captain Ward to wait upon Mr Aston, who named Lord Charles Fitzroy as his friend.†

---

* Aston's full name was Henry Hervey Aston, but his second name is often given as Harvey. He was an early cricketer. A useful batsman, he was a member of the Hambledon Club and made thirteen first-class appearances for the Marylebone Cricket Club between 1786 and 1793, when he sailed for India. He was also a crack shot: 'Two better shots, according to the phrase among men of modern honour, never were pitted', *Gazetteer and New Daily Advertiser*, 26 June 1790. For Aston, see *Memoirs of George Elers: Captain in the 12th Regiment of Foot, 1777–1842*, edited by Lord Monson and George Leveson-Gower (London, 1903), pp. 36–8, 42–3, 45, 47, 53, 55–9, 64, 66–8, 71–2, 75, 78–9, 81–90 and 167–9.
Aston was connected to the earls of Bristol, whose family name was Hervey. He was the grandson of Dr Johnson's friend Henry Hervey, a dragoon officer quartered at Lichfield, where he had met the young Samuel Johnson in 1730. In his *Life of Johnson*, Boswell reports Johnson as saying about Hervey, 'He was a vicious man, but very kind to me. If you call a dog Hervey, I shall love him'. James Boswell, *The Life of Samuel Johnson LL.D.*, 2 vols (London, 1791), i, p. 50. Hervey took the additional name of Aston after marrying Catherine Aston, the daughter of Sir Thomas Aston of Aston Hall, Cheshire, in 1730. He subsequently took holy orders and wrote religious poetry. 'Henry Hervey Aston (1701–48)', *Oxford Dictionary of National Biography*.
† Lord Charles Fitzroy, Aston's second, was the son of the third Duke of Grafton and nephew to the first Lord Southampton, who had bought the area at the foot of Primrose Hill four years earlier. 'Lord Charles Fitzroy (1764–1829)', *Oxford Dictionary of National Biography*. It was customary at the time to address both lieutenants and captains in the army as Mr.

A meeting was then appointed for two o'clock in the morning, at Chalk Farm, near Hampstead, where it was agreed they should both fire by the word of command. Nine paces were measured, and Captain Ward having asked if they were ready, and, when answered, having given the word, Mr Fitzgerald immediately fired, and wounded Mr Aston in the right hand, which was then extended. The ball grazed on to the elbow, and then glanced upon his temple, leaving bare the bone nearly to the ear.

Mr Aston did not fall, and his adversary incautiously broke his ground, and ran up towards Mr Aston, apprehending from the effusion of blood that the wound might have been fatal. Mr Aston, finding his opponent satisfied, did not return the fire; and thus the affair terminated.*

Fitzgerald, who had served in the French army, had brought a sword to the meeting, but on Aston 'saying he should not have recourse to that weapon, he immediately unbuckled it from his side, and flung it away'.[18]

Aston, a wealthy dandy, was a close friend of the Prince of Wales. His wife was the sister of the Marchioness of Hertford, who later became the prince's mistress. Aston fought another duel, against Mr Home Sumner during the Ascot races. Passing the Bush Inn at Staines, he threw an orange at two ladies leaning out of a window but hit Sumner by mistake. In the duel that followed, Sumner was wounded in the hip.[19] After he travelled out with his regiment to India, Aston fought two more duels in Madras in December 1798. In the first, against Major Picton, Picton's pistol snapped and Aston then fired in the air. In the second, the following day, Aston was killed by Major Allen.†

---

* Two o'clock in the morning meant before dinner and was therefore in the afternoon, not at night. Aston later joked, 'I don't know whether I shall be disfigured … but I am sure I was near being defaced', *Gazetteer and New Daily Advertiser*, 26 July 1790. Camden Local Studies and Archives Centre, Hampstead Collection, H 394.8, cutting; *Gentleman's Magazine*, July 1790, p. 660; *London Chronicle*, 26 June 1790. For another account of the origins of this duel, *Memoirs of George Elers*, p. 168. Aston was attended by Mr Tomkins, a surgeon. See also James Gilchrist, *A Brief Display of the Origin and History of Ordeals: Trials by Battle, Courts of Chivalry or Honour, and the Decision of Private Quarrels by Single Combat* (London, 1821), p. 159; and Ben C. Truman, *The Field of Honor: Being a Complete and Comprehensive History of Duelling in All Countries* (New York, 1884), pp. 226, 497.

† Aston, by then a lieutenant colonel, acted with moderation in trying to solve a dispute about the payment for stores. His friend, Colonel Arthur Wellesley, later the Duke of Wellington, advised Aston against issuing an order reprimanding Picton and did his best to resolve the issue. There is a lengthy account of the two duels in *Memoirs of George Elers*, pp. 81–9. See also *Supplementary Despatches and Memoranda of Field Marshal Arthur, Duke of Wellington KG*, i, *India, 1797–1805*, edited by the second Duke of Wellington, 15 vols (London, 1858–72), pp. 141–3; and Elizabeth Longford, *Wellington: The Years of the Sword* (London, 1969), pp. 57–8. Aston left his beautiful Arab charger, Diomed, to Wellesley, but the horse was killed at the

The most famous duel on Primrose Hill was between a soldier and a naval officer, Colonel Robert Montgomery and Captain James Macnamara RN, on 6 April 1803.[20] Both were Irish. Montgomery, who was twenty-eight, was the lieutenant colonel of the 9th Regiment of Foot. Remarkably handsome and with an outstanding war record in Egypt, Malta and the Netherlands, he was a friend of both the Prince of Wales and the Duke of York. At thirty-six, Macnamara was 'a strong, bold, active man', and 'on the eve of marriage to a young lady from Cork, with a fortune of £10,000'.[*] He had fought at the battle of Cape St Vincent in 1797 and had commanded the frigate *Cerberus* with distinction. Recently returned from the West Indies to Chatham, where his ship had been paid off, Macnamara 'had fought two or three duels before; and was remarkable at Cork, for keeping the turbulent in awe'.[21]

The duel, which brought Primrose Hill widespread notoriety, was fought during the brief hiatus in the war against Napoleonic France following the Peace of Amiens in 1802. It was the result of a quarrel about dogs between two men who had never previously met. Both had been in Hyde Park earlier that day. Montgomery, who rode almost daily in the park on 'a beautiful little white Arabian', was riding up and down 'between the bridge and the bar, where the horsemen come in'. His young Newfoundland dog, Wolf, got into a fight with 'another of the same sort, larger and stronger'.[†] Montgomery, seeing that his dog was coming off worse, got off his horse to part them, saying to Macnamara, who had ridden up, 'If you do not call your dog off, I shall knock him down'. Macnamara replied, 'Have you the arrogance to say you will knock my dog down?' The use several times by Macnamara of the

---

battle of Assaye in 1803. Aston was senior to Wellesley and his death created an opening for Wellesley at the siege of Seringapatam, the first major triumph in the latter's glittering career. Andrew Steinmetz, *The Romance of Duelling in All Times and Countries*, 2 vols (London, 1868), ii, pp. 60–4; Shoemaker, *The London Mob*, p. 187.

[*] Both Macnamara and Montgomery had the reputation of being 'dead shots'. A friend of the diarist Joseph Farington, who was acquainted with Macnamara, told him that the latter 'had killed three or four men' and that 'on board a ship, he amuses himself in having fowls that are to be killed placed before him on hen coops and he shoots off their heads with pistol balls'. *The Farington Diary*, ed. J. Greig, 8 vols (London, 1922–28), ii, pp. 199–200.

[†] This quarrel says more about the men involved than their dogs. Newfoundland dogs, although they grow to become very large, are famously docile. According to a subsequent newspaper report, 'Captain Macnamara's Newfoundland dog is one of the most quiet and harmless of his species. He was brought from St Domingo by his master and has always been admired for his beauty and his sagacity', *Ipswich Journal*, 23 April 1803. Lord Byron wrote a moving epitaph for his Newfoundland dog, Boatswain, born the month after the duel between Montgomery and Macnamara. 'Near this spot are deposited the Remains of one who possessed Beauty without Vanity, Strength without Insolence, Courage without Ferocity, and all the Virtues of Man without his Vices. This Praise, which would be unmeaning Flattery, if inscribed over human ashes, is but a just tribute to the Memory of BOATSWAIN, a DOG who was born at Newfoundland, May, 1803, and died at Newstead, November 18th, 1808.'

word 'arrogance' seems to have been the reason why the matter became a serious one. Although the men both left the park, their quarrel escalated shortly afterwards in Piccadilly. On Macnamara's behalf, Captain Barry approached Montgomery and said, 'my friend cannot suffer those words to pass by but insists on a meeting'. He gave Montgomery the choice of time, place and weapons. Montgomery responded 'that the sooner things of that description were decided the better'. He would meet Macnamara 'at Primrose Hill with pistols, the only weapons that gentlemen generally make use of'. The appointment was for two hours later, at 7 o'clock that evening.[22]

Just after five o'clock that afternoon, Captain Macnamara's nephew called upon a surgeon, John Heaviside, and asked him to attend, as his uncle was engaged to fight in a duel:

> On his attending Mr James Macnamara to his uncle, he found Captain Barry along with him, when they got into a hackney coach and proceeded to the ground near Primrose Hill. When they arrived they found Sir William Keir on the ground, but Colonel Montgomery did not appear for some time afterwards; when he arrived, the distance of twelve paces was fixed. The gentlemen took their stands, and fired near together. Colonel Montgomery fell.[23]

On Heaviside going up to him, the colonel said, 'I am shot through the heart'. A post-boy who witnessed the aftermath of the duel stated, 'I assisted in carrying Colonel Montgomery; his eyes were fixed; and he was groaning; I saw the corpse afterwards on a bed in Chalk Farm.'[24]

Montgomery had, however, also badly wounded Macnamara above his left hip, his ball passing through Macnamara, together with the latter's own hip button. At an inquest held at the Southampton Arms in Camden Town on 8 April, Heaviside the surgeon gave an incautiously frank account of the duel, and of his own involvement in it.[25] After the inquest, a charge of manslaughter was brought against Macnamara.[26] Subsequently, however, at the instance of Sir Richard Ford, the chief magistrate at Bow Street, Macnamara, the two seconds and Heaviside were all charged with murder. Macnamara, because of his wound, was allowed to stay under guard at Blake's Hotel in Jermyn Street (attended by his dog). The two seconds had disappeared, but Heaviside was arrested, refused bail and held in Newgate. The grand jury, however, threw out the charge of murder against all of the accused, and restricted the lesser charge of manslaughter to Macnamara himself.

Despite the severity of his wound, Macnamara stood trial at the Old Bailey two weeks after the duel, on 22 April. While witnesses disagreed on the exact words exchanged by the two men during their initial quarrel, there was no doubt that Macnamara's bullet had killed Montgomery. To the judge, Mr Justice Heath, it was an open and shut case: 'the pressure of the evidence, and the prisoner's own admission, left the jury no alternative as to the verdict they were bound to pronounce'.[27]

Macnamara was defended by Thomas Erskine, who was famous for his successful defence of those accused of high treason in the London Corresponding Society trials of 1794.[28] Erskine was remarkably well qualified to appear in the case. Prior to becoming a barrister, he had served as an officer first in the navy and then in the army. He had fought a duel himself, against a surgeon called O'Bryen in Brighton in 1782. He had also acted successfully for the defence in a number of duelling cases.[29] Finally, he had a Newfoundland dog, Phoss, which he trained to sit with his paws on a table, and a wig on his head, in imitation of a judge.* On Erskine's advice, Macnamara admitted the basic facts of the case but claimed that he had been insulted. He rested his defence upon the need to keep up his professional reputation at a time of national danger:

> Gentlemen, I am a Captain of the British Navy. My character you can only hear from others; but to maintain any character, in that station, I must be respected. When called upon to lead others into honourable danger, I must not be supposed to be a man who had sought safety by submitting to what custom has taught others to consider as a disgrace. I am not presuming to urge any thing against the laws of God, or of this land. I know that, in the eye of religion and reason, obedience to the law, though against the general feelings of the world, is the first duty, and ought to be the rule of action: but, in putting a construction upon my motives, so as to ascertain the quality of my actions, you will make allowances for my situation. It is impossible to define in terms the proper feelings of a gentleman; but their existence have supported this happy country for many ages, and she might perish if they were lost. ... Gentlemen, I submit myself entirely to your

---

* Phoss's full name was Aldeborontephosscornio, after a character in Henry Carey's burlesque *Chrononhotonthologos: The Most Tragical Tragedy That Ever Was Tragediʒ'd by Any Company of Tragedians* (London, 1734), a landmark in the history of English nonsense verse. Although he mistakenly names Erskine's dog as Toss, Lord Campbell gives a full description of its judicial activities: 'He had taught the animal to sit with much gravity upon a chair with his paws placed before him on the table, and occasionally he would put a full-bottomed wig on his head and a band round his neck – placing a black-letter folio before him.' John, Lord Campbell, *The Lives of the Lord Chancellors and Keepers of the Great Seal of England from the Earliest Times till the Reign of King George IV*, vi (London, 1847), p. 696. Phoss died in 1814 at the age of twenty (an extreme age for such a large dog) and was described by Erskine as having 'no burlesque belonging to him', but rather as 'the most sagacious and affectionate being ever created'. For Erskine's verses in his memory and his hopes for the dog's immortality, Alexander Fergusson, *The Honourable Henry Erskine, Lord Advocate for Scotland: With Notices of Certain of his Kinsfolk and of his Time* (Edinburgh and London, 1882), p. 529n.; see also, pp. 169–72. The most famous nonsense poet in English, Edward Lear, owned a cat called Foss.

judgments. I hope to obtain my liberty, through your verdict; and to employ it with honour in the defence of the liberties of my country.[30]

Macnamara was also able to call upon a remarkable number of eminent character witnesses. Admiral Lord Hood, with whom he had served on the *Victory*, described Macnamara as 'a man of great moderation and mildness'. Even more impressively, Viscount Nelson, the victor of the battle of the Nile and already a great national hero, stated:

> I have known Captain Macnamara nine years; he has been at various times under my command; during my acquaintance with him, I have not only the highest esteem and respect for him, as an officer, but I always looked upon him as a gentleman, who would not take an affront from any man; yet, as I stand here before God and my countrymen, I do not believe he ever gave offence to man, woman, or child during the time I have known him.[31]

Hood and Nelson were supported by other leading sailors, Lord Minto, Sir Hyde Parker and Sir Thomas Trowbridge, as well as General Churchill and Captain George Martin. William Garrow, who appeared with Erskine for the defence, indeed claimed that 'he could call all the captains of the British Navy, but he thought it was not necessary'.[*] The jury retired from the court for a quarter of a hour before returning to pronounce a verdict of not guilty. The duel did little harm to Macnamara's subsequent career, as he continued in active service until 1814, in the Baltic, the North Sea and off the coast of France, and retired as a rear admiral.[†]

The duel itself had, unsurprisingly, caused a public sensation. In its immediate aftermath, 'Many gentlemen on horseback, and others, went to Chalk Farm to enquire into the particulars yesterday, and crowds of persons were all day viewing

---

* William Garrow had previously acted with Erskine in at least one other duelling case. Two centuries later, Garrow achieved fame as the hero of the BBC series, *Garrow's Law* (three series, 2009–12). He is credited with introducing the principle of 'innocent until found guilty' to the Old Bailey. Banks, *A Polite Exchange of Bullets*, p. 140; 'William Garrow (1760–1840)', *Oxford Dictionary of National Biography*.

† Whatever he may have said in testimony, Nelson's private opinion of Macnamara was less fulsome. A year after the duel he wrote to Emma Hamilton: 'To marry into the family of the Macnamaras, what a prospect. As for Captain Macnamara, it is not difficult to see that he will be shot. He seems to lay himself out for it, and after what has happened no one will pity him. Our friend, Mrs D., seems to think him a nonsuch.' Viscount Nelson to Lady Hamilton, 27 August 1804, Harvard University Library, Houghton MS Eng. 196.5. Macnamara himself married only in 1818. His wife was Henrietta Carleton, the widow of Lieutenant Colonel George Carleton (1781–1814), by whom she had four children. She was the daughter of Henry King of Askham Hall, Westmorland. *Bury and Norwich Post*, 4 February 1818. Macnamara died on 15 January 1826 at Clifton, *Times*, 23 January 1826; *Morning Post*, 24 January 1826. His obituaries devote most of their space to his notorious duel on Primrose Hill.

the spot where Colonel Montgomery fell, which was covered with blood.' It even elicited a short poem, *An Elegy on Colonel Robert Montgomery: Written on the Fatal Spot Where the Lamentable Duel Transpired*, which included the lines

> Oh fatal hill! Engulp'd with sighs and rage,
> Fatal hill! Boast thy pleasantry no more.[32]

Six years later, another duel was fuelled by drink. At 10 o'clock on the morning of 28 February 1809, Viscount Falkland, like James Macnamara a naval captain, fought Arthur Powell at Chalk Farm.[33] 'The distance of ten paces being stepped, and the pistols loaded by the seconds, the parties took their ground, when, by etiquette, Mr Powell being entitled to the first shot, his ball fatally entered the right groin of Lord Falkland.'[34] Following the duel, Falkland was conveyed in a carriage to Powell's house in Devonshire Place, where the surgeon, John Heaviside – who seems to have made something of a speciality of attending at duels – pronounced the wound mortal. Falkland, after hearing the surgeon's opinion, said 'with a faltering voice, and as intelligibly as the agonised state of his body and mind would permit, "I acquit Mr Powell of all blame in this transaction; I alone am culpable".' Falkland died without the ball being extracted two days later.[35] He was visited by the Duke of Sussex on the day after the duel.[36]

This duel was between former friends. Arthur Powell's father had held a lucrative position in the army pay office. Powell himself was a wealthy 'gentleman well known in the polite world, and an intimate friend of his Royal Highness the Duke of Clarence'. He had recently inherited considerable landed property in Fulham and a large fortune in the funds. On its receipt, he had given £10,000 to each of his three sisters, who had previously been scantily provided for.[37] Although separated from his wife, who was living in Ramsgate, Powell was 'esteemed one of the best tempered and most inoffensive men that exist'.[38]

Charles Cary, ninth Viscount Falkland, had succeeded his brother to the title in 1796.[39] Aged forty, he was a drinking companion of Lord Byron, with whom he had dined on 6 February at the Clarendon Hotel in Bond Street at the inaugural meeting of the Neapolitan Club, chaired by the Duke of Sussex, and was described as 'a lively, pleasant man, and by no means of a quarrelsome disposition'.[40] In a note to *English Bards and Scotch Reviewers*, Byron wrote:

> I knew the late Lord Falkland well. On Sunday night I beheld him presiding at his own table, in all the honest pride of hospitality; on Wednesday morning, at three o'clock, I saw stretched before me all that remained of courage, feeling, and a host of passions. He was a gallant and successful officer: his faults were the faults of a sailor – as such, Britons will forgive them. He died like a brave man

in a better cause; for had he fallen in like manner on the deck of the frigate to which he was just appointed, his last moments would have been held up by his countrymen as an example to succeeding heroes.*

It is not clear that Byron saw Falkland presiding at his table on the day before the duel or that he visited him on the day after it.

Falkland had had a successful career in the navy, capturing enemy prizes worth £20,000 to himself. This prize money had made up, to some degree, for the fact that, by the standards of the nobility, Falkland was impoverished. Although the family was English, Falkland's title was a Scottish one. Nor did he own a landed estate. According to a contemporary diary, 'The fortunes of his family have been long reduced and in succession those who have borne the title have received a pension or some employment from government.' [41] In 1802 Falkland had married, for love rather than money, Christina Anton, the beautiful daughter of a merchant in the West Indies. Only the previous month, many of his possessions had been destroyed by a fire at Warne's Hotel in Conduit Street. 'The alarm being made, Lord Falkland ran to save some cash in his secretaire, but he was forced by the flames to retire in great danger, without effecting his object. It is reported his Lordship lost £300.' [42] His naval career had also been at a standstill. In consequence 'of some convivial excesses on board his vessel', he had been 'dismissed the service a year or two ago ... on account of some irregularities arising from too free a circulation of the bottle at his own table'.[43] He had, however, recently been appointed to a new command. Indeed, Byron was due to sail with him on the frigate *Desirée* to Sicily.

On the Saturday night before the duel Falkland had dined in company at Powell's house, where they had disagreed 'respecting the properties of a peculiar description of Burgundy', but then had played together amicably at whist.[44] Afterwards, they went 'arm in arm' to the opera, 'having taken plenty of wine'.[45] Next they went to Stevens's Hotel in Bond Street, where they supped and then drank Madeira negus. After they had parted company, on the most amicable terms, Falkland went on with other friends to the Mount Coffee House, in Lower Grosvenor Street, at 3 o'clock in the morning, where they drank several more bottles of wine. When, at 6 a.m., the coffee-house refused to serve them more, 'the waiter and his master were assailed, and poker, tongs and decanters were put in requisition until a body

---

* Lord Byron, *English Bards and Scotch Reviewers: A Satire* (4th edn, London, 1811), p. 53. In lines 660, 667 and 668 of the poem, Byron wrote:

> Here's Powell's pistol ready for your life ...
> The mangled victim of a drunken brawl,
> To live like Clodius, and like Falkland fall.

Publius Clodius Pulcher was a disreputable Roman politician murdered in 52 BC. His sister, Clodia Pulchra, addressed as Lesbia by Catullus, was the subject of the latter's best poems.

of watchmen took them to the watch-house. Lord Falkland and a Mr Grimsdale were held to bail.'[46]

On Sunday evening Lord Falkland revisited Stevens's Hotel. On espying Powell in the coffee room, he accosted him with the words: 'What drunk again tonight, Pogey?'[47] At this point, neither man was perfectly sober. It was Falkland's public use of his nickname which Powell resented.* Powell

> expressed much displeasure, remarking, 'that he had not the honour of being sufficiently acquainted with him, to entitle his lordship to take so great a liberty'. This drew from Lord Falkland a sarcastic reply, accompanied by some threats; on which Mr Powell rejoined, that 'he had that in his hand (meaning a stick) which would defend him against any menace, even from a lord'. Lord Falkland on the instant snatched a cane from some gentleman in the room, and, as it is reported, struck Mr Powell many severe blows with it. The consequence was a challenge from the latter ...[48]

Physical blows of this kind between gentlemen led, almost inevitably, to a duel. Falkland went the next morning to Powell's house to apologise, but Powell's insistence that an apology be made publicly at Stevens's Hotel, either by Falkland himself or by Powell's brother-in-law, Captain Cotton, on his behalf, was further than Falkland was willing to go. Powell accordingly sent Cotton, as his second, to demand satisfaction. 'Lord Falkland appeared much hurt after he received the challenge, and he did not take wine, as usual, at dinner on Monday, on which day Mr Powell and others, who dined at his house, were to have dined with Lord Falkland. His Lordship did not go to bed on Monday night, but threw himself on a sofa ...'[49]

After he had been wounded by Powell, who shot first, and despite the severity of his wound, Falkland 'stood for above a minute in his position, and then threw his pistol away without discharging its contents. It is well understood that his Lordship never intended to fire at his antagonist, for he was aware he had done wrong, but he conceived his honour called him to the field, rather than make the apology required.'[50]

A coroner's inquest, held at Powell's house, followed two days after Falkland's death. At the inquest the only witnesses examined were Heaviside the surgeon; Powell's butler, Norvell; and Mrs King, the nurse who had attended Falkland. Norvell claimed that Falkland had been brought to the house in a carriage, but

---

* 'He has ever been considered a most inoffensive man, and his familiar friends have long been in the habit of calling him "Pogey Powell"; but though he took no notice of this in private circles, it may readily be conceived that its repetition in public company would be extremely offensive.' *Trewman's Exeter Flying Post*, 9 March 1809.

that he did not know who owned the carriage. Heaviside stated equivocally that he had only been called to examine Falkland after the latter had been brought to Powell's house. All claimed that Falkland had said nothing to them about how he had received his wound. They also told the coroner that Lady Falkland had been unaware of the duel before it took place and had only been informed of its outcome late on Tuesday evening. Neither Powell himself nor the two seconds, Captain Cotton and Mr Ross, were examined. Although the coroner instructed the jury to find a verdict of 'wilful murder against some person or persons unknown', no evidence as to the identity of the perpetrator had been heard and no prosecution followed.[51] Indeed, convictions for deaths caused by duelling remained very rare. Only when the surviving duellist had taken an unfair advantage, failing to obey the conventions that made duels formally equal, was a conviction at all likely. The three sets of juries involved before a conviction was possible – the coroner's jury, the grand jury and the petty jury – repeatedly threw out attempts at prosecution, even when these were made.

The duel had a strange sequel. Falkland's widow was left 'without a shilling', with four young children and pregnant with a fifth. Byron stood godfather to the posthumous baby and generously gave the widow £500, leaving a banknote to that value in a breakfast cup to avoid embarrassment. In 1812 Lady Falkland, after Byron had become famous overnight on the publication of his *Childe Harold's Pilgrimage*, became infatuated with the poet, convincing herself that he was also in love with her, and that passages in *Childe Harold* were about her. On 13 July 1812, she wrote to him, 'You believe that my affections are buried with Falkland in the tomb. Banish all apprehension on that account – I had long ceased to respect or esteem him. It is not a loveless heart I offer you, but a heart whose every throb beats responsive to your own.'[52] Byron, however, did not respond.

The majority of duels on Primrose Hill were either between two officers or between an officer and a non-military opponent, often only identified in newspaper reports by the first and last letters of their surnames.* A typical example was fought in July 1807. 'A duel took place yesterday morning, soon after day-break, in the fields near Primrose Hill, between the son of an earl and Captain B., an officer of Dragoons, in consequence of an altercation which arose between the parties on leaving the Opera on Saturday night. Captain B.'s second fire slightly wounded his antagonist in the arm, when the affair was adjusted.'[53] The cause of the duels included 'a private misunderstanding'; an accusation of pushing off the pavement;

---

*   The disguising of names in this way was a common practice in the newspapers of the day, designed to avoid charges of libel. Protagonists, however, had no objection to the reporting of duels, if this showed that they had been fought fairly. Some may indeed have informed newspapers about the duels themselves.

an argument at the Cavendish Rooms, St Marylebone; a dispute respecting a lady at Covent Garden Theatre; the fairness of a throw at which £3,000 changed hands; and a drunken argument about the relative merits of the army versus the navy.[54]

A foretaste of Primrose Hill's literary reputation was fittingly occasioned by an argument caused by a review. In May 1806 Tom Moore, the Irish poet, published *Epistles, Odes and Other Poems*. It contained little of his best work but did include some erotic verse. A review in the *Edinburgh Review* in July described Moore as 'the most licentious of modern versifiers, and the most poetical of those who, in our times, have devoted their talents to the propagation of immorality'.[55] The reviewer, who refrained from quoting any of the immoral verses, accused Moore of corrupting language, women and the aristocracy:

> There is nothing, it will be allowed, more indefensible than a cold-blooded attempt to corrupt the purity of an innocent heart, and we can scarcely conceive any being more truly despicable than he who, without the apology of unruly passion, or tumultuous desires, sits down to ransack the impure place of his memory for inflammatory images and expressions, and commits them laboriously to writing, for the purpose of insinuating *pollution* into the minds of unknown and unsuspecting readers.[56]

He went on to advise the government 'to put the law in force against this publication'.

Moore discovered that the reviewer, the editor of the *Edinburgh Review*, Francis Jeffrey, was visiting London and challenged him to a duel with the words, 'You are a liar; yes, sir, a liar.' A meeting was arranged at Primrose Hill on Monday 11 August, with Thomas Hume acting as Moore's second and Francis Horner as Jeffrey's.[57] Both principals were very short. As neither owned his own pistols, duelling pistols were borrowed from William Spencer.[58] That Moore was humbly born, and Irish, may have made him keen to confirm his claims to gentility by issuing a challenge. Although he claimed that neither ill-temper nor personal hostility had played any part in his provocation of the duel, that his motives 'were equally free from a certain *Irish* predilection for such encounters, or wholly unleavened by a dash of vanity, I will not positively assert'.[59]

While their seconds discussed the arrangements for the duel and loaded the pistols behind some trees, the principals were forced into an awkward conversation. Jeffrey remarked, 'What a beautiful morning it is', to which Moore replied, 'Yes, a morning for better purposes'. As the seconds seemed to be taking their time with the preparations, Moore told a joke about what an Irish barrister, Billy Egan, had said in similar circumstances: 'Sure, isn't it bad enough to take the dose without being by at the mixing up.'[60] When they were eventually ready to fire, police officers suddenly rushed out from a hedge and prevented the exchange. It transpired that William Spencer had told Lord Fincastle, who had told the authorities. Taken to Bow Street, Moore and Jeffrey indulged in pleasant talk, while heavy sureties were taken, and soon discovered how much they liked one another.

The aftermath of the duel proved more controversial than the duel itself. Rumours soon began to circulate that Moore's pistol had been loaded but that Jeffrey's had not; or that both the pistols had been loaded not with bullets but with paper pellets.[61] According to *The Times*, the following day:

> On the parties being discharged, the pistols were examined, when it appeared that no dire mischief could possibly have ensued from this combat. The pistol of Mr Jeffrey was not loaded with ball, and that of Mr Moore had nothing more than a pellet of paper. So if the police had not appeared, this alarming duel would have turned out to be a game of pop-guns.[62]

A mock ballad, 'The Paper Pellet Duel: or Papyro-Pelleto Machia', appeared in the *Morning Post*:

> And God preserve all writing blades
> Who fain would cut a caper;
> Yet nothing at each other's heads,
> But pellets shoot – of paper.[63]

Lord Byron later joined in the mockery of Jeffrey and Moore, who had published his early poems under the pseudonym of Thomas Little, by verses in *English Bards and Scotch Reviewers*:

> Health to great Jeffrey! Heaven preserve his life,
> To flourish on the fertile shores of Fife,
> And guard it sacred in its future wars,
> Since authors sometimes seek the field of Mars!
> Can none remember that eventful day,
> That ever-glorious, almost fatal fray,
> When Little's leadless pencil met his eye,
> And Bow Street's myrmidons stood laughing by?*

---

* Lord Byron, *English Bards and Scotch Reviewers*, lines 460–8. The poem was first published, anonymously, in 1809. Byron added a note after the first four editions: 'I am informed that Mr Moore published at the time a disavowal of the statements of the newspapers as far as regarded himself, and, in justice to him, I mention the circumstance. As I never heard of it before, I cannot state the particulars, and I was only made acquainted with the fact very lately.' See also Ronan Kelly, *Bard of Erin: The Life of Thomas Moore* (Dublin, 2008), pp. 128–51.

This almost led to another duel, this time between Byron and Moore.[64] The two poets later, however, established a firm friendship.

A more deadly literary dispute was fought out on 16 February 1821, 'in a field between Chalk Farm and Primrose Hill', by John Scott, the editor of the *London Magazine* and Jonathan Christie, a friend of J.G. Lockhart, the editor of *Blackwood's Magazine*. Three articles by Scott, attacking the conduct and management of *Blackwood's*, had led to a paper war involving Christie, Lockhart and Scott. The last called on Christie to demand an apology or instant satisfaction. Refusing to apologise, Christie agreed to a meeting that same night at nine o'clock.

> The moon shone with brightness, so that the parties had a full opportunity of seeing each other, and, having taken ground, they fired together. Mr Scott received his antagonist's ball in his groin, and fell. Every assistance which the circumstances would permit was afforded him, and he was conveyed on a shutter to Chalk Farm Tavern, where he was laid on a bed.[65]

As was often the case with bullet wounds to the stomach at the time, the wound proved fatal. In April 1821, Christie, with his second, James Traill, was tried at the Old Bailey for murder but acquitted.[66] P.G. Patmore, Scott's second and the father of the Victorian poet Coventry Patmore, was later also tried and acquitted. In this duel, the actions of the seconds attracted much criticism. The fatal shot was, in fact, fired during a second exchange. In the first exchange, Christie, who acted with great correctness throughout, had not aimed at Scott. This should have been enough to bring the matter to an end. The seconds had, nevertheless, made the arrangements for a second exchange without Scott being told of Christie's action. Traill also advised Christie not to leave himself a defenceless target again. At the last minute, Scott asked whether Christie had fired away during the first exchange but was told by Patmore that he must not talk but fire. Years later, Thackeray initially refused to be introduced to Coventry Patmore, saying 'I won't touch the hand of the son of a murderer'.[67]

The exact location of another literary duel, fought on 26 November 1823 between the Italian patriot, poet and man of letters Ugo Foscolo and his one-time literary assistant, Samuel Carter Hall, is uncertain, though Barrow Hill was the probable venue. Foscolo, who lived in Digamma Cottage in South Bank in St John's Wood, had three maidservants, referred to as the Three Graces, one, according to John Cam Hobhouse, as 'beautiful as Hebe'. Two of these maids, however, turned out to be prostitutes, and one ran off with Hall. When Foscolo wrote a kindly letter to her, which contained some remarks on Hall's character, she showed it to Hall, who then challenged Foscolo. Foscolo, by his own account, received his opponent's fire at ten paces but then fired in the air.[68]

In February 1826 Byron's publisher, John Murray, was also in danger from an enraged author. Dr Robert Lyall was convinced that his *The Character of the Russians and a Detailed History of Moscow* had been 'shamefully treated' in the conservative *Quarterly Review*, published by Murray. Lyall was unappeased by Murray's disclaimer that 'I neither have, nor ever had, the slightest influence over the editorial staff of the *Quarterly Review*'. Murray suggested that Lyall had the remedy of an action at law, refused to disclose the reviewer's name and threatened that 'if he heard anything further about a challenge, he would answer it by a Bow Street officer'. Lyall was on the point of publishing the exchange, which he claimed showed that Murray was no gentleman, when he received an anonymous note from the actual author of the review, John Barrow, who offered 'to give Dr Lyall the desired satisfaction tomorrow morning at half past six, in the fields between Hampstead road and Primrose Hill'. Lyall disdained the letter, 'delivered by a common porter', and refused to take 'notice of such a communication'.[69]

Other duels were fought for more mundane reasons. On 16 July 1792, a newspaper reported:

> Yesterday morning, about five o'clock, a duel [was] fought in a park near Chalk Farm, Hampstead, between a Mr A......r, a Scotch gentleman, who resides at Kentish Town, and an Irish student, who has country lodgings at the same place: each fired a brace of pistols, but fortunately without injury to either party. On the seconds interposing, the principals left the ground. The dispute is said to have originated the preceding evening at the Assembly House in Kentish Town, from the latter gentleman's throwing some unguarded reflexions on the countrymen of the former.[70]

Another death, that of Thomas O'Reilly on 18 May 1804, followed an incident in Hyde's Rooms in Tottenham Street the previous evening, where O'Reilly, predictably an army officer, had 'very grossly insulted' Humphry Hobart, a student of law at the Temple. Although the origins of the quarrel are obscure, Hobart alleged that 'O'Reilly had used such language to him that no gentleman could put up with'. Nevertheless, the challenge seems to have come from O'Reilly rather than Hobart, or so Hobart maintained. Hobart also claimed that he had wished to settle the business without recourse to a duel. O'Reilly's insistence, however, led to a meeting 'in a field the north side of Chalk Farm' at six the next evening. According to a witness:

> I observed them taking their ground, when I was at the hedge, then I got into the field where they were; I saw the two gentlemen placed in their situations, standing opposite to each other, back to back; they were fifteen or sixteen paces from each other, and a gentleman stood nearly in the centre between them; he gave the signal, I believe that the signal was one, two; he stood wide of them,

then they fired; I saw one of the gentlemen put his hand to the right hand side
of his hip, then I saw them take him to the farm, he did not fall, his friends that
were of the group supported him, or else he would have fallen, he seemed to
totter, and the man that fired ran away.[71]

Although the ball was extracted, O'Reilly died the next day. Tried at the Old Bailey
for murder, Hobart was acquitted.[72]

Another duel, in 1824, stemmed from a dispute about whether a bet had been
made in jest or in earnest:

A duel was fought on Saturday morning, in a field to the westward of Primrose
Hill, between two gentlemen of the names of Littleton and Rogers, in consequence
of a disputed bet on the Doncaster St Leger, whether the bet of 500 sovereigns to
ten against a horse that did not start was named to be play or pay. Mr Littleton
was wounded in the side, but not dangerously, and the affair terminated.[73]

More than one duel was caused by a dispute over a lady:

Yesterday morning a duel was fought in a field adjoining Chalk Farm, between Mr
V. Leander, well known in the musical world, and a Captain Compton: the parties
met, accompanied by their seconds and surgeons, and after having exchanged a
case of pistols each, the affair was proposed by the seconds to be amicably settled,
when the latter gentleman, at whose instigation the duel had arisen, insisted
on further satisfaction, and unfortunately for him his adversary's ball took too
fatal an effect, for little hopes are entertained of his recovery. The cause of this
unhappy catastrophe we understand was occasioned by some trifling civilities
shewn by a lady to Mr Leander, to whom Captain Compton paid his addresses.[74]

Occasionally, the cause of a duel remained uncertain. When Lieutenant Edmund
Bailey of the 28th Regiment, whose father lived in Limerick, fought Theodore
O'Callaghan in January 1818 the motive remained unclear. It was claimed that
they were fighting on behalf of others. O'Callaghan shot Bailey in the right side.
Carried to a house in Ingram's Lane, Bailey died about two hours after the duel,
having first forgiven O'Callaghan. O'Callaghan and both the seconds, Lieutenant
Charles Newbolt and Thomas Phealan, were nevertheless, and unusually, found
guilty of manslaughter and sentenced to three months' imprisonment.[75]

Where the monopoly on duelling by gentlemen was breached, as it occasionally
was, this tended to be by working men rather than by members of the bourgeoisie.
In 1808 Sandoz, a jeweller, and Dubois, a watchcase-maker, were bound over to
keep the peace after it became known that they intended to fight at Chalk Farm.
In February 1819 a dispute about a bet of five shillings, in the Rose in Wigmore
Street, led James Good and George Smith, both gentlemen's servants out of place,

to arrange to meet at Chalk Farm the next morning. Arrested on their way to the duel, carrying loaded horse-pistols, and with a tailor and a barber as seconds, they were bound over to keep the peace.[76] A duel between two journeymen apprentices, both of whom worked for Broadwood, the pianoforte manufacturer, was fought in 1809, most appropriately, over a dispute about tuning.[77]

A later duel on Primrose Hill, on 25 August 1832, was almost certainly the most exotic:

> On Friday morning, at an early hour, a hostile meeting took place at Chalk Farm, between Prince Troubetskoy, a young Russian nobleman of high rank, and Count Tolstoy, Principal Secretary of Legation to the Russian Embassy. The prince was attended by Monsieur Lomanshoff, a gentleman also connected with the Russian Embassy, and Prince Paul Lieven, eldest son of the Russian Ambassador, attended as second to Count Tolstoy.[78]

The duellists were probably Count Ivan Tolstoy (1806–67) and Prince Uri Troubetzkoy (d. 1850), both of whom served in the Russian Ministry of Foreign Affairs.* The two had dined together on Thursday, at the house of Benkhausen, the Russian consul general, where Troubetskoy had heard an observation, made in an undertone by Count Tolstoy, which the prince 'deemed disrespectful to him and the rank he holds as a Russian prince'. He had therefore left the table and returned to Mivart's Hotel, where he was staying, to write the count a challenge to meet him at 5 o'clock the next morning.

> In consequence all the before-named parties met in a field at the foot of Primrose Hill, and in the immediate vicinity of Chalk Farm. The ground having been measured, and the pistols handed to each of the principals, they fired at each other, taking deliberate aim – a mode of duelling, we are informed, which is customary in Russia. Fortunately neither of the shots took effect, and immediately on the report of the pistols four or five policemen hastened to the spot, whereupon the whole party jumped into their cabrioles, which were waiting at a short distance, and drove off to town with the utmost speed, and thereby eluded the police. The above affair has created no small sensation in the diplomatic circle. Prince Troubetskoy has only been in England a few days, and was presented to the king by Prince Lieven at the last Levee. Lord Ranelagh was not upon the ground; but it is said that his lordship lent some very *matériel* assistance to the combatants, both of whom were unprovided for the occasion.[79]

---

*   The Tolstoy and the Troubetskoy families were very extensive, making definitive identification difficult. Count Leo Tolstoy, the novelist, born in 1828, was aged three at the time of this duel. See Nicolas Ikonnikov, *La noblesse de Russie*, xviii (2nd edn, Paris, 1962), p. 139, no. 727 (Tolstoy); and p. 405, no. 105 (Troubetskoy).

Although at first Troubetskoy had wished to fire at five paces, the seconds insisted that this was likely to lead to a charge of murder. The duel was then fought at the much more survivable distance of twenty paces. The two men were subsequently reconciled.

The last duel on Primrose Hill, in May 1837, was the only one fought *à la barrière*, in the continental fashion:

> On Tuesday a hostile meeting took place near Primrose Hill between J.P. J-s-n, Esq., and R. T-k-r, Esq., both connected with the 'turf', and the latter gentleman well known among the sporting circles of the West End. The parties were placed at thirty paces, with the liberty of advancing to within twelve places of each other, and to fire optionally. The belligerents advanced slowly towards each other till within fifteen paces, when both stopped and a pause took place. The seconds were just upon the point of interfering, when both principals fired simultaneously, the ball from Mr J.'s pistol passing through the fleshy part of his opponent's right arm. A surgeon was in attendance, who pronounced the wound to be severe but not dangerous. The parties left the ground in their respective cabs. The cause of dispute was said to have arisen from Mr T-k-r having eloped with Mr J-s-n's sister, a married lady; the eloping party having been pursued by the husband and Mr J.; and the latter, on overtaking the fugitives, having inflicted summary punishment on the seducer.[80]

Despite being denounced by anti-duelling campaigners, and seen as unacceptable by many, duelling in Britain continued into the 1840s. The sensational trial, and acquittal, of James Brudenell, seventh Earl of Cardigan, who later led the Charge of the Light Brigade, before the House of Lords in 1841 highlighted the anachronism of duelling. In May 1840, as colonel of the 11th Hussars, Cardigan had reprimanded Captain John Reynolds, an officer in the regiment, for misconduct at a formal dinner held following an inspection.[81] Reynolds, who had been stationed in India for a number of years, had ordered a black bottle containing Moselle to be brought to the table and then told the waiter to leave it there. This was against Cardigan's instruction that all wine should be decanted. Cardigan may also have assumed that the black bottle contained porter, a favourite drink of Indian officers.

Following the dinner, Cardigan sent a message to Reynolds: 'The colonel has desired me, as president of the mess committee, to tell you that you were very wrong in having a black bottle placed on the table at a great dinner like last night, as the mess should be conducted like a gentleman's table, and not like a tavern or pot-house.'[82] The incident exposed a clash of personalities and a division in the regiment between Cardigan, who wished to bring the regiment up to a high level of polish and activity, and a number of its officers used to the more relaxed life and standards of India, where the regiment had been previously stationed. With neither side prepared to compromise, what seemed a trivial dispute led first to the arrest of Reynolds and, eventually, to his being severely reprimanded.[83] The defence of Reynolds by another 'Indian' officer, Captain Harvey Tuckett, in the *Morning Chronicle*, led to a duel between Cardigan and Tuckett. Fought on Wimbledon Common, on 12 September 1840, Tuckett was wounded after a second exchange. Cardigan was charged with intent to murder but acquitted on a technicality within six hours, after the prosecution team deliberately mishandled the case.[84]

Another notorious duel, between two brothers-in-law, Colonel Fawcett and Lieutenant Munro, was fought near the Brecknock Arms in Camden Town on 1 July 1843. Caused by a dispute over the management of property, it led to the death of Colonel Fawcett. Tried for murder, Munro was convicted and sentenced to death, although this was subsequently reduced to a two-year term of imprisonment. When discussed in the House of Commons, Sir Charles Napier, MP for Marylebone and the leading naval hero of the day, gave it as his opinion that the best way to prevent duels would be only to allow them to be fought across a table. Only one of the two pistols, for which lots would be drawn, would be loaded; and the survivor would then be hanged.[85]

The practice was effectively brought to an end in Britain in 1844, when Sir Robert Peel changed the Articles of War to make participation in a duel a court-martial offence, with the cashiering of any officer convicted. The widows of officers killed in duels, including the widow of Colonel Fawcett, were also no longer entitled to a pension. Although a handful of duels were fought in Britain after 1844, these changes succeeded in bringing the practice to an end within the armed forces, its principal bastion. Elsewhere in Europe, notably in France and Germany, and in America, duels continued to be fought until the First World War and very occasionally afterwards.[*]

Other pistol shots, linked directly to an event unique in British history, were fired on Primrose Hill in 1812. Two half-inch calibre pistols had been bought in April 1812

---

[*] The last duel fought by two Englishmen on English soil was that between two officers, Lieutenant Hawkey and Lieutenant Seton, at Gosport in Hampshire in May 1845, in which Seton was killed. Hawkey was subsequently acquitted of murder. Two Frenchmen, Emmanuel Barthélemy and Frédéric Cournet, fought at Englefield Green in Surrey in October 1852. Cournet was shot dead by Barthélemy, who had killed two men in earlier duels. Barthélemy was acquitted of murder but hanged, three years later, for another homicide. See Banks, *A Polite Exchange of Bullets*, pp. 287, 288; Richard Hopton, *Pistols at Dawn: A History of Duelling* (London, 2007), pp. 260–71.

John Bellingham
(1769–1812), the
assassin of Spencer
Perceval, from a
contemporary account
of his trial.
(*Private Collection*)

JOHN BELLINGHAM.
Taken at the Sessions House
Old Bailey, May 15 1812.

on Ludgate Hill by John Bellingham.* An unsuccessful merchant, born in St Neots in Cambridgeshire but with a wife and children in Liverpool, Bellingham was a man with a grievance. While trading in Russia in 1804, he had been imprisoned for debt in Archangel and then in St Petersburg. On his release, he had sought redress and compensation by writing first to the Marquess Wellesley and then to a sequence of ministers and government departments, as well as by petitioning the Prince Regent.[86] He was particularly aggrieved by the failure to help him of Lord Granville Leveson Gower, the ambassador to Russia during his imprisonment.[87] Receiving no satisfaction, he determined to express his complaint in a direct and sensational manner.

---

*   Andro Linklater, *Why Spencer Perceval Had to Die: The Assassination of a British Prime Minister* (London, 2012), pp. 148–223, provides an elegant but questionable conspiracy theory to show that Bellingham may have had backers among Liverpool merchants affected by Perceval's determination to enforce a ban on the slave trade. The prime evidence for the conspiracy is the ease with which Bellingham paid his washing bills in the weeks leading up to the murder. Ibid., pp. 154–55, 208–23. 'John Bellingham (c. 1769–1812)', *Oxford Dictionary of National Biography*.

Bellingham's grievance was a general one against the government of the day. He learned, however, to recognise its individual members on the Treasury bench during repeated visits to the public gallery of House of Commons. He was also 'so anxious not be disappointed by the failure of the weapons, that, after he had bought the pistols, for which he gave four guineas, he went to Primrose Hill to try how they would go off'.[88] Having tested the pistols to his own satisfaction, and having had his coat pockets specially altered to conceal them, he waited in the lobby of the House on 11 May, after an afternoon spent visiting the European Museum with his landlady. At about a quarter past five, Spencer Perceval, the Tory Prime Minister since 1809, and a man against whom Bellingham felt no personal animosity, entered the lobby, where Bellingham shot him at point-blank range, leading to Perceval's death within minutes.[*] (If Lord Granville had entered the lobby before Perceval, Bellingham would have shot him instead.) Arrested immediately, Bellingham was tried four days later at the Old Bailey, any question of his insanity being summarily dismissed, and was hanged the following Monday outside Newgate Prison.[†]

---

[*]   Perceval himself had a connection with Primrose Hill, in that he had lived at Belsize House until 1807, riding down to Westminster across the fields to its south.

[†]   In July 1812, Lord Granville received a letter signed by someone calling himself Bellingham and challenging him to a duel on Primrose Hill: 'Dear Sir, As you have forced me by your most unnatural cruelty and revenge, I now give you notice that I am your man at any weapon and that I will meet you at Primrose Hill on Monday next, 27 July, at 6 o'clock in the morning. ... It is well known especially at the time you were Consul and Ambassador at St Petersburg your infamous conduct towards my lamented friend John Bellingham Esq. has left a stain which nothing can erase. Would to God that he had met you instead of Perceval and planted a fatal bullet in your breast. Then his triumph would have been glorious. I am determined to revenge the loss of my friend. His blood calls for vengeance and as you were the chief in that unfortunate affair I am resolved to seek your life or lose my own.' National Archives, PRO 30/29/6/11, letter dated 25 July 1812.

1. The Chalk Farm Tavern was for many years the only building of substance near Primrose Hill. At the end of a turning off the Hampstead road, it was a popular venue, hosting a variety of entertainments and with a reputation for rowdiness. Reached easily from the West End, it was a well-known meeting place for duellists. (*CLSAC*)

2. D.T. Egerton, *The Trial of Nerves* (1824). The Chalk Farm Tavern is on the left. Part of the original caption reads, 'when you are compelled to stand fire against one who will not admit the blank cartridge system and who has arrived at the enviable distinction of having "kill'd his man", the pleasure of taking the field is apt to degenerate into a nervous bore as you consider yourself mark'd for crow's meat …'. Sinister black birds hover over the scene. (*CLSAC*)

3. Uniforms were a common sight on Primrose Hill, seen here without trees in its early years as a park. This soldier, with gloves, spurs and riding crop, may have come from the Albany Street barracks of the Life Guards. He is shown on the cover illustration, by Alfred Concanen, of a popular Music Hall song of 1865, 'The Perambulator; or Matilda's Young Guard'. The first lines of the song are: 'I've fallen in love with a pretty young girl, My wife I think I'll make her. I met her first up Primrose Hill, As she drove a perambulator.' (CLSAC)

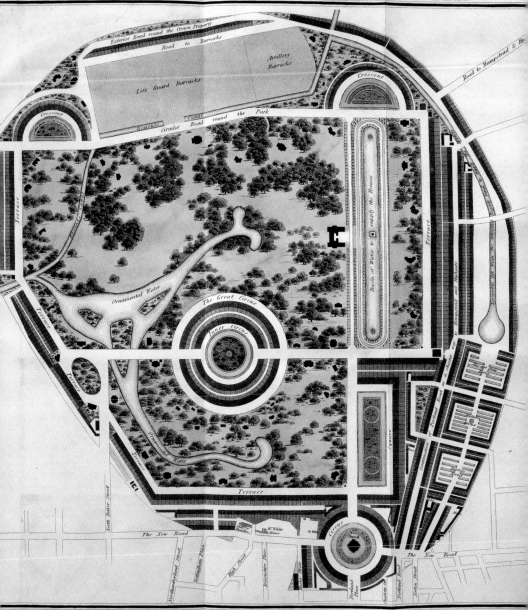

4. John Nash's revised plan for Regent's Park, 1811. The canal still runs through the park and to the south of the giant barracks. The *guinguette* for the Prince Regent is shown facing Cumberland Terrace and is centred on an ornamental stretch of water. The Inner Circle is surrounded by a double circus of housing. (*Private Collection*)

5. The giant Britannia, on top of a terraced Primrose Hill, with trident, helmet and shield, drawn by James Pennethorne as part of his plan to landscape the hill and the wider surrounding area in 1841. No steps to implement the scheme were ever taken. (*National Archives*)

6. One of eighteen watercolours by Charles Anderson, dating from around 1870, which convey a vivid impression of Regent's Park at the time. This view, from near the Broad Walk and across the English Garden, shows Decimus Burton's Colosseum and the tower of Sir John Soane's Holy Trinity Church. (*Westminster City Archives*)

7. Charles Anderson, watercolour of the main open area of Regent's Park, *c.* 1870. The Zoo is to the left, behind the flock of sheep. In the background is a now-vanished bandstand.
(*Westminster City Archives*)

8. Charles Anderson, watercolour of Primrose Hill seen from Regent's Park across the Zoo, *c.* 1870. The summit of the hill, which is still without trees, is crowded with visitors, while sheep graze in the middle distance. The spire to the right of the hill is that of an excessively heightened St Saviour's Church. (*Westminster City Archives*)

9. Two 133 feet high chimneys were conspicuous landmarks seen from Primrose Hill in the early years of the London and Birmingham Railway. They were above the stationary winding engines used to pull early trains up from Euston on an endless rope. The machinery was only used for seven years after the railway opened in 1837. The machinery was then sold and the towers demolished. (*Private Collection*)

10. Primrose Hill Tunnel, completed in 1835, was bored at the insistence of Eton College, which sold access under its land to the London and Birmingham Railway. The small trains used by the railway in its early years were a popular sightseeing attraction. (*Private Collection*)

11. Primrose Hill, seen from what is now Chalcot Square, in 1836. The hedges on the otherwise open hill mark the boundaries between different landowners, with Eton holding the top of the hill and Lord Southampton the area below the middle hedge. The garden of the Chalk Farm Tavern has more trees in it than in earlier views. (*Private Collection*)

(Detail): Below the tavern, a game of cricket (still using underarm bowling) is in progress. Behind the game can seen the Target, attached to the Chalk Farm Tavern and used by soldiers for rifle-practice.

12. The view towards the City from the summit of Primrose Hill, August 2013. The dome of Wren's St Paul's Cathedral can still be seen, though dwarfed by the Shard and the as yet uncompleted 'Cheesegrater' and 'Walkie-Talkie'. (*Alan Jones*)

4

The Gorsedd of the Bards

O N 22 September 1792, at the autumn equinox, a number of men met on the summit of Primrose Hill.[1] Following instructions from an ancient book, the group constructed a stone circle and, as a symbol of peace, sheathed a sword which had been placed on a central stone. Their leader recited odes of his own composition calling for an end to despotism and demanding the return of liberty to Britain. Three years after the outbreak of the French Revolution, and with war looming against Revolutionary France, the meeting and ceremony were clear expressions of Radical views in a city and country shaken by the political upheaval in Paris. More unusually, the main speaker also proclaimed the Gorsedd of the Bards of Britain: a court or moot, derived from a word meaning a mound or hillock in Welsh, held in the open air in accordance with the ancient rites of Bards and Druids.[2]

The speaker on Primrose Hill was a Welsh stonemason called Edward Williams. Williams, however, was far more than just a craftsman with Radical leanings.[3] He was the most influential figure in the revival, part-authentic and part-invented, of traditional Welsh culture.[4] Although the background to the event on Primrose Hill derived, in part, from far-distant history, some elements of the story are relatively straightforward. It is not surprising that a significant and symbolic Welsh public event should have taken place in London or on its then borders. As London was incomparably the largest city in Britain, and by far the largest centre of writing and publishing, it was the centre of minority as well as mainstream cultural activities. The capital, which drew writers such as David Hume and James Boswell from Scotland, and Edmund Burke, Richard Brinsley Sheridan and Thomas Moore from Ireland, was no less of a magnet to writers from Wales. In London, in contrast to any centre in Wales itself, there were sufficient educated and successful men of Welsh origin to provide congenial society and patronage for those with literary talent. The first club to be established for the Welsh living in London was the Society of Ancient Britons in 1715. This was followed by the Honourable Society of Cymmrodorion, which promoted the gathering and publication of material about Welsh history and literature, in 1751; and by the Honourable Society of Gwyneddigion, focused on north Wales, in 1770.[5]

Edward Williams alias Iolo Morganwg (1747–1826), by Robert Cruikshank (1850). Sitting in the chair on which he habitually slept, Iolo holds a manuscript with a Druidic sign at its head. (*Private Collection*)

Born in the village of Flemingston, in the Vale of Glamorgan, in 1747, Edward Williams was christened conventionally. In 1791, however, he assumed the bardic name of Iolo Morganwg. Iolo was an abbreviation of Iowerth, the Welsh version of Edward, and Morganwg the Welsh name for Glamorgan.* Williams's father was also a stonemason, but his mother, who encouraged his intellectual interests, was a *declassée* member of the gentry.† While his first language was English, a language in which he wrote much of his work, Williams was also fluent in Welsh, and was encouraged in his interest in Welsh history and literature by local scholars.[6] He

---

* A rough translation of his name is 'Glamorgan Eddie', reflecting his championship of his county. Ronald Hutton, *Blood and Mistletoe: The History of the Druids in Britain* (New Haven and London, 2009), p. 154.

† Iolo's importance in the history of Druidry has become widely acknowledged in recent years. In an earlier standard work, T.D. Kendrick, *The Druids: A Study in Keltic Prehistory* (London, 1927), he is only given four lines, under the incorrect name of Iolo Morganwy, ibid., p. 27. A later one, Stuart Piggott, *The Druids* (London, 1968), p. 166, refers to the Gorsedd as Iolo's 'nonsense – for it can be called nothing else', in a dismissive account of his life and influence, ibid., pp. 164–74.

was soon producing a mixture of poems in English and Welsh, as well as copious writings on Welsh history and literature, notably on their medieval past. From 1773 to 1777 he lived in London, also working in Kent, and met the leading members of the Welsh societies, some of whom teased him about his 'Hottentotish Glamorgan Welsh'.[7] He failed, however, to find enough support for his writing to allow him to stay in the capital.

Whatever the merits of his work, Iolo was a poor diplomat. Dependent for patronage on those wealthier than himself, he found it difficult to hide his contempt for them, individually and as a group. He was touchy about challenges and imagined slights to his work, and ungrateful to those who supported him, while expressing Radical views that cannot have endeared him to successful Welsh businessmen and other wealthy patrons. His poor health, notably his asthma, had made him early in life dependent on laudanum (a solution of opium in alcohol), which may explain traits in his character.[*] Although energetic and learned, he was poor at finishing work he had begun, as was another laudanum addict, Samuel Taylor Coleridge. Iolo was undoubtedly eccentric, becoming a vegetarian in homage to Pythagoras and sleeping only in a chair in later life, due to his asthma.[†] He was also a notable supporter of Unitarianism, a dissenting sect which deliberately rejected the doctrine of the Trinity, but which he saw, nevertheless, as a uniquely bardic religion. For it he wrote thousands of hymns in Welsh.[8]

After Iolo returned to Wales in 1777, he married a farmer's daughter, Margaret Roberts, and had four children. Despite a series of business failures, and imprisonment for debt in 1786–87, he continued his pioneering work on medieval Welsh literature. In this field he made a number of extraordinary and unlikely advances, notably the discovery and publication of many previously unknown poems by acknowledged writers, including a number by the finest Welsh poet of the Middle Ages, Dafydd ap Gwilym. He also recovered early works copied by later Welsh men of letters, notably a sixteenth-century Glamorgan gentleman, Llywelyn Sion. These sources preserved, often in the form of triads expressing ancient wisdom,

---

[*] A later Welsh poet, Dylan Thomas, who preferred alcohol without opium dissolved in it, also spent much of his time in London. The Irish poet W.B. Yeats was born in London and educated at Godolphin School in Hammersmith. Both lived at times near Primrose Hill, Thomas in Delancey Street and Yeats in Fitzroy Road. Paul Ferris, *Dylan Thomas* (Harmondsworth, 1977), pp. 287 and 294; W.B. Yeats, *Reveries over Childhood and Youth* (London, 1936), p. 5.

[†] 'His food is almost entirely vegetable; and he is a professed Pythagorean with respect to his opinion of animal food. ... In his religious opinions he seems to be inclined to Quakerism, though he professes himself of the Established Church.' *Gentleman's Magazine*, 59 (1789), p. 977. Vegetarianism went hand in hand with Radicalism. Keith Thomas, *Man and the Natural World: Changing Attitudes in England, 1500–1700* (London, 1984), pp. 296–7. See also Ronald Hutton, *The Druids* (London, 2007), p. 21; Hutton, *Blood and Mistletoe*, p. 148.

echoes from the earliest days of Welsh literature. As opposed to what had generally been believed before his discoveries, that most early Welsh literature had been produced in the Welsh-speaking strongholds of north Wales, Iolo showed that his own county, Glamorgan, had in reality been the hub of early Welsh literature. Ancient bardic customs, which had once been common over the whole of Britain, were now preserved only there.[9]

Even more remarkably, Iolo found extensive proof of the connection between Wales and the Druids, with a wealth of detail about the survival of Druidic learning in Wales from its earliest beginnings. This included evidence of the continuity of the Druidic system, extending from ancient times to the Middle Ages and beyond. He was able to describe the division of Druids into the specialised orders of Bards, Druids and Ovates, with their correct costumes and duties, their rites of initiation and their beliefs. He was even able to reveal details of the runic alphabet they had used. The Druidic system of belief, which Iolo claimed was fully compatible with his own admittedly idiosyncratic brand of Christianity, had strong elements of reincarnation, with souls working their way up from the darkness of the lowest level of Annwn, via the world itself, Abred, to the bliss of Gwynvyd. Druidic belief had also included a strong dose of Radicalism, with a marked dislike for tyrants and war.[*]

The meeting on Primrose Hill in September 1792 may have followed earlier meetings there, including one in 1717.[†] In 1791 Iolo had issued a proclamation in archaic Welsh, inviting all those who wished to become Bards to come to Primrose Hill at 9 o'clock on the day of the summer solstice of 1792, but no record of a meeting then survives.[10] He also claimed to that the Gorsedd had previously been

---

[*]   Iolo staked a claim to being the only remaining Bard, other than his friend the Reverend Edward Evans of Aberdare, in a letter written by himself and published in the *Gentleman's Magazine*, 59 (1789), pp. 976–7. In it Iolo described himself, in the third person, as 'remarkably sober and temperate ... naturally reserved, very bashful, and has been unfortunate in his little concerns through life hitherto'. He later claimed that 'communications and assistance' from Evans had allowed him to give a full account of the Bards. William Owen, *The Heroic Elegies and Other Pieces of Llywarç Hen, Prince of the Cumbrian Britons, with a Literal Translation* (London, 1792), p. lxii. Hutton, *Blood and Mistletoe*, pp. 166–7; Hutton, *The Druids*, pp. 59, 60.

[†]   It has been claimed, but not substantiated, that the Mother Grove or Grand Lodge of the Circle of the Universal Bond, under its Gaelic name of *Gairdeachas*, was proclaimed on Primrose Hill at the autumn equinox of 1717, following a meeting at the Apple Tree Tavern in Covent Garden presided over by the freethinker John Toland. Toland was only one of many eminent men to be named, now or later, as early Druids. The Universal Bond, set up by George Watson Reid in 1907, claimed a long history and a past membership including Francis Bacon, John Aubrey, William Stukeley, Charles James Fox, William Blake, Iolo Morganwg himself and, for good measure, Charles Dickens. See Hutton, *Blood and Mistletoe*, pp. 125–6, 348–73.

revived in Wales itself at the spring equinox of the same year, on Plynlimon in central Wales, by himself and two other Bards:

> When in the year of our Lord one hundred seven hundred and ninety-two, and the sun in the point of the vernal equinox, a summons and invitation was given in the hearing of the country and the prince ... to repair to the top of Pumlumon, in Powys, at the expiration of the year and the day, in the hours of noon, where there will not be a naked weapon against them ... for the purpose of pronouncing the judgment of a Gorsedd, in the eye of the sun, and face of the light, on all with respect to genius and moral conduct, who may seek for presidency and privilege, according to the privilege and custom of the Bards of the isle of Britain. The Truth in Opposition to the World.*

For this meeting the only evidence is that of Iolo himself, in his introduction to poems by the early medieval bard, Llywarç Hen, published in 1792.†

In contrast, the autumn meeting of 1792, on Saturday 22 September, and another at the winter solstice, were recorded in London newspapers:

> This being the day on which the autumnal equinox occurred, some Welsh Bards, resident in London, assembled in congress on Primrose Hill, according to ancient usage. ... The wonted ceremonies were observed. A circle of stones formed, in the middle of which was the Maen Gorsedd, or altar, on which a naked sword being placed, all the Bards assisted to sheathe it. The ceremony was attended with a proclamation, the substance of which was, that the Bards of the Island of Britain (for such is their ancient title) were the heralds and ministers of peace, and never bore a naked weapon in the presence of anyone. ... The bardic tradition, and several odes, were recited.[11]

At the meeting the Welsh claim to having been both the founders and preservers of bardic and Druidic learning was also spelt out clearly:

> The bardic institution of the Ancient Britons, which is the very same as the Druidic, has been, from earliest times, through all ages, to the present day,

---

* Owen, *The Heroic Elegies and Other Pieces of Llywarç Hen*, pp. lii–liii. Although published under the name of William Owen, much of the work in the book, including the introduction, was by Iolo. It includes, more than once, the phrase that became his motto: 'Y Gwir yn Erbyn y Byd' ('The Truth against the World'), ibid., pp. xlvii, xlix, liii.

† In his seventy-five page introduction to *The Heroic Elegies and Other Pieces of Llywarç Hen*, Iolo set out his Druidic system in a form recognisably the same as that proclaimed upon Primrose Hill. After establishing the connection of Llywarç Hen ('Llywarç the Aged') to the court of King Arthur, ibid., pp. viii–ix, and his heroic life, pp. xii–xv, Iolo gives a general account of Bardism, pp. xxi–lxxx, which includes a description of its orders, pp. xxxvi–xliii, and the proper way of holding a Gorsedd, pp. xlv–liii.

retained by the Welch. Foreign writers, ancient and modern, have fallen into a great mistake, in considering the Bards and Druids as different orders; or at least, as one subordinate to the other. This is very wrong; for the three orders are, and always have been, by the Welch and the Bards themselves, considered as being on the most perfect equality with each other.

Druidism (which the Welch rightly call Bardism) has been sought for in vain by historians, in Greek, Roman, and other foreign authors: they are now informed, if they will attend to it, that any regular Welch Bard can, in a few minutes, give them a much better account of it than all the books in the world; and at the same time the most convincing proofs, that it is now exactly the same that it was two thousand years ago.[12]

Only Iolo attended the meeting as a Druid, but three leading members of the Welsh community in London, Edward Jones, William Owen and David Samwell, came as Ovates. Two women, Owen's wife, Sarah, and the author Anna Seward, were also initiated.* Odes were read by a number of those present. Sheathing a sword was a clear protest against the looming possibility of war against France, with the added benefit of demonstrating to the authorities that they were not intent on armed rebellion. It was also reported that at the next meeting, to be held at the winter solstice, an ode to Rhitta Gawr, 'a famous Chief of the Ancient Britons, who exterminated so many despots, that he made himself a robe of their beards', would be read.[13]

At the winter solstice of 1792, another meeting was held on the hill. This meeting was presided over by William Owen, as a Druid, and those attending came in the coloured robes which marked their rank: Druids in white; Bards in sky blue; and Ovates in green. Although Iolo gave an address on the ancient bardic order, Edward Jones, the harper to the Prince of Wales, led the singing of a version of the National Anthem:

> Hark! from the trump of Fame
> George is the glorious name!
> Loud echoes ring:

---

* Jones was an important collector of traditional Welsh melodies. Owen (who adopted the additional surname Pughe in 1806, following an inheritance) compiled a Welsh-English dictionary and translated *Paradise Lost* into Welsh. He later became an ardent follower of the prophetess Joanna Southcott. Samwell was a naval surgeon who had sailed with, and been present at the death of, Captain Cook. Seward, known as 'the Swan of Lichfield', was a friend and critic of Dr Johnson. She was admired by Sir Walter Scott, who edited her poems and wrote a short biography of her. See entries for 'Edward Jones (1752–1824)', 'William Owen Pughe (1759–1835)', 'David Samwell (1751–98)' and 'Anna Seward (1742–1809)', *Oxford Dictionary of National Biography*.

> George, with true glory crown'd,
> Bid we the song resound
> Through the wide world around
>   God save the King.[14]

This cannot have been to the liking of Iolo, whose favourite toast in these years, according to Robert Southey, was to 'the three securities of liberty: all kings in hell; the door locked; the key lost'.[15] Although Mrs Owen and Miss Harper were admitted as Ovates, and as candidates to become Druidesses, the Gorsedd had split politically, something emphasised by the expulsion of a Bard at the meeting, for an unknown offence.[16]

While it is unclear whether further meetings followed on Primrose Hill, or elsewhere in London, by 1795 Iolo was back in Wales, where he lived until his death in 1826 in Flemingston, the village where he had been born.* In the years after he returned, he held a number of bardic meetings, but others were broken up by magistrates suspicious of the Radical and pacifist tendencies on display.[17]

These events on Primrose Hill can only be explained by returning both to the ancient world and to a range of political and intellectual developments in the three hundred years before the meeting. In classical literature, notably in Julius Caesar's *De bello gallico* and Tacitus's *Annales*, there are a number of references to Druids, in Caesar as a learned class in what is now France and in Tacitus as priests leading desperate resistance to a Roman army led by Suetonius Paulinus on the island of Anglesey. These sources raise as many questions as they answer about the identity, influence and beliefs of the Druids, who are mysteriously absent from the subsequent history of the Roman Empire. Little or no interest in them was shown by the Christian writers of the Middle Ages.[18] For such a celebrated group, and one credited with such influence, it is remarkable that no single archaeological discovery has ever been linked with certainty to the Druids.[19]

Such inauspicious beginnings did not prevent the Druids from a sensational and varied later career. The Renaissance brought with it a renewed interest in the literature and learning of the classical world, with the recovery, editing and printing of Roman and Greek authors. Tacitus, whose writings were unknown during the

---

* In November 1792, relations between the principals were so bad that Iolo issued a challenge to Jones to meet him in the fields behind the British Museum, a well-known duelling ground. Dillwyn Miles, *The Secret of the Bards of the Island of Britain* (Llandybie, 1998), p. 66, claims a Gorsedd, attended by Anna Seward and the Prince of Wales, was held on the hill at the autumn equinox of 1793, but cites no source. A bardic meeting on Primrose Hill, led by David Samwell, was advertised in 1798. Hutton, *Blood and Mistletoe*, pp. 159–60, 168, 444–5.

Middle Ages, was rediscovered in the fifteenth century. The emergence of modern nation states also brought about a focus on the early histories of the territories these states incorporated. This included a wish to see those they assumed to be distant ancestors in a positive light.[20]

The Druids were notable beneficiaries of this search. From the beginning of the sixteenth century to the end of the seventeenth, many of the nations of Europe discovered links to the Druids. First off the mark were the French, relying on Caesar, but also on spurious detail published by Annius of Viterbo in 1498. The French were followed by the Germans, who had a proprietary interest in Tacitus, as the author of the *Germania*, the earliest description of the German people. Later on the Scots and the English came to see the Druids as ancient Britons; and as the ancestors of the two peoples united by the accession of James VI of Scotland to the throne of England in 1603.

One of the main attractions of the Druids was of course their flexibility. They could be patriots or traitors, heroes or bogeymen, according to choice. As resistance fighters against the Roman Empire, they could be depicted as early nationalists. As astronomers, doctors, musicians, naturalists, philosophers, poets, rulers and sages, they could lay claim to a tradition of learning and civilisation distinct from that of Greece and Rome. For some, they were the last devotees of a religion of peace once universally observed. For others, outside Catholic countries, they could be taken as the forerunners of the priestly cast which had duped the people of Europe before the Reformation and still held the countries of southern Europe in thrall. At their most sinister, they were depicted as the votaries of a nightmare cult practising human sacrifice, an image memorably captured in the depiction of a wicker man, inside which massed victims are about to be burned to death.[21]

The eighteenth century saw the Druids rise to ever greater prominence while shedding much of their sinister reputation. A learned priesthood with scientific interests, and not associated with either Protestantism or Catholicism, appealed to the rational temper of the eighteenth century. The key figure in the history of English Druidry was William Stukeley (1687–1785), the father of British archaeology, who associated the Druids with Stonehenge and Avebury; and made them respectable precursors, with the Jews of the Old Testament, of both monotheism and deism.[22] Indeed, Stukeley portrayed them as distinguished and civilised early British leaders. In a career that saw him reinvent himself several times, Stukeley even took on a Druid identity under the name of Chyndonax. He knew north London well, as from 1759 until his death he lived in Kentish Town, where he had a garden with a 'Druid Walk'.[23] He must have visited Primrose Hill and Barrow Hill.

Druid friendly societies, embodying similar rites to those of freemasons' lodges, also grew across Britain following the foundation of the Ancient Order of Druids by Henry Hurle in 1781. Although meetings followed a fixed ritual, and initiates were told that the order traced its history back to a ancient British chieftain, Togodubline, members were more interested in conviviality, expressed in music and drinking, than in arcane scholarship.[24]

Iolo Morganwg was the inheritor of all these traditions. His greatest achievement, however, was the lasting capture of the Druids for Wales. This, until he accomplished it, was an unlikely feat.[25] While Druids had been claimed as the ancestors of many European nations, there had been no particular link between them and Wales, other than in the description by Tacitus of Anglesey as the site of a last stand against the Romans. This is not perhaps surprising, as Welsh history and identity had long lain dormant, with interest in it restricted to a handful of antiquaries. Only the legends of King Arthur and his Welsh magician, Merlin, had lent a distant allure to early Welsh history. Although Wales had once incorporated several independent kingdoms, the last independent king, Llewelyn ap Gruffydd, the ruler of Gwynedd, had died fighting Edward I in 1282. A final flicker of independence had vanished with the death of the rebel, Owen Glendower, in the early years of the fifteenth century. While it provided, in the Tudors, the ruling house of both England and Wales throughout the sixteenth century, Wales itself was absorbed into the English state in 1536.[26]

Unlike Scotland and Ireland, Wales played no more than a minor role in the English Civil War; and by 1700 many of its people spoke English as well as Welsh. The Welsh gentry, who in previous centuries had supported Welsh-speaking poets, now looked to English literature rather than their own. Such poets as there were tended to come from humble ranks.[27] Nor was Welsh literature easy to turn to modern use. Medieval Welsh was sufficiently distant from eighteenth-century Welsh as to be difficult to understand. Much of it, in any case, consisted of poetry marked by obscure allusions. While the names of a number of medieval bards, including Taliesin and Aneirin, were remembered, the date and meaning of much of their work was unknown or obscure.[28] The difficulties of certainty in this field are reflected in two translations of the same lines of medieval Welsh verse. A translation of what was judged by an expert in 1803 to be part of a Druidic hymn read:

> O son of the compacted wood, the shock overtakes me!
> We all attend on Adonai, on the area of Pwmpai.

In contrast, in 1858 another expert considered the same lines were taken from a satire on monks:

> Like wood-cuckoos in noise they will be,
> Every one of the idiots, banging on the ground.[29]

Wales was, however, by no means immune to the wish to establish, or re-establish, a glorious past for itself and to distinguish itself from its overmighty neighbour. Ironically, this movement gathered pace just at the moment when traditional Welsh culture was disappearing, with the beginnings of industrialisation in south Wales. While others before and after him also contributed to the discovery of an early Welsh cultural heritage, there is no doubt that the central figure in this process was Iolo Morganwg. There was, however, an inescapable problem about all his work. Although undoubtedly a learned man, who made numerous genuine contributions to the study of Welsh literature and history, Iolo was also a fantasist and a forger on an heroic scale.[30] Among a host of other forgeries, not a single one of the poems by Dafydd ap Gwylym, which Iolo claimed to have discovered, was genuine. He covered his tracks in his forgeries of Welsh sources copied by Llywelyn Sion by claiming that Llywelyn had read them in the library of Raglan Castle, which had been destroyed in the Civil War.[31] The scale and brazenness of Iolo's invention can be gauged from the fact that in 1791, when Dr John Williams revived the legend of a Welsh prince, Madoc, discovering America in 1170, Iolo immediately and independently forged a corpus of documents to support the claim.[32]

From early in his literary career, Iolo specialised in plausible deception.[33] As has been seen, he often 'discovered' unknown poems by known writers, mixing old and new in learned editions. He reported other men of letters, conveniently no longer alive, as having once seen significant verses in manuscripts that had later been unfortunately, or perhaps fortunately, destroyed. His own facility in both modern and medieval Welsh composition, his formidable reputation as the leading expert on the subject, and his typical mixture of true and invented learning, made his forgeries difficult to detect. At a time when philology was often highly speculative and the true history of early Britain unclear, it is not surprising that the extent of his forgeries was not established until well over a century after his death.

Why Iolo embarked on his career of deception remains uncertain. One element in it may have been to a wish to establish his own work vicariously under the names of famous predecessors. In the end, his forged Welsh poems certainly brought him greater fame than his English verse. (His English poems, published as *Poems, Lyric and Pastoral* in 1794, had failed to establish him as the Welsh Robert Burns.)* Possibly, having failed to find them in genuine Welsh literature,

---

* Iolo Morganwg, *Poems, Lyric and Pastoral, in Two Volumes* (London, 1794). As well as the poems which failed to match those of Burns, the collection included further details of the bardic and Druidic tradition, ibid., ii, pp. 194–203; an 'Ode on the Mythology of the Ancient British Bards, in the Manner of Taliesin, Recited on Primrose Hill', pp. 203–16; and 'An Account of, and Extracts from, the Welsh-Bardic Triades', ii, pp. 217–56. The list of subscribers to the volumes

Iolo decided to introduce the themes he wished it to have himself, whether in his detailed account of Welsh bardic and Druidic learning, or in his ascription to Glamorgan of a glorious literary heritage. Perhaps, under the influence of laudanum, he found it difficult to distinguish truth from falsehood.[34] His career, in a lower key, echoed that of the Scot James MacPherson. MacPherson's *Ossian* poems, purportedly written by a Gaelic bard and translated into English by their discoverer, swept Europe before being unmasked as forgeries.[35] While Iolo's scholarship was challenged by others even while he was still alive, the gradual unravelling of his forgeries fatally destroyed his reputation. By the time this had happened, however, one at least of his goals had been achieved: the establishment of Wales as the home of Druidry, celebrated by Iolo's successors and institution-alised by the holding of *eisteddfodau*. Iolo's brazen motto, 'Y Gwir yn Erbyn y Byd', 'The Truth against the World', is a succinct but telling comment on his own life, work and influence.[36]

Paradoxically, despite their origins in Radicalism and deceit, the Welsh Druids went on to become highly respectable. Building on a genuine earlier tradition of poetic and musical gatherings, Thomas Burgess, the Bishop of St David's, organized an *eisteddfod* at Carmarthen in 1819 run by the Cambrian Society for Dyfed. Although Iolo attended, and forced the meeting to listen to his account of Bardism, he could not prevent later meetings becoming conservative celebrations of local patriotism. *Eisteddfodau*, which became the natural forum for the promotion of Welsh culture, were later held regularly, growing in size and stature under the patronage of the Welsh clergy, with nonconformist ministers taking a leading role.[37] Costumes and ritual, including the ceremonies of the Gorsedd, were retained for symbolic rather than polemical reasons. The National Eisteddfod, first held at Aberdare in 1861, incorporated a sanitised Gorsedd of the Bards. Its conservative credentials were strong enough by the 1890s to allow the Prince and Princess of Wales to accept initiation as honorary Ovates.[38]

Iolo Morganwg was by no means the only contemporary poet to have visited Primrose Hill and certainly not the greatest one. Unlike Morganwg, William Blake was not a temporary visitor to London but rather lived in it nearly all his life. Born in 1757, he spent most of his life in obscurity, despite his brilliance as an engraver. He told Henry Crabb Robinson, 'I should be sorry if I had any earthly fame,

---

was an impressive one and included not only the Prince of Wales but George Washington, Horace Walpole, Tom Paine and William Wilberforce. The opening poem in the collection is an 'Ode to Laudanum', ibid., i, pp. 1–5: 'Thou canst repel venom'd rage, the fever'd anguish canst assuage, and blunt the tooth of pain.' For an assessment of the merits of Iolo's poetry, see Morgan, *Iolo Morganwg*, pp. 24–39. See also, Hutton, *Blood and Mistletoe*, p. 160.

for whatever natural glory a man has is so much taken from his spiritual glory. I wish to do nothing for profit. I wish to live for art. I want nothing whatever. I am quite happy.'[39] Like Morganwg, Blake was also a Radical, at one point standing trial on the accusation of having cursed the king, a serious charge on which he was acquitted.[40]

Although his imagination fed on many sources, including the Old Testament, as a poet Blake was supremely reliant on his own visionary inspiration rather than on tradition. Unlike Morganwg, Blake was searingly honest, if often obscure. He turned the everyday world of London into a cosmic reflection of Jerusalem, with the spiritual and everyday mixed. While his longer works are often impenetrable, Blake had a sublime ability to see the latent significance of everyday things and to express profound ideas in deceptively simple terms:

> To see a World in a grain of sand
> And a Heaven in a Wild Flower,
> Hold Infinity in the Palm of your hand
> And Eternity in an Hour.[41]

The subject of *Jerusalem*, written between 1804 and 1820, was the fallen condition of Man and the forces which will redeem him. London is imagined as the historical Jerusalem.[42] In it Blake memorably declared that:

> The fields from Islington to Marybone,
> To Primrose Hill and Saint John's Wood,
> Were builded over with pillars of gold,
> And there Jerusalem's pillars stood.*

On Primrose Hill itself Blake had a vision of the sun.[43] He told Henry Crabb Robinson, 'I have conversed with the spiritual Sun. I saw him on Primrose Hill. He said, "Do you take me for the Greek Apollo? – "No", I said, "that" (pointing to the sky) "is the Greek Apollo. He is Satan".'†

---

* William Blake, *Jerusalem*, 'To the Jews', lines 1–4, *The Complete Writings of William Blake*, ed. Geoffrey Keynes (London, 1957), p. 649. In *Jerusalem*, Blake also wrote that 'From London to York and Edinburgh the furnaces rage terrible. Primrose Hill is the mouth of the furnace and the iron door', ibid., p. 714. In *Milton*, he wrote of Albion that 'his left foot near London covers the shades of Tyburn: his instep from Windsor to Primrose Hill stretching to Highgate and Holloway', ibid., p. 531.

† In his *A Vision of the Last Judgement* (1810), Blake provided another highly original perception of the sun: 'What,' it will be questioned, 'when the sun rises, do you not see a round disk of fire somewhat like a guinea?' 'O no, no, I see an Innumerable company of the Heavenly host crying, "Holy, Holy, Holy is the Lord God Almighty". I question not my Corporeal or Vegetative Eye

Blake also had a typically idiosyncratic view of the Druids. He believed that they had once been the benign priests of the earliest religion, founded in Britain. This religion had spread across the world, before then becoming corrupt and bloody. In *Jerusalem* he repeatedly associated them, and their stone circles, with ritual murder. Their crimes, however, were not those of Gothic monsters but the result of Blake's identification of them with deists and with the philosophers of the Enlightenment, whose reason removed direct religious revelation and a personal relationship with Christ. An even more unlikely identification was made by Blake between the Druids and the industrialists of his own day.[44]

Henry Crabb Robinson accompanied another poet across Primrose Hill, though the latter's reaction was in an infinitely lower key to that of Blake. In June 1812 William Wordsworth recorded, 'On Sunday morning I had a most pleasant walk with Henry Robinson through the fields and over Primrose Hill to Highgate; we crossed the intended Prince Regent's Park at Mary bone which will be of vast extent, but the ground has in itself no variety for it is a dead flat, but it will have agreeable views from certain parts of Hampstead and Highgate hills.'[45] Robinson also recorded the walk: 'At half-past ten joined Wordsworth in Oxford Road; we then got into the fields, and walked to Hampstead. I read him a number of Blake's poems, with some of which he was pleased. He regarded Blake as having in him the elements of poetry much more than either Byron or Scott.'[46]

Wordsworth's poetry also featured Druids from his earliest years. Later he included them in both *The Prelude* and *The Excursion*. His feelings about them, though at times memorably expressed, fluctuated between shuddering at their practice of human sacrifice and admiring their scientific knowledge.[47] In a single passage in *The Prelude*, within the space of a few lines, he has it both ways:

> It is the sacrificial altar, fed
> With living men, how deep the groans, the voice
> That crowd the giant wicker thrills ...

> I saw the bearded teachers, with white wands
> Uplifted, pointing to the starry sky
> Alternately, and Plain below, while breath
> Of music seemed to guide them, and the waste
> Was chear'd with stillness and a pleasant sound.*

---

any more than I would Question a Window concerning a Sight. I look thro' it and not with it.' *The Complete Writings of William Blake*, p. 617.
* The obsolete word 'thrills' means 'thralls'. William Wordsworth, *The Prelude*, xiii, lines 331–3 and 349–54.

Wordsworth had abandoned his early Radicalism by 1812. This was not the case with another poet, Percy Bysshe Shelley, born in 1792 the eldest son a Sussex baronet. His early-expressed Radical and atheistic views led to his expulsion from Oxford and estrangement from his father, an estrangement compounded by his elopement with the sixteen-year-old Harriet Westbrook. Reduced to poverty, the couple lived at a number of addresses in Kentish Town. Shelley's proclaimed disregard for conventional marital fidelity led to the couple's separation; and his meeting with the Radical writer William Godwin brought about an acquaintance with Godwin's daughter, Mary, and her stepsister, Claire Clairmont. Mary, the future author of *Frankenstein*, who became Shelley's second wife, was also the daughter of Mary Wollstonecraft, the author of *A Vindication of the Rights of Women* (1792), who had died giving birth to her.

Unlike the Lake Poets, whose passion was for walking, Shelley from an early age had an obsession with boats. At this time, he was restricted to expressing this by sailing paper boats. The novelist Thomas Love Peacock described a walk with the poet over Bagshot Heath, where they 'came on a pool of water, which Shelley would not part from till he had rigged out a flotilla from any unfortunate letters he happened to have in his pocket'.[48] Mary described watching him sailing paper boats on one of the pools on Primrose Hill for three days in October 1814:

Sunday 2 October. Peacock comes after breakfast – walk over Primrose Hill – sail little boats return a little before four ...

Monday 3 October. Read *Political Justice*. Hookham calls – walk with Peacock to the lake of Nangis and set off little fire boats. After dinner talk and let off fireworks ...

Wednesday 5 October. Peacock at breakfast. Walk to the lake of Nangis and sail fire boats ...*

The lake of Nangis was a private name, after the French town where the party had been a few weeks earlier, for one of the pools on Primrose Hill, the last of which was filled in in 1902.

Shelley's love of lakes and boats had two tragic sequels. In 1816 his first wife,

---

* *An Essay Concerning Political Justice* (1793) was the most famous book by William Godwin, Mary's father and Claire's stepfather. Thomas Hookham was a publisher who acted as a mediator between Shelley and his first wife, Harriet. Although Shelley showed no interest in the Druids, Peacock was the author of a poem, 'The Genius of the Thames', which is about a Druid fleeing from the slaughter on Anglesey to London. See Hutton, *Blood and Mistletoe*, p. 211. *The Journals of Mary Shelley*, ed. Paul R. Feldman and Diana Scott-Kilvert (2 vols, Oxford, 1987), i, pp. 30–1. See also *The Journals of Claire Clairmont*, ed. Mary Kingston Stocking (Cambridge, Massachusetts, 1968), p. 47.

Harriet, drowned herself while pregnant in the Serpentine. Then, on 8 July 1822, at the age of twenty-nine, Shelley was himself drowned in the Bay of Spezia sailing his yacht, *Don Juan*, in a storm. In his pocket was found a copy of Keats's poetry.* His body was burned on a pyre on the beach by his friend, Lord Byron, whose mistress Claire Clairmont had become.

There is no record of Byron on Primrose Hill, although in *Don Juan* he tersely dismissed the Druids in a couplet:

> The Druid's groves are gone – so much the better:
> Stonehenge is not – but what the devil is it?[49]

The hill, however, does have one unlikely connection with Byron. His marriage to Annabella Milbanke had been notoriously difficult, with his cruelty towards her being compounded by his incestuous relationship with his half-sister, Augusta Leigh. Ostracised by society, Byron left England in 1816 and spent the years until his death in 1824 at Missolonghi in exile. His widow, however, lived on until 1860, when she died in a house overlooking the hill.†

---

* It is impossible that Keats did not know Primrose Hill, on the route between Hampstead and the West End, but it is not mentioned in his poetry or his letters.

† She died on 16 May 1860 at 11 St George's Terrace, still directly next to the hill before the construction of Primrose Hill Road. Ethel Colburn Mayne, *The Life and Letters of Anne Isabella, Lady Noel Byron* (London, 1929), p. 429.

5

Regent's Park

I F the last decade of the eighteenth century and the early decades of the
nineteenth century saw both duellists and poets upon Primrose Hill, as well as
Londoners enjoying an escape from the smoke and hubbub of the city, they also
saw changes around the hill that determined its setting in the future.[1] The most
striking was John Nash's creation of Regent's Park, between 1811 and 1826, part
of a wider scheme connecting the park to Westminster via Regent Street. Another
component of the plan, the Regent's Canal, begun in 1812, ran through the north
of the park. A section of park was given over to the Zoo, the hill's immediate
neighbour to its south, from 1826. These years also saw the beginnings of building
in St John's Wood and Camden Town.

In 1800, however, Primrose Hill and Barrow Hill remained small hills set
amongst fields. A survey of Eton property by Thomas Milton, dated October 1756,
provides an early source for the college's land on the hill: the four main fields were
Rugmoor, Blue House, Sheppard's Hill and Primrose Hill. They were all meadows
and made up just under sixty acres. Milton's survey also shows a footpath running
over the hill from Marylebone Park to Upper Chalcot Farm, making its way
through Rugmoor and Primrose Hill fields before veering right over Sheppard's
Hill and through two fields behind the hill, together called Thirteen Acres.[2]

Milton's survey is confirmed, with only minor variations, by a more detailed
survey, drawn up for Eton College by Abraham and William Driver in November
1796. This valued the Chalcots Estate (divided into Upper and Lower Chalcot
Farms) as a whole at £860 a year, an increase of almost £400 on the value of the
farm in 1770, when its annual value had been £480 a year.[3] This no doubt reflected
the growth of the London, with its appetite for dairy products, and the increase
in prices due to the war with France. Of 206 acres, only ten were arable. The
Drivers reported that:

> The foregoing farm is in general very good land and in a high state of cultivation,
> which is occasion'd in a great measure from its contiguity to London, from
> whence manure is so easily obtain'd. The crops of hay it produces annually are

very great, and being mostly strong land seldom fails in dry seasons, which renders it the more valuable.[4]

The surveyors already had an eye to the possibilities of building on the estate, though primarily on the part of it bordering the Hampstead road rather than on Primrose Hill itself:

> A considerable part of this estate is very eligibly situate for building, being within three miles of London and adjoining the turnpike road for a considerable extent and, provided sufficient encouragement could be given to the tenant with respect to the length of the term ... we have no doubt it might be easily accomplished in which case the land contiguous would be considerably increas'd in value and of course the college would ultimately derive great advantage probably doubling the present fines.[5]

At the time, however, there were only a few houses on Upper Chalcot Farm, at the end of the modern England's Lane. The two farms were rented out by Eton's tenant, Thomas Earle, to the large-scale dairy farmer, Thomas Rhodes, who sublet the houses: 'There are three dwelling houses and a cottage upon this farm let by Mr Rhodes to under tenants which in general are in good repair, having lately had several sums of money laid out upon them.'[6] The good condition of the houses was in contrast to that of the fences, which were in disrepair, partly because of the many cows kept on the hill and partly because the wood was stolen by pilferers.[*] Because of the growth of London, Primrose Hill attracted large numbers of visitors, especially in the summer and on traditional holidays.

London itself was also coming nearer to the hill. In the 1780s, short building leases issued on the Southampton Estate, to the west of the Hampstead road and to the east of Marylebone Park, had seen poor-quality houses built along the line of the road. On the same estate, Park Street (later Parkway), previously a track known as Slip Shoe Lane, ran up from the Mother Red Cap, where the roads to Hampstead and Kentish Town divided. Park Street linked up with Green Lane, on the line of the present Albany Street, near the later site of Gloucester Gate.[7] To the east of the road the beginnings of Camden Town were erected on an estate belonging to Charles Pratt, first Earl of Camden. He took his title from his

---

[*] Rhodes had almost a thousand cows on his farm, the farmhouse of which was just north of the later site of Euston. For farming practices near London, see John Middleton, *General View of the Agriculture of Middlesex* (2nd edn, London, 1793), pp. 52, 414–24. The cows were intensively farmed, being fed grain in the middle of the night to increase their milk yield. London milk was often unappetising and sometimes dangerous. 'A cow-keeper informs me that the retail milk-dealers are, for the most part, the refuse of other employments; possessing neither character, decency of manners, nor cleanliness. No delicate person could possibly drink the milk, were they fully acquainted with the filthy manners of these dealers in it.' Ibid., p. 424.

estate near Chislehurst, where Camden House, named after the great Elizabethan historian and antiquary, William Camden, was his country retreat.[8]

The most significant change in the early years of the nineteenth century was to the south of the hill. In early 1811 the leases to the farms in Marylebone Park, held by the Duke of Portland, fell in and were resumed by the crown. The lands belonging to the crown, exchanged in return for the payment of the civil list at the beginning of each reign, were in fact administered by the Office of Woods and Forests, a government department controlled by the Treasury. Under William Pitt the Younger, Prime Minister with one short break from 1783 to 1806, government was made far more efficient, with the aim of reducing waste and of maximising revenue. As one part of this, the crown lands were put under regular audit. Rather than leases being used as items of patronage to be given to courtiers or placemen, they were now to be issued or renewed only on market terms. Over two decades before 1811, plans had been made for developing Marylebone Park, a property of great potential value. The lead in this was taken by the surveyor general, John Fordyce. It was he who recommended that the crown turn down a proposal by the Duke of Portland for a road across the park linking his main St Marylebone estate with his estate at Barrow Hill, north of the park. Fordyce's advice was based on the perception that such a road would inhibit the crown's freedom to develop the park. Further action, however, had to be put on hold during the wars against Revolutionary France, which lasted almost continuously between 1793 and 1815.[9]

The imminent termination of the Duke of Portland's leases brought about the revival of a competition for the best plan to develop Marylebone Park. Under Fordyce's auspices, an open competition, with a prize of £1,000, had attracted no entries when it had first been first announced in 1794. Now the government narrowed the competition to its own employees. The winner was the architect of the Department of Woods and Forests, John Nash. He submitted a plan, combining villas and terraces in a Picturesque landscape, offering the government a very large return for an attractively low outlay. In its initial outline, it would have left very little land available for public recreation. The plan for the park went through a number of evolutions, notably after Spencer Perceval, the then Prime Minister, discussed the park with Nash at Downing Street in August 1811 and insisted that the park should have more open space and fewer buildings.[10]

John Nash was a man for the grand scale. After a rackety and unsuccessful early career as an architect and developer, which had included bankruptcy and exile to provincial Wales, he had built up a country house practice, collaborating with the leading landscape designer of the day, Humphry Repton. This taught Nash the virtues and the flexibility of the Picturesque, in which the strict rules of Classical and Neo-Classical architecture were replaced by the doctrine that

Gloucester Gate, Regent's Park, engraving by Thomas H. Shepherd,
from James Elmes, *Metropolitan Improvements: or London in the Nineteenth
Century* (London, 1827). St Katharine's Hospital is in the background.
(*Private Collection*)

houses should *look* as if they were in a natural setting, whether or not this was
an illusion. Under the Picturesque, the outside and inside of a house no longer
needed to match each other. The buff-coloured palaces of Regent's Park, covered
in stucco to give the illusion of stone, were built as terraced housing for the upper
middle class.[11]

Nash, a man of great energy and boundless charm, was a born salesman who
inevitably offered more than he delivered. His commitments at the time he planned
Regent's Park were enormous: not only was he responsible for the park and Regent
Street but also for the rebuilding of Buckingham Palace and the Royal Pavilion
at Brighton. He was not someone for detail, as the failings of a number of his
buildings proved.[12]

As well as being the principal architect of Regent's Park, Nash was the prime
mover behind the Regent's Canal. He had not been its initiator, as schemes for
digging a canal through the north of London to the new docks to the east of the
City had been in train for years. He became, however, the principal shareholder
in the enterprise and the main driving force behind it. His deputy at the Office
of Woods and Forests, James Morgan, was given the responsibility for most of its
construction, even though Morgan had no previous experience of work on canals.
Nash had originally considered allowing the canal, as an ornamental feature,

to run through the middle of his park and connect to its lake. The realisation, however, that barges full of industrial materials would lessen the attraction of the villas in the park, and interfere with the privacy of their residents, led the commissioners and Nash to a decision to change the route of the canal to the north of the park.[13]

With capital raised, and the Prince Regent's name given to what had originally been advertised as the London Canal, digging began in 1812. Running from the hub of the Grand Union Canal at Paddington, the canal crossed Maida Vale and entered the new park at its north-west corner. Avoiding the need for any locks before Camden Town, the route of the canal was excavated in a wide cutting, further sheltering the inhabitants of the park from the chance of exposure to the cargoes carried by barges. The canal also neatly completed Nash's intention to preserve the privacy of the park by limiting the number of entrances to it. Until the 1840s, the only bridges across the canal to the north of the park were Macclesfield Bridge, opposite what became Avenue Road, and a footbridge where the Tyburn crossed the canal by a small aqueduct between Macclesfield Bridge and St John's Wood. The nearest other entries to the northern half of the park were at Gloucester Gate and Hanover Gate.[14]

Just to the south of Primrose Hill, the canal divided at Water Meeting Bridge, with the main branch running down to Limehouse via Camden Town and Islington. A second branch, known as the Cumberland Market Branch, ran down from 1812 to 1942 under Gloucester Gate towards Cumberland Basin.* This was the hub of the service area established by Nash to the east of his park, of which the principal artery was Albany Street. Nash hoped to establish three markets there: Cumberland Market for hay, Clarence Market for fruit and York Market for meat. In the event, only Cumberland Market ever opened for business.[15] In the early years of operation, the take-up of the quays around Cumberland Basin was so poor that Nash had to rent nearly all of them himself.

Regent's Park was laid out and most of the houses in it and around it built between 1811 and 1826. Its basic plan was of two circles, one within the other. The park's principal decorative feature, its lake, was created by excavation in 1816 and filled by the damming of the River Tyburn. Nash also landscaped the trees in the park to create an illusion of privacy for each of the projected villas. A series of terraces, of differing degrees of grandeur, surrounded the south of the park from Gloucester Gate to Hanover Gate. Others, named on plans as Munster and Carrick

---

*   The canal, also known as the 'Collateral Cut', was declared redundant in 1937 under the provisions of the Railway and Canal Traffic Act of 1888. Dammed in 1942, it filled not with rubble from bombed houses but with clay from excavated Tube shelters. National Archives, Works 16/1879.

Terraces, are shown on early maps of the park on its northern boundary but were never built. A double circle of terracing around the Inner Circle was another early plan, as was an offer of the inside of the circle to the Duke of Wellington as the site for a grand villa. Many other villas, including one for the Prince Regent himself, with an ornamental canal in front of it, were also planned but never built.[16] What was built, however, was not dependent upon Nash but upon the housing market. Following the practice of other major estates, the crown looked to lease out land on ninety-nine-year building leases, under which the builder or his tenant met the costs of building, after their designs had been submitted for Nash's approval. The completed buildings would not only produce an income for the crown but would revert to it after the expiry of the leases.[17]

Although considerable interest had been expressed when the plans for the park were first revealed, the actual uptake was disappointing, with very few offers being made for plots in its first years. An upturn in the economy, and in public confidence, once the country had begun to recover from the Napoleonic Wars, made up for the slow start, with all the terraces between Gloucester Gate and Hanover Gate built by the end of the 1820s. Only a few of the over fifty projected villas were ever built. Of these no more than six were built inside the Outer Circle.[18]

The slow take-up of plots, and the convenience to the government of space under its own control, led to the allocation of land in the park to several extraneous bodies. Of these the first to stake a claim was the military. The army asked for 'barracks, and the exercising ground for the troops, comprising about forty acres ... to be formed near Primrose Hill'.[19] With the country at war with France, and the government conscious of the dangers of popular unrest in the capital, the War Office came up with a plan to build a large barracks for the Life Guards, later increased in size to include the Artillery. This would have replaced the existing Life Guards barracks in King Street, off Baker Street, and would have brought in the Artillery from St John's Wood, where troops had been quartered since 1804. Nash's early plans for the park all show versions of the proposed barracks, though these was never designed in greater detail than as three parallel streets.[20] In one of the early plans, the canal was to have run to the south of the barracks, which would have placed the barracks themselves immediately next to Primrose Hill. Nash advised that the canal would 'pass so near those barracks as to afford great convenience in bringing hay, straw, fodder and provisions and carrying away manure'.[21] He also considered access roads to the barracks and proposed, to give an idea of the finished buildings, 'forming a scaffold that when we shall ride round the park we may see the mass which the barrack will occupy'.[22]

There was, however, considerable resistance. The Department of Woods and Forests had no wish for a substantial and valuable part of the park to be taken over by large barracks and, in particular, objected to a suggestion that half the park should be kept in military hands for exercising the cavalry and artillery horses: 'the appropriation of two hundred to three hundred acres of Marylebone Park as exercising ground for the troops to be quartered in the intended barracks there might materially interfere with the general plan ... for the improvement of that estate'.[23]

Several MPs objected to what they saw as the excessive size and cost of the project: the barracks would have a wall over a mile in length around it and cost £170,000, the equivalent of £400 for every man and horse.[24] Others, including the leading Radical Sir Francis Burdett, spoke out strongly against the barracks on the grounds of the threat that soldiers so close to the centre of the capital posed to the freedom of the people.[25] According to the like-minded Sir Thomas Fremantle:

> It was a most serious matter, to consider whether they would give government the power to raise a military depot, in such a city as London, a sort of Praetorian camp that could not but be hostile to the feelings of the people, and might eventually be dangerous to their liberties.[26]

In the end, it was private rather than public pressure that had most influence on the government's decision. The Duke of Portland had no wish for barracks next to his estate at Barrow Hill. Part of his price for agreeing to the construction of Regent Street through his land to the south of the park was the removal of the barracks from its north.[27] The War Office had to accept a smaller barracks for the Life Guards in Albany Street (in the business rather than the Picturesque part of the park) and to continue to lease the barracks for the Artillery in St John's Wood, building a fine riding school there in 1825.

The pressure to replace London's old quays with purpose-built docks led to a surprising addition to the park. St Katharine's Dock, to the immediate east of the Tower of London, was built by Thomas Telford by excavating land previously belonging to and centred around the medieval hospital of St Katharine. To compensate the hospital, a new church, and accommodation for its brothers and sisters, was built on land given to the hospital on the Outer Circle, just south of Gloucester Gate, between 1825 and 1827. They, and a villa for the master of the hospital in the park itself, were designed by Ambrose Poynter, a disaffected ex-pupil of Nash, who deliberately ignored the stucco used by Nash on his terraces and villas, building instead in brick with stone facings.[28]

South of Cambridge Terrace, Decimus Burton designed the Colosseum, an ambitious sixteen-sided building erected between 1824 and 1827 for the surveyor and entrepreneur Thomas Horner. With an impressive portico, the building was based more on the Pantheon in Rome than on the original Colosseum. It was intended to house a panorama of London painted by E.T. Parris from hundreds of preliminary drawings made by Horner from a cabin on top of the dome of St Paul's

Cathedral, while the dome was being repaired. Due to spiralling expenses, and the failure of Parris to complete the panorama, Horner and his backers were already ruined by the time it was opened to the public in 1829.[29]

Whatever his difficulties with Cumberland Basin, Nash and his architectural heir, James Pennethorne, developed two distinctive and attractive sets of small, Picturesque villas on either side of the Cumberland Market branch of the canal. Park Villages West and East, which date from between 1823 and 1835, consist of individually designed villas set in small plots of land. At the top of Park Village East, near Gloucester Gate, Nash also designed his only pub, the York and Albany.[30]

The change that had most impact on Primrose Hill, being the closest to it physically, was the establishment of the Zoo. The Zoological Society of London was founded in 1826 by Sir Stamford Raffles. Raffles, also the founder of Singapore, had collected a range of exotic animals during his time in the Far East.[31] Originally restricted to five acres on the south side of the Regent's Canal, the Zoo quickly proved itself a success, as it drew on the British Empire for animals to exhibit. It gradually expanded to thirty-six acres, including land to the north of the canal.[32] The Zoo filled the vacuum where the giant barracks would have been.

The Zoo, a name which it gave to all other languages, was the first major institution in the world specialising in the keeping, breeding, study and exhibition of wild animals. It was also for many years the largest zoological collection in the world, with the best library on its subject. The Zoo, however, was not open to the general public until 1846, before which entrance was only available to fellows of the society, and to their families and friends. While it drew large numbers of Londoners, and many others from further afield, as a private and fenced institution it formed a barrier between Primrose Hill and Regent's Park. The Zoo's existence, however, ensured there would be no domestic housing to the south of the hill. For its first ninety years, all the Zoo's buildings were also mostly no more than one storey high. Only with the building of the Mappin Terraces in 1914 did the height of the Zoo buildings interfere with the sightlines between the park and Primrose Hill.[33]

The land inside the Inner Circle had been let out in 1812, as a market garden, to Thomas Jenkins and George Gwyther of the Portman Nurseries, which supplied many of the trees for the park. The cost of buying out their lease served as a deterrent to the founders of the Zoo, whose preferred site it was. The land was subsequently refused to the founders of the newly established King's College, London, on the grounds that one zoo was enough for the park.[34] In 1838 it became the gardens of the Botanic Society of London.

The 1820s saw the completion of a road running directly in front of Primrose Hill itself, originally called Primrose Hill Road, joining Park Street (the later Parkway) and Gloucester Gate to St John's Wood. This completed the third of the east to west lines of communication, the others being the Outer Circle of Regent's Park

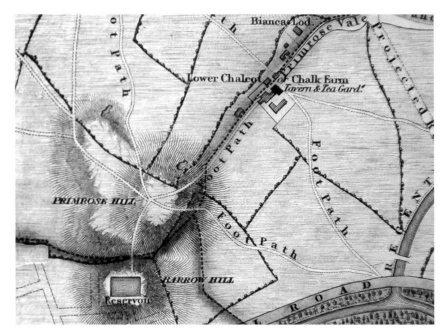

Greenwood's map (1827) shows the newly built West Middlesex Reservoir.
Primrose Vale, a turning from the Hampstead road, leads to the still isolated
Chalk Farm Tavern and Tea Gardens. A 'Projected Road' runs across the
Southampton Estate. (*Private Collection*)

and the Regent's Canal, which still separate Primrose Hill from Regent's Park. In
the same decade, a turnpike road was built running north from St John's Wood
to Finchley, with a branch leading from Swiss Cottage to Macclesfield Bridge.[35]

Although the main reason that the Duke of Portland wanted a road built to
the north of the canal was to allow him to develop his Barrow Hill estate, delays
and arguments about who should repair the road, and about the rights to connect
the drains of new houses to existing sewers, vitiated the project from the start. In
1822 four of the builders who had taken plots on the estate complained to Samuel
Ware, the duke's surveyor:

> We the undersigned beg leave to state to you that after petitioning and making
> other repeated applications to the vestry, for the repair of the Primrose Hill Road,
> which for these nine months past has been in an almost impassable state, the reply
> of the vestry is 'that they will in no way contribute towards it'.
>
>   We therefore solicit your assistance in bringing before His Grace the
> Duke of Portland the peculiar hardship of our case, and the great injury and
> inconveniences we labour under – our houses in wet weather, being positively

inacceptable [sic], earnestly hoping, as we do, that His Grace will render us some assistance either through his representations to the vestry, or in what other way he may think proper.[36]

In 1827, however, the Portland Estate was still wrangling with the crown about the road:

I have received your letter of 1 March in which you propose to forward to me some account relating to the Primrose Hill Road 'in order that measures may be taken for ascertaining what portion thereof is to be paid by the Duke of Portland'. I never considered His Grace liable to any further sum than was demanded and paid – on the contrary I considered that His Grace and his tenants have claims for compensation from the delay and neglect in completing the road.[37]

Under these circumstances, which must have been extremely discouraging to anyone trying to build there, the development of the Barrow Hill estate was unsuccessful. Although a number of villas and terraces were built in the prime locations facing Regent's Park, most of the land between Primrose Hill and the St John's High Street was filled by unprepossessing houses and workshops, including a sizeable saw-mill, during the 1820s and 1830s. According to an opponent of the proposed Finchley Road in 1824:

There is a mass of new and inferior buildings near to Colonel Eyre's land in Marylebone, which are called Portland Town, and are inhabited by persons of the lowest orders, on which account it is spoken of as the St Giles of Marylebone parish.[38]

Portland Town indeed acquired a reputation for rough behaviour that it kept throughout the nineteenth century. Walpole Eyre, who ran the Eyre Estate for his brother, wrote in 1830, asking for it to be properly policed: 'I need not state to you that Portland Town is principally inhabited by persons of the lowest description, and as that place and the neighbouring district are not included in any system of parochial management, it is highly desirable that there should be an effectual police establishment in that quarter.'[39]

At least the new houses were supplied with plentiful water by the end of the 1820s, a decade which saw the removal of the summit of Primrose Hill's immediate neighbour, Barrow Hill. The initiative for this came from the Duke of Portland, as part of his promotion of his nearby estate. As Samuel Ware explained to the secretary of the West Middlesex Water Works, 'The estate is partly let on building leases and it is important to obtain a good supply of water to the houses erected, and to be erected on it.'[40] A reservoir on Barrow Hill would also provide water for the duke's main St Marylebone estate. There was already a well there: 'On the summit of the lower hill ... about twenty-eight years ago was dug a well 280 feet deep, five feet diameter in the clear about 250 feet deep, and in the lower thirty feet reduced in lengths so that at the bottom it is three feet diameter in the clear.'

> His Grace proposes to be made on the summit a reservoir, and to be erected thereon a steam engine or other powerful machine to raise water from the well into the reservoir. The ground both in respect to shape and soil is well calculated to a reservoir.[41]

The company's view, however, was that the well would not supply sufficient water by itself, even with a steam engine. It therefore drew up plans to draw its water from the Thames. According to *The Times*:

> The vast increase of building in this quarter has suggested the necessity of constructing a reservoir for the supply of water to the new neighbourhood. A work of this kind has being going on for some months, and being now near its completion, attracts a good deal of curiosity. It is advantageously situated on Little Primrose Hill, from which its elevation, being 175 feet above the level of the Thames, the liquid body will flow from a point higher than any building in Marylebone, and be enabled, consequently, to invade the topmost chamber in the parish with ease. The basin will be twenty feet deep, and cover an area of two acres, and when finished will be enclosed by a wall with an ornamental palisade, so as to render it an object of embellishment to the park. It will contain 18,000 tons of water, considered to be adequate to the supply of as many houses; and the fluid will be brought from the Thames above Hammersmith, a distance not less than seven miles. The increase of houses in the parish of Marylebone has been from nine thousand to fourteen thousand within last two years. The cost of the work has been computed at £25,000.[42]

Completed by the end of 1825, the reservoir was originally open to the elements until a scare about the dangers of cholera saw it roofed over in 1853, in compliance with the Metropolis Water Act of 1852, which obliged all reservoirs within a radius of five miles of St Paul's Cathedral to be covered. The Act also prohibited the extraction of water from the Thames below Teddington Lock. This made the company draw its water at Hampton, before pumping it seven miles to filter-beds at Barnes and then to Hammersmith, crossing the Thames twice in conduits.[43]

The first houses in the main part of St John's Wood were in the southern part of the Eyre Estate, opposite Hanover Gate, rather than to the north of the park.[44] Ambitious plans for a grand circus further north came to nothing. After the Napoleonic Wars, however, the Eyre Estate was developed successfully, establishing the suburban villa as a type. In 1812 St John's Wood also became known as the principal home of cricket. Thomas Lord, a Yorkshireman who as a cricketer had played at the White Conduit Club in Islington, had been instrumental in setting up a cricket ground just north of the New Road, on the site of what is now Dorset Square. The plans of the Portman Estate to build the square led to Lord moving his cricket ground further north. This move, however, was short-lived, as the construction of the Regent's Canal entailed a third, and final, move to its present site.[45]

By 1840, with so much building activity around Primrose Hill, it seemed only too likely that its fields would soon be turned into building land. As landowners knew:

> The richest crop for any field
> Is a crop of bricks for it to yield.
> The richest crop that it can grow
> Is a crop of houses in a row.[46]

6

London's Crowning Glory

UNLIKE Regent's Park, and indeed many other parks, Primrose Hill has no buildings on or in it, other than the solitary lodge at its south-west corner and the playground. By becoming a park, it avoided being covered with houses. Its remarkable escape from being built over does not mean, however, that no attempts were made to do so.

Barrow Hill or Little Primrose Hill had disappeared in 1825, after the West Middlesex Water Company bought it from the Duke of Portland and built a reservoir on it. That it should have become a reservoir was not, however, inevitable, as other plans for the hill had been raised at the end of the eighteenth century. It was Barrow Hill, not its neighbour, that was referred to in a brief report in *The Times* in 1791. This noted that 'Primrose Hill, which commands a view of London, Hampstead, Harrow, and the neighbouring places, is fixed upon for the spot on which a magnificent Mansion is to be erected for the Marquis of Titchfield'.[1] The title was a courtesy one belonging to the heir of the Duke of Portland, the owner of the Barrow Hill estate. The mansion was soon abandoned, but only a month later it was announced: 'A place of entertainment is to be erected on Primrose Hill, where it was reported the Marquis of Titchfield's mansion was to have stood.'[2]

Although Primrose Hill's owners were certainly willing to consider the building of conventional housing on their land, the hill also attracted grandiose proposals from a variety of architects, developers and visionaries. While none of these buildings – which ranged from grand villas and giant statues to a replica of the Parthenon, a pagoda and a pyramid taller than St Paul's Cathedral – was in the end built, the plans for them confirm the attraction and presence of the hill in the minds of the Londoners of the day.[3] Taking their cue from John Nash's connection of Regent's Park and Westminster via Regent Street, a number of later town planners also included Primrose Hill as a pivotal point on avenues intended to sweep through London.[4]

News of the creation of Regent's Park produced a rumour about the government's plans for Primrose Hill. Tom Moore, who five years earlier had met Francis

Jeffrey in an abortive duel on the hill, in 1811 reported on the Prince Regent's plans, 'There's no news that you'd care to hear of except that the prince is to have a villa upon Primrose Hill, connected by a fine street with Carlton House, and is so pleased with this magnificent plan that he has been heard to say, "It will quite eclipse Napoleon".'[5] Moore was partly right. A major feature of Nash's plan for Regent's Park was to connect it via what is now the Broad Walk in Regent's Park, via Portland Place and Regent Street, to Carlton House, the Prince Regent's London house, and then to St James's Park and Westminster.[6] Primrose Hill is indeed now connected to the Broad Walk by St Mark's Bridge over the Regent's Canal, at one remove, but it has never been aligned directly with Nash's famous route.

Nor was Moore entirely wrong about the plans for a villa for the Prince Regent. Nash's early plans for Regent's Park included a *guinguette*, a villa named after one of the French places of entertainment on the banks of the Seine outside normal licensing control. This, with an ornamental canal in front of it, was planned for the park opposite Cumberland Terrace, which is perhaps for that reason the grandest of all the terraces. Though shown in outline on early plans of the park, it was never designed in detail.[7] The government of the day, faced by Nash's massive overspending on Regent Street and Buckingham Palace, which he was enlarging for the Prince Regent to replace Carlton House, had no wish to open another bottomless pit of expenditure.[8] In 1829, by which time the cost of work on Buckingham Palace had become a scandal, a newspaper proclaimed: 'The king, as we long since said, ought to have asked for three millions of money to build a decent palace at Primrose Hill, and not for £300,000 to repair Buckingham House, which being in swampy ground will never be desirable to live in.'[9]

Following victory in the Napoleonic Wars in 1815, Parliament voted £300,000 for monuments to those who had fallen at the battles of Trafalgar and Waterloo, these two victories representing all the battles in which British sailors and soldiers had died fighting the French. This large sum, which was offered during the euphoria of victory, was remarkably slow to be paid out. It nevertheless excited numerous proposals for fitting tributes.[10] These included John Martin's design for a huge triumphal arch spanning the New Road to the north of Portland Place, surmounted by a column with a statue of Wellington on top of it;[11] an ornamental tower in Regent's Park by William Wilkins and John Gandy; and an 'elevated building terminating in an Observatory' by Robert Smirke in Greenwich Park. In the end, the principal monument to the victory, John Nash's Marble Arch of 1828, was not finished until thirteen years after Waterloo. Nelson's Column in Trafalgar Square had to wait until 1843.

James Elmes is remembered for his *Metropolitan Improvements* of 1827, which celebrated recent additions to London's architecture, including Regent Street and

Regent's Park. Although he had a less successful career as an architect, he was quick off the mark when, in 1816, he proposed a double celebration of Waterloo on and near Primrose Hill.[12] On Primrose Hill itself, Elmes proposed to build a temple in honour of Wellington, with statues of Blücher and the pope. Nearby he planned the village of Waterloo, tagging a fashionably named commercial development onto his grandiose national monument.*

> This new village, as its name imports, is intended as a humble tribute of commem- oration to one of the most splendid military achievements that ever embellished the page of history – an achievement that envelopes in its refulgent glories, and brings to one focus, the warlike character of Great Britain and her Allies, which overwhelmed the vaunted and invincible host of the greatest military despotism of modern times – an event, the memory and effects of which will descend to the latest posterity to be for ever immortalized by the glorious and ever-memorable names of Wellington and Waterloo. ... This commemorative village affords ample choice for the selection of an healthy residence, amidst the ground plots marked out on a most fascinating and beautiful spot of ground, situate between Primrose Hill and Belsize Park, commanding extensive and picturesque views over the country ...[13]

In addition, the new village would also be a place of public entertainment:

> The proprietors of this ground (an area of nearly forty acres) have subdivided it into a commemorative plan of two parts; the first, being the new village of Waterloo, encircles the second, which will be formed into a brilliant place of national public amusement, in which every effort will be employed ... to record the glory of the hero of Waterloo ... by a decorative display of tributary offerings of the plastic arts: creating by their means an inseparable association of ideas, of reverence and gratitude. ... This place of public recreation, intended to be superior to any in the metropolis or its vicinity ...[14]

On appropriate anniversaries, salutes would 'be fired from a redoubt thrown up on an islet in the public gardens intended for the display of fireworks, which multiplied and reflected from the expansive surface of the lake must be raised in brilliant effect'.[15]

In the surrounding village the names of the individual plots had not yet all been allocated, though they were to be either those of victories in the Napoleonic Wars or those of one of the Allied generals or leaders, including Blücher and Kutusoff.[16]

---

* [James Elmes], *Description of the New Village of Waterloo: Formed into a Limited Number of Allotments for Building, on a Most Enchanting and Salubrious Spot Contiguous to the Regent's Park, near Primrose Hill, in the County of Middlesex* (London, 1816).

There were to be six islets in the lake and, in commemoration of the campaign of Waterloo itself, one part of the approach road was to be called La Belle Alliance (a farmhouse on the battlefield) and an intersection Quatre-Bras, the successful British action at a nearby crossroads two days before Waterloo.[17] Hoping to attract widespread interest, the brochure ended by stating that 'The plan may be seen of Mr James Elmes, architect, Great Coram Street, Brunswick Square, who will generally be at home between the hours of two and four'.[18] He waited in vain.

Another equally ambitious plan to celebrate the British victory, conceived at the opposite end of the scale from his usual work, was proposed by the Scottish miniature painter Andrew Robertson. His plan involved the removal of much of Primrose Hill. 'The situation I have chosen is Primrose Hill, close by the canal in Regent's Park, from which the hill is to be cut away, so as to form a sheet of water.'

> I did not mean to offer any plan for the Waterloo monument, but an idea has occurred so noble, so appropriate and so economical, that I cannot resist offering it: this, therefore, fills up my evenings ... as an architectural design, it will be more beautiful than anything produced for two thousand years. I need only mention that it is to *rebuild the Parthenon* – since we have now in this country its most valuable remains ... I propose, in the pediment, to have sculpture expressing the contention of Neptune and Minerva renewed. ... In one, Minerva brings in her car, or is surrounded by, Wellington, Abercrombie, etc. ... In the case of Neptune, Nelson, Howe, etc. ... To render the situations equal, I place the building east and west instead of north and south. The interior will admit of due combination of the two services. On the frieze outside, instead of the centaurs, I represent a soldier of each cavalry regiment. Under the platform or terrace on which it stands, there will be a cemetery for those who fought in the war, as they did. Immediately under the building for those at Waterloo. This will afford ample space for cenotaphs to the memory of those who fell, and to record the names of every private, statues of the generals, admirals, and statesmen, to be disposed about the building and terrace, together with the king and Prince Regent ...
>
> A magnificent stair and avenue, on three sides, forms the approach, at the end of one is to be the Caledonian Asylum, corresponding in character to the Parthenon. At the end of the opposite approach a similar building, as it is in contemplation to build a royal palace, and one for the Duke of Wellington, I would combine all into one great plan, by placing the one to the south, the other to the north.
>
> The expense of what relates to the Parthenon would not exceed £200,000, which will be a great recommendation. The architects are all mad raising piles to cost millions, whereas, by a choice of situation, elevation and consequence are at once obtained. ... God grant me success, it promises well.[19]

In order to work out the likely cost of his plans more accurately, Robertson, living at 33 Gerard Street, Soho, proposed to get a quotation for 'preparing at Aberdeen, and removing and erecting in London, a Doric column 35 feet high, six at the base, or rather bottom of the shaft (there is no base) and about 14 feet of the entablature which is 14 feet high, above it'.[20] Cautiously, and so as to avoid anyone in Aberdeen guessing what his project might be, he asked his correspondent to avoid mentioning that no less than fifty-six of these columns would be needed.

Robertson's proposal, though never built, at least attracted some public support, as reflected in a letter to *The Times* in April 1817:

> In regard to the monuments now to be erected, whether separate, or united in one, there can be no doubt of its being the universal feeling that the object should be accomplished on a scale, and in a perfection, becoming the gratitude of a country standing as high in power and in civilization as Great Britain does; and that, far from sacrificing good taste for magnitude, the work should be so executed as most effectually to benefit and to improve those arts which are capable of being employed in the execution of it. ... It consists in an exact representation of the Parthenon of the Acropolis of Athens, to be erected on a platform moderately raised on Primrose Hill.[21]

Statues would be commissioned, for which inspiration was readily at hand, as 'a large proportion of the original sculpture belonging to it is now in the British Museum', to fill 'as much as may be, at first, wished of the capacious pediments, the ninety metopes, the 450 feet of friezes'.[22] The inside walls 'would furnish an equally unbounded scope for the genius of historical painting in immortalizing the glories of the nation'. A crypt, fifteen feet in height, would receive 'the remains of departed heroes or departed friends, and such monuments as gratitude or affection may wish to raise there'. The writer optimistically envisaged the completion of the structure in little more than a year, at a cost 'at the utmost' of £150,000, saving £50,000 from Robertson's own estimate. Much of this would go to 'employing manual labour ... among the lower classes of the community', while competition to provide the sculpture and paintings would 'furnish occupation to a very great number of artists'.[23]

A faint echo of Robertson's plan could still be heard in 1846, during the debate on where a giant equestrian statue of the Duke of Wellington, astride Copenhagen, the charger he had ridden at Waterloo, should be placed. Sculpted by Matthew Cotes Wyatt, at thirty foot high and weighing forty tons, it was the largest equestrian statue ever to have been cast in Britain.[*] Although the duke himself

---

[*]   The statue, costing £14,000 and paid for by subscription, was placed directly opposite Apsley House, No. 1 London, the Duke of Wellington's London residence. John Martin Robinson,

sat for the sculptor, Copenhagen was dead; so another horse, Rosemary, claimed by critics to be a poor likeness, was used as a model. After numerous delays, and many exchanges in Parliament, the statue was finally erected on the Victory Arch at Hyde Park Corner in October 1846, against the wishes of Decimus Burton, the arch's architect. The statue was immediately seen to be out of proportion to the modestly sized arch, raising a debate about alternative sites which was only ended by the Duke of Wellington's own veto on its being moved.

Bell's Life saw the advantages of placing the statue on Primrose Hill:

> It has been suggested that Primrose Hill would be an excellent site for this statue. A better locality cannot be chosen. It would look extremely well from Portland Place and the Regent's Park, and would command the attention of the surrounding country for miles – including the passengers of the Great Western and Birmingham Railways, and would even be visible from the Surrey hills.[24]

Punch approved the choice of Primrose Hill, but examined the practicalities of such a transfer:

> 'Oh Where, and Oh Where?' The question is being asked by everyone in reference to the intended position of the Wellington statue. It is, we believe, in contemplation to place it on the brow ... of Primrose Hill, where it would be discernible from a considerable distance. Some difficulty has arisen, on account of the disturbance of vested interests which must take place by the dislodgement of the brandy-ball dealers, and other merchants of saccharine, who resort on Sundays to the summit of the mount; but this may be remedied by opening the four legs of the horse as stalls for sweet-stuff.[25]

In the end, the statue was moved first to Green Park in 1883 and then, in 1885, to the Round Hill, close to the Royal Garrison Church at Aldershot.[*]

An edifice for the benefit of the people, rather than to the glory of the nation, was proposed in 1844, soon after Primrose Hill became a public park. A 'well-known

---

The Wyatts: An Architectural Dynasty (Oxford, 1979), pp. 173–88; 'Matthew Cotes Wyatt (1777–1862)', *Oxford Dictionary of National Biography*; M.H. Port, 'The Wellington Statue', *The History of the King's Works*, vi, *1782–1851* (London, 1973), pp. 494–5. Port restricts the statue's height to twenty-seven feet. Decimus Burton's arch had been built in 1826–28.

[*] In 1883 the Wellington Statue Committee briefly considered Primrose Hill as a possible new site for the statue, *The Times*, 1 May 1883. In 2004 the Aldershot Garrison undertook its renovation, clearing away nearby bushes and rebronzing the statue.

In 1870, the *Pall Mall Gazette* suggested using Primrose Hill as a warning to speculators. It claimed there were no memorials to 'our own folly which might serve as useful warnings to posterity. ... For instance, a large structure at the top of Primrose Hill in memory of the railway mania a few years ago might be of inestimable benefit to succeeding generations.' *Pall Mall Gazette*, 17 November 1870.

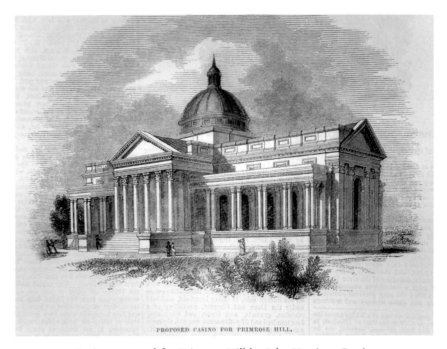

PROPOSED CASINO FOR PRIMROSE HILL.

Casino proposed for Primrose Hill by John Harrison Curtis,
an ear specialist and a promoter of outdoor exercise for all classes.
From the *Magazine of Science* (1845). (*CLSAC*)

aurist and oculist', Mr Curtis, submitted an illustrated plan to the Commissioners of the Woods and Forests for a substantial casino on the hill, with a portico of six Corinthian columns. 'Casinos, although hitherto unknown in England, are common enough on the Continent, and are found to be exceedingly agreeable adjuncts to parks and other places of public resort.'[26] The word casino at the time meant a small villa used for pleasure, not necessarily for gambling. On Primrose Hill it was to be a place for physical and spiritual refreshment: visitors would be 'furnished with breakfast or tea in the open air, in fine weather, the novelty of the thing would attract many, and thus induce some to leave their beds an hour or two before the usual time, and inhale the morning air before it is impregnated with smoke'.[27]

John Harrison Curtis, the man behind the proposal, had made a reputation for himself as an expert on hearing problems.[28] His *Treatise on the Physiology and Diseases of the Ear* (1817) went through four editions. His Royal Dispensary for the Diseases of the Ear, in Dean Street, Soho, boasted two kings, three royal and six other dukes, three marquesses and eight earls amongst its patrons. While many of his treatments of the ear were misguided, Curtis was a gifted self-publicist whose general recommendations for the preservation of health contained much shrewd common sense.* This quality was the chief merit of his *Observations on the Preservation of Health in Infancy, Youth, Manhood and Age* (1837), which prescribed cheerfulness, excursions to the countryside, exercise and fresh air.† He also stressed the need for more public parks:

> although much has been done in this way, there is still room for improvement. On the Continent, greater attention is paid to procuring places of exercise and amusement for the inhabitants of towns than in this country; but there are indications that give us reason for hoping that our inferiority in this respect will not be suffered long to continue.[29]

One of Curtis's patients was Robert Peel, later to be Prime Minister when Primrose Hill became a public park. When Peel asked Curtis what he was hoping to achieve in applying an enormous syringe to his ear, Curtis replied, aiming the tip of the syringe directly at his patient's ear canal and giving it a little dig: 'Mr Peel, if you don't hold your tongue, I shall certainly do you a mischief.'[30]

As well as being proposed as the site of a mansion, a place of public entertainment and the site of a national monument, Primrose Hill was repeatedly seen as part of the answer to one of the most pressing questions facing London, and other British cities, in the first half of the nineteenth century. Primrose Hill might have been covered by housing not for the living but for the dead – and not just for the bodies of national heroes.

The enormous expansion in population, with London reaching almost a million inhabitants by 1800, meant not only that there was not enough room for living worshippers in the existing churches, should they all choose to attend, but that there

---

* One of the attractive features of his book on health in general is an un-Victorian tolerance of children: 'Another characteristic of childish exercise is noise – screaming and bawling invariably accompany it; and if such expressions of delight are prohibited, the children cannot proceed with their diversions. Here, as everywhere, we may discover the wisdom and beneficence of the arrangements of nature. This noise, which, to the adult, appears so useless, and which is to him a source of annoyance, and is therefore forbidden, is produced by the exertion of those delicate organs – the lungs. By this exercise they are developed and strengthened, and thus rendered capable of resisting the morbific influences to which they are, in our variable climate, peculiarly exposed.' John Harrison Curtis, *Observations on the Preservation of Health in Infancy, Youth, Manhood and Age: With the Best Means of Improving the Moral and Physical Condition of Man* (London, 1837), p. 31.

† An impressive list of patrons, including King William IV and Queen Adelaide, Leopold I, King of the Belgians, and the then Princess Victoria, takes pride of place before advertisements for Curtis's other books at the end of the volume.

was no space for their bodies when dead in existing churchyards. St Marylebone, with its small parish church and burgeoning population, twice tried to alleviate its problem by opening additional burial grounds south of the New Road.[31] St Pancras, whose population increased hugely between 1760 and 1850, also bought additional land for burials near to its old parish church.[32]

By the early years of the nineteenth century the problems associated with the burial of the dead, eighty years before the first legal cremation in 1885, were becoming a national scandal.[33] In the main cities, churches themselves and churchyards were crammed with far more bodies than they could hold, with graves being reused and churchyards rising above the level of surrounding streets, as coffins were piled one on top of the other in them. The effluvia from the dead was also suspected of causing disease. Repeated incidents of coffins breaking open and of bodies being desecrated drew frequent attention to the problem. With a premium on space, any semblance of decent burial also became extremely expensive. As well as this, the breaking open of graves by 'resurrectionists', taking newly buried corpses to supply the shortage of bodies needed by anatomists, made a sensational addition, even if in England no resurrectionists went as far as the notorious Burke and Hare, who in Edinburgh in 1827 and 1828 supplied the bodies of those they had murdered, cutting out the need for exhumation.[34] All of this was increasingly unacceptable in a society that was beginning to value decency and decorum, and to disdain the rough manners of the eighteenth century.[35]

Provision of burial space had indeed been involved in the genesis of Regent's Park. As a measure to ease St Marylebone's problems, the principal landowner in the parish, the third Duke of Portland, had offered six acres of land for a burial site on his Barrow Hill estate to the immediate west of Primrose Hill, on the condition that the parish promoted an Act for a public road across the park to join his extensive estates in St Marylebone with those to the north of Marylebone Park. Discouraged in part by the thought of an unending line of funeral cortèges crossing the park, the government's decision to refuse the duke permission to build the road signalled its plan to develop the park itself.[36]

The parish's dilemma remained unresolved until 1814, when St John's Wood Chapel, designed by Thomas Hardwick and with a burial ground to its north, was opened. Fittingly, this was on the site of an old plague burial ground bought from the Eyre Estate in 1807.[37] One of the early burials in the new ground was almost certainly the most notorious. Joanna Southcott, a farmer's daughter from Devon who had become a prolific author and considered herself a channel of divine revelation, had declared herself the Bride of Christ in 1792. Promising salvation to her followers and issuing prophecies, she built up a sizeable following which included members of Eyre family. In 1813, at the age of sixty-four, she declared herself pregnant with Shiloh, the new Messiah. She died, just after Christmas, on

27 December 1815, leaving a box of sealed prophecies to be opened only in the presence of twenty-four bishops of the Church of England at a time of national emergency.* As St Marylebone grew, it provided a steady stream of corpses. By 1833 40,000 people had been buried in the cemetery. By 1886, when the burial ground was closed as a graveyard, this figure had risen to 60,000. There were 26,676 burials in the graveyard of St Pancras church between 1827 and 1847.[38]

Burying so many bodies in a confined area made it impossible to allow the individual commemoration of the great majority of the dead.[39] With London's population continuing to soar, a new solution emerged, taking the problem of burial away from parishes, and solving it both commercially and hygienically. George Carden, a barrister of the Inner Temple, campaigned from 1824 for a public cemetery on the lines of Père Lachaise in Paris, which he had visited in 1821 on a tour of inspection of burial places at home and abroad. He provided gruesome evidence of the shortcomings of the existing provision for burial and made a positive case for the advantages of properly planned cemeteries. 'To those who have travelled into foreign countries, where cemeteries are generally provided on an elevated site and at a short distance from populous towns, a remedy for many of the evils justly a cause of deep regret, if not of animadversion, must, as soon as they beheld them, have instantly occurred.'[40]

Cemeteries outside towns, Carden claimed, were often favourite places of resort for the neighbouring population. He gave a glowing account of the attractions of the landscaped gardens of Père Lachaise. The cemetery he proposed would also be secure from resurrectionists, as it would be surrounded by a high wall 'watched and guarded so as to prevent the possibility of the sepulchres being violated'.[41] In 1825 Carden petitioned Parliament to set up an official enquiry into the existing burial system. He also launched a General Burial Grounds Association on the London Stock Exchange, appealing to investors to back his scheme to lay out an extensive cemetery, intended not only to be attractive and hygienic but also profitable.† In contrast to the squalor of churchyards and the limited space of St Marylebone's graveyard extension at St John's Wood, Carden's cemetery offered ample space for

---

* A neo-Southcottian sect, the Panacea Society, founded in 1919, claims to be the guardian of the box in Bedford. See the society's website: www.panacea-society.org. When a rival box was opened in 1927, without the necessary twenty-four Anglican bishops being present, it was found to contain a few unimportant papers, a lottery ticket and a horse-pistol. 'Joanna Southcott (1750–1814)', *Oxford Dictionary of National Biography*.

† Early cemeteries were indeed potentially profitable. Two of the earliest were in Liverpool, at Low Hill (1825) and St James's (1825–29). The latter, designed and landscaped by John Foster, paid an 8 per cent dividend in 1830. The Glasgow Necropolis, opened in 1832 on a hill near the cathedral, was meant to be seen as a communal monument as well as to remind citizens of their dead. James Stevens Curl, *The Victorian Celebration of Death* (Thrupp, 2000), p. 44.

individual burials. It would allow the bereaved, or at least those who were able to pay for the privilege, to commemorate the dead by individual monuments or in a family mausoleum.

A meeting for subscribers was called for 20 December 1825, at the Crown and Rolls Rooms, 110 Chancery Lane. The nominal capital was to be £150,000, with shares at £50 each, with Carden himself willing to take a thousand. Before the meeting took place, Carden wrote again to the subscribers announcing that he had had a positive reaction from the clergy he had approached and claiming the 'liberal and zealous aid of the public press'. He also announced: 'I am happy to state that the Society can obtain a very eligible spot, on a rising ground, almost contiguous to Primrose Hill.' [42] In the event, the meeting was cancelled on 15 December due to a national financial crisis and Stock Exchange crash which made it unlikely that the scheme would attract backers.

Carden's proposal, nevertheless, drew considerable interest and encouraged the production of a number of designs for the cemeteries. In 1826 and 1827 Augustus Charles Pugin, who had earlier provided a panorama of John Nash's scheme for Regent's Park before it was officially accepted, exhibited three designs for cemeteries at the Royal Academy, one of which was intended for Primrose Hill. [43] At a meeting in February 1830 intended to relaunch the float of a public burial ground company, the chairman announced that he had received two communications, one 'from Mr Goodwin, relative to the consideration of his design for a public cemetery' and the other 'from Mr Willson respecting his plan of a pyramid'. [44]

Francis Goodwin (1784–1835) subsequently exhibited his plan for a 'Grand National Cemetery' on Primrose Hill at the National Cemetery Office in Parliament Square. Whether he knew of Andrew Robertson's plans for a Parthenon on Primrose Hill is unclear. According to a newspaper report, his aim was

> to obtain for the metropolis of this country an advantage similar to that enjoyed by the metropolis of France, in having one large and general place of interment, beyond the boundaries of the city. The burying-place of Père la Chaise [sic], near Paris is well known. Mr Goodwin's object appears to be to surpass the famous Parisian cemetery, in the advantage of situation and the picturesqueness of arrangement. For this purpose he has chosen for its site (supposing that he should succeed in forming the joint stock company) Primrose Hill and its neighbourhood. The grand outline of his plan embraces no less a space of ground than one hundred and fifty acres, but to the centre parcel of this — about forty-two acres — he has confined his more striking design. This space he proposes to surround with a double cloister, which will afford a promenade in case of unfavourable weather, while its walls will be dedicated to the reception

of tablets and memorials. To this cloister there are to be three grand entrances, one a copy of the Propylea, and the others, right and left, after the famous arches of Constantius and Septimius Severus: these entrances are, by means of terraces, to conduct to a temple built on the model of the Parthenon, probably the grandest and most perfect Grecian building that ever was erected. The building will be consecrated so as to admit of divine worship being performed. ... The whole superb arrangement is to conclude with a magnificent crescent, of several hundred feet in the span, surmounted at the base by a copy of Trajan's pillar. ... The whole of the cloisters, and the more extensive edifices are to be founded on catacombs, calculated to contain an immense number of corpses.[45]

At each corner of the walls surrounding the cemetery would be copies of the Tower of the Winds in Athens, intended not only as ornaments but also as watchtowers.

The second proposal for a cemetery at Primrose Hill, in the shape of a pyramid, was by Thomas Willson. Born in about 1780, Willson had won the gold medal for architecture at the Royal Academy Schools in 1801.[46] His plans included a Royal Military College for the Emperor of Russia (1805) and a National Mausoleum to Naval and Military Heroes (1815), neither of which was built. After a short-lived experiment in emigration to South Africa in 1819–20, Willson returned to England and started work on one of the most extraordinary designs in British architectural history. Willson exhibited an initial version of his scheme as early as 1824. Then, in May 1829, he announced that he would be making an application to Parliament for a charter to bring his plan into effect. He also submitted an outline of his plan to Carden's public meeting in 1830. As Carden, however, was committed to a garden cemetery in the style of Père Lachaise, Willson's plans can have had little appeal to him.

Willson published his scheme in 1830 as *The Pyramid: A General Metropolitan Cemetery to be Erected in the Vicinity of Primrose Hill*. His plan was for a pyramid at the centre of a large, landscaped cemetery. Its exact proposed location is unclear, but Willson, whose address was given as 11 New Cavendish Street, Portland Place, stated that 'the site has been wisely chosen in the vicinity of Primrose Hill, where it will possess the advantage of being equally accessible from every part of the Metropolis'.[47]

It was not the outline of the pyramid that was so unusual. Made of brick faced with granite, it was to be based on the Roman pyramid of Cestius in Italy, rather than on any of those in Egypt, with an obelisk on its summit. It was the stupendous size proposed that set it apart.[*] Described by its architect as 'a massive, imposing

---

[*] It was not, however, the only giant pyramid proposed in the early nineteenth century as an adornment for London. In 1815 Colonel Frederick Trench had proposed a pyramid 364 feet high (one foot less than the height of St Paul's) at the King's Mews in Westminster, the future

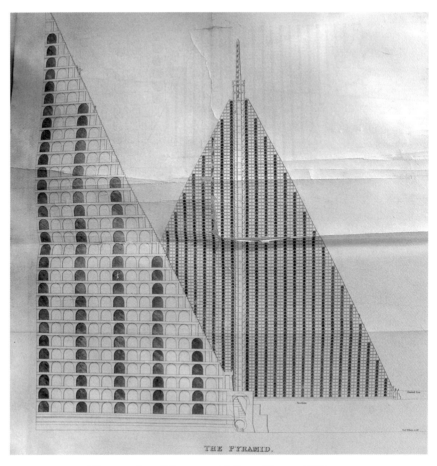

THE PYRAMID.

The exterior of the pyramid, from Thomas Willson,
*The Pyramid: A General Metropolitan Cemetery to be Erected in the Vicinity
of Primrose Hill* (London, 1830).

and awful structure, surpassing in magnitude the great pyramid of Egypt', the
pyramid had ninety-four stories, two underground and ninety-two above.[48] It was
to be nine hundred foot square and higher than St Paul's Cathedral. With four
entrances, and approached by a 'lofty Egyptian portal', it was designed to have
215,296 catacombs, each holding twenty-four coffins. In all, when full, the pyramid
would contain 5,167,104 bodies.[49]

---

site of Trafalgar Square. The pyramid would have had twenty-two tiers, one for each year of
the war against France, decorated by martial friezes. Pyramids were in vogue, partly due to the
French and British campaigns in Egypt during the Napoleonic Wars. Felix Barker and Ralph
Hyde, *London as it Might Have Been* (London, 1982), pp. 68–9; 'Sir Frederick William Trench
(c. 1777–1859)', *Oxford Dictionary of National Biography*.

Willson was confident in the attractions of his scheme. 'It will rise in solemn majesty over its [London's] splendid fanes and lofty towers, to proclaim by its elevation, the temporary triumph but final overthrow of Death, teaching the living to die, and the dying to live for ever.'[50] At its top, a circular stone staircase would terminate in a small astronomical observatory, surmounted by 'a plain and appropriate obelisk'. 'To trace the length of its shadow at sun-rise and at eve, and to toil up its singular passages to the summit, will beguile the hours of the curious, and impress feelings of solemn awe and admiration upon every beholder.'[51] It would be 'ornamental to the Metropolis, an impressive *memento mori* to every passing age, and an object of pious veneration to posterity'.[52]

The architect had few doubts about the commercial attractions of his design: 'while it is the mightiest work that was ever undertaken, it is the ONLY ONE that can meet the exigencies of the case, and that is at the same time PRACTICABLE, ECONOMICAL, and REMUNERATIVE'.[53] Providing an excellent public task for the unemployed, it would cost £2,500,000 to build, but would earn £15,000,000 for its shareholders in a century. Alternatively, an early freehold sale of individual catacombs and niches would realise a profit of £10,764,800. The bodies from the city churches could be moved there as early clients, while good drainage and ventilation would assure its salubriousness. 'The present is not an age when a scheme is to be rejected, because it is stupendous, and soars beyond the comprehension of the multitude.'[54] 'The grand Mausoleum will go far towards completing the glory of London!'[55] Willson was also prescient in recognising the attraction of the skyscrapers of the future to their developers: 'The base comprehending eighteen and a half acres, being multiplied by the several stages to be erected one above another, *when required*, will generate nearly *1000* acres! self-created out of the void space over head, as the building progresses upwards.'[56]

Goodwin's and Willson's grandiose designs were never realised. Carden's campaign, however, soon reached fruition. His cemetery company bought fifty-five acres of farm land bordering the Grand Junction Canal and Harrow Road in 1831. With government support assured by the outbreak of a cholera epidemic in 1831, Kensal Green Cemetery opened in 1833.[57] Between 1832 and 1847, Parliament approved the establishment of eight commercial cemetery companies, including the London Cemetery Company, which bought the site for Highgate Cemetery in 1836.[58]

Following an Act of Parliament in 1842, Primrose Hill was opened as a public park. This did not end suggestions for the use of the hill by those with ambitious building plans. First off the mark, indeed jumping the gun after hearing a rumour that the government was about to buy Primrose Hill, were the directors of the West Middlesex Waterworks, who wrote to the Department of Woods and Forests to propose a large tower not on Primrose Hill but on Little Primrose Hill, at their reservoir on Barrow Hill. As the secretary of the company explained:

> A plan has been suggested to the company to erect a hexagon tower at the eastern end of their reservoir of a great elevation – one side to have a projecting turret for a steam engine chimney, one for the chimnies of the several stories, and one for an internal staircase to those rooms. That the exterior should also have a spiral staircase projecting from the faces of the tower. In the other faces of the tower would be doors to the landings of the external staircase and windows to light the several rooms.
>
> A building of this character in such a position, it has been conjectured, would by a moderate payment for ascent to the several rooms, and for a contemplation of the panoramic views combined with subjects of attraction in those rooms, produce an annuity to compensate the outlay of money in the erection of it.
>
> The West Middlesex Water Works Company understanding that government has obtained a property in the greater Primrose Hill, and contemplates the erection on its summit of some kind of observatory building, for the recreation of the people – the West Middlesex Company is desirous that the Commissioners of the Office of Woods ... consider whether any scheme having such a building as that before described, and uniting the two hills in one plan of public use, recreation and beauty, could not be effected on some joint plan.
>
> The West Middlesex Company has reserved the land about its reservoir, in order to remove to a distance from the water in it the soot of chimneys; and the chimney which it contemplates for its own use, and the tower containing it is proposed to be of a very great height.[59]

Nor was the Department of Woods and Forests itself above thinking about a dramatic use of its new acquisition. In 1841, the year before the Act that made Primrose Hill a park was passed, but when the government's acquisition of the hill was already settled, James Pennethorne, Nash's adopted stepson and architectural heir, who was the nearest equivalent to an official government architect of the day, drew up a radical new landscape for the hill, incorporating other land to its north and east. The hill itself was to be crossed by a wide path to its east, incorporating a terrace, while several concentric paths ran round the hill. Pennethorne's most striking suggestion for the new park was, however, a giant statue of Britannia seated on a terrace at the top of the hill. While no further action was taken to commission this spectacular addition, Pennethorne was no crank or outsider. It was his plans which were implemented in the landscaping of two other later London parks, Victoria Park and Battersea Park.[60]

Even after its transformation into a public park, Primrose Hill and the area

A pagoda on Primrose Hill, from W.H. Twentyman,
'Proposed Royal Champs Elysées', c. 1860. (*Private Collection*)

around it still attracted ambitious proposals. The Regent's Canal had never proved as successful as its projectors had hoped, with many of the bulk goods which were its staple being transferred to the railways after 1840. The logic of this led to a series of proposals either to construct a railway line parallel to the canal or to fill in the canal completely and lay a railway line over its bed. Early schemes in 1836 and 1845 failed to get parliamentary sanction or were unable to raise sufficient capital. A scheme for a railway parallel to the canal, passing Regent's Park and the Zoo in a covered way, was scotched by the Department of Woods and Forests in 1847, but as late as 1882 the Regent's Canal, City and Docks Railway Act was passed, even though the railway itself was not built.[61]

In 1853, the leading architect C.R. Cockerell unveiled a plan for a curved three hundred feet wide avenue to run from Regent's Park over Primrose Hill to Belsize Park.[62]

Taking our course from the Regent's Park, the road proposes to pass over the commanding height of Primrose Hill, and thence to ascend gracefully by a magnificent park-ride and avenue, or boulevard – reminding us of the most enchanting continental arrangement – till it enters the Hampstead road, by the existing beautiful avenue of Belsize Park, improving the surrounding building land by situations for the most desirable villas and gardened habitations.[63]

From there it was to reach the Heath via Pond Street, with a second branch running from the East Heath to the Spaniards, then reaching Hampstead at Telegraph Hill.[64]

A more localised and westerly version of the same idea was published by W.H. Twentyman, a major developer in St John's Wood, in 1860.* Twentyman proposed a 'Royal Champs Elysées' beginning in Regent's Park, running to the west of Primrose Hill and reaching Telegraph Hill via Frognal. In this scheme, Primrose Hill itself was to be crowned by a pagoda.[65] In 1864, John Leighton looked closer at hand for inspiration. His avenue ran across Regent's Park from Park Crescent and over the west side of Primrose Hill before turning left to reach the Finchley Road at Swiss Cottage. Instead of a pagoda, Primrose Hill was to be topped by a statue of William Shakespeare, 'ten or twelve feet high, in marble, mounted on a pedestal proportionate in height', with 'an ornamental shrine of iron and glass to enclose it', to commemorate the tercentenary of his birth.[66] Estimated to cost £3,000, it was hoped to raise the money from public subscription: 'a little more than 50,000 shillings, 100,000 sixpences, or 500,000 pence will be amply sufficient to place an elegant and imposing structure and work of art on Primrose Hill ...'[67] Not enough money was forthcoming to fund the cost of this statue, but a small statue of Shakespeare was erected in 1864 outside the Queens public house in Regent's Park Road, looking out over the hill.

The idea for a statue of Shakespeare was not a new one.[68] In 1854 the French sculptor Pierre-Joseph Chardigny (1794–1866), who had lived in London and had exhibited at the Royal Academy in 1842–43, proposed 'erecting a colossal statue of Shakespere on Primrose Hill'.

> He calculates the expense at 700,000 francs, or, in round numbers, a million. M. Chardigny, a pupil of the Bosio school, is the son of a distinguished sculptor, who was killed by a fall of scaffold while finishing his bas-relief of Juno at the Louvre. The son is known by his statue of Jean Goujon in front of the Hôtel de Ville, at Paris. For his statue of Ferdinand VII he received the decoration of the order of Isabella the Catholic, and other badges of honour from the King of Holland and the Queen of Portugal. ... If carried out, it will surpass the German statue of Bavaria and that of St Charles Borromeo on the shores of the Lake

---

* For a proposal for a road across the side of Primrose Hill, put to St Marylebone Vestry, see the *Observer*, 17 December 1860. This was justified by its proposer, Mr Freeth, on the grounds that Primrose Hill's paths were unsafe at night: 'In fact, after nightfall, these paths were quite useless, and no respectable people, especially women, dare venture across them.' For William Holme Twentyman, see Mireille Galinou, *Cottages and Villas: The Birth of the Garden Suburb* (New Haven and London, 2010), pp. 182–3.

Maggiore. It will surpass even Napoleon's grand triangle of bronze elephants in the Place Bastille, to commemorate his campaign in Egypt. M. Chardigny, who is at much at home in the foundry as the studio, has been devising means to simplify the mode of execution. He proposes to divide the colossus into ten fragments, which are to be placed on each other horizontally. Many of these fragments, too large for easy transportation, might be divided vertically, and then put together with screws, which would not be seen in perspective.[69]

This statue would answer 'the frequent remark by foreigners that there is in this country no monument to Shakespeare' on a scale to match the colossal statues of St Charles Borromeo in Italy or of Peter the Great in Russia.* Chardigny intended the statue to be a hundred feet high above a stone pedestal. It was to be made of cast iron, formed by a new process he had himself invented:

In the statue it is proposed to have three floors, with a staircase for ascending to the top or head of the monument. These three floors will divide the statue into three rooms, of about eighty feet in circumference and fifteen feet each in height, the sides of which the artist proposes should be adorned with *bassi-relievi*, in cast iron, representing all the chief scenes of Shakspeare's plays. In the middle of the first floor are to be statues, in cast iron, of the Queen and Prince Albert. The third floor of the statue, reaching to the head, will afford a most splendid panoramic view of London, through the apertures for the eyes, which, following the proportions of the rest of the statue, will be more than two feet wide.[70]

This would allow those ascending to the top of the statue to see all of London through the eyes of the playwright.

Chardigny, who seems to have had neither official backing nor a patron for his proposal, was not well known in England. Many of the press reports about it indeed refer to him as 'Signor Chardigni', assuming he was Italian. His timing may also have been premature, as his proposal was made ten years before the tercentenary of Shakespeare's birth. While therefore news of the idea of the statue received wide coverage, it was never likely to become a reality. It did, however, provoke the *Art Journal* to address the question of 'Scale for Portraiture in Sculpture':

As regards effort of the imagination, the idea of great size appears to us rather puerile than grand. It is as easy also to suppose a mile of altitude as a hundred

---

*   The statue of Borromeo in Arona, by Giovanni Battista Crespi, is seventy-five feet high on a plinth thirty-nine feet in height. The equestrian statue of Peter the Great in St Petersburg, known as the Bronze Horseman, by Etienne Maurice Falconnet and unveiled in 1782, is twenty feet high on a twenty-five-foot pedestal, consisting of the 1,250 ton Thunder Stone. The most famous giant statue of the Ancient World, the Colossus of Rhodes, constructed between 292 and 280 BC and destroyed by an earthquake in 226 BC, was 107 feet in height.

or two hundred feet. That size is an element of grandeur there is no doubt, for what would the pyramids be a foot high! but it is only good and effective as other qualities are when it is rightly applied; and too vast a scale is not appropriate to obtain a just or even the grandest effect in a portraiture.[71]

Despite the disappointment of Chardigny's own hopes, a giant statue by a French sculptor, Frédéric Bartholdi, conceived in the 1860s but not finished for another twenty-five years, quickly became one of the world's most famous symbols. A gift from France to America, the statue of Liberty, standing 151 feet above its pedestal, was erected on Bedloe's Island in New York Harbour in 1886.

7

Public Walks

WHILE Primrose Hill was seen as a desirable site for the erection of a major monument or for a profitable cemetery, considerations other than glory or profit came into play and, in the end, preserved the hill as a park. Worried about the unprecedented expansion of London, the government came to see the desirability of ensuring that there were places where citizens could get away from the fumes of the city and have the opportunity for outdoor relaxation.

The rapid growth of Britain's cities, and in particular the unprecedented expansion of London until it was the largest city in the world, with just under a million inhabitants in 1800 and almost two and a half million in 1850, was a cause of disquiet to politicians and many others. The population of the parish of St Pancras, which included part of Primrose Hill, exploded from around a thousand inhabitants in 1760 to 31,000 in 1801, and to 160,000 in 1852.[1]

In his *Principles of Population*, which went through six editions between 1798 and 1826, Robert Malthus prophesied that the rise in population would outstrip the ability of nations to feed themselves, leading to mass starvation and to catastrophic epidemics to restore a sustainable level. There was also widespread anxiety about the potential for public unrest and, perhaps, revolution. Nor was there any lack of precedent to alarm those of a nervous disposition. The French Revolution, which had disturbed the peace of Europe for twenty-five years, had begun in France's capital and largest city, Paris, in 1789.[2]

The English government had reacted to the French Revolution by introducing a range of repressive measures to ensure that discontented, and disfranchised, members of the population did not follow the example of their fellows across the Channel. Although the war against Napoleon brought about a surge of patriotism, with great public rejoicing greeting the victories of Trafalgar in 1805 and Waterloo in 1815, widespread disillusionment followed the end of the war. In its aftermath a slump replaced the booming war industries, while disbanded soldiers and sailors faced unemployment.

Industrial recession and political discontent under a reactionary Tory government led to the Peterloo Massacre in August 1819 in St Peter's Square in Manchester. As a result of the local magistracy overreacting to the calling of a large Radical meeting, Hussars supporting the local Yeomanry charged the crowd with sabres drawn, killing eleven people and injuring hundreds.[3] This fed political unrest rather than crushing it. An extreme reaction was the Cato Street Conspiracy of 1820. In a stable-block just to the south of Regent's Park, plotters led by Arthur Thistlewood hatched a spectacular plot to murder the entire British Cabinet when it met for dinner at the house of the Earl of Harrowby in Grosvenor Square. The conspirators got no nearer to their targets than Cato Street itself, where their meeting was interrupted by a force of police and soldiers.[4] Less direct methods were brought to bear on the chronic imbalance of the political system, which gave two seats in Parliament to the handful of voters of the virtually uninhabited borough of Old Sarum and none to the citizens of industrial Manchester. There was also a sustained attack by Radicals, in Parliament and the press, on unearned privilege and on the corruption of aristocratic nepotism. The Tory government finally lost power in 1830, bringing in the Whig government of Earl Grey and paving the way for the First Reform Act of 1832.

Although the Whigs were led by a wealthy, exclusive and interrelated aristocratic set, they had won power in alliance with the middle classes of the cities, including many urban nonconformists, and with Radicals who supported the extension of suffrage. Whig governments were therefore more sensitive to the problems of the growing cities than the Tories, who drew their main support from the countryside and the established church. One major result of the Whig victory was a wholesale reform of local government by the Municipal Corporations Act of 1835, which ended the powers of closed corporations.[5]

The growth of cities, and of London in particular, presented national and local government with many challenges besides that of public order. These included disease, poverty and sanitation. While at the beginning of the eighteenth century only one in five people had lived in towns, by 1850 half the population did so. The huge increase in the built-up area of London had led to the disappearance of open areas that had once been available for public recreation, as the names of Bethnal Green, Covent Garden, Moorfields and Spitalfields recall. Because of London's sheer size, it was no longer easy for citizens to reach the countryside. Most of London's squares were also closed, with entrance only available to keyholders.[6] Many other smaller open spaces disappeared under bricks and mortar, while those that remained had to cater for a greatly increased number of users. Hyde Park, Green Park and St James's Park were open to the public, but Kensington Gardens only admitted those who were respectably dressed. All four parks, however, were in the West End and well away from many of the newly built-up areas.[7]

An awareness of the need for the better provision of open spaces led the Whig government to appoint a Commission on Public Walks to report on their availability, addressing three acknowledged facts:

PLATE 1 Primrose Hill was a popular place of excursion from the middle of the eighteenth century. This engraving, from about 1790, shows its top full of people. (*CLSAC*)

PLATE 2 The Chalk Farm Tavern in 1810. It was entered through an archway, shown in many illustrations of it, and had an upstairs gallery. Over the years it was altered several times, before being pulled down in 1853 and replaced by what is now a Greek restaurant, Lemonia. (*CLSAC*)

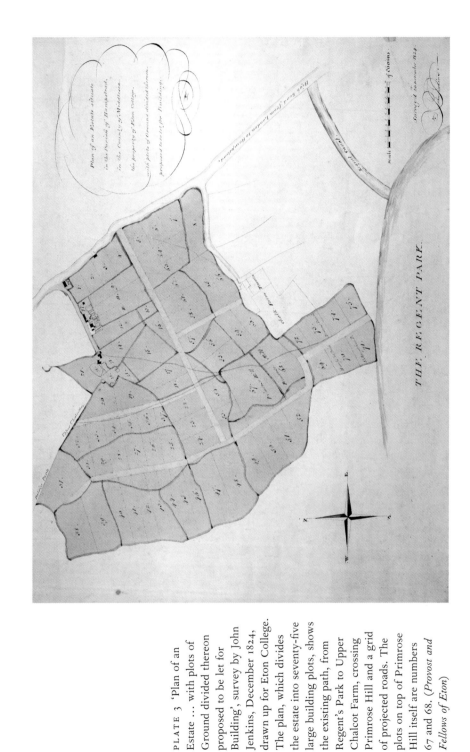

PLATE 3 'Plan of an
Estate … with plots of
Ground divided thereon
proposed to be let for
Building', survey by John
Jenkins, December 1824,
drawn up for Eton College.
The plan, which divides
the estate into seventy-five
large building plots, shows
the existing path, from
Regent's Park to Upper
Chalcot Farm, crossing
Primrose Hill and a grid
of projected roads. The
plots on top of Primrose
Hill itself are numbers
67 and 68. (*Provost and
Fellows of Eton*)

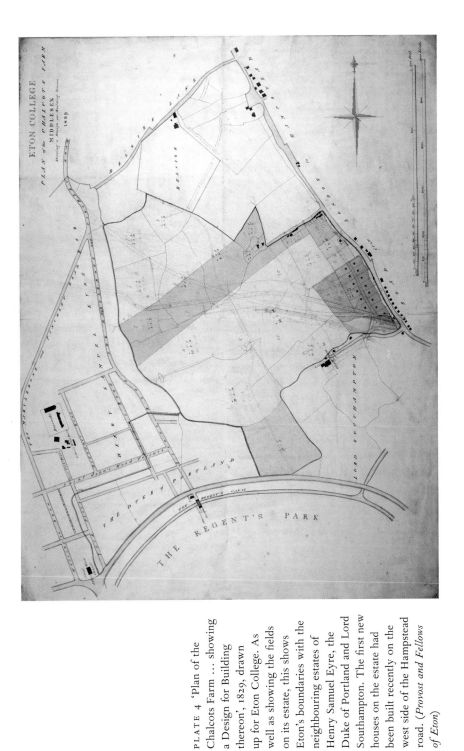

PLATE 4 'Plan of the Chalcots Farm ... showing a Design for Building thereon', 1829, drawn up for Eton College. As well as showing the fields on its estate, this shows Eton's boundaries with the neighbouring estates of Henry Samuel Eyre, the Duke of Portland and Lord Southampton. The first new houses on the estate had been built recently on the west side of the Hampstead road. (*Provost and Fellows of Eton*)

PLATE 5 Sir Edmund Berry Godfrey (1621–78), the
discovery of whose corpse on Primrose Hill unleashed
the Popish Plot. (*Private Collection*)

PLATE 6 William Stukeley (1687–1765), the father of
English archaeology. Keenly interested in the Druids,
he assumed the Druidic identity of Chyndonax.
(*Private Collection*)

PLATE 7 Thomas Moore (1779–1852),
the Irish poet, whose duel with Francis
Jeffrey in August 1806 was interrupted
by the arrival of law officers.
(*Private Collection*)

PLATE 8 Anne Isabella, Lady Byron,
née Milbanke (1792–1860), the widow of
the poet, died at 11 St George's Terrace.
(*Private Collection*)

PLATE 9 The naturalist Philip Gosse (1810–88) and his son Edmund (1849–1928), from the latter's memoir, *Father and Son* (1907). Their joint expedition to the top of Primrose Hill in 1855 was not a success. (*Private Collection*)

PLATE 10 The largest equestrian statue ever cast in Britain, Mathew Cotes Wyatt's giant statue of the Duke of Wellington on his horse, Copenhagen, was ridiculed for being out of proportion to Decimus Burton's Victory Arch at Hyde Park Corner. Proposals for moving it included placing it on the top of Primrose Hill. Roger Fenton's photograph of the statue was taken in about 1857.
(*Royal Photographic Society*)

PLATE 11 'The Proposed New Church of St Mark's, Albert Road', 1849, showing Thomas Little's design. The finished church, consecrated in 1853, was different in a number of its features and in its alignment, with its main entrance from St Mark's Square rather than what is now Prince Albert Road. (*CLSAC*)

PLATE 12 The celebrated photographer Roger Fenton lived at 2 Albert Terrace and was one of committee behind the building of St Mark's. One of his earliest photographs, from 1852, shows the hoardings surrounding the church, which was then being built. Frustratingly, Fenton took a number of photographs of Regent's Park but none of Primrose Hill. (*Société Française de Photographie*)

PLATE 13 A high-profile casualty of the Second World War, St Katharine's Lodge, in Regent's Park near Gloucester Gate, was hit by a flying bomb in 1944 and subsequently demolished. (*Private Collection*)

PLATE 14 The only house on Primrose Hill, the lodge at its south-west corner, has stone dressings and mullioned windows. It was built in 1860 at the cost of £672 and has been lived in since then by park-keepers and then policemen. (*Sandra Lousada*)

First, that during the last half century a very great increase has taken place in the population of large towns, more especially as regards those classes who are, with many of their children, almost continually engaged in manufacturing and mechanical employments.

Secondly, that during the same period, from the increased value of property and extension of buildings, many enclosures of open spaces in the vicinity of towns have taken place, and little or no provision has been made for public walks or open spaces, fitted to afford means of exercise or amusement to the middle or humbler classes.

Thirdly, that any such provision of public walks and open places would much conduce to the comfort, health and content of the classes in question.[8]

Chaired by Robert Slaney, the MP for Shrewsbury, it heard evidence from seven witnesses from London, four from Manchester, two from Birmingham and Liverpool, and one each from Blackburn, Bolton, Bradford, Bristol, Bury, Hull, Leeds, Sheffield and Walsall.[9]

On 13 March 1833 the committee heard from John White junior, the surveyor of the parish of St Marylebone, about Primrose Hill:

You know the spot called Primrose Hill on the northern side of Regent's Park? – I have been intimately acquainted with it from a youth.

Is it not a spot to which the humbler classes resort? – It has been resorted to, to a very great extent, to my knowledge between forty and fifty years.

Do you not think it would be much lamented if that should be built over, so as to deprive the humbler classes of the recreation they have been accustomed to enjoy on the spot? – It would be taking away one of the lungs of the metropolis.

To whom does the land belong? – Primrose Hill is the property of Eton College; the next adjacent property is Lord Southampton's, the Regent's Park, which belongs to the Crown, and the Duke of Portland, and also to Colonel Eyre.

Do you happen to know that Eton College had it in contemplation if eligible offers were made, to divide that land and to let it on building leases? – They put forth proposals to that effect in the year 1829.

If they should be accepted, would the consequence be a division and an inclosure of this land which hitherto has been in a great measure enjoyed by the humbler classes on their holidays? – Their favourite walk used to be over Primrose Hill to Hampstead, and most unquestionably it would be interrupted.[10]

In its report, the committee made one of its few specific recommendations to the government:

Your committee beg to state that they have heard with much regret that it is in contemplation to inclose and build upon the pleasant rising ground called Primrose Hill, situate to the north of the Regent's Park. Such a course will much diminish the beauty and salubrity of the park; it will also shut up a healthy open spot which the humbler classes have been in the habit of visiting with their families time out of mind. No one who has seen the throng resorting thither in the summer months, and the happiness they seem to enjoy, but must lament that this spot, commanding a fine view and good air, should be taken from them. It is understood that it belongs to Eton College, and your committee humbly suggest that means should be taken by government to secure it in its present open state.[11]

The recommendation of the committee came at an opportune moment. Eton had indeed been contemplating developing the Chalcots Estate, including Primrose Hill, but had to date made limited progress in doing so. Its attention had been drawn to possible development as long ago as 1796, when a survey of the estate had reported that a considerable part of the estate was very eligible for building.[12] Over the intervening years, the college had received a number of proposals for the use of its land for public buildings and other institutions. Well aware of the potential value of its land for housing, even before it acquired a private Act of Parliament in 1826 that allowed it to offer building leases of ninety-nine years on the whole of the Chalcots Estate,[*] it had a plan drawn up in 1822 dividing its estate into plots suitable for villas. In this it was claimed that:

The estate from its proximity to London and from its elevated situation is so well adapted for the erection of villas with a small quantity of land attached thereto that it would be eagerly sought after by the wealthy citizens of the metropolis – and builders would readily speculate in taking the plots.[13]

Each of the seventy-seven plots in the 1822 scheme was of half an acre or more. The most desirable plots were those near the Hampstead road, with the annual ground rent of the most expensive set at £140. Those on the top of Primrose Hill, numbers 67 and 68, were valued at £44 and £38 a year respectively, though it was admitted that the fourteen acres on the top of the hill were not suitable for building. A second plan drawn up two years later by John Jenkins divided the entire estate into seventy-five large plots.[14]

As many potential developers found, issuing advertisements in praise of the advantages of their own land, as Eton did in 1829, was one thing; attracting builders was another.[15] There were always fewer middle-class buyers, let alone

---

[*]   'An Act to Enable the Provost and College of Eton, in the County of Bucks, to Grant Building Leases of Lands in the Parishes of Hampstead and Marylebone, in the County of Middlesex, and for Other Purposes', 7 George IV, c. 25 (1826).

upper-class ones, than there were building plots and houses available. The Chalcots Estate also had few of the advantages that builders hoped for. Eton's governing body, the provost and fellows, was itself half-hearted in its wish to promote building. Agricultural renewals from the estate came directly as personal income to themselves (with a double portion for the provost), whereas ground rents from building went to the college's general fund.* The years of the war had been particularly remunerative to them, although the building of the Regent's Canal brought alternative dairy supplies to London and had reduced the profits from local farming. Eton also showed itself unwilling to incentivise builders by sharing the cost of the infrastructure or providing loans. This infrastructure, in terms of roads and sewers, was therefore slow to develop. Although the college made a start on Adelaide Road in 1830, possibly as a bargaining counter to negotiate good terms with the London and Birmingham Railway then being planned, the road did not reach Swiss Cottage for another twenty years. Nor did the college's sale of land to the London and Birmingham Railway in 1834 add anything to the attraction of the estate to potential builders or householders, even though the railway passed under the college's land in a tunnel.† These weaknesses were not remedied by the position on the south of the hill, where the crown estate had failed to find takers for its plots in the northern half of Regent's Park before building in the park was brought to an end in 1826. To the west of the hill was the unprepossessing housing of Portland Town, consisting mainly of low-quality housing and including a number of industrial workshops.

Even if these obstacles to development had been overcome, Primrose Hill was protected to a degree by itself. According to a surveyor,

> The land is a bed of very rank clay, exceedingly wet, very unfavourable to habitations – and will at any rate require a considerable outlay to render it adapted to building. Besides which the neighbourhood is not at all desirable from the

---

* This practice was legally improper but had become customary. In March 1839, Eton received a remarkable proposal from a major developer, which might have seen its estate emulate the impressive terraces of Regent's Park to the south. William Kingdom, a large-scale developer in west London, wrote to the college proposing to erect a series of high-quality terraces on a line approximately of Adelaide Road. Because this might have profited the college but would not have benefited the provost and fellows, the proposal fell through. The college was unwilling to grant leases of building plots at a rate that would have compensated Kingdom for the expense of paying for the roads and sewerage. See F.M.L. Thompson, *Hampstead: Building a Borough, 1650–1964* (London, 1974), pp. 223–5.

† The college received £600 per acre for the land sold to the railway and was also able to insist that the tunnel under its land was dug as a tunnel rather than by cut and cover. The tunnel was excavated, with considerable difficulty, between 1834 and 1837. John Shaw to George Bethell, 23 April 1834, Eton College Records, 49, no. 64; Thompson, *Hampstead*, p. 220.

howling of the beasts in the Zoological Gardens and the constant hissing and noise from the railroad.[16]

Not all the approaches that the college received, however, were for building houses, even if one excludes the threats of Primrose Hill becoming the site of a new Parthenon or London's principal cemetery. In 1831 Eton was approached by Mr Bromley, a solicitor of Gray's Inn, with a proposal for 'a botanical institution to be established by a society' on Primrose Hill. The proposal was taken seriously by Eton's agent, John Shaw. He and his father, the previous agent, had numerous meetings with Bromley, who, having tried to find other sites, thought it 'difficult to believe that any other site could be found in the neighbourhood of London in all respects so eligible as the one in question'.[17] John Shaw junior told Eton that Mr Bromley was 'a gentleman of great respectability, that he and the members of the proposed society are impelled by the desire of promoting the science and have great reason to believe that they will be assisted by the public in so desirable an institution, which is likely from the great success of the Zoological Society in the neighbourhood: their architect Mr Clarke appears a man of considerable talent and is the son of an old friend of my father's'.[18]

Although Bromley was confident of acquiring sufficient funds, once it was made known that the land was definitely available, Shaw reported that 'in the present stage of the business my father feels it his duty to act with the greatest caution, but at the same time he feels that the successful establishment of a great public institution on the college estate must add very greatly to its value, and that the land could not be better employed on their obtaining for it a fair and well secured rent'.[19] A plan of the proposed garden shows it taking eighteen acres of land on the south-west side of the hill, while the architect, William Clarke, exhibited plans for the site at the Royal Academy exhibition of 1832.[20] A prospectus, aimed at selling six hundred shares at £50 each was issued as 'A Proposal for the Establishment of a Botanical and Ornamental Garden in the Neighbourhood of Regent's Park', informing investors that 'a site at the back of the northern side of the Regent's Park, nearly opposite to the grounds of the Zoological Society has been chosen for this purpose'.[21] In the event, Bromley and his society failed to raise sufficient funds. This was not, however, the end of plans for a botanical garden in the area. In 1838 the newly founded Botanic Society of London took over the lease of the eighteen acres inside the Inner Circle in Regent's Park.[22]

Despite the recommendation of the Committee on Public Walks, the Whig government did nothing immediate to acquire Primrose Hill.* Committed to

---

* Although Radicals, including J.A. Roebuck and Joseph Hume, made some progress, including the Enclosure Act of 1836, which exempted common fields near towns from enclosure, little was done in the short term to implement the committee's recommendations. In 1841 the

William Clarke's plan, exhibited at the Royal Academy in 1832,
for an eighteen-acre botanical garden on Primrose Hill. (*CLSAC*)

reducing the expense of government to a minimum, it was loath to incur any outlay
which could be avoided or deferred. When asked directly by Sir Samuel Whalley,
the MP for Marylebone, whether the government intended to purchase Primrose
Hill, Lord Duncannon, the First Commissioner of Woods and Forests, replied that
he 'feared that the purchase of Primrose Hill would be impracticable, on account
of the number of proprietors'.[23] The key to forcing its hand came from a renewed
threat to turn the hill into a cemetery. In 1836 the London Cemetery Company
acquired an Act of Parliament allowing it to establish 'cemeteries for the interment
of the dead, northward, southward and eastward of the metropolis'.[24] It approached
Eton to explore the possibility of leasing Primrose Hill.

Eton's agent, John Shaw, reported to Thomas Batcheldor at Windsor that
'the solicitor of the London Cemetery Company recently established has made
application for the site of Primrose Hill and the eighteen acre field next the park;
he is desirous of knowing whether the college would sell it if the company obtained
an Act of Parliament to enable them so to do, and for what price; he also requires

government made a grant of £10,000 to encourage the provision of parks near towns. The
restrictions on its disbursement, however, ensured that it was not fully distributed until 1856.
For the parliamentary impact of the committee's recommendations, see Hazel Conway, *People's
Parks: The Design and Development of Victorian Parks in Britain* (Cambridge, 1991), pp. 39–40.

to know the extent of term for which it would be let, and whether the term could be made renewable upon the payment of a fine'.[25] Shaw asked for instructions as to whether the college wanted him to negotiate with the company, but noted that 'in all probability the object will be objectionable, however respectable the parties may be'.[26] Refused by Eton, the company purchased the former park of Ashurst Manor, a seventeenth-century house demolished in 1830 to provide a site for Vulliamy's St Michael's Church in Highgate. The park, landscaped by David Ramsay, became Highgate Cemetery.[27]

A year after the London Cemetery Company's tentative approach, a far more dangerous and insidious threat to Primrose Hill came from another new cemetery company. The Portland Cemetery Company introduced a Bill allowing it to enclose fifty acres anywhere in north London and to stop existing rights of way through its chosen ground. Its board included Walpole Eyre, who controlled the main St John's Wood estate, and a number of MPs sitting on the parliamentary committee examining the Bill. The Bill, submitted as the North Metropolitan Cemetery Bill, had gone through most of its stages between February and May 1837 before the threat to Primrose Hill was recognised. When the company's intentions became clear, there were vigorous protests in the press, in parish meetings and in Parliament.

The first newspaper to sound the alarm was the *Observer*, on 14 May 1837. It exposed the conflict of interests inside the parliamentary committee examining the Bill and complained about the danger of a 'Cemetery Mania' allowing the seizure of public land for the benefit of the rich:

> We are led to these observations by the attempt to introduce new Bills with extraordinary powers for inclosing ground sacred to the public, and, among others, we understand the Portland Cemetery Company, which originally as their Bill stood was a speculative building company, are now endeavouring to get a Bill through the House for enclosing a great proportion of Chalk Farm and the field approaching Primrose Hill.[28]

A letter to *The Times* the following day, entitled 'Another Liberal Job', provided more details of the threat:

> Being an admirer of the proposed mode of interment of the dead, I applied for and received a copy of the Bill, and finding, that instead of a cemetery for the interment of the dead, it was a Bill to establish a building company to enclose and lease out Primrose Hill, that it took power to stop up or turn, or discontinue any highway or footpath leading thereto, and well knowing that the college to which Primrose Hill belongs have no power to alienate to build thereon, I petitioned the House to permit me to be heard against it. I attended the committee and found the majority composed of the trustees and directors of the proposed company

– viz. Mr G. Grote, Mr Price, Mr Ramsbottom and Mr Villiers.* The committee proceeded to read the petitions of several persons opposed to the measure, but decided that there was no parliamentary ground alleged in the petitions, and they were denied a hearing; and, on the Bill being opened, it was found that since the petitioners had received their copies of the Bill twenty clauses had been taken out, and at least thirty entirely new ones introduced, of which the petitioners had no knowledge.[29]

The Portland Cemetery Company responded the following week through its parliamentary counsel, John Wickey Stable, who stated that Eton's 1826 Act allowed it to 'let the said hill and its vicinity on building leases, "for public squares, streets, crescents (or any form of building), roads, sewers, etc"'.[30] As opposed to spoiling the hill, he went on to claim that the company would save the hill from disappearing under housing and that the company would lay it out 'in ornamental walks, parterres and terraces, in such a manner as to bring out and heighten the picturesque beauties of the spot'. Thus improved, it would be 'thrown open to the public'.[31]

A 'very numerous meeting of parishioners assembled at the vestry room' at Hampstead on 25 May. They heard from Standish Motte, the parliamentary counsel of the rival London Cemetery Company, that the Portland Company's Bill allowed it 'to enclose the Chalcots Estate, or Primrose Hill, or any land within ten miles of London', and that it also gave Eton the power to sell the Chalcots Estate (which it could not, as a charitable foundation, otherwise do). The vestry clerk noted that the parish had not been duly notified of the Bill. The meeting vociferously supported a decision to petition against the Bill.†

---

* Although the Whig government of the 1830s was often accused of allowing its supporters, including MPs, to enrich themselves, not all four MPs were Whigs. S. Grove Price was the Tory Member for Sandwich, while John Ramsbottom, who promoted the establishment of the first cemetery in Reading, was the Radical Member for Windsor. Charles Pelham Villiers, the brother of the fourth Earl of Clarendon, was a Benthamite Whig and keen free trader who represented Wolverhampton in Parliament between 1835 and 1898, when he was the Father of the House at the age of ninety-five. As a personal gift, to mark her Diamond Jubilee in 1897, Villiers presented Queen Victoria with a parasol dressed in Chantilly lace, *The Times*, 8 March 2012. George Grote, whose family bank acted for the Portland Cemetery Company, was the Radical MP for the City of London. Grote disliked banking and is better known for his twelve-volume *A History of Greece: From the Earliest Period to the Close of the Generation Contemporary with Alexander the Great* (London, 1846–56).

† *The Times*, 26 May 1837; the Hampstead Vestry minutes of the previous day reflect the vestry's anxiety about the likely loss of income from its own 'additional burial ground' rather than any concern about the loss of Primrose Hill. Its minuted meeting seems to have been on the same day, but earlier than, the public meeting reported in *The Times*. Camden Local Studies and Archives Centre, Hampstead Vestry Minutes, 25 May 1837.

The previous day, the vestry of the parish of St Marylebone had passed a motion which both protested against the Portland Cemetery Company's Bill and demanded that Primrose Hill be acquired for the public:

> it would be a great deprivation to the surrounding inhabitants were Primrose Hill enclosed or built upon, and having learnt with apprehension that it is contemplated to do so, and that there exists a power under a private Act for the provost and authorities of Eton College to let that spot on building leases, do appoint a committee of five members to request the Commissioners of Woods and Forests and the Home Secretary to urge upon the government the propriety of securing that portion of the Chalcots Estate for the free and unrestricted use of the public ...[32]

The vestries of Paddington and St Pancras also sent petitions, protesting at not having been informed about the Bill.[33]

In Parliament itself, the Portland Cemetery Company's Bill, which had once looked as if it would pass into law almost unnoticed, began to meet stiff resistance. Standish Motte presented Hampstead's petition to the parliamentary committee, which tried to limit the scope of his objection to Hampstead's own interest. 'After a strenuous and energetic appeal by Mr Motte on behalf of the parishioners of Hampstead, the committee would only consent to hear him against one clause. ... Mr Motte contended that all the parishes within ten miles of London *were* interested, and ought, by the standing rules, to have had notice of the Bill ...'[34]

By now the whole matter of the Bill had become scandalous. The surreptitious attempt to pass a private Bill affecting public rights, the packing of the committee with those with clear interests in the company involved, the failure to give notice of the Bill to the parishes affected, and the changing of clauses and wording in the Bill, amounted in combination to a clear abuse of parliamentary procedure, bringing the system of private Bills into disrepute.[35]

The proceedings then fell almost to the level of farce when the solicitor of the Portland Cemetery Company, John Wickey Stable, submitted a petition to the House of Commons. In it he claimed that one of the committee sitting on the Bill, Sir Samuel Whalley, the MP for Marylebone but not a director of the company, had added the words 'or any part of it' to the committee's resolution without due authorisation.[36] Given a severe grilling at the bar of the House, on 8 July and again on 13 July, Stable contradicted himself on a number of central issues.[37] He was also shown to have threatened Sir Samuel Whalley with submitting his petition, alleging misconduct, unless Sir Samuel withdrew his opposition to the Bill.

Sir Samuel Whalley explained that, though he had helped introduce the Bill, after being asked to do so by several of his constituents, he had not realised until after the second reading that it 'gave the promoters of it a roving commission to establish a cemetery anywhere within ten miles of the metropolis'. Thomas Wakley, the Radical MP for Finsbury and another member of the committee who was also not a director of the company, 'had called for a plan of the site, and on the plan being produced it was found that the intention of the promoters was to wrest Primrose Hill from the public'.[38] The committee had therefore added the words to the Bill: 'Provided that nothing in this Act do allow the said company to use Primrose Hill for any of the purposes of the company.'[39] The words 'or any part of it', which Whalley had added in unclear circumstances to reinforce the exemption of Primrose Hill, and which Stable wanted removed, might if removed have allowed the Portland Cemetery Company to restrict the extent of the excluded part of Primrose Hill to as small an area as six acres.

In the debate on the third reading in the Commons, on Friday 16 June 1837, the Bill was proposed by Thomas Duncombe.[40] It was opposed by Sir Samuel Whalley; by Joseph Hume, the Radical Member for Middlesex, who claimed that 'ever since the time of the great plague in London Primrose Hill had been a place of resort with the public'; and by Thomas Wakley, who said that 'Primrose Hill was the Hyde Park of the working classes'. Wakley asked the House how it would treat a proposal to convert Hyde Park into a cemetery.[41] In the vote, the Bill was lost by 133 votes to 47. As the *Observer* remarked: 'Should the infamous attempt of the Portland Cemetery Bill to enclose Primrose Hill be the means of bringing a change in the system of the private Bills committees, it will be one of the objects which, in the last few years, the public have seen accomplished by moral influence.'[42]

On 5 June a St Marylebone delegation, led by Dr Robert Fellowes, the Rector of St Marylebone, had already succeeded in presenting their case directly to the Prime Minister, Lord Melbourne. They reported back:

> Dr Fellowes stated that the deputation which had been appointed by the vestry on the subject of Primrose Hill had waited on Lord Melbourne on Monday last, and that his lordship seemed very favourable to the purposes of the deputation and professed his willingness to promote the object which they had in view. Lord Melbourne appeared quite alive to the importance of preserving the site of Primrose Hill for the use and recreation of the public, and consequently of preventing it from being occupied by houses or converted into a cemetery, and the deputation have no doubt that the vestry will find in his lordship a sincere and zealous auxiliary in effecting an object so essential to the health, exercise and enjoyment of the metropolis and particularly of the parish of St Marylebone.[43]

Melbourne, as a Whig, believed in yielding to popular pressure where doing so was inevitable in the longer term and when prompt acquiescence prevented further pressure for change from building up.

A week after the visit of the delegation, Lord Duncannon, the First Commissioner of the Department of Woods and Forests, was instructed to buy Primrose Hill for the public:

> The attention of Lord Melbourne and the Chancellor of the Exchequer has been called to the intended enclosure of Primrose Hill as a public burial ground, and a very general wish having been expressed both in and out of Parliament that the public should not be deprived of this spot, which has so long tended to the health and recreation of the people of this metropolis, they request Lord Duncannon to take such steps as he may deem expedient for ascertaining the value of the property and such particulars connected with it as may enable His Majesty's government to judge whether this land can now be obtained for the public on terms which they could feel justified to submitting to Parliament.[44]

While this decision undoubtedly reflected the government's embarrassment, as well as its wish to promote the creation of public spaces available to the growing population of cities, there were other reasons behind it as well. An explicit reason was the wish to wean the poor away from their favourite pursuits of drink and gambling, and to make them more industrious. Open places

> reserved for the amusement (under due regulations to preserve order) of the humbler classes would assist to wean them from low and debasing pleasures. Great complaint is made of drinking-houses, dog fights and boxing matches, yet, unless some opportunity for other recreation is afforded to workmen, they are driven to such pursuits. The spring to industry which occasional relaxation gives seems quite as necessary to the poor as to the rich.[45]

Although the government was in favour of new cemeteries around London and elsewhere, it had no wish for one immediately next to the crown's own estate in Regent's Park. Regent's Park itself was also under pressure from the public, as much of it was still closed to them. There were large private grounds surrounding the villas in the park and, in its early years, the Zoo was only open to fellows and their guests rather than to the general public. In Nash's last report on the park, in 1832, he had recommended making the north of the Broad Walk accessible to the public. Rather than opening up all the other private areas in the park, allowing the Broad Walk to extend across the Regent's Canal and to connect the park to Primrose Hill was an excellent safety-valve.

From Eton's point of view, it is unsurprising that John Shaw, Eton's agent, came to the conclusion that allowing part of the Eton Estate to become a public park would benefit the estate as a whole. Turning Primrose Hill over to housing would have caused a major protest, in the press and in Parliament, unwelcome to Eton and the government. At a time when the privileges of the landed elite, and their access to government posts and emoluments, were contentious political issues, it was not the moment for a wealthy school, where a great many of the aristocracy, including leading politicians, had been educated, to draw condemnation on itself by depriving the people of London of a traditional pleasure so as to enhance its own coffers.

While not a common, as its ownership by Eton was clear-cut, Primrose Hill was used in many ways as if it were one. The hill, 'hitherto viewed as common ground', was 'a place resorted to by the inhabitants of London as the nearest elevated point of observation where a pure atmosphere can be obtained, with a view of some extent and beauty'. Although it was 'not common ... the use of numerous ancient footpaths over it gave a sanction to its enjoyment by tourists from the smoky and foetid regions of the interior ...'[46] It was a popular place of recreation, as well as the site of a fair over many years, with large numbers reported there at Easter, Whitsun and on summer weekends. It had been used as one of the sites for public fireworks to celebrate the coronation of George IV in July 1821.[47] Its status as a public site had been reinforced by the duels fought there and by its occasional use for public meetings, while the Chalk Farm Tavern was a well-known place of excursion for Londoners. There was also an assumption by the public that they had a right of access to the hill, which was crossed by farm tracks and long-established footpaths, as well as by other paths established more recently; and a right to use it as they pleased. Nor were its fences of much value as a deterrent: 'the fences are very bad which is partly occasioned by the great stock of cows fed upon the farm and, being so near the metropolis, the wood is daily stolen and carried away'.[48]

As with many sales of property, the actual transaction which led to the crown acquisition of Primrose Hill was a slow and tortuous one, with both sides fighting their corners with tenacity over the price. Eton demanded £350 per acre for its fifty acres, but this was strongly opposed by the land agent employed by the crown, Edward Driver, who thought that £300 per acre was the maximum that should be paid, 'considering the purpose to which it was being appropriated and the benefit thereby to the rest of the estate'.[49] Eton was slow in its responses and held out for the higher price, emphasising the value of its estate as building land. There was also haggling about who should be responsible for buying out the existing lease, currently held by Giles Clarke.[50] At one stage negotiations were broken off for a year.

In the end, the problem was resolved by exchange rather than by straight purchase. John Shaw, the surveyor of Eton's Chalcots Estate, identified a number of buildings and pieces of land in the heart of Eton, some very close to the college, which Eton did not own. Of these, the Christopher Inn, within a hundred yards of Eton Chapel, was a particular concern to the college authorities as a temptation leading their pupils to drinking and gambling. In an official note, the provost and fellows concluded:

That it is highly desirable for the good discipline, health and recreation of the youth educated at the said college that the buildings and land in the immediate vicinity should be under control ... so as to preclude the risk of additional buildings being erected, or trades and businesses carried out which might by the noise and traffic attending to them prove of annoyance to the college by disturbing attention and interfering with the orderly rules and regulations of the establishment.[51]

The Christopher Inn, and the other houses and pieces of land desired by the college, were unsurprisingly, given the proximity of Windsor Castle, owned by the crown. Transferring them to Eton in an exchange had the great benefit from the government's point of view of allowing Primrose Hill to be acquired for the public without any public money being spent.

Edward Driver was confident in the power of the crown's position. He pointed out the constraints on Eton's freedom of action and offered the inducement of access from south of the hill to the rest of the college's estate:

it cannot have escaped your observation that the very numerous public footpaths, which are claimed over this property in almost all directions, must ever so interfere with any eligible appropriation for building purposes that it appears next to impossible so to appropriate it, except partially. And further there not being any frontage in communication with the high road. ... Whereas provided the college should feel disposed to cooperate with the crown in the object I now propose, it might be stipulated that the crown should offer a handsome communication from the public road somewhere in the direction which I have marked in the sketch, so as to communicate with the remaining land on the north side belonging to the college.[52]

Eton's own agent, John Shaw, endorsed Driver's comments:

Valuable as this part of the property undoubtedly is, its circumstances as regards the right of entrance from the Park Road, and the long continued liberty or rather trespass of the public on it in all directions, would render an exchange perhaps desirable; and if it were beneficial to the college in its more local interests some sacrifice might perhaps be advisable as regards the property.[53]

In March 1841 *The Times* was able to report:

The Provost and Fellows of Eton have just concluded an arrangement with the Commissioners of Woods and Forests for the exchange of some land belonging to the college at Primrose Hill for a large plot of ground, now covered with buildings, at Eton, directly opposite to the college. It is the intention of the college authorities ... to pull down the old tenements, and erect, on their site, some first-rate houses, which will be occupied by the several masters and others connected with the college. The whole of that delightful and salubrious spot, Primrose Hill, being now in the hands of the crown, it may fairly be presumed … that that healthy and recreative outlet from the smoke of the metropolis will be suffered to remain undefiled by bricks and mortar.[54]

The final exchange was of thirty-two acres at Eton for fifty-three acres on Primrose Hill. Both parcels of land were valued at £15,112 5s. 0d. Eton's property had initially been valued at £16,275, but a deduction to cover the cost of paying out the remainder of the existing lease on Primrose Hill led to a reduction of this by £1162 15s. 0d., balancing the sums exactly. The crown paid the cost of passing the Act of Parliament required to allow Eton to alienate land given to it in perpetuity. Eton was also given a future right of access from what became Regent's Park Road to the rest of its estate, though this land was not turned into a road until thirty years later, with the construction of Primrose Hill Road.

8

Lord Southampton

B Y F A R the greater part of what became Primrose Hill Park came from Eton College. It was the threat to cover Eton's land, and above all Primrose Hill, with a cemetery or housing that had caused uproar in 1837 and led to the crown's decision to acquire the land for the public. Eton, however, was not the only contributor of land to the park. While the protracted negotiations which led to the exchange with Eton were still in train, an opportunity to add to the future park from an adjoining estate arose unexpectedly.

To the east of Primrose Hill and of Regent's Park lay the Southampton Estate, owned by Charles Fitzroy, third Lord Southampton. The estate, at its south, stretched from Fitzroy Square to Euston; and, further north, between Regent's Park and the Hampstead road. It included the Chalk Farm Tavern and all of the modern area between Regent's Park Road and Gloucester Avenue, as well as half of Camden Town and a substantial block of land to the east of Haverstock Hill. Another large part of the estate, including Fitzroy Park, was in Highgate, bordering Kenwood at the north and Parliament Hill at the south.

The fortunes of the Fitzroy family stemmed from the attractions of one of their forebears during the reign of Charles II. Barbara Villiers, who became Duchess of Cleveland in her own right, was one of the king's favourite, or certainly longest-term, mistresses. She bore him five children, all of them acknowledged and ennobled. Their surname, Fitzroy, recognised them as the king's illegitimate children. The pair's second son, Henry Fitzroy, was created the first Duke of Grafton in 1675. He had married Isabella, the daughter of one of the king's chief advisers, the Earl of Arlington, in 1672, when he was nine and she was four. She brought him substantial lands in Northamptonshire and an estate in Suffolk, centred on the village of Euston, as well as the lease of the ancient manor of Tottenhale.[1]

The second duke's will split the estate, following his death in 1757, between his two grandsons, with the younger, Colonel Charles Fitzroy, inheriting his London holdings, with their great future potential. These were consolidated while Colonel Fitzroy's elder brother, Augustus, third Duke of Grafton, was Prime Minister between October 1768 and January 1770. Within six months of assuming office,

Grafton was instrumental in passing an Act of Parliament giving the freehold of the manor of Tottenhale, held by the canons of St Paul's, to his younger brother in return for the payment to the canons of £300 a year.[2] This very favourable transaction, from the point of view of the Fitzroy family, was later supplemented by Fitzroy's purchased acquisition of the freehold of most of the land in the manor of Rugmere in 1786.[*]

A terrier, a register of landed property, of Colonel Fitzroy's land near Primrose Hill, based on a survey of 1771, lists the fields under what is now railway land and Primrose Hill Village.[3] These fields, shown on two maps and stretching from Parkway, then a track known as Slip Shoe Lane, to the Chalk Farm Tavern, made up 121 acres in total. There were seven fields, all of them meadows with names giving their size, such as 'Twelve Acres'. The exception was the eight-acre field nearest to Primrose Hill, called 'Hilly Field'. The map shows Chalk House Lane running from the Hampstead road to the Chalk House, which was already a tavern, and terminating there. Chalk House, later the Chalk Farm Tavern, is listed as having a 'house, barn, gardens and small plot'.[4] The map shows a path across the land from the Mother Red Cap, the tavern where the roads to Hampstead and to Kentish Town divided, and another crossing Marylebone Park, cutting through the 'Fifteen Acre' field before coming to an Eton field named as 'Fryers Rugmore' and then reaching the top of Primrose Hill. Other than the Chalk House, a few houses to the east of Haverstock Hill and a one or two along the Hampstead road, the only housing marked on the maps is a short terrace on the west side of what became Camden High Street.

---

[*] According to the *Morning Chronicle* in 1837: 'In the year 1768 the Duke of Grafton was Prime Minister. His brother, Mr Fitzroy, was lessee of the manor and lordship of Tottenhall, the property of the Dean and Chapter of St Paul's London. Dr Richard Brown, the then prebendary of the stall of Tottenhall, having pocketed the emolument attending the renewal of the lease, and there being little chance of any further advantage to him from the estate, readily listened to a proposal of Mr Fitzroy for the purchase of the estate. The thing was agreed, and the Duke of Grafton, with his great standing majority, quickly passed an Act of Parliament, in March 1769, diverting the estate, with all its rights, privileges, and emoluments from the prebend, and conveying the fee-simple entire, and without reserve, to Mr Charles Fitzroy and his heirs for ever. The Act states it to be with the consent of Richard, Lord Bishop of London, and the privity of the Dean and Chapter of St Paul's.' For this transaction the church received the relatively small sum of £300 a year; a little over six times the annual rental (£46) that was being charged for the leasehold. The *Morning Chronicle* went on to claim that by 1837 the Fitzroy family had already made £1,500,000 from the development of the estate. The Survey of London, xxi, *Tottenham Court Road and Neighbourhood* (London, 1949), p. 6, in contrast states that the Fitzroys only really obtained the development rights to 255 acres of the demesne land of the manor, since most of the occupiers of customary or copyhold land had enfranchised themselves by paying quit rents over a great many years.

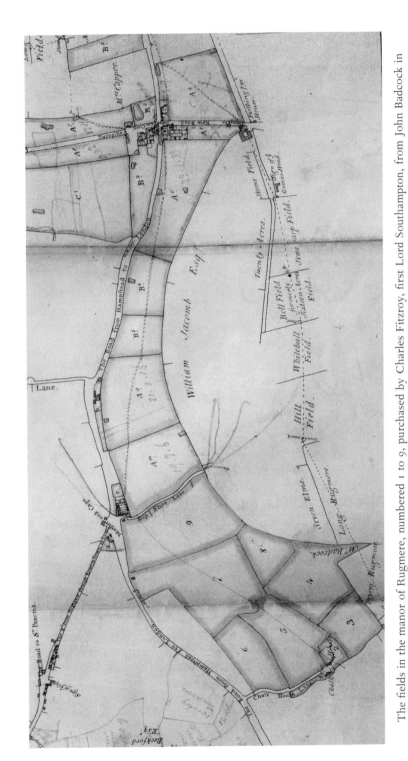

The fields in the manor of Rugmere, numbered 1 to 9, purchased by Charles Fitzroy, first Lord Southampton, from John Badcock in 1786 (the map is dated 1771 but was probably drawn at the time of this purchase). Chalk House Lane is shown leading to Chalk House – the Chalk Farm Tavern. Slip Shoe Lane, later Parkway, leads up from the Mother Red Cap. The curve below the fields marks the boundary of Marylebone Park, later Regent's Park. (*Southampton Estate*)

A clearer view, with more precise measurements, of Lord Southampton's estate, in what was the ancient manor of Rugmere, can be seen on Tompson's 1804 map of St Pancras.[5] On this 'Hilly Field', at the foot of Primrose Hill, is named as the Upper Pitt Field (with the small 'Pitt Field' between it and the Chalk Farm Tavern). The other fields in the 1771 terrier are named as the Lower Pitt Field, the Chalk Field, the Shoulder of Mutton Field, the Old Twelve Acres and the Old Barn Field. All of these, with the exception of the Pitt Field and Upper Pitt Field, leased by Thomas Rutherford, the licensee of the Chalk Farm Tavern, were rented out to Thomas Rhodes, the cattle farmer, who also rented many of the fields on the Eton Estate. The map also shows two footpaths leading from the south across these fields to the Chalk Farm Tavern.

Charles Fitzroy, who acted as his elder brother's political manager before falling out with him, had an active military career, fighting at the battle of Minden in 1759, as well as a political one.[6] A courtier and confidant of Queen Charlotte, the wife of George III, and a philanthropist, he was ennobled as Lord Southampton in 1780. He was closely connected with George, Prince of Wales, and was the Controller of his Household.[*] His title then descended in 1797 to his son, George Ferdinand, and in turn to the latter's son, Charles, the third Lord Southampton, in 1810.[7]

In the sixty years after 1771, the main change to this part of what became the Southampton Estate in 1780 was not the addition of houses but the excavation of the Regent's Canal between 1812 and 1816. The estate drove a hard bargain when letting the canal pass through it, insisting not only on a good price but on extensive safeguards against industrial works being set up on the canal banks.[8] They also extracted a commitment from the canal company to build bridges within six months of the Southampton Estate demanding them: 'Three substantial brick, stone or iron bridges shall be erected and built, of the width of at least thirty feet in the clear, with proper parapets or balustrades, and for ever maintained and kept in repair, over the said canal ...'[9] These bridges, Fitzroy Bridge, Grafton Bridge and Southampton Bridge, although not built until 1825, were the earliest signs of an intention to develop the estate.

The third Lord Southampton, born in 1804, succeeded to the title on the death of his father in 1810. He was brought up by his mother, Frances Isabella Seymour, a granddaughter of the first Marquess of Hertford. She was austerely religious and given to whipping her sons herself. In later life, she took to wearing a black

---

[*] Southampton had been one of the four men who had called on Mrs Fitzherbert in 1784 in an attempt to persuade her marry the prince. For Southampton's links with the future Prince Regent, see Saul David, *Prince of Pleasure: The Prince of Wales and the Making of the Regency* (London, 1998), pp. 30, 61–2, 65, 72 and 157.

poke bonnet and preaching in public from the top of a barrel. Once, when her younger son, Henry, asked her for a horse, she sent him a tract instead.[10] Privately educated, Southampton did not attend Oxford or Cambridge; or, like many of his family, go into the army. The overwhelming passion of his life was foxhunting. He was master of the Quorn Hunt between 1827 and 1831, renaming it Lord Southampton's Hounds during his mastership. He then became the master of the Grafton Hunt, which he hunted, 'entirely at his own cost without a subscription of any kind', for the next thirty years.[11] As a huntsman, he was clearly highly regarded: 'No man knew better what a pack of hounds should do, and how they ought to do it.'[12] In the field, Lord Southampton was in his natural element: 'His lordship possessed an extraordinary faculty for getting to the end of a run without much jumping. He rode rather small horses for a sixteen-stone man; knowing the country thoroughly, and being such a good judge of what hounds were doing, he seemed to see everything that passed.'[13]

Although he was active locally, as a JP and as chairman of the local quarter sessions, he took little part in wider public life.[14] In his youth a Whig, he voted against the Reform Act of 1832 and was a Tory thereafter. The only national political question that aroused his passion, other than that of the London and Birmingham Railway, which closely affected his personal interest, was the Corn Laws controversy of the 1840s, when he headed the local agricultural interest in Northamptonshire in demanding the retention of these controversial laws. Belatedly, he became Lord Lieutenant of Northamptonshire, five years before his death in 1872. For most of his adult life, his principal home was at Whittlebury Lodge, near Silverstone, conveniently placed for hunting and not far from the Duke of Grafton's own hunting lodge, Wakefield Lodge, which was the heart of the Grafton Estate in Northamptonshire.

Lord Southampton has at least a minor claim to fame based on dynastic longevity. He inherited his title at the age of five and lived to be sixty-nine. His first marriage, to Harriet Stanhope, was, however, childless. Remarrying in 1867, to Ismania Nugent, he rapidly sired a family of five, of whom the heir, his son Charles, was the fourth. The fourth Lord Southampton, born in 1870 and succeeding to the title at the age of two, survived until 1958, giving a tenure of the barony between father and son of 148 years.[15] Only a Scottish peer, the thirteenth Lord Sinclair, has held a peerage for longer than the fourth Lord Southampton, for eighty-seven years and 104 days against Southampton's eighty-six years and 144 days.

The lives of the immediate family of the third Lord Southampton were less centred on foxhunting than his own. His younger brother, Henry, was a minor Whig politician.[16] He was more remarkable, however, for his marriage.[17] Henry, like his brother a fine horseman, fell in love with Hannah Rothschild, the daughter of the founder of the English branch of the Rothschild family, Nathan Mayer Rothschild.

Charles Fitzroy, third Lord
Southampton (1812–72), by
Andrew Duncan, from the
New Sporting Magazine (1836).
Southampton was the Master
of the Grafton Hunt for
thirty years from 1831.
(*Private Collection*)

Their love survived six months apart, demanded by Hannah's brothers in the
hope that separation would cool the couple's attachment. This exile Henry spent
on a prolonged tour of Europe, accompanied as far as Constantinople by his elder
brother.[18] On his return, Henry and Hannah's determination remained unchanged.
They were married by Anglican rite at St George's, Hanover Square, on 29 April
1839. Hannah's mother drove with her daughter to the church but did not enter
it. Hannah could afford to disregard the usual Rothschild imperative of marrying
a cousin because she had inherited £12,500 on the death of her father three years
earlier, as well as having £50,000 invested in the family bank. Marrying against
her family's wishes, however, cost her a further £50,000 in dowry.*

Although Hannah was estranged from her family, and Henry cut off by his,

---

* Hannah had, prior to her father's death, already attracted a proposal from a gentile, Prince
Edmond de Clary. The Rothschilds, who looked askance at other Jewish suitors, expected their
daughters to marry their cousins. Niall Ferguson, *The World's Banker: A History of the House of
Rothschild* (London, 1998), pp. 337–46, 1110–11.

which led to the brothers not speaking to each other for fourteen years, the couple lived happily together and had two children, though the elder child, Arthur, died young.[19] Henry, a prodigiously hard worker, was on the verge of promotion to Lord Aberdeen's cabinet when his health collapsed. He died in December 1859, aged fifty-four. At Hannah's own funeral, in 1864, 'the Duke of Grafton, Lord Charles Fitzroy and Lord Southampton, who had known and seen the deceased so little ... never alluded to her but talked of railroads, horses, etc.'.[20] Henry Fitzroy's ambition to become Speaker of the House of Commons was fulfilled vicariously by his nephew, the third lord's second son, Edward Fitzroy, who was Speaker of the Commons between 1938 and 1943, in the darkest days of the Second World War.[21]

The progress of development on the Southampton Estate in London was in many ways conventional. Fitzroy Square, the centre of Fitzrovia (named after the family), was a handsome square begun by the Adam brothers in the 1790s, with good quality streets nearby, such as Warren Street (named after the first Lord Southampton's wife, Anne, the daughter of Admiral Sir Peter Warren). The first Lord Southampton built a house on his Highgate estate, Fitzroy Farm, with grounds landscaped by Humphry Repton. For a time it rivalled its neighbour, Lord Mansfield's Kenwood; but it was not used by the family after the death of the second Lord Southampton in 1810, being let until 1825, when it was demolished. In the late eighteenth and early nineteenth century, the Southampton Estate let out various small building plots to the west side of the Hampstead road, near Mornington Crescent, to speculative builders on short leases, which resulted in notably poor quality housing.[22] There is no reason, however, to think that the Southampton Estate was incapable of better quality development elsewhere. In 1826 the estate was bringing in a handsome income of £9,571 19s. 8d. a year.[23] The 1830s saw villas being built on ninety-nine-year leases on the estate in Highgate. There were also plans for a row of villas to the east of Regent's Park, between Gloucester Gate and Primrose Hill, even if these were criticised for being too closely spaced.

Into this unspectacular but not abnormal pattern of development came something completely new, the first trunk railway into a capital city anywhere in the world. After the success of the Stockton and Darlington Railway, opened in 1825, followed by the Liverpool and Manchester Railway in 1830, the conditions were ripe for a railway link to join London to Birmingham and to the great commercial cities of the north.[24] The London and Birmingham Railway, which raised a prodigious sum in capital and retained Robert Stephenson as its engineer, faced two major problems in trying to work its way into the centre of London. The first was a physical one. The route had to come into London from the west, past Harrow and Willesden, so as to use the Tring Gap through the Chilterns. This also enabled the company to avoid the Northern Heights, the hills of Hampstead and Highgate. Secondly, the company needed to acquire land on which to build its line, avoiding wherever possible the expense of driving it through existing houses. The crown estate of Regent's Park had no wish or incentive to allow the railway to cross its land. The company at one point considered terminating its line at Paddington, the solution later adopted by Isambard Kingdom Brunel for his Great Western Railway. The map accompanying its first attempt in 1832 to get a Bill through Parliament showed its line ending near Battle Bridge, the future site of King's Cross. This Bill passed the Commons but was thrown out arbitrarily by the Lords committee examining it. The net result of this (other than increasing the already substantial unpopularity of the House of Lords) was greatly to increase payments to landowners along the line, raising the total cost of land acquisition from a budgeted £250,000 to £750,000. In London itself, the company persuaded the third Lord Southampton to sell the company land for a depot at Camden.

In a second sale, Southampton provided the railway with access to central London, via a corridor running from just to the east of Fitzroy Bridge over the Regent's Canal down to Euston, where the railway built its terminus. Euston, the country house at the centre of the Duke of Grafton's Suffolk estate, had already been used to name the square facing the terminus. The company erected Philip Hardwick's magnificent Doric Arch in 1837 at the entry to the station as a symbol of the arrival of the age of the railway.[25]

The construction of the London and Birmingham Line took place between 1833 and 1838 under the direction of Robert Stephenson. A number of its most notable features were in the vicinity of Primrose Hill. The tunnel under the Eton Estate, dug between 1834 and 1837, and with an ornamental entrance, was an outstanding early feat of engineering, though built at the cost of numerous lives.[26] The spoil from the tunnel and the cuttings was used to build up the railway's land between Primrose Hill and Camden Town, resulting in the level of the railway being up to fourteen feet higher than that of the surrounding land. One reason for building up the land was the need for the railway to cross the Regent's Canal by bridge rather than tunnel on its way to Euston. This added to the incline of the slope. The difficulties early engines had in pulling trains up the steep gradient, and the need to placate local landowners, who objected to engines near to their land, led to a decision to haul early trains up to the canal by a system of ropes drawn by stationary winding engines to the north of the canal. The twin chimneys of the winding engines stood 133 feet high and made a conspicuous landmark during the seven years the machinery was in operation. The railway yard was also the reason for the building in 1846–47 of the Round House, an engine shed for goods engines. The building of the railway did little, however, to improve the local links with the rest of London. Plans to make Chalk Farm the terminus of the railway were abandoned before the railway opened, by which time the line had been extended to Euston. As the early railways were aimed initially at carrying freight rather than people, the first passenger stop after Euston was Harrow.[27] The area between Primrose Hill and Camden Town, however, became the railway's London depot, which for over a hundred years was the area's leading employer.

The sale to the London and Birmingham Railway was by no means the last of Lord Southampton's sales. Although he was still planning his development along the edge of Regent's Park in 1836, and was willing to sell Eton a triangle of land at the eastern end of Primrose Hill in 1838, two years later he took an unusual and radical step. Under the hammer of George Robins, the leading auctioneer of the day, the freehold of most of Southampton's London estate was sold in a three-day auction in August 1840.[28]

The auction, widely publicised by Robins, drew a great deal of attention. The week before the sale Robins had to announce a change of venue, away from the London Auction Mart near the Bank of England:

> Mr George Robins begs respectfully to intimate to the public, that, in consequence of the unprecedented number of applicants for particulars of this important sale of freehold ground rents, and valuable building ground (already exceeding two thousand), and the utter impossibility of accommodating his auditery [sic] in the largest room of the Auction Mart, he has engaged the spacious room at the London Tavern, in Bishopsgate Street, where the sale will positively take place on Monday, 10 August, and two following days, at twelve for one most punctually.[29]

Robins had issued a handsome catalogue of the land for sale, with clear maps showing existing buildings and projected roads, as well as details of each lot. The projected roads were exceptionally wide and have remained so to the present day. All the plots are shown as suitable for villas, reflecting the aspiration that the estate should have a smaller number of prestigious houses rather than a higher density of terraces. Robins was not bashful in proclaiming the attractions of the lots. Lord Southampton's estate, with upwards of 200 acres of freehold building land, was offered on 'a grand building plan, where the word "certainty" may be used in the place of speculation'. The Highgate estate was described as being 'within two miles of the metropolis; and yet throughout Mr Robins' great experience he has never yet come in contact (even at a remote distance) with a park so full of natural beauty. … Nature (always kind) has been bountiful here.' Nor was the London and Birmingham Railway seen as a disadvantage: 'The Birmingham Railway has given an impetus to the Southampton Estate which will render it annually of greatly increasing value.'[30] The auctioneer's own copies survive for the most of the lots,

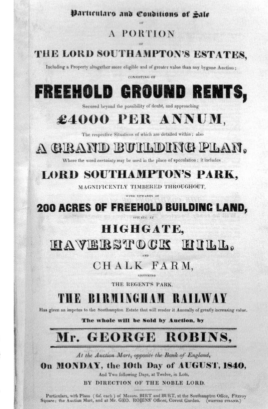

Particulars and Conditions of Sale
OF
A PORTION
OF
THE LORD SOUTHAMPTON'S ESTATES,
Including a Property altogether more eligible and of greater value than any bygone Auction;
CONSISTING OF

FREEHOLD GROUND RENTS,
Secured beyond the possibility of doubt, and approaching

£4000 PER ANNUM,
The respective Situations of which are detailed within; also

A GRAND BUILDING PLAN,
Where the word *certainty* may be used in the place of speculation; it includes

LORD SOUTHAMPTON'S PARK,
MAGNIFICENTLY TIMBERED THROUGHOUT,
WITH UPWARDS OF

200 ACRES OF FREEHOLD BUILDING LAND,
SITUATE AT

HIGHGATE,
HAVERSTOCK HILL,
AND
CHALK FARM,
ADJOINING
THE REGENT'S PARK.

THE BIRMINGHAM RAILWAY
Has given an impetus to the Southampton Estate that will render it Annually of greatly increasing value.

The whole will be Sold by Auction, by

Mr. GEORGE ROBINS,
At the Auction Mart, opposite the Bank of England,
On MONDAY, the 10th Day of AUGUST, 1840,
And Two following Days, at Twelve, in Lots,
BY DIRECTION OF THE NOBLE LORD.

Particulars, with Plans (6d. each) of Messrs. BIRT and BURT, at the Southampton Office, Fitzroy Square; the Auction Mart, and at Mr. GEO. ROBINS' Offices, Covent Garden. (WRITING STRAND.)

Interest of the 1840 auction Lord Southampton's London estate was so great that George Robins had to move the auction from his usual auction rooms to the London Tavern in Bishopsgate, where it was held over three very hot days, 10–12 August 1840. (*Southampton Estate*)

with the prices reached and the names and addresses of the buyers.[31] Another copy contains a complete list of the hammer prices in guineas. In all 265 lots were on offer.

On Monday, 10 August, the holdings to the east of the Hampstead road and Haverstock Hill were sold. As well as existing houses in Ferdinand Street, Southampton Terrace and Grafton Place, there were almost one hundred building plots of about an acre each. Robins had drawn attention in his publicity to one possible, but not unexpected, use: 'This land, from its elevated position, is especially adapted for a commodious cemetery on an extensive scale.'[32] In the event, no cemetery company took the bait. The first day's sale realised 37,350 guineas or £39,217.

On Tuesday, 11 August, it was the turn of Highgate. A substantial part of the advertised lands had already been sold by private treaty prior to the auction to Lord Mansfield, the owner of Kenwood, who bought the lots adjacent to his existing park. The reduction of the land available, and the knowledge that the remaining lots would border parkland, produced exceptional prices: 'The result was not merely obtaining £500 an acre from Lord Mansfield, but it gave such an impetus to the

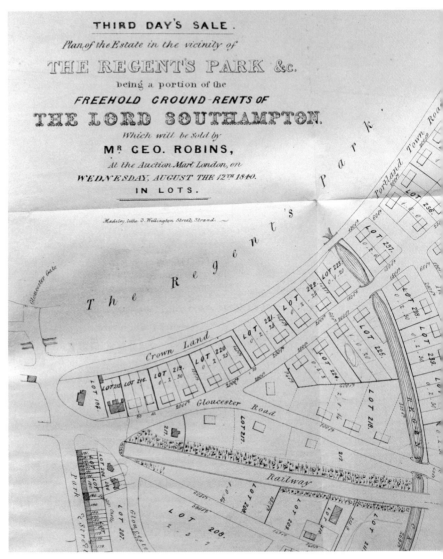

The map accompanying the third day's sale shows the location of all the lots. It also shows the exceptionally wide roads which became a conspicuous feature of the neighbourhood, even if few of the projected villas were ever built. The crown bought lots 229 to 234 to add to Primrose Hill Park. Only houses, for instance along Park Street (later Parkway), shown darkly coloured were already built. The line of Gloucester Road (the 'Road to Hampstead') was later moved further in from the edge of the land belonging to the London and Birmingham Railway. (*Southampton Estate*)

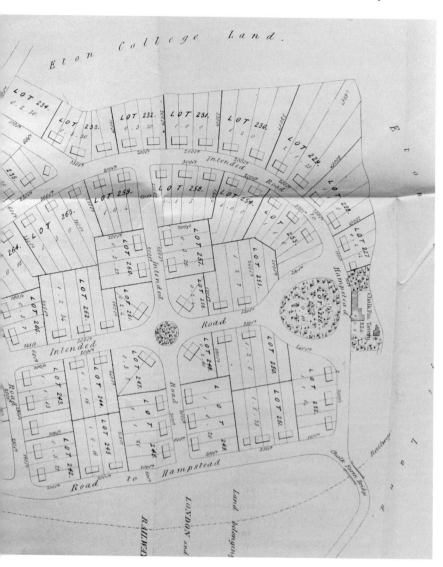

adjoining lots, from the knowledge they would still have the beauteous park for their boundary, that the land adjoining in many instances averaged £1,000 per acre.'[33] Lord Mansfield bought forty acres for £20,000 and the other lots realised 27,320 guineas or £28,686, giving a total of £48,686 for the day.

Before the third day's sale, that of the lots near Primrose Hill, George Robins addressed the expectant buyers. He

announced that he had effected an important arrangement with the Commissioners of Woods and Forests, by selling them twenty acres of Lord Southampton's

land, near to Chalk Farm; in return for which they undertook to keep it all as
an ornamental ground for the public; in fact to be a continuation of park and
shooting-ground from Primrose Hill to Chalk Farm.[34]

Prospective buyers, who clearly knew of the plans for Primrose Hill to become a
park, realised at once that the crown purchase would increase the value of the lots
now nearest to the new park: 'consequently all the lots that will now have a park
for their neighbour instead of never-ceasing houses, rose in value so much as to
double the amount per acre given by the commissioners'.[35] As the *Age* reported:

> The public must rejoice at this event, and it proved most beneficial to Lord
> Southampton, for every lot in the vicinity of this intended park, which had
> formerly been estimated at £300 and £400 an acre was sold from £700 up to
> £1,200 an acre; in fact, such a result was never before noticed on record.[36]

The six lots on the edge of Primrose Hill bordering the Eton Estate, numbers
229 to 234, and one other lot, number 237, had been withdrawn at the last minute.
The crown, represented by its agent, Edward Driver, had reached a bargain with
Lord Southampton's solicitors, Birt and Burt, at £300 per acre for the seven lots.
In all, the crown paid £2,284 for a little over eight acres.[37] It was a lasting tragedy
that Driver failed to buy Lots 235 and 236, which separated the two areas purchased
and which would have allowed a direct link between the Broad Walk and Primrose
Hill.[38] The other lots, despite the withdrawal of Lots 183–205, consisting of houses
in Camden Town, from the day's sale, made 38,760 guineas or £40,698. Few lots
remained unsold, though the Chalk Farm Tavern, Lot 226, the subject of an existing
lease, was one of them.

On the day after the auction Driver wrote to Alexander Milne, one of the
Commissioners of the Woods and Forests, to tell him what had happened:

> I could not succeed in realizing my hopes of getting the land at £250 per acre
> which I had offered to Mr Birt, the solicitor for the Southampton Estate. I having
> another interview with him and Mr Robins before the auction opened yesterday, I
> found they would not sell for less that £300 per acre, so I left them without buying
> and prepared by getting two gentlemen to bid for me at the auction. Finding,
> however, that the company was very numerous and half crazy for buying, I was
> afraid to trust to the auction and therefore, a little time before the lots in question
> were about being offered, I wrote a letter to Mr Birt agreeing to give his price
> of £300 per acre ...[39]

On the corner nearest Park Road (later Prince Albert Road), Lot 234 had an
unusual difficulty attached to it, as Lord Southampton had some years previously
leased the site to the brewers, Felix Calvert and Co., for a still unbuilt public house.

The bargain between Edward Driver and the Southampton Estate left the crown with the liability of buying out the lease. This was the reason for the crown's final purchase, Lot 237, next to the Regent's Canal and on the line of the Broad Walk in Regent's Park. Driver bought this lot with the intention of exchanging it with Calverts as the site of their pub:

> I stipulated that Lot 237 should be added to the purchase, as that would afford the crown the opportunity of making an exchange with Mr Calvert, as it would be a better situation and so I concluded the contract as per enclosed memorandum.
>
> According as the other lots sold at the auction, I have no doubt 237 would have sold for 600 or 700 Guineas at least and Lot 234 would have produced a still higher price, whereas I have secured them at £300 per acre ...[40]

In the event, while Calverts were content with the proposed exchange, the buyers of the two blocks of lots facing the park on either side of the canal were decidedly unhappy about a public house being opened between their planned developments. The Reverend Dr Edward Thompson, who had bought the block between the canal junction and Primrose Hill, wrote indignantly to the Earl of Lincoln, the First Commissioner of Woods and Forests:

> As neither I nor my agent have heard anything definite or official respecting the piece of land adjoining mine on the outside of the Regent's Park, I am sure you will excuse my bringing again the subject under your consideration. We only wish to know if it be the intention of the Woods and Forests to allow Messrs Calverts to build a public house (which would be most objectionable to the neighbourhood) on the plot of ground, which you purpose to grant a lease.
>
> As I before observed in a former letter, I am the largest freeholder among those who purchased land of Lord Southampton in that part. My intention was to have built first-class houses, but if a public house is to be built, or there is an uncertainty about it, it will be a question with me, whether third-class houses, or a cemetery, would not answer my purpose better.[41]

The developers Joseph Guerrier and Peter Pearse, who had bought the lots facing Regent's Park between Lot 237 and Gloucester Gate, wrote with equal vigour, complaining that they already had to deal with the blight caused by the York and Albany, Nash's only public house, at Gloucester Gate.[42]

The matter was resolved when a consortium of those who had bought lots in the auction, headed by Thompson, Guerrier and Pearse, grouped together to buy out Lot 237 from the Department of Woods and Forests, which then compensated Calverts. This made it available as the site of a public building even more necessary to a successful estate than a pub.[43] After a fund-raising campaign orchestrated by Dr Thomas Dale, the Vicar of St Pancras, money was raised for the erection of

St Mark's Church, designed by Thomas Little and consecrated in 1853. Calverts had in any case increased their presence in the area by their purchase in the auction of Lot 241 for £1,533. Adjacent to the Regent's Canal, and on the corner of two of the projected roads, this became the Engineer pub.

Four of the principal buyers at the third day's auction were developers or architects.

Buyer	Lots	£
William Tringham	180–2, 209–10, 249	5,164
Charles Oldfield	208, 225, 258	3,496
George and Henry Bassett	207, 217–18	3,076
Peter Pearce and Joseph Guerrier	220–3	2,782
Thomas Little	259, 263–5	2,758

William Tringham, the leading purchaser, was the exception to this. With addresses in Cunningham Place, St John's Wood, and Long Cross, in Chertsey, he was a wealthy landowner.[44] Oldfield's lots were the future sites of three fine terraces: Regent's Park Gardens, fronting the new park to the east of Fitzroy Road; St Mark's Terrace, overlooking what would have been a Calverts pub on Lot 237 but became St Mark's Church; and Regent's Park Terrace in Oval Road. George Bassett was the surveyor to the Southampton Estate. His son, Henry, designed a number of Italianate villas in Gloucester Crescent; villas on what became Gloucester Avenue; and a terrace between the Chalk Farm railway bridge and the garden of the Chalk Farm Tavern. Pearce and Guerrier, who had come to an agreement with the Commissioners of Woods and Forests about a narrow strip of crown land between their purchases and the park, built the villas between St Mark's and Gloucester Gate. Thomas Little was the architect for Dr Thompson, who had bought two lots for £2,541. Little designed not only St Mark's, and the houses between St Mark's and the new park, but also the houses on Regent's Park Road between Princess Road and Fitzroy Road, on three lots he himself bought at the auction.*

In a second auction, the following year, Lord Southampton sold lots which had been withdrawn from the previous year's sales or had failed then to reach their reserve prices.[45] Auctioned in sixty-one lots by Robins in his Great Room in Covent Garden on 4 and 5 May 1841, the houses on offer were those to the immediate

---

* These lots were nos 259, 263 and 264. Little, whose address was 36 Northumberland Street, New Road, also designed the now demolished church of All Saints, St John's Wood, very much in the same style as St Mark's, for Dr Edward Thompson, as well as chapels at Highgate and Nunhead cemeteries. In the years before St Mark's was completed, a temporary church existed on the northern corner of Princess Road and Regent's Park Road.

south of the Regent's Canal in Camden Town, while the building plots were well away from Primrose Hill in Gospel Oak. The sale, however, included the Chalk Farm Tavern, with its garden and other buildings, but not the adjacent field used for shooting at the Target. Robins made light of its proximity to the London and Birmingham Railway:

> The fame of this Tavern has extended over a great number of years, indeed, from the number and variety of events that may be traced to this spot, it becomes a matter of history. It has recently acquired considerable additional value by means of the RAILWAY, the Station being close at hand, rendering the Hotel a delightful abode wherein to repose the night previous to the train commencing its daily vocation.[46]

Sold with a lease which had thirty-seven years still to run, the freehold of the tavern went for £1,974 to Keith Barnes of Spring Gardens, Westminster. Details of the buyers and how much they paid only survive for the odd-numbered lots, so the exact figures for the proceeds of the auction are unknown. If, however, the even-numbered lots can be assumed to have matched the odd-numbered ones, the auction would have raised £27,666.

Because the lots had been sold freehold, the area was no longer controlled by an estate office. The result was a variety of different developments over the following fifty years, ranging from the villas of Bassett, Pearce and Guerrier to low-grade railway cottages and numerous workshops, many to do either with piano manufacture or the railway. Away from the park frontage, the area resolved itself mainly as terraces, not villas.

To calculate the total realised by Lord Southampton's cumulative sales, the additional sums received from Lord Mansfield and the crown must be added to the proceeds of the 1840 and 1841 sales. Before the auctions, Lord Southampton had also received money from the Regent's Canal Company and from the London and Birmingham Railway Company.[47]

	£
First Day's Sale	39,217
Second Day's Sale	28,686
Sale to Lord Mansfield	20,000
Third Day's Sale	40,698
Sale to the Crown	2,284
1841 Sale	27,666
Sale to the Railway	50,000
Total	190,551

What triggered the auctions of 1840 and 1841 is not immediately clear. No reason was given in the newspapers of the day or in later accounts of the sale. Nor can one be found in the records of the auction or in the papers of the Southampton Estate office, which was in Fitzroy Square. Lord Southampton himself took little interest in the day to day administration of his London estate, which was run by his agent Henry Beauclerk and then by the solicitor Jacob Birt. No letters from Southampton to them survive to give a date to, or an explicit reason for, the decision to auction a major part of his London estate. It is likely, however, that the sales to the London and Birmingham Railway helped prompt the subsequent auctions of 1840 and 1841. There may, however, have been longer-term problems. Lord Southampton's mother, though beautiful, had brought no money into the family.[48] Even during his minority, the estate had been selling off assets. These included the land on which New St Pancras Church was built, sold to the parish for the high price of £6,695 in 1818.[49]

On the other side of the ledger, it is clear that Lord Southampton spent much of the capital realised on the acquisition of a sizeable estate around Whittlebury Lodge, his country house in Northamptonshire, near Towcester. This estate was built up in the 1830s and 1840s by a steady series of purchases in the parishes of Whittlebury, Silverstone and Wappenham. These acquisitions included land bought from the Duke of Grafton in Northamptonshire; and the manor of Luffield in nearby Buckinghamshire, acquired from the trustees of the Stowe Estate. Southampton's aim was clearly to build up a substantial country estate, ideal for hunting and not far from the Duke of Grafton's own Wakefield Lodge.[50]

By the time of Southampton's death in 1872, however, both the London and the country estates were heavily indebted. Most of the income generated by the two estates was being used to pay the interest on a series of large mortgages. How pressing the position had become is evident from the sale of £7,500 of family silver to Garrards in January 1867.[51] After 1872, Southampton's trustees quickly came to the conclusion that there was no alternative to selling the country estate, which was bought at auction on 2 May 1873 by Robert Loder for £304,000, plus £50,000 for the timber. Even then the trustees had to sell much of the best property in the London estate, including all of Fitzroy Square and most of the houses near Euston.[52]

How Lord Southampton managed to run through so much capital, as well as the £10,000 a year income from his London estate, is difficult to explain. The attractive theory that he was a compulsive gambler has no evidence to support it. Indeed, according to a man who knew him well, 'a more sensible and reasonable man than Lord Southampton never lived'.[53] The most obvious answer to the question may have some truth in it. Southampton was a passionate foxhunter in the heyday of hunting, yet he was not a man of unlimited wealth, on the scale of his cousin the

Duke of Grafton, or of other leading huntsmen such as the Duke of Beaufort and the Duke of Rutland. Providing hunting for the local community was an expression of leadership in the county and brought great personal esteem, yet it was a highly expensive commitment.

At the beginning of the nineteenth century Lord Fitzwilliam was spending up to £2,500 a year on riding horses, apart from those in his racing stables.[54] To buy a pack of hounds might cost £3,000 and their annual upkeep £1,000 or more. To this the cost of paying and mounting the hunt servants, maintaining coverts, gates and bridges, and keeping on good terms with farmers by compensating them for any damage done, must be added. When Master of the Quorn, Southampton 'was unremitting in his endeavours to show sport; he considered the farmers' interests and was extremely popular with them, while his affability gained him friends everywhere'.[55] As Master of the Grafton, Southampton

> hunted the pack entirely at his own cost without a subscription of any kind. Keepers and earth-stoppers were all paid by him in the most liberal manner. He was a good customer to the farmers, buying many horses and much provender. I heard him ask one old gentleman, who did not hunt, if he had threshed his oats. 'No, my lord, but I soon shall', was the reply. 'Very well, let me know and I will ride over and buy them.' Not a bad way, this, to keep things pleasant in a country![56]

Southampton's first wife, Harriet, also liked to live in some state. She was accustomed to luxury and 'when taking her afternoon drive in the country round her estate at Whittlebury, would appear in a barouche drawn by four grey horses and outriders'.[57] The Southamptons 'entertained very largely; many of the single noblemen came, and brought their hunters to the village of Whittlebury, and stayed some time …'[58]

In return for spending for his open-handed spending, Southampton was assured of both status and popularity:

> The hunting interest, based on a common excitement at the thrill of the run, sharing common memories of frustration, disappointment and exhaustion as well as achievement, informed by respect and admiration for a great Master, was perhaps the most real and fundamentally influential element in county society. The brotherhood reached far beyond the loyalties bred by estates, and embraced men from a great many stations in life, for alongside the lord, the squire and the parson, the farmer, the doctor, the solicitor and even the village sweep could all be seen at the meet; the labourer alone perhaps had no representative there. As loyalties founded on emotions outrun the calculus of economic interests, so the fox did more for the unity and strength of the landed interest than rent

rolls, and barbed wire did more to destroy the ties of county society than death duties.[59]

Perhaps Southampton's willingness to spend capital was reinforced by the childlessness of his first marriage and by his estrangement from his brother. The lack of an effective entail was also a precondition of his ability to sell his land.[60] He became master the Quorn at the age of twenty-four and hunted the Grafton until he was fifty-nine. Only in the last years of his life, with a new young wife and family, did Southampton cut back on his hunting. He built a new house at Whittlebury for his second wife and young family, after his existing one burnt down in January 1867.

If Lord Southampton had disposed of the freehold of a sizeable area of what is now inner London, the crown had achieved its objective of 1837 of acquiring Primrose Hill for the recreation of the people. The map appended to the Act of Parliament of 1842 shows exactly what had been acquired by the crown. From Eton it had acquired just over 53 acres, in four fields, Blue House, Primrose Hill, Sheppards Hill and Rugmoor (and small sections of three others, Square Field, Thirteen Acres and Ten Acres), plus a small triangle of land on the south-eastern corner of the new park which the college had itself acquired from Lord Southampton in 1838. It had, however, given up the future use of a small corridor of land on the east of the hill to the Eton Estate. The lots bought at Lord Southampton's auction amounted to just under eight acres, excluding Lot 237, which was not intended to be part of the park. In all, the government had acquired 61 acres, 3 roods and 31 perches of land for the public at the direct cost to the crown of little more than £2,000.

The finished bargain with Eton was sealed by an Act of Parliament, 5 & 6 Victoria, c. 78, passed in 1842. An Act for Effecting an Exchange between Her Majesty and the Provost and College of Eton, was passed not by a Whig government but by the Tory government headed by Sir Robert Peel, which had come to power in August 1841. Introduced by the Earl of Lincoln on 24 May 1842, it passed through the Houses of Parliament with only very minor changes. On the committee which examined it were a number of those who had previously taken an interest in the future of Primrose Hill, including three local MPs, Sir Benjamin Hall, Sir Charles Napier and Dr Thomas Wakley. It received the royal assent on 5 August 1842.[61]

9

The New Park

H UNDREDS of parks and smaller public spaces, of which Primrose Hill was only one, opened in cities and towns throughout Britain in the last sixty years of the nineteenth century. Some, following the earlier example of Regent's Park, were deliberately intended to improve the value of housing in and around them. Many more were opened after they were acquired by local councils, reformed under the Municipal Corporations Act of 1835 and now reflecting the aspirations and civic pride of Victorian rate-payers. Others, such as Waterlow Park in Highgate, were the result of the munificence of individual benefactors. Under a series of Acts, it also became easier to turn commons into public parks. These new areas added to the piecemeal pattern of existing public spaces, including town squares and churchyards, and to the small number of public gardens in older cities and towns, such as Northern Hay in Exeter, dating back to 1612 and the Quarry in Shrewsbury, established in 1719.[*]

While not the first public park to be established in the nineteenth century, Primrose Hill was one of the earliest in what was to become a national campaign to preserve and create open spaces. Only a handful parks of any size were opened before it, all of them outside London, with the exception of the special case of Regent's Park. The Royal Victoria Park in Bath was leased by the local council in 1830, following a successful subscription campaign, in an attempt to draw residents to Bath in the summer as well as the winter. It was opened by Princess Victoria seven years before she became queen. Moor Park in Preston was opened in 1833 after the burgesses successfully claimed rights over it. The Arboretum in Derby (1840), landscaped by J.C. Loudun, was the gift of a benefactor, as was Norfolk Park in Sheffield (1841).[1] Regent's Park itself, developed between 1811 and 1826, had been formed from land already belonging to the crown. It was a commercial

---

[*] Open spaces which were not public parks were sometimes treated as if they were commons. Hampstead Heath is a good example of this, attracting large numbers of visitors on summer weekends and holidays. Hazel Conway, *People's Parks: The Design and Development of Victorian Parks in Britain* (Cambridge, 1991), pp. 15–16. Later in the century a number of disused churchyards and burial grounds were turned into public gardens, ibid., pp. 214–20.

development intended to bring profit to the crown; and, in its early years, public access was limited to the Outer and Inner Circles. Rather than providing more space for the public, the creation of the park stopped them crossing what had once been the fields of Marylebone Park. Bushy, another royal park, was opened to the public in 1837, but it was at a distance from London and well away from its masses. Primrose Hill, in contrast, was the first park in England directly acquired by the government with the intention of providing recreational space for the general public, and in particular for members of the working class, even if the government acted more out of embarrassment than from fixed intent.*

As with many other government decisions in the nineteenth century affecting the lower classes, the acquisition did not stem simply from philanthropy. It was hoped that the availability of parks would help wean the lower classes from drinking, gambling and violence, particularly on Sundays (their only day of leisure), and

---

* The acquisition of Primrose Hill preceded three other government purchases of land in London for parks in the following two decades. Two of these were on a larger scale than Primrose Hill. The obvious lack of open spaces for recreation in the East End of London was addressed, following a public campaign, by the purchase of land to make Victoria Park. While an Act for acquiring the land for Victoria Park was passed in the summer of 1842, the crown's actual purchase of the land was not completed until 1844. This was funded by the sale of York House, previously the residence of the Duke of York, brother to George IV and William IV. While it was hoped that the terraces surrounding the park would provide the crown with a return, on the lines of Regent's Park, the slow uptake of leases constrained the development from the start. Victoria Park was nevertheless landscaped by James Pennethorne, with ornamental entrance lodges, a pagoda and two lakes, and was planted with flowers and trees under the supervision of John Gibson. Other attractions were added subsequently, including the magnificent Gothic fountain given by the philanthropist Angela Burdett-Coutts in 1862. Battersea Park, opened in 1856, provided a park south of the river. It was also elaborately landscaped by James Pennethorne. The third space was Kennington Common, the scene of the great Chartist rallies of 1848, acquired in 1852. Geoffrey Tyack, *Sir James Pennethorne and the Making of Victorian England* (Cambridge, 1992), pp. 87–114. See also, Conway, *People's Parks*, pp. 24–5, 38, 41–3, 87–8, 94.

Another project, for a sizeable royal park, never came to fruition. Albert Park, for which Pennethorne drew up a plan in 1851, was intended to provide Islington with a park running north from the line of the North London Railway as far as Finsbury and Stoke Newington. This ambitious but expensive scheme fell victim to government parsimony. In the end, a far smaller area in the north of the area originally designed as a park was opened by the Metropolitan Board of Works as Finsbury Park in 1867. Tyack, *Sir James Pennethorne*, pp. 114–18. There seems to have been some suggestion of calling Primrose Hill 'Albert Park', as this name appears on early maps of the park and in contemporary correspondence. It may help account for the naming of Prince Albert Road. This appears on early maps as Portland Town Road, Park Road and Primrose Hill Road, but changed to Albert Road soon after Queen Victoria's marriage to Prince Albert in 1840. It only achieved promotion to Prince Albert Road in 1937, when the London County Council wished to reduce the number of Albert Roads in London.

towards peaceful and healthy family recreation. The acquisition of Primrose Hill was also part of a campaign, born from the fear of political protest and social unrest, to bring popular meeting places under formal control. If there were to be mass meetings, they had much better be held on Primrose Hill, well away from the centre of government and the fashionable houses of the West End, than in Hyde Park.

Before it was opened, the architect of the Department of Woods and Forests, James Pennethorne, drew up a layout for the new park. As well as paths circling the hill, this included a level terrace at its summit, dominated by a huge seated statue of Britannia, and another terrace to its east.[2] His plan, however, was ignored by the commissioners, who had a very different agenda to that which had led to the development of Regent's Park.[*] The government had indeed assured the Eton Estate that it had no intention of building on the hill during the negotiations that led to the hill's acquisition. The deal reached just before the 1840 auction with the Southampton Estate was also contingent on the lots bought by the crown not being built on, allowing the houses facing the park an uninterrupted view.[3]

The promise not to build in the park was respected. The commissioners indeed seem to have had little interest in their new acquisition. They certainly had no strategic plans for it. The early history of Primrose Hill as a park was largely one of benign neglect. Its status was low, as a separate park, administered by the Superintendent of Regent's Park, but not itself a royal park. Unlike Regent's Park, which had been completely landscaped by Nash with an artificial lake, new roads and the planting of thousands of trees, Primrose Hill was left largely untouched other than by removals. In the 1840s all its existing trees were felled, with the exception of a few on the perimeter of the park, at the same time as the other internal boundaries were removed. The boundaries between the Chalcots Estate fields had disappeared even before the park was created, but the boundaries between the three areas acquired in 1840 and 1841 lasted a few years longer.[†] The early landscape of the park was therefore one of open pasture. This approach was rationalised in the longer term by the contention that Primrose Hill should be deliberately kept open and wild, to contrast with the artificial and manicured Regent's Park. The hill has always been, as it in many ways remains, the poor relation of its august neighbour. Nor could it count on positive support from any of the parishes around it, as it lay in three separate parishes: those of Hampstead, St Marylebone and St Pancras. Because it was not all in any one or even two of these parishes, and was

---

[*] 'The hill, and land adjoining it, from the suspension bridge over the Regent's Canal, comprising 150 acres, will be converted into plantations, serpentine and other gravel walks, and small pieces of ornamental waters', but nothing came of this. *Builder*, 9 August 1845, p. 38.
[†] The fields exchanged with Eton included a small parcel of land acquired by the college from Lord Southampton in 1838, and still with boundary hedges, as well as the lots bought at Lord Southampton's sale.

well away from the centre of each of them, the new park attracted no monuments to local patriotism or pride.

The Broad Walk in Regent's Park was opened to the public in 1841. In 1843, when James Dredge's iron suspension bridges, on either side of the Zoo, were built, access to the hill was open again to walkers across the park, as it had not been since Nash had closed Marylebone Park to the public thirty years before. Unfortunately, Dredge's bridges proved inadequate, partly because of skimping on the cost of their construction. A report in 1862 recommended that they should be replaced. Both bridges were rebuilt by 1870 and again in the early twentieth century.[4]

The one public facility provided by the government in the first years after the park's opening was a gymnasium, near to the new park's south-west corner, opened in 1848.

> By desire of Viscount Morpeth, the Chief Commissioner of her Majesty's Woods and Forests, a gymnasium has just been erected for the use of the public, near the foot of Primrose Hill, and was opened on Good Friday. The attendance was then but trifling, owing to the unfavourable weather; but on Easter Monday and Tuesday the spot was visited by many persons. The apparatus is inclosed, and a keeper is in attendance to preserve order.
>
> The regulations to be observed by the public are inscribed upon a large board within the ground. Among these, no person is allowed to occupy any one part of the apparatus exclusively longer than fifteen minutes; any person wilfully damaging the apparatus will be prosecuted; use of gross or abusive language is to be punished by exclusion from the gymnasium during that day; and the public are requested, by another regulation, to assist the keeper, if required, in maintaining order.[5]

Here was an epitome of the government's aims. The public was to devote itself to healthy exercise under regulation and supervision, eschewing bad language and rougher pastimes. Women and girls, however, as can be seen in contemporary illustrations of the gymnasium, did not go on the equipment. A later set of rules explicitly banned women even from spectating: 'No females, or children under eight, are allowed in the enclosure.'[6] While it marked Primrose Hill out as being different from the royal parks, none of which had one, the new gymnasium was pioneering in that it was the first set of exercise equipment provided by the government for the public anywhere in Britain.[7]

An early description of the park emphasised both the openness of the hill and the opportunity it provided for healthy exercise:

> Almost adjoining Regent's Park on the north-west side is Primrose Hill, to which the public have free access, and which is a very favourite spot for a

The gymnasium on Primrose Hill, opened in 1848, contained the first exercise equipment provided by the government for public use. (*Private Collection*)

summer ramble. It is in the form of a large roundish swell or knoll, and, being unplanted, affords views of a very ample and diversified character, besides yielding admirable exercise to those who are vigorous enough to run up and down its face.[8]

Even fencing in the new park took a surprisingly long time. Although in 1843 workmen were already reported 'erecting the boundary fences on the eastern side near Chalk Farm Tavern',[9] it was not until 1845 that 'immense numbers of workmen commenced, by the orders of the Commissioners of Woods and Forests, fencing in the whole of the land, including Primrose Hill on the north side of the Regent's Park ... for the purpose of increasing the Regent's Park, and securing a public thoroughfare to the top of Primrose Hill';[10] and it was 1847 before 'the enclosure of the new park at Primrose Hill ... was completed'.[11] Initially the boundaries of the hill consisted of wooden three-rail fencing reused from Regent's Park, though with walls and iron railings on its western boundary. Most of this early fencing was replaced by oak palings by the end of 1845. By 1847 new paths linked the five main gates to the summit of the hill.[12] The paths were surfaced by gravel. The later installation of barrier fencing at path junctions showed that these paths were heavily used.

Rights of way had been an important consideration in the acquisition of Primrose Hill. Although Eton was clearly the owner of most of the hill, one of the reasons it had been willing to effect the exchange with the crown was the certainty that any attempt to lease out the land on the hill for building would be hotly contested. The long-term public use of Primrose Hill, both as a place of enjoyment in itself and as part of a widely used route between St Marylebone and Hampstead, had established rights of way that might well have been defended successfully in the courts. Eton's own complaints about trespass on its land and damage to its fences were reflections of its awareness of widespread public use. Even if it had won a legal battle to close the paths across the hill, the college would have generated a storm of criticism in the press in doing so. It was indeed the Portland Cemetery Company's threat to close the rights of way across Primrose Hill that had focused opposition to its plans and had led to the public campaign against its Bill.

If the rights of way over Primrose Hill itself were preserved, the new park was badly served by the loss of other long-established rights of access. A deliberate denial of access from the west, where the land belonged to two large estates, proved a major limitation to the longer-term use of the new park. The Duke of Portland's Barrow Hill estate was the hill's immediate neighbour north of Regent's Park, with the estate running back as far as the eastern side of St John's Wood High Street. The fenced West Middlesex Water Works reservoir, leased from the Portland Estate, already blocked access immediately to the north of St Edmund's Terrace. Above the reservoir, a developer, William Fry, held adjoining building leases on the Portland and Eyre estates.* Another developer, William Twentyman, held building leases on the land bordering Primrose Hill up to the boundary with the Eton Estate.† Fry clearly wished to stop the right of access across his land, while Twentyman, whose houses fronted onto Avenue Road, had no wish to allow trespassers access to the gardens of his villas. Although it was the leaseholders who blocked the rights of way from St John's Wood, it was unlikely that this would have brought them into conflict with the owners of the two estates. Both the Duke of Portland and Walpole Eyre, who ran the Eyre Estate, needed to attract good-quality developers, not discourage them. If

---

* William Robert Fry, originally a timber merchant in Limehouse, also made good-quality bricks. Although bankrupted in 1835, he recovered and, with his son, continued building on the estate until 1862. Fry was also granted a lease to build four houses on the Portland Estate in July 1829. For Fry, see Mireille Galinou, *Cottages and Villas: The Birth of the Garden Suburb* (London and New Haven, 2010), pp. 146–8, 153–4, 408–9, 438, 451, 452, 454, 455, 472–3 and 481. A map, ibid., p. 146, shows the plots taken by developers on the Eyre Estate. For his Portland Estate lease, London Metropolitan Archives, 58/WM/A/03.

† William Holme Twentyman (1802–84), was the main developer of Avenue Road inside the Eyre Estate. He specialised in large, expensive villas. Born in Liverpool, he had made a fortune as a watchmaker and jeweller in Mauritius before returning to England in 1837. His first building lease on the Eyre Estate was in 1838. Although his main agreement with the estate, which led to the building of the prestigious Regent's Villas on the east side of Avenue Road, was not signed until 1843, the estate's own plans for the plots may date to well before this. Galinou, *Cottages and Villas*, pp. 181–5, 480–1. See also ibid., pp. 146, 150–3, 306, 453–4, 474 and 479.

it had come to a court case, the estates would have supported the developers, not the campaigners.

In 1838 it was reported that the main St John's Wood estate had been busy blocking all access to Primrose Hill:

> In the Marylebone vestry, on Saturday, Mr Kensett stated, that he had received a great number of communications from individuals upon the subject of the wall now in course of erection on the estate of Colonel Eyre, which would prevent all access from the Avenue Road to Primrose Hill. Many of these letters were from people far advanced in years, bearing testimony to the existence of the path in question by having passed over it upwards of forty years ago, and expressing their willingness to come forward and prove their assertion. He would suggest that the surveyor be directed to assist the committee by collecting all possible information from the localities which surrounded Primrose Hill. This was agreed to.[13]

Three years later, a report to the St Marylebone Vestry complained:

> Mr Kensett here read the report of a committee, of which he was chairman, appointed to inquire into a recent infringement of the public right of way leading to Primrose Hill from the Avenue Road. It set forth that a footpath and a right of way, running from the south west to the north east, and leading over a stile from the Avenue Road to Primrose Hill, which path had been known to exist for upwards of thirty years, is now about to be closed by a Mr Fry, a builder, who occupies under the Duke of Portland. The stile had already been taken down, and a bank and hedge planted. A granite stone, with the parish mark, designating the boundary, had also been taken up and laid at a distance from the spot where it originally stood, the boundary line forming two-thirds of the path thus stopped, and the public excluded from access to Primrose Hill, which, by the beneficence of the crown, has been recently purchased for the use of the people in perpetuity. ... The stoppage of this thoroughfare prevented access to Primrose Hill from all parts of Westbourn and Avenue roads, and, in fact, shut out a large portion of the inhabitants of Marylebone and the whole of Paddington from that place of public resort and recreation, without going round for a considerable distance to the Hampstead or the St Pancras side.[14]

Whatever the vestry's indignation, it was a losing battle. Although a committee, accompanied by the MPs for Marylebone, Sir Benjamin Hall and Sir Charles Napier, visited the hill in 1842, 'when the borough members were satisfied that the public had a right of way which had been infringed on by Mr Fry', the vestry had no appetite, and the local campaigners themselves no funds, for taking on the risks and costs of a series of law suits in defence of rights of way.* This unwillingness was undoubtedly reinforced by the fact that any legal action would almost certainly have been opposed by the two largest landowners in the parish. The Duke of Portland was also one of richest men in England.

A few years earlier, in 1835, Hampstead Vestry had faced a very similar dilemma. A committee was set up to report on the unilateral closure of three existing rights of way, one from Pond Street to the Load of Hay on Haverstock Hill and two running towards Primrose Hill. On the first, the committee members reported that the landowner involved, Mr Lund, had refused even to see them and had asked that all future correspondence should be with his solicitor. On the second, the committee had

> lately viewed the ancient footway which led from Belsize Park near the corner of the park wall across Mr Bliss's meadow to the hedge and thence over a stile (the situation of which is still observable from the nails in the trees) to the fields leading to Primrose Hill. Its course as laid down in the Newton plan of the parish is well known to Mr Field who used to frequent it. As stated in the surveyor's report, this last mentioned path and also the path which led from the Load of Hay across the fields belonging to Eton College to Chalk Farm are now obstructed.[15]

Although the parish surveyor was asked to prepare a legal case to force Lund to reopen the path across his land, a vote by vestry members promptly stopped this being taken any further. It was decided

> that whatever the matter of fact as to the right in question it is not desirable or expedient that the rate payers of this parish should incur the expence of litigating the right in order to disturb a respectable inhabitant in the occupation of his property.[16]

It is not therefore surprising to find St Marylebone Vestry adopting a similarly pragmatic attitude in the following decade. It is easy to sympathise, however, with those who were disappointed by its failure to defend existing public rights. Four years after the opening of the park, St Marylebone Vestry were addressed by a local campaigner:

> An exceedingly strange and youthful-looking personage, with his collar turned down *à la Byron*, who stated his name to be Henry Dowell Griffiths, secretary

---

* *The Times*, 26 July 1842. Napier was a swashbuckling naval hero whose exploits pre-echo those of Hornblower. Admired by Palmerston, as an MP he was a Radical Whig. For Hall and Napier, see 'Benjamin Hall, Baron Llanover (1802–67)'; and 'Sir Charles Napier (1786–1860)', *Oxford Dictionary of National Biography*.

of the West London Central Anti-Enclosure Association, came before the board, on the part of that association, to enforce on the attention of the vestry their duty, as the conservators of the parish, to prevent the rights of the rate-payers and the public being invaded by the blocking up of certain rights of way and ancient footpaths, especially on the Kilburn or Marylebone side of Primrose Hill.

Mr Griffiths, in a very excited manner, proceeded to explain the nature of the various encroachments, which he said were no less than seven in number, all in the Avenue Road, and which had completely stopped up as many as twelve ancient footpaths over that delightful place of recreation, Primrose Hill.[*]

While the members of the vestry undoubtedly regretted the loss of the rights of way, their sympathies must have been quickly alienated when Griffiths went on to attack property rights in general. He 'declared that neither the duke or the colonel ever possessed a foot of ground but what they had robbed from the people, and said that it was duty of the vestry, as a representative body, to wrest it from their grasp'.[17] Griffiths had addressed the vestry while holding 'several hundred bills upon the subject of the enclosure'.[18] When asked to retire, so that the vestry could consider his application, Griffith pelted the chairman and vestrymen with 'compact bundles of his bills'.

> After the applicant had fully satisfied himself with this achievement, he retired, and the vestry, believing the young gentleman to be only a fit companion for 'the wild savage' and slightly touched in the upper story, got rid of the matter by moving and adopting the next order of the day.[19]

Opposing the closure of the rights of way had by now changed from a practical possibility, supported by the public representatives of the parish, to a grievance held by an eccentric Radical campaigner. The result of the closure, however, had a major long-term effect on Primrose Hill. The Eyre Estate, in particular, turned its back

---

[*] *Observer*, 13 July 1846. Griffiths listed the encroachments: 'The obstructions consisted in the garden rails of the Elms villa and garden walls of the villa, no. 14, on the opposite side of the Avenue Road. The garden walls of enclosure no. 4 Woodstock Place; the garden walls of no. 23, opposite; the wall at the end of the stable passage (facing Acacia Road) between Woodstock Place and the Regent's Villas; the garden walls of what is intended to be the fourteenth of the Regent's Villas, and through the garden wall of the villa opposite.' The original misprints 'Arcadia Road' for 'Acacia Road'. Griffiths' behaviour may reflect a long-term frustration at the failure of his campaign. He had written to the Commissioners of Woods and Forests in July 1843, inviting them to attend a meeting on Primrose Hill of 'the committee appointed by the vestry to enforce the reopening of the Kilburn footpaths to Primrose Hill'. Writing from 4 Phillpott Terrace, Edgware Road, Griffiths described himself as 'one who has interested himself in the movement ever since the spring of 1841 ...', Henry Dowell Griffiths to the Commissioners of Woods and Forests, 24 July 1843, National Archives, Cres 2/794.

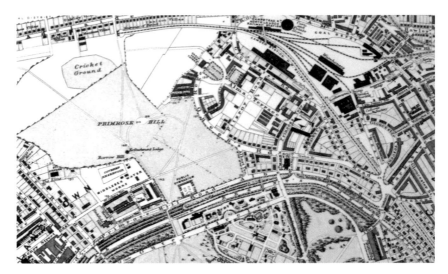

Stanford's map of 1862 still shows fields to the north of Primrose Hill, as well as the Eton and Middlesex Cricket Ground, while villas stretch along Avenue Road. Primrose Hill Road has not yet been built and many of the building lots on either side of Fitzroy Road remain empty. The massive engine shed and other buildings emphasise the area's link to the railways. (*Private Collection*)

on the hill. All the houses on the east side of Avenue Road were built with only the back walls of their gardens bordering onto the hill and with no direct access onto the hill other than through a few private entrances. To this day there is no road, lane or public path leading directly to the park from St John's Wood, except to the south of Barrow Hill Reservoir. The result has been that Primrose Hill has always been far less connected to St John's Wood, despite the latter's proximity to the hill, than to Chalk Farm and Camden Town.

Gradually additions were made to the park. A modest kiosk, which had originally been part of the Great Exhibition of 1851, was transferred to near Barrow Hill Reservoir when the Crystal Palace moved to Sydenham in 1852. This was upgraded to tea rooms known as the Queen's Pavilion, built in 1859. These tea rooms were, in turn, pulled down in 1905 and replaced by new ones a few years later.[20]

The lodge at the south-west corner of the park dates from 1860. With high chimneys, painted stone dressings and mullioned windows, plans for it were drawn up by the surveyor John Phipps, given a budget of £600. Thomas Mills, of 28 York Street, Westminster, quoted £592 to build it with cement dressings, but £672 for Bath stone dressings. Phipps accepted the higher estimate and reported to the Office of Works on 11 January 1861:

the New Lodge, Primrose Hill, is now completed (with the exception of the paper to the walls which it is proposed should be done in the spring) and fit for occupation; and I should suggest that Sherlock the Inspector, who is now receiving a weekly allowance in lieu of East Lodge, Park Crescent, which cannot for some time be occupied, in consequence of the Metropolitan Railway, should be placed in the New Lodge.[21]

The building of the world's first underground railway line, to the south of Regent's Park, resulted in the new lodge being allocated to the head park-keeper.*

The new park was now subject to supervision and to rules. Except for those regulating the gymnasium, no rules for the park in general exist for its early years, though there were certainly park-keepers from at least 1851, when it was reported that 'The park-keepers appeared on Wednesday in their new uniforms'.[22] The earliest set of rules to survive dates from 1872:

1. No unauthorised person may ride or drive in the park, or bring in any wheelbarrow, truck, or cycle.

2. No cattle, sheep or pigs are allowed to enter, except for pasturage.

3. Bath chairs and perambulators are not allowed on any paths where they are prohibited by notice.

4. No unauthorised person shall drill, or practise military evolutions, or use arms, or play any game or music, or practise gymnastics, or take photographs, or sell or let any commodity.

5. No chairs or other seats may be placed for hire, except with the license of the Commissioners of Her Majesty's Works and Public Buildings, and subject to the terms and conditions of such license.

6. The use of the gymnasium is allowed only on condition of observing the rules of the place and the directions of the park-keepers in charge.

7. No unauthorised public address may be delivered in this park ...

8. The persons in charge of dogs must prevent them from causing annoyance to any person, and from worrying or fighting with other dogs, or injuring

---

* Subsequent inhabitants of the lodge, who with their families have been the only inhabitants of Primrose Hill other than the men of the Anti-Aircraft unit in the Second World War, were Inspector George Court (1863–81); Inspector Joseph Page (1881–1907); Inspector Edward Wickham (1908–12); Sergeant Elijah Ladbroke (1912–19); Henry Balchen, probably a sergeant (1919 until 1922 or later); Sergeant Albert Sherriff (until 1934); Inspector William (or Walter) Simmonds (1934–37); Inspector Arthur Huggett (1937–45); Sergeant Harold Clement (1945–54); and Sergeant Ken Gillies (1954–81). Information from Mark Watson.

or disturbing any animal in the park. No person shall take into or have in the park any dog not led by a chain or string, or other sufficient fastening, during such time as notices are exhibited, prohibiting the admission of dogs unless led.

9. Any dog brought into the park which may reasonably be suspected to be in a rabid state will be destroyed.

10. Climbing the trees, railings or fences is forbidden.

11. Birds' nesting and taking, destroying or injuring birds or animals are forbidden.

12. The distribution of handbills, advertisements and other papers is forbidden.[23]

These rules were revised and updated in 1886, 1932 and subsequently. Until 1974, when they were absorbed into the police, the park was patrolled by park-keepers in distinctive uniforms.

The hill was unlit until 1868, despite numerous complaints about the inconvenience and dangers that this caused. A contemporary saying held that one gas light was worth three policemen. Following a deputation from the vestries of St Marylebone and St Pancras to Lord John Manners, the First Commissioner of Works, the hill was finally provided with lighting.[24]

On Thursday night week the permanent gas lights erected on Primrose Hill, to the number of eighty-six, were lighted, and the effect was a strikingly brilliant illumination of the whole surface. The lamps, of which thirty-two are in the parish of St Pancras, thirty-three in Marylebone and twenty-one in Hampstead, are distributed at short intervals along each of the paths from every approach to the top of the hill. The appearance of this large collection of lights in such close proximity is a sight worth the trouble of a visit, whether viewed from the foot or the crown of the hill. ... The result of the illumination will be most beneficial in facilitating the communication between the important parishes previously mentioned and in abolishing the nuisances which a short time back so prominently claimed public attention.[25]

No water was provided for visitors to the hill for forty years after the opening of the park, other than from the ponds on the hill or the drinking trough for sheep and cattle next to the gymnasium. Only in 1864 was a fountain previously used in Hyde Park placed near the lodge. At its centre was a metal figure from which flowed jets of water. On its arrival in Primrose Hill it was placed on a stone plinth. An inscription was added the following year: 'All creatures have their joy, and man has his. But as birds drink and straight lift up their heads; so must he sip and think if better drink he may attain to after he is dead.' The fountain was moved to the children's playground in 1927, but no longer exists.[26] A second drinking-fountain, outside the park itself at the corner of Regent's Park Road and Albert Terrace, was given privately in memory of Judge Joseph Payne, 'a zealous total abstainer and a faithful friend of Bands of Hope', who died in 1870.[27]

Few benches were provided in the London parks of the first half of the nineteenth century. 'A Pedestrian' complained in 1845:

> There ought to be, as is found everywhere all over the Continent, large seats under almost every tree, instead of which the benches are carefully distributed over the grounds, as if they were most rare and costly specimens of art, and so the same stinginess is to be observed in Hyde and all the other parks.
>
> Look at Primrose Hill again; why, there is not one single seat of any description whatever to be found on its summit, as is so naturally expected and desired by all who, on a fine sunny day, have been tolling up it to breathe a little fresh air.[28]

Some, however, had clearly been provided by 1851:

> A spacious carriage-way has been formed from the Hampstead road through the grounds of the Chalk Farm Tavern, leading into the Regent's Park and Camden Town. A number of gravel walks have been laid down, and seats placed for the accommodation of visitors.[29]

By the 1880s, 'the placing of chairs' was noted as one of the improvements that had helped make Primrose Hill a 'place of public recreation and enjoyment'. It was claimed that 'whereas a few years ago private chairs were not required on the hill, today these number several hundred'.[30]

The top of the hill remained a favourite viewing spot. In 1860 a resident of St Edmund's Terrace, William Smee, wrote: 'I am an observer of light, and am conversant with the changes in the landscape created by variations of light and of clouds and of mist. I think few better places than Primrose Hill could be found near London for seeing the effect of light during an eclipse ...'[31] Unlike Greenwich Hill, Primrose Hill never had an observatory, but in 1854 permission was given to William Wood to exhibit a telescope there.[32] Not all observations from the hill were, however, to a high degree of accuracy, as a letter to *The Times* pointed out in 1863:

> The 'large meteor' seen by Mr Crumplen on Monday evening at 8.27, three times as brilliant as Venus, and moving from west to east, was a fire balloon sent up shortly after 8 o'clock from the Eton and Middlesex Cricket Ground, Primrose Hill, as a finale to some athletic sports which had taken place during the afternoon.[33]

A dial was placed on top of the hill in 1904, identifying buildings to its south.

To raise money, the boys of the Home
for the Maintenance of Destitute Boys
not Convicted of Crime sold and
delivered firewood to houses in the
neighbourhood.
On the corner of Regent's Park Road
and King Henry's Road, this well-run
institution taught the boys crafts, with
woodwork a speciality. (*CLSAC*)

By the end of the nineteenth century, the perimeter of Primrose Hill had been settled, including the construction of the houses that were to mark its periphery until the Second World War. Villas and terraces, built in the 1840s and 1850s on plots purchased in Lord Southampton's sale, lined Regent's Park Road and Albert Terrace. St George's Terrace, just to its east, had direct access to the park until the construction of Primrose Hill Road. A large and handsome terrace, Regent's Park Gardens, faced the park to the east of Fitzroy Road. Behind Albert Terrace the spire of St Mark's Church, consecrated in 1853, reflected the growth of the local population.

An obvious opportunity to connect Primrose Hill to the Broad Walk in Regent's Park had been lost by this stage. The lots bought by Dr Edward Thompson in Lord Southampton's auction in 1840, which occupied the whole block between the bridge over the canal leading from the Broad Walk and the hill, had remained unbuilt upon for a number of years.* (These were Lots 235 and 236, which the

---

* One reason for the delay in resolving the question of the site of St Mark's Church was the possibility that the land would be needed for a station on a railway built alongside or replacing the Regent's Canal. In early 1847 G.F. Hudson, who acted for Dr Edward Thompson, wrote to the railway company: 'I am only just informed that your Bill proposes to take away, and use for the purpose of the rail, the site of a proposed church near Primrose Hill towards the erection of which a committee of a few gentlemen, including myself, have taken some trouble and obtained some subscriptions, having obtained also the appropriation of the site for such purpose.' G.F. Hudson, 12 February 1847, National Archives, Cres 2/794.

crown failed to buy when it bought the adjoining lots for the park.) It would have made an obvious extension to Primrose Hill Park, as would two acres of land belonging to the Duke of Portland to the west.[34] The Department of Woods and Forests, or rather its master the Treasury, set its face against any further purchases. As Viscount Morpeth, the Chief Commissioner of the Woods and Forests, wrote to the indefatigable campaigner Henry Dowell Griffiths in 1846: 'I should be very glad to be enabled to purchase some of the land adjoining Primrose Hill, but I have not the command of any funds for the purpose.'[35] As a paper sympathetic to Griffiths commented:

> Lord Lincoln, when Chief Commissioner of the Woods and Forests, was willing to extend Primrose Hill Park beyond its present insignificant space, had it not been for want of 'sufficient funds'; his successor in that office, Viscount Canning, also promised to take the question 'into consideration', and doubtless would have done so, had not a change in the administration caused a change in the Woods and Forests. Lord Morpeth avows himself heart and soul for the 'extension'. ... By the bye, the indolence of the government, with respect to this park, is worthy of remark. The ground has now been purchased about five years, yet not a single tree has been planted in it ...[36]

After many delays, the housing of Eton's Chalcots Estate covered the whole area to the north and east of the park by 1900. The earliest part of the estate to be developed, to the west of the Hampstead road and north of what became Adelaide Road, dates from the 1830s. The church of St Saviour provided a centre for the area when completed in 1856. Villas then spread slowly down Adelaide Road. Using the strip of land acquired from the crown at the time of its exchange of Primrose Hill, Primrose Hill Road was driven through from Regent's Park Road (originally Queens Road) to Adelaide Road, after Eton resumed the land for its 'Intended Road' in 1868, with the fields behind being built over by the developer Samuel Cuming to create Ainger Road and Oppidans Road. Primrose Hill Road itself, which cut off St George's Terrace from direct proximity to the park, was lined with villas facing the park from Ainger Road to King Henry's Road. To service this new estate, the church of St Mary's Primrose Hill was completed in 1872.*

---

* The first vicar was Charles Fuller, originally the minister of a temporary church between Ainger Road and Oppidans Road. Fuller's high-church leanings alienated the governors of the Boys' Home in Regent's Park Road (its full title was 'The Home for the Maintenance of Destitute Boys not Convicted of Crime'), whose spiritual welfare he had previously supervised. Instead, he attracted a group of pious young women. His efforts to raise money for a permanent church were greatly eased by the gift of £3,000 by one of them, Miss Mary Emily André (1838–1900), but the gift came with one condition, which he accepted, which was for him to marry her. Information from Christopher Kitching, archivist of St Mary the Virgin Primrose Hill.

Elsworthy Road, on the northern border of the park, for many years stopped at Elsworthy Terrace, which still provides a main entry to the park. It had been built on what had been a cricket ground, which now moved west, to between the end of Elsworthy Road and Avenue Road. The Eton and Middlesex Cricket Ground, covering over eleven acres, remained in existence until 1890. Unusual in having inside the ground the very sizeable vent-shaft of the Primrose Hill Tunnel, it was much used by local sporting clubs as well as the Volunteers. Its continued existence was testimony to the slow growth of building on the Eton Estate.

In 1873 William Smee wrote to the then Prime Minister, W.E. Gladstone, stressing the desirability of adding the Eton and Middlesex Cricket Ground to the existing park:

> Knowing the great and arduous duties you have to perform, I regret being obliged to call your attention to a very small affair, but the case is urgent, and in a few months buildings will be placed upon a portion of the ground. ...
>
> It may, therefore, be worthy of your consideration whether the government should not purchase the Eton and Middlesex Cricket Ground, which adjoins, and consists of about twelve acres. This is a private ground, and, I believe, does not pay.[37]

Smee rightly claimed that 'This would make a splendid addition to the park and, perhaps, £20,000 would purchase the whole.'[38] He concluded: 'a great nation can find no better and no more economical use for a little mite of surplus revenue than its judicious employment in providing space for healthy, innocent, and cheap outdoor entertainment'.[39] Gladstone himself did not reply, though Smee did receive an official acknowledgement.

The disappearance of the ground was the result of the activities of two of the leading house builders of the late nineteenth and early twentieth centuries. William Willett the senior, the chief builder of Kensington, also developed Eton Avenue and the roads off it with large, high-quality houses in the 1870s and 1880s.[40] In 1890 he took the reversion of the lease of the cricket ground and the land around it, in total over sixteen acres.[41]

The alarm was sounded by *The Times*:

> The inhabitants of South Hampstead and the neighbourhood have become alarmed at the rumour that on the expiration of the lease in September of the Eton and Middlesex Cricket Ground, which has been used by the public there for over twenty-four years, it is likely to be let for building purposes. ... There is no other open space in the neighbourhood where sports can be carried on by the middle-class residents, and it is feared that if the ground is closed and built upon it would materially depreciate the value of the surrounding property.[42]

A campaign to save the ground for cricketers or the general public, led by the philanthropist Lord Meath, was unable to raise enough money to meet the Willetts' price of £50,000 to allow the land to continue undisturbed as a cricket field. Hampstead Vestry had no money to spare, due to its efforts at this time towards the preservation and acquisition of Hampstead Heath Extension, while St Marylebone Vestry refused to contribute, describing the ground as

> a low-lying field abutting upon Primrose Hill, for which the outrageous price of over £3,000 per acre was asked. There was no need for adding sixteen acres to the beautiful open space of Primrose Hill and Regent's Park immediately adjoining; and even if it were desirable to acquire the land, the price was most exorbitant.[43]

Although the Eton and Middlesex Cricket Ground disappeared, it was replaced by some of the best houses in north London. This development was largely overseen by the second Willett. William Willett junior is better known as a tireless campaigner for daylight saving. He had conceived the idea out riding early one summer morning near his house in Chislehurst, when he had noticed how many blinds were still down. His pamphlet, *The Waste of Daylight*, went through nineteen editions between 1907 and 1914, with 'Summer Time' being finally adopted only after his death as a war measure in 1916, to reduce the usage of coal.[44] Employing Ambrose Faulkner as architect, the Willetts built over one hundred houses in Elsworthy Road and Wadham Gardens between 1895 and 1902, creating in 'Elsworthy Village' what has been described as the first garden suburb.

> The Willetts in effect put Norman Shaw on the production line, going in for gables, tiled roofs, bay windows, red brick exteriors, and above all abandoning decisively the near uniformity of town housing, which had permitted only minor variations in ornamental detail, and going in for deliberate contrasts in shape and elevation between adjoining houses. It was the effective beginning of twentieth-century suburban architecture, on a grand scale and for wealthy customers, producing houses which offered great comfort without compelling the stiffness and formality which mid-Victorian household management had had to provide in order to make the mid-Victorian house function.[45]

From St Mary's along Elsworthy Road, and then down Avenue Road, all the houses had their backs to the park, unlike those in Regent's Park Road, Albert Terrace and Primrose Hill Road and, to the west, Ormonde Terrace. From the time it acquired Primrose Hill, the crown resisted attempts by householders to establish private entrances into the park. This, and the fact that there were no public entrances onto the hill between Elsworthy Terrace and St Edmund's Terrace, has always meant that this part of the hill has far fewer visitors than the south and east.

Behind the immediate border of the park, other housing sprang up in the second half of the nineteenth century, with most available building plots filled by 1900. The area behind the villas fronting Primrose Hill in Regent's Park Road and Primrose Hill Road was filled with terraces by 1870, but included many workshops and a block of modest housing for men working at the railway depot which separated the area from Camden Town. A more pretentious mix of villas, without its own stabling but also without nearby workshops, was built on the Eton Estate. The villas set in gardens of St John's Wood contrasted with the low-quality housing of Portland Town to its south. During the nineteenth century the area around the park remained very largely middle-class, as can be seen from Charles Booth's 'Descriptive Maps of London Poverty' of 1889, where the villas facing Primrose Hill and in Avenue Road are coloured with the confident gold of 'upper-middle and upper classes: wealthy'. Many other houses near to them are in the red of 'well-to-do: middle class'. The only pockets of the light-blue 'poor' in what is now Primrose Hill Village were in the railway cottages, the mews behind St George's Terrace and the east side of Sharpleshall Street. Portland Town had large areas of 'poor', but even here there was no dark blue for 'very poor, casual: chronic want', let alone black for 'lowest class: vicious, semi-criminal'.[46]

London by 1900 had of course extended far to the north of Primrose Hill, which drew visitors from a wide surrounding area. While it is impossible to say how people reached the hill, or how many came from close to hill and how many from further away, the nineteenth century was a great age of walking. Although the wealthy may have had horses to ride and carriages to ride in, most members of the population were still reliant on their feet. Large numbers of office-workers and labourers walked miles to work and back each day. Walking was also a popular leisure activity for all classes, and walking in company with members of their family or with friends was an acceptable activity for respectable young women. Many visitors to the new park of Primrose Hill undoubtedly reached it on foot, whether from nearby or further afield. Cycling, beginning with the boneshakers and penny-farthings of the 1870s, had become widespread and fashionable by the 1890s. Bicycles liberated women from the need to be chaperoned, even if bicycles themselves were not allowed in the park.

The growth of public transport, nevertheless, made it increasingly easy for those who lived at a distance to reach the hill. The London and Birmingham Railway had had little interest in serving local destinations, with its first stop after Euston being at Harrow. A local station on the North London Line was, however, opened in 1844.[47] The first bus route in England was not far away. George Shillibeer started to operate his service along the New Road in 1829. This was followed by the General Omnibus Company, with services running around the park by 1840. A horse-bus terminus was set up at the Adelaide Hotel, near what was later to become Chalk Farm Tube Station.

The branch of the Metropolitan Line from Baker Street to Swiss Cottage dates from the 1870s. Two stations on this branch of the line, Lord's and Marlborough Road, were later closed, with St John's Wood Station being opened between them. Chalk Farm Tube Station itself, on the Northern Line, opened in 1907.

The land, particularly that on the north-west side of the hill remained very damp in wet weather, despite repeated attempts to solve the problem. A first campaign, by which the southern slope was drained into a culvert discharging into the canal, was completed by Hewitt Davis in February 1854.[48] Many problems, however, remained unsolved. In 1880 a local resident reported that 'after heavy rains the ground at the lower part of Primrose Hill becomes a lake, and for days afterwards the water may be seen running over the pavement in the Regent's Park Road, and in many parts of the park itself the stagnant water lies for hours after rain'.[49]

A second drainage campaign, in 1882, undertaken by James Gridwood following complaints of flooding in Avenue Road from the northern outflow as well as on Primrose Hill itself, was carried out in preparation for tree planting.[50] Following it, the hill was planted in the autumn of 1883 with black Italian poplars along its main paths, and with white and pink hawthorns in between. There were three larger plantations behind the top of the hill, with a grove on its summit. This grove remained a notable feature of Primrose Hill until it was felled to make way for anti-aircraft guns in 1938: 'No more looking at the view from seats beneath its branches', according to Louis Macneice.[51] As well as these, there were a number of individual species, including a line of walnut-leaved ash near Barrow Hill Reservoir. Although five ancient hollow oaks were removed by Gridwood, an oak was planted with a great deal of ceremony in 1864 to mark the tercentenary of the birth of Shakespeare. As a journalist described the park in 1883:

> crossing the Canal by the footbridge we are soon at Primrose Hill, on which within the last year some five hundred young trees have been planted. ... In a very short time they will leave far behind them Shakespeare's oak, planted on the south side of the hill some twenty years ago, and still not much taller than the railing which surrounds it. Primrose Hill, covered with umbrageous plane trees will be a real ornament to London. It is curious that the trees near its top are flourishing the most. May the powers that be carefully watch the staking of these young trees, and protect their bark from the teeth of sheep and the pocket knives of yet more destructive boys.[52]

The Shakespeare oak, despite its provenance in the royal nursery at Windsor, never flourished and needed to be replaced at Shakespeare's quatercentenary in April 1964.

In the early twentieth century, a third drainage campaign finally led to the disappearance of the last of the Tyburn ponds, when it was filled with soil in 1902. Between 1902 and 1911 twenty acres north of the hill were 'reclaimed and laid out as a recognised ground for cricket and football'. According to A.D. Webster, ten games of cricket could be played there at a time. This was, however, by no means the beginning of games on Primrose Hill. As long ago as 1851 the Commissioners of Woods and Forests had 'issued instructions to fill up the different hollows in Primrose Hill Park, in order that the lower portion may be converted into a cricket field'.[53] Even before that a watercolour of the hill dating from 1836 shows a game of cricket being played at its foot. More formal cricket was also played on the Eton and Middlesex Cricket Ground. This mostly hosted matches between local sides, though occasionally more prestigious matches were played there.* Following the completion of the Eton Estate, the northern boundary was established as a brick wall, inside which there was a single avenue of trees.

The oak palings around Primrose Hill, which had been put up in 1845, were in poor repair by 1913. They survived until 1929, when they were pulled down, leaving the park open to the south and east.[54] Iron fencing had been planned as a replacement for the oak palings, but this was postponed during the First World War. Rescheduled after the war as part of an Unemployment Relief Programme in 1925, at a cost of £1,000, this scheme was never implemented. In the late 1920s the London Society and the Committee of London Squares ran a campaign to remove fencing around public spaces. As there were no gates to Primrose Hill, the fencing served no obvious purpose, while removing the fencing (which cost nothing to do, as the contractor took the wood in lieu) also saved the cost of erecting a replacement. The fencing was removed in July 1929, other than around the gymnasium and playground, and where there was a steep bank on Primrose Hill Road. According to Hugh Johnston, writing from 31 Fitzroy Road, 'It is difficult to explain just what a sense of open space, freedom and trustfulness the absence of a fence has created'.[55] Heavy wear near the entrance between Regent's Park Road and Primrose Hill Road led to a shrubbery being planted there.

Some, but not all, of the railings on top of the hill were removed at the same time:

> The removal of the railings from the greater part of the circular open space on the top of the hill is also a great improvement: but, unfortunately, the north-west arc of this circle is still fenced in, owing to the fact that a few shabby and undecorative shrubs are growing on the adjacent plot of ground. As it exists at present,

---

* Until they were built over in the 1860s, there were two other cricket grounds to the north and north-west of England's Lane, respectively the 'Subscription Cricket Ground' and the 'Tradesmen's Cricket Ground'. See Stanford's 1862 map of the area.

this shrubbery is not worth fencing in at all: and it seems disproportionate that
a particularly vulgar spiked fence should be employed for the purpose.[56]

The final addition to the park before the Second World War was the playground.
There was a playground, with a wooden shed, next to the gymnasium from the
1920s. This was replaced in 1930–31 by a more formal arrangement, including a
building which provided a staff mess room and storage accommodation for tools
and an ambulance, as well as lavatories and a children's shelter. A turret was added
on top of the latter to house a clock. Money for this was provided by a legacy from
Mr George Bridcut of Yew Tree House, Ombersley, who left £500 to Primrose Hill
'for the purpose of erecting a clock in some suitable place'.[57]

Sheep were regular visitors to the hill until the Second World War and indeed
afterwards. Straying sheep and cattle had caused problems early in the park's
history, as the crown did not erect proper fencing around its new acquisition until
1845.* A flock of sheep, feeding on both Regent's Park and Primrose Hill, was
used to keep down the length of the grass.[58] Because there was no fencing round
Primrose Hill between 1929 and 1954, sheep had to be brought there and returned
to Regent's Park during the day, as they could not be left on the hill overnight.
According to the park manager:

> There never has been much grazing on Primrose Hill owing to it being open
> all night. There is great difficulty in getting the sheep across to Regent's Park
> at night and rather than run the risk of accidents the sheep are kept in Regent's
> Park. Therefore there will be very little difference, if any, if there is no grazing.[59]

The years after 1890 saw the beginning of a decline in all the areas around
the park. Although the grander villas still remained in demand, many of the
terrace houses started to be sublet. This process was accelerated by the growing
difficulty of finding servants, which became particularly acute after the First
World War. Without servants, middle-class life became unviable in houses with
many stairs. Large numbers of middle-class Londoners now joined the exodus to
the more modern and convenient suburbs. The houses they left were split up into
multiple occupancy, with some becoming hostels and others providing single-room
accommodation for individuals or even families. Social decline was accompanied

---

* In 1845, Giles Clarke, who leased part of the Eton Estate, complained that, when he had sold
his interest in Primrose Hill: 'I expressly stipulated that the whole of the lands taken by the
crown should be forthwith fenced off from my land (of which I have about 150 acres immediately
adjoining the land in question). ... From that period, however, to the present time no steps have
been taken on the part of the crown towards fencing off the land agreed to be purchased and by
which I and my tenants have been subjected to the most serious loss and inconvenience.' Giles
Clarke to Office of Woods and Forests, 1 May 1845, National Archives, Work 16/180.

by physical decline, as the houses became blackened by the soot of coal fires, a problem added to by the constant smoke from the engines coaling at the Chalk Farm engine shed and from the six hundred trains passing every day.

10

Across the Hill

W HEN Primrose Hill became a park in 1842 there were few houses or other buildings near it. Twenty years after its opening, in 1862, the journalist George Rose Emerson gave an impression of the changes since the beginning of the century. He began by drawing an idealised portrait of its distant past, as part of a forest that had lasted undisturbed until the end of the eighteenth century: 'It is difficult even to recall later aspects of the place, when the rounded hillock was covered with primroses which gave it its name, and at its feet were swamps intersected by green lanes from Marylebone fields and Tottenham Court. Sixty years ago even the hill was as secluded and rural, as completely removed from the hum and bustle of a great city, as any Sussex or Devonshire hillock.'[1]

If Emerson failed to remember the large numbers of trippers from London who had frequented the hill in the eighteenth century, and the popularity of the Chalk Farm Tavern amongst duellists, he gave a good sense of what could be seen from the summit of Primrose Hill at the time:

Now, as we look Londonwards, we find that the metropolis has thrown out its arms and embraced us, not yet with a stifling clutch, but with ominous closeness. We do not look, as our grandfathers did, on waste uncultivated fields, where the hare still crouched and burrowed in silent safety, but on a charming picture, where art, indeed, has superseded uncultivated nature only to adorn it. A trim park, with green sward and shell paths, flower-patches and gymnasium, is immediately at our feet; then the narrow stream of the Regent's Canal, designed by Nash, but now in imminent hazard of being converted into a railway; and beyond spread, like a variegated carpet, the Regent's Park, with its broad walks, lakes, villas, and the gardens of the Zoological Society, the slender spires of St Katherine's Church and the massive dome of the Colosseum breaking the lines of the stately terraces marking the outline of the park.*

---

* This was written at a time when the plans to turn the Regent's Canal into a railway had not been abandoned. The spires of St Katherine's Church were those of the hospital of St Katharine on the Outer Circle beyond Gloucester Gate. It is now better known as the Danish Church. The

Whatever the attractions of Regent's Park to the south, on all other sides London was growing inexorably:

> In the background, like a dusky giant, lies the Great City, with its thousand spires and tall chimneys piercing to the cloud which overhangs the mighty mass. St John's Wood, spruce and trim, invades us on the right, and on the opposite side are huge railway stations, circular engine-factories, house upon house, and street upon street. We turn away from London, only to find that bricks and mortar are fast invading the pleasant Hampstead fields, dear to our boyhood for the buttercups and hedgerows, the myriads of wonderfully-coloured moths, and the lark singing far away in the blue expanse. A huge cutting traverses the valley at our feet, and pierces the bowels of the green hill, and the snorting and panting of mighty engines have long since scared away the lark and the goldfinch, the throstle and the thrush, for whom the cunning bird-catcher used to set his snares on this very spot. ... But the tall trees crowning the ridge of Hampstead Hill are yet untouched; there, too, is the spire of the church, still, as of old, a landmark; and away to our right, beyond the groves of Caen Wood, the white church of Highgate, gracefully conspicuous, overtops the sombre cedars of the cemetery; and we willingly forget, that further eastward, the once green slopes are crowded with houses, and that castellated prisons rear their dismal and defiant towers.[*]

Thirty years earlier, in 1830, a local magistrate had described the attractions of Primrose Hill. Turning from what could be seen from the hill to the hill itself, he recognised the opportunity it offered to the poor to escape from the noise and pollution of London, even if he combined this with a rose-tinted view of the innocent pleasures of an earlier generation:

> Until about twenty or thirty years ago, the fields around London ... were alive with players at cricket, trap-ball, foot-ball, prisoners' base, and other healthful and inspiriting amusements. At the present day, where the fields are not overrun with buildings, they are enclosed against the use of ancient and animating pastimes.[2]

Colosseum, designed by Decimus Burton to display a vast panorama of London, was on the same side of the Outer Circle beyond Chester Terrace. It was pulled down in 1875. Cambridge Place is now on its site. George Rose Emerson, *London: How the Great City Grew* (London, 1862), pp. 254–5.

[*]   Emerson was presumably referring to the five-winged Pentonville Prison, built in 1842; and Holloway Prison, built in 1852. The original Holloway, a mixed prison until 1903, was built in castellated style, with a grand turreted gateway. This was all swept away in the utilitarian rebuilding of the prison in the 1970s. Emerson, *London*, pp. 254–5.

There were two spots near London, however, 'on which some traces of the former cheerfulness are yet suffered to remain', Primrose Hill and Greenwich Hill:

> My observations have been chiefly drawn to Primrose Hill, and frequently have I climbed it, and enjoyed the stream of pure air that pours over it, in contrast with the murky atmosphere of the metropolis; and I delight to see the lower orders, as those are called who work, with their children, of a fine Sunday afternoon, effect their escape from the unwholesome air of the lanes, and alleys and workshops they toil in during the week, also climb this hill and run down it, and then toil up it again to run down it again, with more spirit than might be expected from their stinted and emaciated frames.[3]

He went on, however, to qualify this vision of a people's paradise with an alarming report of the dangers facing unaccompanied women on the hill:

> But the hill is free to all, to the blackguards, properly so called, as well as to decent people, and through the absence of all police, and under the pretence of fun, the blackguards are suffered to commit most shameful outrages. It is the practice of these ruffians, whenever unprotected young women walk over the hill, to come up behind them with a rope, or handkerchiefs tied together, to cast it round them, and drag them down the hill until they are thrown head over heels. ... I was on Primrose Hill upwards of an hour yesterday afternoon, and every young woman who walked up the hill, unless well protected, was subjected to this brutal treatment. ... There had not been a policeman near the hill all the afternoon, as I am informed; but I saw many of them uselessly parading in the promenades of Regent's Park. ... The presence of one or two policemen would keep ruffians within bounds, and enable the decent part of the commonalty to receive the benefit of air and exercise, and the enjoyment of innocent recreation, free from personal outrage.[4]

In this he was repeating a claim made twenty years previously, in 1808, which gave more credit to the police: 'The most indecent outrages are now frequently committed by a set of blackguards, in the fields near Primrose Hill, without regard to age or sex, and robberies not infrequently take place. The police officers, however, now exercise the utmost vigilance in that direction.'[5]

The mixture of innocent pleasure and occasional depravity reflects two aspects of the history of Primrose Hill. While a place of pleasure, exercise, relaxation, conversation and innocent amusement to most of the men, women and children who visited it, it also had a rougher side. This side can easily be made too much of, as most of those who crossed Primrose Hill without incident never recorded their experiences. Those involved in the unusual and criminal activities which found their way into the newspapers and court records of the day represent a tiny fraction of the hill's visitors.

The contrast between the reports of innocent pleasure and occasional depravity also reflects Primrose Hill's reputation as a place of popular rather than genteel amusement. Newspapers reflected the suspicions of their readers about the lower classes, especially now that the latter had acquired a taste for leisure. In July 1845 a newspaper reported on 'Cockney Sundays':

> If you want to see the Cockneys in their holiday suits, now is the time. If your conscience will permit you to take a walk ... it matters little which way you go; if the day be fine you will see the citizens lining the road by thousands, and spreading themselves over the green sward wherever they can find access to it. ... Primrose Hill is a living mass on a Sunday evening. Hampstead and Highgate have more inhabitants than their houses could contain.[6]

Newspapers in the first half of the nineteenth century repeatedly, and always condescendingly, associated Primrose Hill and Cockneys. 'The true Cockney has never travelled beyond the purlieus of the metropolis, either in body or spirit. Primrose Hill is the *ultima Thule* of his most romantic desires ...'[7]

While most people who visited the hill did so privately as individuals or in small groups, often as a family outing, Primrose Hill also had a public face. It was a place of public celebration, with firework displays drawing large crowds. It was used for military exercises, by the Volunteers during the Napoleonic Wars and from 1860, and by the Life Guards during much of the nineteenth century. It was also a place for public meetings, including those demanding political reform. During the first half of the nineteenth century it regularly attracted large numbers of people on public holidays and summer Sundays, with the Chalk Farm Fair at Easter and Whitsun being especially popular. Throughout this time, the Chalk Farm Tavern remained a notable place of entertainment, with large numbers of people enjoying a variety of entertainments.

Public celebrations with fireworks on Primrose Hill go back at least as far as the coronation on George IV in 1821, when a newspaper promised: 'At night, several of the largest rockets will be thrown up from Primrose Hill, by which light balls will be suspended by parachutes in the air, nearly a mile high, where they will continue to burn for many minutes, and will be visible from every part of the town.'[8]

The end of the Crimean War was marked by widespread rejoicing throughout Britain. This included a grand firework display on Primrose Hill in June 1856:

> It was generally rumoured throughout the metropolis that the fireworks on Primrose Hill would be on a scale of magnificence surpassing the other centres of attraction, and there was an immense concourse to witness the pyrotechnic display which was announced to take place. The persons assembled within the inclosure were mainly of the middle and lower classes, but there was a

Primrose Hill was a
well-known venue for
firework displays, with grand
displays being put on for the
coronation of George IV in
1821 and for the celebration
of the end of the Crimean
War in 1856, illustrated here.
(*Private Collection*)

much larger collection of 'roughs' than might have been anticipated. They
did not, however, occasion any annoyance to the more respectable portion of
the spectators; but having secured early in the evening such positions as they
deemed most favourable for viewing the fireworks, they amused themselves by
singing in chorus the 'Ratcatcher's Daughter', and other popular songs of the
same class, and by 'chaffing' one another. ... From a comparatively early part of
the evening there was a surprising flow of population, some in carriages, many
in cabs, omnibuses and vans, and most on foot. ... Along the road lining the
northern side of Regent's Park, ranks of vehicles, three deep, were drawn up,
and it required no small amount of patience, perseverance, and pilotage to steer
through their perilous interstices. In hundreds of instances were to be seen the
wives of the working classes, with children in their arms, and children around
them, seated along the rails which surround the hill, and well content, at the cost
of personal toil, with the opportunity of witnessing the national display.

The time appointed for the commencement of the display of fireworks was half-past nine o'clock, and just previously the wind, which blew from the eastward, freshened into a gentle gale, threatening to mar very materially the effect of those specimens of the pyrotechnic art upon which so much labour had been expended. Fortunately, however, the wind subsided, and the exhibition took place under the most favourable circumstances, for scarcely a breath of air influenced the flight of the aerial fireworks, while the darkness of the sky added greatly to their effect. From that moment, in quick and unremitting succession, discharges of rockets, pearl streamers, parachute-shells, mines, squibs, tailed stars, and tourbillions, continued till a quarter past eleven o'clock. The people seemed highly delighted with the manner in which the display had been effected, and they gave expression to their satisfaction in loud and frequent applause.[9]

While the coronation and Crimean fireworks were harmonious and officially sanctioned occasions, other gatherings and encounters on Primrose Hill and nearby were not. In 1790, three years before the outbreak of war in 1793, an attempt to press men for the navy had led to bloodshed:

A most violent affray took place in a field near Primrose Hill, leading to Hampstead, between a press gang and a number of young men who were enjoying the innocent recreations of the day. In the contest several were wounded desperately on each side; but numbers increasing, the gang was compelled to fly, not, however, until their leader was so severely bruised, as to require the assistance of his party to carry him off the field of action.[10]

Twenty years later, indignation at the part the army had recently played in putting down civil disturbances, at a time of widespread food riots, led to a sustained attack on five regular soldiers:

A considerable degree of popular displeasure has been expressed against the Life Guards, in consequence of their conduct during the late disturbances. ... On Sunday afternoon five of the Life Guardsmen, who were walking together on Primrose Hill, were assailed by a number of people collected there, in so serious a manner as to endanger their lives. They backed up against a ditch, and defended themselves with their swords until twenty-five of their comrades arrived to their assistance and rescued them.[11]

The French Revolution had brought both a sharp increase in Radical activity amongst its admirers in Britain, notably by the members of the London Corresponding Society, and a crack-down by the government on political meetings.[12] Although government suppression was at its height during the early years of the war with France, suspicion of Radicals, especially those from the working classes, formed the background to official reaction to popular demands until at least the middle of nineteenth century. The Radicals, in turn, countered official repression by protests, newspaper campaigns and rallies, culminating in a demand for the acceptance of the People's Charter. Although Radical activity slackened after 1800, it revived again after the end of the war in 1815 and the Peterloo Massacre of August 1819. Primrose Hill was reported as a Radical training ground in the November of that year:

> Next Monday week is said to be the day of meeting in Smithfield market place. Those who intend to go armed to the meeting, it is said, will carry pistols openly in belts, and swords by their sides, It is reported that a number of the Radicals, who call themselves the Physical Force men, meet regularly to instruct each other in the manual exercise, and on Sunday morning last numbers were practising the military exercise near Primrose Hill.[13]

After the passing of the Reform Bill in 1832, the Radicals campaigned for the removal of the tax, aimed at working-class readers, on newspapers. A meeting called by the Radical Association of Marylebone was held on Primrose Hill on Easter Monday, 11 April 1836. 'Great exertions had been made by the Radicals of the metropolis for many days previous, to ensure what they termed "an overwhelming expression of public opinion", upon the necessity of the entire abolition of the duty on newspapers.'[14] To the amusement of a reporter, who arrived after 'walking nearly up to his knees in mud through two fields', the weather limited the turn-out to the Radical Association's leaders and a few enthusiasts, together with

> several nurserymaids with children in their arms and attached to their gowns, a few of the holiday folks, a considerable number of itinerant dealers in ginger-beer, nuts and oranges, bearing their wares before them, many of the labourers engaged on the Birmingham Railroad, and others, in all from 150 to 200 living beings.[15]

The largest Radical meeting of the decade on the hill was addressed by a maverick Chartist and ex-Wesleyan minister, the Reverend J.R. Stephens.[16] On Sunday 12 May 1839 he held three political meetings in London, at Shepherd and Shepherdess Fields, at Kennington Common, and on Primrose Hill. At the meeting on the hill, in what was ostensibly a sermon, Stephens protested vehemently against the highly unpopular New Poor Law of 1834, which he saw as a deliberate attack on the working classes:

> He said he would never acknowledge the power of Parliament to pass the New Poor Law, and, so help him God, he never would. He never would pay rates under it. His chairs, his tables, everything he had, might be sold, the house might be

pulled down over his head, but he would not acknowledge that law. Everything might be taken from him, except his wife, his child, and his life. If necessary he would repel force by force – he would resort to the knife and the bullet – he would sell his life sooner than obey the law.[17]

Repeated use of such inflammatory language led to his prosecution, in August 1839, and imprisonment for eighteen months in Chester Castle.

The Chartist movement of the late 1830s and the 1840s drew mass support from working men across Britain. The People's Charter, issued in 1838, demanded universal male suffrage, a secret ballot, annual elections to Parliament and the payment of MPs. It was promoted over the following decade by Radical newspapers, mass meetings and petitions, the largest of which had over three million signatures. Most of its activities were peaceful, though it was tarred in the eyes of the propertied by a minority of extremists, such as John Frost and Feargus O'Connor, who advocated strikes and violence. In 1848, a year that saw the outbreak of revolution across much of Europe, the Chartists held two great rallies on Kennington Common on 10 April and 12 June, when the government recruited a hundred thousand special constables to counter the threat of disorder. In the event, the days went off peaceably and proved to be the high-water mark of Victorian Radicalism.[18]

A large rally on Primrose Hill in 1856 harked back to earlier times, rather than presenting any sort of threat to law and order or to the government. It celebrated the release of the Chartist John Frost, a Radical martyr who had been sentenced to be hanged, drawn and quartered for levying war against the queen by leading a short-lived Chartist rising in Newport, Monmouthshire, in 1839: the last armed rising against the government on the British mainland. His sentence was commuted to transportation for life to Van Dieman's Land.[19] Pardoned in 1854, Frost returned to Britain in 1856. A march through central London and the City to celebrate his return was held in September 1856 but failed to attract mass support, though a good number turned out on Primrose Hill, the march's final destination. *The Times* reported the event with a mixture of disdain and self-congratulation:

Under the pretext of presenting an address of congratulation to this person on his liberation from slavery and exile (to which he was sentenced for the remainder of his life), an attempt was made for the moment to drag the Charter, with all its bitter reminiscences, from the oblivion to which it has long been consigned; and for several hours, in the height of the day, the continuous current of traffic which pours through the thoroughfares of this great city was obstructed by a political procession. Perhaps in no capital in Europe, except that of England (which these men count unworthy of them), would such a demonstration have been tolerated, composed, as it was, of men whose open and avowed object is to overturn the whole political constitution of the country in which they live, and to substitute one propounded by themselves.[20]

The greatest turnout of the century on the hill, matched only by that for the victory firework display for the end of the Crimean War, was not to express Radical demands but to show support for a foreign hero, Giuseppe Garibaldi, whose defence of Rome against the French in 1849 had caught the popular imagination in England. As the liberal and nationalist opponent of the pope, Garibaldi appealed to Protestant Londoners, who regarded the papacy as the epitome of clerical and political reaction.[21] Described by the Radical *Reynolds's Newspaper* as 'the greatest man by whom England has ever been visited', Garibaldi had arrived at Nine Elms Station on 11 April 1864.[22] His progress by carriage to Stafford House, where he was to stay as the guest of the Duke of Sutherland, took five hours to cover three miles, such was the size of the crowd that greeted him. Over the next ten days, Garibaldi was fêted by high society and met all the leading politicians of the day, as well as the Prince of Wales (though not Queen Victoria, who disapproved strongly of revolutionaries). On his way into the opera at Covent Garden, 'Women, more or less in full dress, flew upon him, seized his hands, touched his beard, his poncho, his trousers, any part of them they could reach.'[23] A national tour including all of Britain's major cities was planned for him, when, suddenly and unexpectedly, he left the country.

Garibaldi's departure without explanation, other than for alleged reasons of health, led to the suspicion that he had been made to leave.[24] A crowd, estimated by the police at hundred thousand, met on the hill for a pro-Garibaldi rally on 23 April 1864, protesting at what they thought was the arbitrary expulsion of their hero. It coincided with a meeting for planting an oak in commemoration of the tercentenary of Shakespeare's birth, though scheduled to start after it. Both events were organised by the Working Men's Shakespeare Committee.

Although the Shakespeare meeting had been officially authorised, that for Garibaldi had not. This led to the police banning any speeches by the committee organising the rally. According to Police Inspector Stokes:

> At 5.45 p.m. (after the ceremony) a large number of persons assembled on the top of the hill, and several men, calling themselves 'the Working Men's Committee', were in the centre, one of whom was standing on a seat addressing the people, to the effect that 'Garibaldi was sent home by the English Government to please the French Emperor'. I, accompanied by a sergeant and two constables, went to him. I said I wished to speak to him. He got off the seat, and I told him he could not be allowed to address any meeting there.[25]

Although the chairman, the highly respectable barrister Edmond Beales, agreed to disband the meeting without further speeches, the affair raised important questions about the right to public assembly.

A letter from Robert Hartwell, the secretary of the Working Men's Shakespeare Committee, expressed the point. He protested that the

> interference and violence of the police was uncalled for and unconstitutional. The meeting had been openly convened, the proceedings had commenced, the greatest order prevailed, and there was not any, the slightest, symptom of disturbance until after the police had refused to allow the chairman to continue his address; and there can be no doubt but for the police interference the meeting would have passed off as quietly as did the proceedings about an hour previous, on the same spot, connected with the Shakespeare Commemoration.*

The right of the public to meet and to express their political views, however unwelcome these were to the government, was proclaimed repeatedly at or near Primrose Hill between the meeting of the London Corresponding Society at the Chalk Farm Tavern in 1794 and the Garibaldi rally of 1864. It was a right only finally conceded by the government following riots in Hyde Park in 1866 and 1867. By this date, however, there was little appetite for revolution anywhere in England.

Non-political gatherings on or near Primrose Hill were often more violent than political ones. Chalk Farm Fair, held at Easter and Whitsun, had a well-earned reputation for boisterous behaviour. In May 1853 a St Marylebone court was 'crowded in consequence of its having become known that, owing to an alarming riot at Chalk Farm, Primrose Hill, Regent's Park, some soldiers and others had been guilty of most ruffianly behaviour towards the police'.[26] In the dock were two soldiers, Edward Bowerman, a private in the Grenadier Guards, and George Murden, a private in the Coldstream Guards, and four labourers. A policeman who had tried to arrest Bowerman, who was drunk and who had used a whip to strike a lady and gentleman, had been knocked down. Things soon escalated into a general brawl:

> A great many more constables arrived without loss of time at the spot, and several of them were seriously injured by stones and other missiles, which were thrown at them from all directions. The two soldiers were the most ruffianly-conducted of the whole party by whom the police were attacked. The rest of the prisoners

---

* The willingness of Edmond Beales to obey a questionable police instruction not to address the Garibaldi rally was a far cry from the early days of the London Radicalism. *The Times*, 25 April 1864; see also, ibid., 26 and 28 April, 6, 7 and 12 May 1864.

PLATE 15 Postcards provide the best visual record of Primrose Hill in the years before the First World War. The view from the top of the hill about 1910. (*Private Collection*)

PLATE 16 A view of the top of Primrose Hill, with benches and a grove of trees. (*Private Collection*)

PLATE 17 Engines steaming near the Round House in the early years of the twentieth century.
(*Private Collection*)

PLATE 18 St George's Terrace, showing the small statue of Shakespeare on the outside the Queens.
The pub opened in 1854. (*Private Collection*)

PLATE 19 Regent's Park Gardens before the First World War, showing its separate access road. This fine terrace, demolished in the 1960s, had a mews behind it. (*Private Collection*)

PLATE 20 Fitzroy Road before the advent of the car. (*Private Collection*)

PLATE 21 Mabel Dearmer (1872–1915)

PLATE 22 Percy Dearmer (1867–1936)

The Dearmer family, who lived from 1907 in the vicarage of St Mary the Virgin
Primrose Hill at 7 Elsworthy Road, lost two of its members in the First World War.
(*Juliet Woollcombe*)

PLATE 23 Geoffrey Dearmer (1893–1996)

PLATE 24 Christopher Dearmer (1894–1915)

PLATE 25 The twin-engined Junkers 88 bomber, shot down by night-time anti-aircraft fire, which landed on Primrose Hill. RAF men prepare it for removal, 10 October 1940. (*Imperial War Museum*)

PLATE 26 A rangefinder on Primrose Hill in 1940. Later in the war there was a radar-net at the back of the hill. (*Imperial War Museum*)

PLATE 27 One of the single-barrelled 4.5 inch anti-aircraft guns on Primrose Hill in 1940. The guns, installed in 1939, contributed to the defence of London during the Blitz. (*Imperial War Museum*)

PLATE 28 One of the later twin-barrelled 5.25 inch anti-aircraft guns used on Primrose Hill. Photographed by Lieutenant Taylor on 27 August 1943. (*Imperial War Museum*)

PLATE 29 Lance-Bombardier Harold Danks, an anti-aircraft gunner on Primrose Hill between May 1940 and February 1941. His diary records life there during the Blitz. A photograph taken in early 1942, at Cardington Cross, Bedfordshire, shortly after he left the hill. (*Imperial War Museum*)

PLATE 30 Sigmund Freud (1856–1939) in the garden of 39 Elsworthy Road.
He lived there from June to September 1938, after arriving in London from Vienna via Paris, before
moving to Maresfield Gardens in Hampstead. Here Freud is being presented by Griffith Davies with
the Charter Book of the Royal Society, for his signature, on 23 June 1938. (*Freud Museum*)

joined in the outrage, and some of them used their best exertions to rescue those who were legally in custody. Many of the police were injured by the missiles which had been hurled at them.[27]

Sentencing the soldiers to four months in the house of correction, the magistrate, Mr Broughton, 'strongly expressed his opinion as to the necessity of doing away as speedily as possible with so great a nuisance as Chalk Farm Fair'.[28]

On Easter Monday 1852, the flamboyant Victorian journalist George Augustus Sala visited Chalk Farm Fair on a bright April day, with a strong wind 'eddying round corners viciously, catching nursemaids cunningly and drifting them all, drapery, ribbons, parasols and baby, against old gentlemen of mysogynic appearance; smiting little boys on the hip, and savagely sending their caps into interminable space, and their hoops between the legs of grown-up people'.

> The fair ground was not extensive, on this Easter Monday. It was an anomalous, irregular-shaped patch of broken ground, resembling a dust-heap on a large scale, somewhat; bounded on the north by Primrose Hill; on the south by the railway bridge; on east and west, and on all intermediate points of the compass, by unfinished houses, and fantastic traceries of scaffold-poles. There were booths where the traditional kings, queens and cocks in gilt gingerbread were dispensed; and where, in gaily decorated tin canisters, the highly-spiced nuts appealed to the senses of the holiday makers. There were shabby little pavilions, stuck all over in front with the profiles of gentlemen with very black features and coats, and very white shirt-collars: together with a stock offer in moustaches, a vermillion habit, and epaulettes like knockers; the whole being intended to give you an extensive idea of the resources of the 'Royal Chalk Farm Artist's Studio', where you could have your portrait taken by the instantaneous magic process for sixpence – a fact that the artist himself (in a wideawake hat and a blouse) seemed never weary of reiterating.*

---

* *Household Words: A Weekly Journal Conducted by Charles Dickens*, Saturday 8 May 1852, pp. 165–6. The article continues: 'There were Royal Pavilion Theatres and Royal Cobourg Saloons and Royal Amphitheatres, where the story of woebegone clowns, dirt, rouge, tarnished spangles, and soiled fleshings, was told for the thousandth time. There were a "giant and a dwarf", some "bounding brothers", a "bottle equilibrist", a "strong man", a "professor of necromancy" and a "sword and ribbon swallower". There were weighing-machines, "sticks" (the speculation of swarthy gipsies), at which you might throw for pincushion prizes and never get any; and there were Swiss bell-ringers, Ethiopian serenaders, juveniles, who turned over three times, or threw "cartwheels" for a penny; sellers of cakes, sweet-stuff, tarts, damaged fruits, slang songs, whistles, catcalls, and penny trumpets. Finally, there were many swings, roundabouts, and turnovers, which, crammed to overflowing with men, children, and women, revolved, oscillated, or performed demi-summersaults incessantly; the motive power being given by brawny varlets in corduroys and ankle-jacks. Add to this a little fortune-telling, a

The Chalk Farm Tavern itself had a reputation for hosting sports, often drawing sizeable crowds and with betting one of the main attractions. While events also included races and cricket matches, as well as the use of the 'target' for shooting competitions, the best-documented sport there was wrestling. Competitions put on by the Society of Cumberland and Westmorland Wrestlers at Easter and Whitsun in the 1830s drew sizeable crowds. Many of the wrestlers were soldiers, with other soldiers supporting them, but the contests seem to have been good-humoured, with a prize-giving dinner afterwards at the tavern.[29] In other years Cornish wrestling was on offer instead.[30]

In 1850 the landlord of the tavern announced a new race ground at Chalk Farm on a poster: 'Mr Price begs leave to inform his friends and the public that the splendid grounds (adjoining Primrose Hill) will be opened for foot races for the Whitsuntide Holidays and will be continued throughout the season.'[31] On Whit Monday that year Mr Robert Makepeace, the 'American Stag', was to leap over one thousand hurdles, ten yards apart and three feet six inches high, in three hours and five minutes, 'one of the greatest feats ever attempted by man'.[32] On the following day a silver watch was offered to the winner of a novices walking match over seven miles and a silver snuff box to the winner of a mile handicap race.[33]

Other amusements at the tavern included magical shows starring Monsieur

---

little fighting, and a great deal of music, noise, and bellowing, with a great deal of dust to cap all, and you will have a fairish notion of Chalk Farm Fair on Easter Monday.

Imagine in this broken, dusty, confined patch of building-ground, a compact, wedged-in, fighting, screaming, yelling, blaspheming crowd. All manner of human rubbish licensed to be shot there. There was more crime, more depravity, more drunkenness and blasphemy; more sweltering, raging and struggling in the dusty, mangy backyard of a place, than in a whole German principality. ... You could not move, or try to move, ten paces without hearing the Decalogue broken in its entirety – the whole Ten Tables smashed at a blow. By sturdy ruffians, with dirty "kingsman" 'kerchiefs twisted round their bullnecks like halters, with foul pipes stuck in their mouths, and bludgeons in their hands, jostling savagely through the crowd, six and eight abreast, with volleys of oaths and drunken songs. By slatternly, tawdry, bold-faced women, ever and anon falling to fighting with one another; and in a ring formed by a "fancy", composed of pickpockets, costermongers, and other intense blackguards, clawing, biting, pulling each other's hair, rending each other's garments, giving in at last breathless, almost sightless, all besmeared with blood and dust. By some of the defenders of their country with their side-belts (happily bayonetless) all robbed of pipeclay, and besmirched with beer-stains. By beggars and tramps, shoeless boys and girls, thieves, low prize-fighters, silly "gents" and here and there, perhaps, a decent mechanic, or little tradesman, who has taken his family to the Fair, in sheer ignorance, and expectation of some innocent entertainment out of doors.' For Sala's authorship of articles in *Household Words*, see *Household Words: A Weekly Journal, 1850–1859, Conducted by Charles Dickens: Table of Contents, List of Contributors and their Contributions*, compiled by Anne Lohrli (Toronto, 1973), pp. 421–6. For Sala's rackety but highly productive career, see 'George Augustus Sala (1828–95)', *Oxford Dictionary of National Biography*.

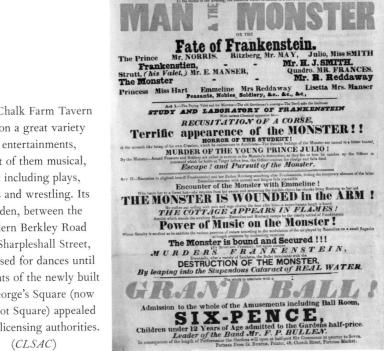

The Chalk Farm Tavern put on a great variety of entertainments, most of them musical, but including plays, races and wrestling. Its garden, between the modern Berkley Road and Sharpleshall Street, was used for dances until residents of the newly built St George's Square (now Chalcot Square) appealed to the licensing authorities. (*CLSAC*)

Davitzer, the 'Great Wizard'; and *Man and the Monster: or The Fate of Frankenstein*, a 'romantic Ballet of Action in Two Acts', with Mr R. Reddaway as the Monster. After many harrowing episodes, including the murder of Prince Julio and the abduction of the heroine, Emmeline, the Monster is charmed by the power of music and his ferocity soothed by an 'air played by Emmeline on a small flageolet'. He allows himself to be bound but breaks free again and murders Frankenstein, only being finally destroyed when he leaps into a 'Stupendous Cataract of Real Water'.[34] A Whitsun Bazaar in 1850 combined a Royal Quilt Exhibition with Mr Thompson, 'the King of the Tambourine Performers', playing on ten tambourines, and Mr Gellene's 'much admired Nondescript Dance'. The entertainment included tableaux vivants of marble statues, ranging from the murder of Abel to the execution of Charles I.[35]

Nearly all entertainments at the tavern ended with music, with concerts in the garden ('supported by a double company of vocalists') or a 'grand ball' ('admission to the whole of the amusements including ball room sixpence'). While this caused little trouble when the tavern stood alone, or almost alone, in the fields at the foot of Primrose Hill, it inevitably brought on complaints from the residents of the nearby houses built in the 1840s and 1850s.

In 1860 a petition from local residents in the newly built Chalcot Square, then called St George's Square, to the Middlesex Quarter Sessions, asked for the entertainment licence not to be renewed. It set out their grievances:

> That fronting the said Chalk Farm Tavern is a small piece of land or garden ground of about three quarters of an acre in extent which belongs to the same tavern and which some time since was enclosed by a brick wall.
>
> That during the present summer and autumn entertainments have been given in the same garden ground at which a band of music plays in an elevated tent open to all sides from an early hour in the evening until a very late hour at night with very slight intermission – that in addition to such music some acrobat has been engaged for and has walked or performed upon a rope suspended from elevated positions in the midst of fireworks accompanied by a band of music and by great tumult at a very late hour at night.
>
> That rockets and other fireworks of a dangerous and alarming kind have upon the same occasions and at or near midnight been discharged from the same gardens and in such a careless and dangerous manner that burning sticks and sockets belonging thereto have descended in the gardens of the houses of St George's Square and your petitioner has now in his possession two of such rocket sticks and sockets which descended in the garden of the house no. 9 and he was informed that another fell in the front area of the house no. 7 St George's Square so as to endanger life and even to injure one person.
>
> That such entertainments bring together a large number of bad characters of both sexes, who conduct themselves in a very noisy and offensive manner, and after such entertainments amuse themselves by pulling bells and wrenching off bell handles lowering the character of the neighbourhood and most seriously deteriorating the value of the property.[36]

In the face of united local opposition, it is not surprising that not long afterwards the Chalk Farm Tavern's garden was sold off for housing.* Two roads with housing dating from the 1860s, Berkley Road and Sharpleshall Street, preserve the outline of the old gardens, while the stables of Eglon Mews filled its interior until converted first into a lathe-making business and then into an early motor car works at the turn of the century.[37]

---

* The licensee of the Chalk Farm Tavern saw it in a much more positive light: 'Chalk Farm Tavern, near Primrose Hill. Season 1860. The public are informed that these delightful and popular gardens are open during the summer, for a succession of galas and fêtes on a scale of splendour never before attempted. The beautifully decorated Chinese Orchestra is 36 feet high, and tastefully illuminated with profusions of variegated lamps, Chinese lanterns etc, together with a Leviathan platform, capable of accommodating a thousand persons.' Heal Collection, A IX, 22.

An impression of what the hill was like on a busy day in 1875 has been left by an Italian, Giuseppe Maria Campanella, then living near to the hill at No. 13 St John's Terrace, at the western end of Adelaide Road. Campanella was a political exile from Italy after the failure of the revolution of 1848. He was a talented singer who had once sung in the choir of the Sistine Chapel.

> To the right is the well-known Primrose Hill, which commands one of the best views of the great metropolis. From its summit the eye ranges over the immense mass of houses, public buildings, and churches. Regent's Park is seen just below you towards the south, with its Zoological and Botanical Gardens. ... The rising of the sun from Primrose Hill, with all the interesting associations, is not to be described; it must be seen to have an idea of its interest and grandeur.[*]

Campanella described how far Primrose Hill had come from the days of duelling and of the rough behaviour described by George Augustus Sala:

> It is well worth to be present at some of these popular English holiday meetings, which take place six or eight times in the course of the year, and to be one amongst them. But above all on the three days of Easter. Then in fine weather you would see these people clean and homely in dress – father and mother, with their whole family, baby and all, with or without perambulator – seated in family groups on the slopes of Primrose Hill, in the simple, but, to them, only too rare enjoyment of the fresh air and the warm sunshine. Some girls and boys enjoyed running down the steepest part of the hill, arriving out of breath at the bottom. Boys performed feats of gymnastics on cross-bars, placed there for the purpose; a man and his wife or two men swing long ropes, and young children tried how often they could jump. It was surprising to see how well some of them kept time. My wife and I enjoyed walking up and down amongst them, for we saw they did not notice us at all, so full were they of the rare enjoyment.
>
> It was a surprise and pleasure to me, as an Italian, to see how the English, on festive occasions, like these, keep order amongst themselves. Not a *gendarme* – not a national guard – not one spy. Nor, at that time, did we see even English policemen; and the people that day, we were assured, had numbered 20,000.[38]

Campanella's view confirmed that of Frederick Miller, an early historian of St Pancras, published the previous year:

---

[*] Giuseppe Maria Campanella, *An Italian on Primrose Hill: A Narrative* (London, 1875), pp. 6, 7. Campanella had fled Italy after taking part in Daniel Manin's defence of Venice against the Austrians. Giuseppe Maria Campanella, *My Life and What I Learnt in It* (London, 1874), pp. 279–375. Campanella published a second part of his autobiography, catering to Victorian suspicions of the pope and of monastic orders, as *Life in the Cloister, in the Papal Court and in Exile* (London, 1877).

Forty, thirty, even but twenty years go, Primrose Hill was the resort of the roughest and rudest classes of people, at holiday time and on Sundays. A certain class of caterers for the bodily wants of the multitude then made a din with their cries, the remembrance of which contrasts most unfavourably with the conduct of the orderly law-abiding people who now frequent the hill and repose on the grass or on the excellent seats around its summit.[39]

As opposed to the semi-professional events organised by and near the Chalk Farm Tavern, amateur sport was a feature of Primrose Hill both before and after it became a park. In April 1873, William Smee gave an account of the limitations on the games played on the hill. He bewailed the number of boys and young men who were unable to find sufficient space to play football or cricket:

Primrose Hill Park is very much used by boys as a cricket or football ground, and on Saturdays there is not enough space. Even today, with the ground wet and the weather not inviting, it was full, and in the summer months boys go away because there is not room to play.[40]

On Saturdays, the young of more than half a million people come to Primrose Hill, or would come if there were space. This afternoon there were between two thousand and three thousand, and if the day had been finer there would have been many more.[41]

If most people's experience of Primrose Hill was of peaceful and innocent enjoyment, free from any kind of trouble, there were also unusual events on the hill over the years. Unlike the anonymous, everyday experiences of mainstream visitors, these incidents, crimes and tragedies attracted notice at the time, in the newspapers and the courts, and have left a record of what happened very largely lacking for uneventful visits.

It would be difficult to find a more unusual incident than that reported in the press in August 1850:

On Monday morning about nine o'clock, two young buffaloes were being driven from the terminus of the Great Western Railway at Paddington; when in the Edgware Road some sweeps shaking a soot bag alarmed them, and they started at a terrific pace in the direction of Lisson Grove. Several persons were knocked down and seriously injured, and a Mrs Le Blanc, of Alpha Cottages, had her ribs fractured. The animals dashed through Regent's Park into Primrose Hill Park, leaping fences with the greatest ease, and were not secured till 10 o'clock at night, and after seven persons had been seriously injured.[42]

Crime on the hill, however rare statistically, has of course left a more vivid record than innocent recreation. Primrose Hill's reputation for disorder and violence, however, diminished over the nineteenth century, undoubtedly reflecting growing civility in the population at large. Even after the Chalk Farm Fair went into decline in the 1850s, there was still occasional rough behaviour on hill. In August 1866 two doctors were walking up the hill, 'where about two hundred and fifty people, most of them respectably dressed men, women, and children, were enjoying the evening. There appeared to be no meeting of any kind, and the appearance of the hill was the same as on any other evening.'[43] As they were returning, however,

> A crowd of thirty or forty boys, of between fourteen and eighteen years of age, came running round the hill, and as soon as they came near us a dead cat was flung at one of us, knocking off his hat, which was at once seized by some boys and pulled about. Remonstrances were answered by a volley of gravel and dirt into our faces, so that the only course open to us was to run down as fast as possible to the gate.[44]

Chased down the hill by some of the boys, and fighting their way through others coming up to meet them, the two men reached 'the wide path on the lower part of the hill, where we met some people who shared our indignation at such treatment, but were unable to help us against such a number of roughs'. After losing the hat and an umbrella, the men sought refuge in the nearest public house, 'where for some time we heard the yells of the boys, evidently waiting for our reappearance'.[45]

There were annual Guy Fawkes Night celebrations on 5 November. While mostly peaceful and good-humoured, these could also be marked by disorder. In 1868 W.C. Galloway reported:

> Last evening, about 8'oclock, a friend of mine and myself, like many others, went on to Primrose Hill to see the fireworks. After we had been there about half an hour we were suddenly set upon by from a dozen to fifteen roughs. Before I had time to raise an arm in self-defence I was knocked down and robbed of all the money about me. My friend fortunately managed to escape. Afterwards he accompanied me to the Albany Street police station, where we were treated with coolness by the sergeant who took the charge, and on telling him that others had received a similar treatment he took the precaution of sending one policeman to the hill. This man, who returned with us, when he arrived at the gates met two other members of the force, who informed him that a riot was going on, and that it was unsafe to venture on the hill; he accordingly ventured no further.[46]

Nor is vandalism a modern invention. A local resident complained in 1877: 'I reside near Primrose Hill, which is provided with a number of handsome lamps, and it is really deplorable to see the number which are deliberately broken. A short time since I counted close upon two hundred panes, and taking twelve consecutive lamps I found that thirty-two panes of glass out of forty-eight were broken – smashed to pieces.'[47]

Along with its reputation for duelling, Primrose Hill had a lesser notoriety, dating back to the eighteenth century, as a place for armed robberies, though there were many more robberies on the Hampstead road than on the hill itself. In November 1764

> A gentleman on his return to town was robbed on Primrose Hill, near Hampstead, by three men in soldiers' cloaths, of eight guineas and some silver, which they were not contented with, but afterwards stripped and bound him to a tree and there left him; he was afterwards released by some persons passing by, who gave him a waistcoat to preserve him from the inclemency of the weather.[48]

Forty years later, in 1802,

> A few days since, as a gentleman was coming to town from Kilburn Wells, crossing a field near Chalk Farm, a man rushed up to him from behind a tree, with a pistol in his hand, who demanded the gentleman's money. The gentleman had only eighteen pence on him. The fellow not being satisfied with this, searched his pockets, and took a spectacle case from him. The gentleman entreated very much to have it back, as his eyes were dim, and he had business to transact in town, which he could not transact without them. They were accordingly returned.[49]

In September 1821 Thomas Fitzgerald, aged thirty-one, was tried for robbery at the Old Bailey. Nicholas Peters, an infirm elderly gentleman, had been walking near Primrose Hill on the afternoon of 10 August when Fitzgerald presented a large horse-pistol to his breast and demanded his money. Peters, who was terrified, immediately gave him four shillings, which was all the money he had about him. Fitzgerald then said: 'You have got a watch; I must have that also'; and Peters gave it to him. Fitzgerald tried to pawn the watch the same day, but left it on the counter when questioned. Subsequently arrested by a Bow Street patrol, Fitzgerald was convicted and sentenced to death.[50]

In an echo of the duels that had made Primrose Hill famous, two greengrocers from Portland Town, Thomas Birmingham and a man named Good, quarrelled in 1847 about 'the amount of business done at their respective shops'. Accompanied by four other men, the two settled their differences 'in a field near Primrose Hill, it being then eleven o'clock at night'. They fought one round, at the end of which both were on the ground. 'Good rose immediately, but while the deceased was striving to do so he fell again, as it was supposed from a blow struck by Good'. Birmingham was picked up in an insensible state and never recovered consciousness. Although there was no obvious external injury, Mr Britton, a surgeon, gave the cause of death as a rupture of the right lateral sinus of the brain. Good was charged with manslaughter.[51]

Sexual crimes, though uncommon, were not unknown. In 1810 it was reported that:

> For some days past a fellow genteely dressed in black has infested the fields in Marylebone, to the annoyance and terror of ladies who are so unlucky as to meet him. Two young ladies out of Baker Street, and a little boy, were indecently accosted by the monster on Wednesday morning, in the fields leading from Portland Road to Primrose Hill, and he literally tore the cloaths off one of their backs, and brutally scourged her with a switch. The other young lady was treated in a manner too indecent to be described. Some ladies from a boarding-school were molested by the same fellow in the fields on Monday.[52]

Other sexual offences brought prosecutions: In 1825, for instance, 'The court was occupied a considerable time in trying an old wretch named Nash, for atrocious practices with a soldier at Primrose Hill. ... The evidence for this was of that very disgusting nature, that we, in common with every person in court, were happy when the trial terminated.'[53]

A highly unpleasant case showed that paedophilia is not simply a modern phenomenon.[54] On Saturday 18 August 1900 Florence and Amy Hobart, aged eight and six, of Crogsland Road, Chalk Farm, were playing near the gymnasium on Primrose Hill, when Harry Hope, a twenty-eight-year-old porter, of Orchard Street, Westminster, came up to them and, holding up a pear, said, 'Who wants this?' Florence

> replied that she would like it and he gave it to her, at the same time giving one to her sister. He then said that he would take the latter for a little ride down the street and thereupon took her by the hand and led her away. The witness stayed where she was for the some time, but when she saw them getting on an omnibus she tried to overtake them.[55]

Hope took Amy by train to Chingford:

> The compartment was empty, and on the way he tore off some of her underclothes, threw them out of the window, and beat her. He behaved in an outrageous manner towards her ... and when she resisted he beat her with a stick, tied her hands and feet together, and thrust something into her mouth to prevent her screaming. During his violence he also forced all her front teeth down her throat.[56]

Amy was lucky to be found alive the following morning in Chingford Forest. Abrasions and bruises showed clearly that 'an attempt had been made to outrage her'.[57] Hope was swiftly arrested. Convicted on 11 September of 'unlawfully taking Amy Hobart ... with intent that she should be carnally known', Hobart was sentenced to two years' hard labour.[58]

Not all violence was directed at other people. In August 1795 it was reported that 'Last Tuesday the body of a man was found in a pond near Chalk Farm. Four £10 bank notes, three guineas, and three halfpence, were found in his pockets. He proves to be a native of Switzerland, and was lately dismissed from the service of Lord Stanhope.'[59] In 1807 a double tragedy was narrowly averted:

> On Saturday last a gentleman's servant, who was out of place, was discovered hanging from some railing over a hollow, in a field near Primrose Hill. An unfortunate indigent female, who first saw the body in that situation, procured assistance, and had it cut down. She afterwards attended the inquest, which was held at the Volunteer, at the top of Baker Street. From different circumstances that came out before the jury, it was thought that poverty and a weak mind was the cause of the rash act. The jury, therefore, humanely gave their verdict as Lunacy. The woman who first saw him appeared both at that time, and at the time of the inquest, to be very much afflicted; but the shock appeared most strangely to operate in an inverse ratio on her mind, for on Tuesday morning she hung herself in the very same spot. She happened to be discovered in time, and her life was saved.[60]

The discovery of what he intended to do came too late to save the victim of another sad history played out on the hill and at the Chalk Farm Tavern. On 21 June 1828,

> About eleven o'clock, a very respectably attired elderly gentleman was observed pacing Primrose Hill, apparently in deep meditation, and alone. ... Shortly after, the waiter at the tavern, and several gentlemen, observed the same individual descending the banks of the target bank towards the house. On his arrival, he appeared cheerful in his manner, and walked about the gardens for about half an hour, when on observing the waiter at the entrance to the tavern he, addressing him, asked if he could rest himself in that room (pointing to the Assembly Room), as he was fatigued, having walked a long distance.[61]

Shown up to the room, the gentleman ordered a pint of red wine and mutton chops. When the waiter went to lay the cloth for the meal, he found the door locked. Climbing onto the balcony in front of the window, he 'saw the gentleman still sitting at the table, with the decanter, and a phial and some white paper before him'. Upon the waiter threatening to force the door, the gentleman opened it and exclaimed, 'I am dying; I have taken arsenic for soda powders.' A surgeon, Mr Curtis of Camden Town, came quickly and administered an emetic. The gentleman had meanwhile produced a card with his name: Mr Dupin of 30 South Bank, Regent's Park, and 6 Cecil Street, Strand. Conveyed by a coach to South Bank, Dupin 'lingered in the most excruciating agony till eight o'clock, when he expired in the presence of several members of his family'.[62]

On the morning of 4 May 1861, as James Glover, a bricklayer, 'was proceeding to his work over Primrose Hill, he observed a respectably dressed man on the eastern side, near the Eton Cricket Ground, deliberately place a loaded pistol to his right ear. A loud report followed, and the man fell dead instantly.'[63] Fashionably dressed, with gold studs in his shirt, the man had a piece of paper in his pocket which read: 'Friend: you who shall find this body take it to the nearest public house, and deliver the letters as addressed.' One was to a Roman Catholic priest, Mr Eyre, of Hill Street, who recognised the handwriting as belonging to Richard Goring, of Hamilton Street, Camden Town. The other was to George Goring, an engineer in Limehouse. 'From the contents of the letter addressed to the Reverend Mr Eyre, that gentleman is led to believe that the cause of the commission of this desperate act was a love affair in which the unfortunate man had been disappointed.'[*]

Death caused by natural agencies was also not unknown on the hill. A strange sequence of events led to a death in 1805:

> On Monday evening, as a gentleman and lady were walking across the fields from Hampstead road to Primrose Hill, they met a person of gentlemanly appearance, who flew at the lady and grasped her round the neck. The gentleman was astonished at the stranger's conduct, and concluded that he was a lunatic; but while in the act of attempting to disengage him, the unfortunate man fell and expired in a fit. It has since appeared that he was a gentleman who was on a visit at Hampstead for his health.[64]

In July 1849, an inquest was held into the death of James Stewart, aged thirty-three. On the previous Sunday, Stewart had been 'on the top of Primrose Hill, nearly all the day, exposed to the sun, selling ginger beer, and about five o'clock in the evening he was observed to drop suddenly upon the earth'. Mr Bail, a surgeon who examined him, pronounced that he had died from 'a sun stroke or *coup de soleil*'.[65]

Seen from the point of view of the park management, it was not the criminal, the unusual or the unlikely which presented the real challenge. In the years up to the Second World War there were numerous instances of low-level damage, usually

---

[*] Nine years later, James Dennison, a clerk aged twenty, shot and killed himself early in the morning at the foot of Primrose Hill 'because he considered he had been wronged by his superior officers'. *Pall Mall Gazette*, 6 January 1870; *Reynolds's Newspaper*, 7 January 1870.

focused around the playground and gymnasium, with incidents of vandalism and even arson. In 1934 the see-saw was smashed, a swing was missing and the giant stride was out of order. In 1936 it was reported that 'The Primrose Hill Gymnasium would appear to be a rendezvous for all types of individuals of varying ages and is frequented by the hooligan element who have little respect for the apparatus provided or for the railings which have been erected to protect the gymnasium'.[66] Yet in September, after the gymnasium was closed early, 'temporarily at the urgent request of the police on account of several serious complaints ... regarding the noise made by lads frequenting it after dark and their unseemly language, and also because of evidence that it was becoming a training ground for prostitutes', there were many protests.[67] George Lewis wrote to say, 'When I left school seven years ago my height was four foot five inches. My height is now five foot six inches, thanks to that gym on Primrose Hill.'[68]

If it is impossible to know who all the men, women and children who visited Primrose Hill over the years were, or what they thought, a number of unusual men and women left memories to do with it. Charles Lamb, the essayist, recalled a missed opportunity:

> I do not remember a more whimsical surprise than having been once detected
> – by a familiar damsel – reclined at my ease upon the grass, on Primrose Hill
> (her Cythera), reading *Pamela*. There was nothing in the book to make a man
> seriously ashamed at the exposure; but as she seated herself down by me, and
> seemed determined to read in company, I could have wished it had been any
> other book. We read on very sociably for a few pages; and, not finding the
> author much to her taste, she got up, and – went away. Gentle casuist, I leave it
> to thee to conjecture, whether the blush (for there was one between us) was the
> property of the nymph or the swain in this dilemma. From me you shall never
> get the secret ...*

The far less coy Harriette Wilson, the most celebrated courtesan of the Regency, walked a prospective lover to the top of the hill before rejecting him.† Having

---

* Samuel Richardson's *Pamela: or Virtue Rewarded* (London, 1740), an eighteenth-century bestseller, is the story of a nobleman's attempts on the virtue of the beautiful Pamela Andrews, a maidservant aged fifteen. Charles Lamb, 'Detached Thoughts on Books and Reading', in *The Last Essays of Elia* (London, 1833); *Elia and the Last Essays of Elia*, edited with an introduction by Jonathan Bate (Oxford, 1987), pp. 199–200.

† Harriette Wilson's memoirs, published in 1825, make up in enterprise what they lack in veracity. Their famous opening lines read: 'I shall not say why and how I became, at the age of fifteen, the mistress of the Earl of Craven. Whether it was love, or the severity of my

arranged to meet Lord Granville Leveson Gower in Marylebone Park, she decided on first sight that he was not what she was looking for:

> Having brought a man up to Marylebone fields, on such a terribly hot morning, it would not not have been fair, or lady-like, to have dismissed him, until I had given his talents and powers of pleasing a fair trial. I walked him up to the tip-top of Primrose Hill, and then towards Hampstead, and then back again to Great Portland Street. At last his Lordship made a full stop, while he took off his hat to wipe his face, declaring he could go no further, as he was quite unaccustomed to walking, and the sun was so very oppressive.[69]

Herman Melville, the author of *Moby Dick*, recorded his impressions of Primrose Hill in 1863:

> The view was curious. Towards Hampstead the open country looked green and the air was pretty clear; but cityward it was like a view of hell from Abraham's bosom. Clouds of smoke, as though you looked down from Mount Washington in a mist.[70]

In 1890 William Michael Rossetti, the younger brother of Christina and Dante Gabriel Rossetti, was living at 3 St Edmund's Terrace, 'a line of streets raised well above the level of Regent's Park, and not far below the summit of the closely adjoining Primrose Hill. It is not a cloud-capt summit, but in London it counts as the nearest approach to a hill that we have to show'. He liked its 'noiseless quiet (for there is scarcely any of the London rattling and rumbling)' and its ability to stand above the fog:

> In this Primrose Hill locality my old friend the London fog (for which I have always had a sneaking kindness) is considerably less demonstrative than at a lower level and in closer environments: many times when there has been a dense fog in London streets, and even in Regent's Park, there has only been a whitish mist in St Edmund's Terrace.[71]

William Rossetti's father-in-law, the painter Ford Madox Brown, lived at 1 St Edmund's Terrace at the end of his life.

---

father, the depravity of my own heart, or the winning arts of the noble lord, which induced me to leave my paternal roof, and place myself under his protection, does not much signify; or if it does, I am not in the humour to gratify curiosity in this manner.' Harriette Wilson, *The Memoirs of Harriette Wilson Written by Herself*, 2 vols (London, 1924), i, pp. 255–6. See also, Frances Wilson, *The Courtesan's Revenge: Harriette Wilson, the Woman who Blackmailed the King* (London, 2003), pp. 52, 108, 199–220, 251–6, 260. Lord Granville Leveson Gower, when ambassador to Russia, had refused assistance to John Bellingham, later the murderer of Spencer Perceval, when Bellingham was imprisoned there for debt.

He usually wore a shiny top-hat and a black cape, and he used to take my grandmother's little dog out for a walk on Primrose Hill. He couldn't walk very fast because he had the gout, but the little dog was very old and couldn't go fast either, so it didn't mind. He would stop from time to time to look behind to see if it was coming, and then it used to stop too, and sit down and look up at him, and hang its tongue out and wag its tail, and then they went on again.[72]

Eleanor Farjeon's memories, speaking for generations of children, add a touch of realism:

At twelve o'clock it was time to go for a walk. 'Let's go to Regent's Park', said Joe. 'And take some bread', added Bertie, giving the show away. Bread meant the delight of ducks and water. 'Wouldn't it be nicer, dears, to go to Primrose Hill? It is such a clear day, and I can show you St Paul's from the top.' We disliked Primrose Hill, the grass was so bare, and the trees were so dull, and you never got away from the feeling of iron railings, and however clear it was *I* couldn't see St Paul's and, even if I could, I didn't want to. However, when Miss Milton said firmly, 'Yes, we'll all go for a nice walk to Primrose Hill', we knew there was no hope.[*]

Two men with a darker vision of society who must often have looked over London, the undoubted centre of world capitalism, from the top of Primrose Hill, and whose works were used to justify class warfare and many actual wars after their deaths, were the German refugees, Friedrich Engels and Karl Marx. Engels lived from 1870 to 1894 at 122 Regent's Park Road, with a direct view on to the hill.[†] Marx lived at 41 Maitland Park Road, across the railway bridge on the other side of the Hampstead road, from 1875 to 1883. There are more records of the men, and Marx's family, picnicking on Hampstead Heath, but it is impossible to believe that they did not also walk on Primrose Hill. Indeed when the Marx family moved from their cramped rooms in Dean Street to Grafton Terrace, near to Maitland Park Road, in 1856, Marx's wife Jenny wrote that they had moved into 'a small house at the foot of romantic Hampstead Heath, not far from lovely Primrose Hill'.[73]

Their association with the hill was undoubtedly one of the reasons that a

---

[*] In the 1890s the Farjeon children and their governess were living at 196 Adelaide Road. Miss Milton was one of those people who 'seemed to go against everything I wanted to discover. ... However, if we took our hoops we could play the game of Greeks and Trojans which Harry had invented for us, after the *Iliad* had been shared out fairly among us.' Miss Milton, predictably, 'thought we had better leave our hoops at home'. Eleanor Farjeon, *A Nursery in the Nineties* (Oxford, 1935), pp. 384–5.

[†] He died, however, at 41 Regent's Park Road, a house belonging to his friend Dr Ludwig Friedburger, the pathologist to London County Council, in 1896. *From Primrose Hill to Euston Road*, ed. F. Peter Woodford (2nd edn, London, 1995), p. 77.

climb to the top of Primrose Hill was the favourite London excursion of their principal follower, and the man who lived to bring revolution and civil war to Russia. Vladimir Ilyich Ulyanov, better known as Lenin, and his wife Nadezhda Krupskaya, lived in Holford Square in Clerkenwell between 1902 and 1903, as Dr and Mrs Richter (most people thought they were Germans). According to the latter's memoirs:

> It was also our custom to ride out to the suburbs. Most often we went to Primrose Hill, as the whole trip only cost us sixpence. Nearly the whole of London could be seen from the hill – a vast smoke-wreathed city receding into the distance. From here we got close to nature, penetrating deep into the parks and along green paths. We also liked going to Primrose Hill because it was near the cemetery where Karl Marx was buried. We paid visits there.*

Despite their liking for country walks around London, and living peacefully amongst their neighbours, Lenin's conviction that revolution would come was not affected by his time in London:

> He loved going on long rides about the town on top of an omnibus. He liked the movement of this huge commercial city. The quiet squares, the detached houses, with separate entrances and shining windows, adorned with greenery, the drives frequented only by highly polished broughams were much in evidence – but tucked away nearby, the mean little streets, inhabited by the London working people, where lines with washing hung across the street, and pale children played in the gutter – these sights could not be seen from the bus top. In such districts we went on foot, and observing these howling contrasts in richness and poverty, Ilyich would mutter through clenched teeth, and in English: 'Two nations!'[74]

---

* As Marx is buried in the east cemetery at Highgate, either Krupskaya's judgement of distance is at fault or she may here have been confusing Primrose Hill and Parliament Hill. Nadezhda Krupskaya, *Memories of Lenin* (1930; this edition, London, 1970), p. 68.

11

The Martian Invasion

F EW PLACES in Europe were untouched by the ripples caused by the French Revolution of 1789, with the execution of Louis XVI in January 1793 leading to war between Britain and France in the following month. Primrose Hill was no exception. Iolo Morganwg's proclamation of the Gorsedd of the Bards on it in September 1792 was partly an anti-war protest. The subsequent declaration of war, however, led to the government introduction of a series of measures designed to curb the activities of Radicals such as Morganwg and to ensure that there would be no revolution in Britain.

Despite some early successes, including the naval victory of the Glorious First of June in 1794, it soon became clear that the war would last far longer than had first been hoped. Even if revolution could be prevented at home, there remained the danger that it might be imposed by conquest. A mass movement of Volunteers was raised from 1794, ready to serve in the case of invasion but also to put down insurrection at home.[1] By 1804 the numbers of Volunteers had reached an astonishing 400,000 men in 4600 different corps, representing 18 per cent of men of military age.

Although the Volunteer movement was a national one, it was well represented in London, with parades held in Hyde Park (including one of ten thousand men inspected by the Duke of York, the Commander-in-Chief) and elsewhere.* There are numerous reports of Volunteer units practising their shooting skills at the 'target' near the Chalk Farm Tavern. In 1804, for instance, the first battalion of the Queen's Royal Volunteers, having mustered at Ranelagh House and after being inspected in Hyde Park, marched to the Chalk Farm Tavern to practise their shooting skills, with gold medals being presented by the colonel for the best two

---

* The miniature painter Andrew Robertson wrote on 27 July 1801, 'I am told that about ten thousand were reviewed by the Duke of York and Prince of Wales', *Letters and Papers of Andrew Robertson, A.M., Miniature Painter to his Late Royal Highness the Duke of Suffolk* (2nd edn, London, 1897), p. 51. For a discussion of which hill the Grand Old Duke of York may have marched his men up, see *The Oxford Dictionary of Nursery Rhymes*, edited by Iona and Peter Opie (Oxford, 1952), pp. 176, 442.

marksmen.* Following their exercises, the officers and men celebrated by drinking and eating in the tavern, as the Volunteers, who were not under military discipline other than in the case of invasion, and who were drawn from the respectable members of the public, were socially far more cohesive than their contemporaries in the regular army.

> After the ball firing the corps marched up stairs by companies to the Long Room, where they found an excellent dinner was provided for them, by order, and at the expence of Colonel Robinson. After dinner the health of the king was drank with three times three; and then 'God Save the King' was sung by the whole corps.[2]

After numerous other toasts, including the health of their gallant colonel drunk with the utmost enthusiasm, the corps joined in singing 'Rule Britannia' in full chorus. 'A few adjourned to other parts of the house, according to the custom of soldiers, to associate with their favourite companions, and they spent the evening together in the utmost harmony, and parted at dusk, perfectly well satisfied with the day's excursion.'[3]

Faced by a series of French military victories in Europe, and under the threat of invasion by the French *Armée d'Angleterre* in 1797, the British high command commissioned a number of reports on natural defensive features to the south and north of London. These were incorporated in the recommendations of Lieutenant-General Sir David Dundas in his report on the defence of the capital. In case of an invasion based on landings in Essex and Suffolk, the Northern Heights of Hampstead and Highgate were seen as a natural line of defence protecting London.† In 1798 Major Thomas Vincent of the 30th Regiment drew up detailed suggestions for the deployment of forces behind a front line stretching from Highgate to Child's Hill:

> About a thousand yards in the rear of the front is another branch of the Hampstead Heights on which a corps of cavalry (sixteen hundred strong) may draw up with intervals equal to a third of a squadron, having Belsize in front of their right and their left posted on Primrose Hill.[4]

The immediate threat of invasion was lifted in June 1798 when Napoleon

---

* Several of the old oak trees on the hill contained large numbers of 'ounce' bullets, as did the soil around the site of the target. A.D. Webster, *The Regent's Park and Primrose Hill: History and Antiquities* (London, 1911), pp. 88–9.
† Later, Dundas made a critical impact on outcome of war with France by exercising his influence to secure Sir Arthur Wellesley, later the Duke of Wellington, the command of British forces in the Iberian peninsula. Roy Allen, 'The Hampstead and Highgate Citadel: Defence Plans against Napoleon', *Camden History Review*, 10 (1982), pp. 7–9; 'Sir David Dundas (1735?–1820)', *Oxford Dictionary of National Biography*.

Bonaparte, the revolutionary regime's leading general, abandoned any immediate hope of conquering England to embark on an expedition to Egypt. He returned, without his army, the following year to seize power in Paris. After a short-lived peace in 1802–3, the threat of invasion was renewed, with Napoleon (who crowned himself emperor in 1804) concentrating 130,000 men at Boulogne in 1805, with 2,240 barges to carry them across the Channel.[5] All that stood in his way was the Royal Navy. The French fleet's attempt to elude Nelson, and to give the French mastery of the Channel long enough to allow the barges to cross, led first to a British chase across the Atlantic to the West Indies and then to a decisive battle. At Trafalgar, on 21 October 1805, Nelson destroyed a joint French and Spanish fleet. With this defeat, any prospect of a successful French crossing of the Channel was lost, although this did not prevent speculation, fuelled by paranoia, about other ways the French might arrive, whether by balloon or by tunnel.[*] Napoleon broke up the camp at Boulogne and marched his army south to defeat the Austrians and Russians at Austerlitz on 2 December. A medal, designed to commemorate victory in his *Descente en Angleterre*, and showing a naked Napoleon as Hercules overthrowing a fish-tailed England, remained unissued.[6]

Following the victorious conclusion of the Napoleonic Wars in 1815, Primrose Hill was little affected by military matters during most of the rest of the nineteenth century, other than as a potential site for a monument to victory in the Napoleonic Wars, though the Life Guards regularly exercised on its south side before and after it became a park. Soldiers from both St John's Wood and Albany Street were a not-infrequent sight on the hill, made conspicuous by their scarlet uniforms. In the latter part of the century, they were also joined by Volunteer units drilling.

The Crimean War of 1854–56 showed the shortcomings of the British army in fighting another European power on land. As the Russian fleet presented no challenge to the Royal Navy, and with the war's principal theatre being set around Sebastopol, to the north of the Black Sea, there was never any threat of a Russian invasion. Relief at the end of the war was, however, celebrated in style, with a spectacular firework display on the hill in June 1856, put on by the government and watched by a huge crowd drawn from all classes.[7] Less ephemerally, the photographer Roger Fenton, who lived at 2 Albert Terrace, had been sent out to record the war. His images have defined the war ever since, giving him an unassailable claim to have been the world's first major war photographer.[8]

There was a brief scare early on the morning of 2 October 1874, when Primrose

---

[*] During the Second World War, a section of Royal Engineers buried microphones in the sand on a ten-mile stretch of coast to the east and west of Dover to listen for any sounds of the Germans tunnelling. Nothing was heard. For a history of invasion threats, see I.F. Clarke, *Voices Prophesying War, 1763–1984* (Oxford, 1966). For examples of British paranoia, see Keith Wilson, *Channel Tunnel Visions, 1850–1914* (London, 1994), pp. 22–32, 178–81.

Hill was rocked by a massive explosion. It brought the Life Guards, fearing an
enemy attack or a terrorist outrage, hurrying from their barracks in Albany Street.[9]
In reality, the explosion, on the Regent's Canal near Macclesfield Bridge to the
west of the hill, was caused by gunpowder, carried by a barge, the *Tilbury*, being
accidentally set alight by one of its crew of three, all of whom were killed.[10]

In 1898, however, hostile invaders, armed with massively superior weapons and
immune to late-Victorian artillery, conquered London, most of whose inhabitants
fled in panic. With large parts of the city destroyed, the invaders consolidated
their gains and planned their next moves in their principal redoubt on Primrose
Hill. There, as they regained their strength, ingesting captives while uttering an
eerie hooting noise, they began building a great flying machine for the conquest
of the world.

Fortunately, the need to save London and the world was fictional rather than real.
The Martian invasion in H.G. Wells's *The War of the Worlds* (1898), nevertheless,
gave Primrose Hill a central role in one of the most remarkable novels of the late
nineteenth century. It addressed not only Britain's place in Europe and the world but
also mankind's place in nature. H.G. Wells (1866–1946) knew Primrose Hill well.
From 1888 to 1891 he lived with his aunt, Mary Wells, at 12 and then 46 Fitzroy
Road, at the foot of the hill. He married his cousin, Isabel, in 1891.* In the years
after 1889, he taught science at Henley House, a preparatory school in Mortimer
Crescent in Kilburn, where A.A. Milne, the son of the school's headmaster, was
one of his pupils and Alfred Harmsworth, later Lord Northcliffe, another. Wells
described Henley House as 'not very successful', but admired J.V. Milne and very
much enjoyed the school lunches: Mrs Milne 'was rather concerned if I did not eat
enough, because I was still, she thought, scandalously thin'. Although A.A. Milne
later described Wells as not being a great schoolmaster – 'He was too clever and too
impatient' – Wells was clearly a success at the school. At the same time as teaching,
he sat and passed the licentiate of the College of Preceptors with great distinction.
J.V. Milne announced in the school magazine in May 1890 that 'our popular Science
Master, Mr H.G. Wells' had won three prizes: 'It is rather rough on the other
gentlemen that all three prizes should thus be carried off by one man, and shows

---

*   The marriage did not last long, as by 1894 Wells had moved to 7 Mornington Crescent with
his mistress (later to be his second wife), Catherine Robbins. By the time of writing *The War of
the Worlds*, he was living in Woking in Surrey, near many of the Martian landing sites. His very
substantial earnings then allowed him to build a house on the south coast at Sandgate. From 1930
Wells had a London flat in Chiltern Court, Baker Street. He returned to nearer Primrose Hill
in 1936, living for the last ten years of his life at 13 Hanover Terrace, Regent's Park. Michael
Sherborne, *H.G. Wells: Another Kind of Life* (London, 2010), pp. 107–34, 282, 314–48.

a want of consideration quite foreign to Mr Wells's character.'[11] Wells's teaching
and the school outings he led, including at least one visit to Primrose Hill, were
clearly memorable. Twelve years later, A.A. Milne wrote to Wells from Cambridge:

> Do you remember a small-sized boy with long hair to whom you taught at one
> time all the geology he ever knew? He sat at the front desk in what was known
> as the 'first class room' and hazarded ideas on the strata of Primrose Hill. ... I
> am the long-haired kid ...[12]

A prolific writer and novelist, with what became a worldwide reputation, Wells
had been born in humble circumstances in Bromley in Kent in 1866. His parents
kept a shop. His father was an ex-professional cricketer and his mother had been a
lady's maid. After leaving school at fourteen, Wells was an assistant in a pharmacy,
before being apprenticed as a draper in Southsea and then working as a pupil teacher
in Midhurst. After strenuous efforts to educate himself, at the age of eighteen he
won a scholarship to the Normal School of Science in South Kensington, where
he attended lectures by T.H. Huxley, the leading populariser of Darwin's theories.
Wells soon determined to become an author.[13]

After writing two scientific textbooks, Wells published his first scientific fantasy,
The Time Machine, in 1895. In it a Victorian scientist is transported forward in time
to 802,701 A.D. on a bicycle. This was followed by *The Island of Dr Moreau* (1896),
in which a shipwrecked traveller finds himself on an island where the sinister Dr
Moreau is turning animals into humans. In *The Invisible Man* (1897), the eponymous
hero, Jack Griffin, recalls the day before he became invisible:

> I remember that morning before the change very vividly. I must have gone up
> Great Portland Street. I remember the barracks in Albany Street, and the horse
> soldiers coming out, and at last I found myself sitting in the sunshine and feeling
> very ill and strange, on the summit of Primrose Hill. It was a sunny day in
> January – one of those sunny, frosty days that came before the snow this year.
> My weary brain tried to formulate the position, to plot out a plan of action.[14]

Griffin is singularly unsuccessful in his plans to benefit from his own invisibility,
which leads him only to frustration, unhappiness, crime and death.

Wells's most famous scientific fantasy, however, was undoubtedly *The War of
the Worlds*, serialised in *Pearson's Magazine* in 1897 and published in book form in
1898.[15] In *The War of the Worlds* the Martians land on Earth in cylinders shot from
a giant gun on Mars. Their accuracy at such an enormous distance is remarkable,
as seven, out of a total of ten, cylinders land within twenty miles of each other.
The first arrives at Horsell Common, north of Woking in Surrey, with subsequent
landings on a golf links between Woking and Byfleet, at Pyrford, Bushy Park,
Mortlake, Wimbledon and, finally, on Primrose Hill.[16] Human curiosity about the

object on Horsell Common and attempts to investigate the first cylinder, which slowly unscrews itself, soon turn to horror.[17] A delegation, bearing a white flag and including Stent, the Astronomer Royal, seeks to negotiate with whatever is in the cylinder but is destroyed by a white flame, after three puffs of green smoke are seen accompanied by a deep humming noise.[*]

The Martians themselves, who possess 'intellects vast and cool and unsympathetic', have a degree of scientific knowledge far beyond that of humans.[18] They have 'a big greyish rounded bulk, the size, perhaps of a bear'. They have peculiar V-shaped mouths, but no chin, immense eyes and oily brown skin. They have heads, rather than bodies, with a pair of very large, dark-coloured eyes and a kind of fleshy beak, around which are sixteen slender tentacles, like whips, arranged in two bunches of eight.[19]

The invaders' weaponry, backed up by versatile handling-machines used for its construction, soon proves itself overwhelmingly stronger than the forces of artillery and sappers sent against them. As well as the heat-rays that destroy the delegation and burn down anything in their path, the Martians control giant war-machines, walking tripods of immense destructive power, from which not only heat-rays can be unleashed but also black smoke:

> These canisters smashed on striking the ground – they did not explode – and incontinently disengaged an enormous volume of heavy, inky vapour, coiling and pouring upward in a huge and ebony cumulus cloud, a gaseous hill that sank and spread itself slowly over the surrounding country. And the touch of the vapour, the inhaling of its pungent wisps, was death to all that breathe.[20]

It soon becomes clear that the Martians, who destroy everything that resists them as well as burning down numerous towns, are invincible. They do not, however, always kill the human beings they encounter but sometimes capture them as a prelude to ingestion:

> Strange as it may seem to a human being, all the complex apparatus of digestion, which makes up the bulk of our bodies, did not exist in the Martians. They were heads – merely heads. Entrails they had none. They did not eat, much less digest. Instead, they took the fresh, living blood of other creatures, and *injected* it into their own veins.[21]

The Martians have also brought with them a red weed that grows in profusion and chokes the waterways near London, including the Thames.

---

[*]   A mysterious deep humming noise, witnessed by four people, was heard on Primrose Hill on 3 February 2012 and reported to the UK UFO Sightings website. *Hampstead and Highgate Express*, 9 February 2012.

There is inevitably universal panic in London. Among the millions trying to flee, the brother of the anonymous hero and narrator of the book fails to get on board a North-Western train at Chalk Farm, where the crowd in the goods yard is so thick that trains trying to leave plough into shrieking people. He is lucky to get hold of a bicycle, from a sacked bicycle shop in the Chalk Farm Road, but finds Haverstock Hill impassable due to several overturned horses.[*]

The hero of the book, a scientific journalist who has many narrow escapes from the Martians in Surrey, makes his way back into London and towards Primrose Hill, via Kensington, Marble Arch and Baker Street. After being puzzled by seeing Martians standing still and making a wailing sound of 'Ulla, ulla, ulla', he is encouraged to discover a wrecked handling-machine in St John's Wood. Its Martian driver has lost control of it and, helpless, has been torn to pieces by dogs. The hero determines to discover what has happened on Primrose Hill.

He approaches it across the Regent's Canal, 'a spongy mass of dark-red vegetation' after being choked by the Martians' red weed, and via St Edmund's Terrace, where he 'waded breast-high across a torrent of water that was rushing down from the waterworks towards the Albert Road':

> Great mounds had been heaped about the crest of the hill, making a huge redoubt of it – it was the final and largest place the Martians had made – and from behind these heaps there rose a thin smoke against the sky. Against the sky line an eager dog ran and disappeared. The thought that had flashed into my mind grew real, grew credible. I felt no fear, only a wild, trembling exultation, as I ran up the hill towards the motionless monster. Out of the hood hung lank shreds of brown, at which the hungry birds pecked and tore.
>
> In another moment I had scrambled up the earthen rampart and stood upon its crest, and the interior of the redoubt was below me. A mighty space it was, with gigantic machines here and there within it, huge mounds of material and strange shelter places. And scattered about it, some in their overturned war-machines, some in the now rigid handling-machines, and a dozen of them stark and silent and laid in a row, were the Martians – *dead!* – slain by the putrefactive and disease bacteria against which their systems were unprepared. ...
>
> Across the pit on its farther lip, flat and vast and strange, lay the great flying-machine with which they had been experimenting upon our denser atmosphere when decay and death arrested them. Death had come not a day too soon.[22]

The Martians are not proof against terrestrial bacteria. By this fortunate accident, the world is saved from conquest.

---

[*]   Wells, *The War of the Worlds*, p. 93. A later bicycle shop in the Chalk Farm Road, Evans, was looted by the London rioters of August 2011.

While the climax of *The War of Worlds* takes place on Primrose Hill, a London landmark known to many of H.G. Wells's readers and on which an artilleryman might well have placed a battery to overawe the city below, the novel has a much wider national and international context. Britain in the nineteenth century was the predominant world power. At its height the British Empire ruled a third of the land on Earth. London was the greatest city in the world, in population, wealth and sophistication. Britain also had the most powerful navy, maintaining it at a level equal to the two next largest navies. In contrast, its army, even if capable of winning easy victories over tribal opponents in the creation of Britain's far-flung empire, was much weaker than those of the main powers on the Continent, France, Germany and Russia. One consequence of this disparity was a fear, held by the government and shared by many patriotic Britons, of invasion.

Despite the final defeat of Napoleon at Waterloo in 1815, British paranoia about the threat of French invasion continued for the greater part of the nineteenth century. Under Palmerston as Prime Minister, massive forts, later known as Palmerston's Follies, were built around the coast of England, including ones in the Solent to protect Portsmouth from invasion. When William Gladstone, as Chancellor of the Exchequer, opposed these on the grounds of their expense and threatened to resign in 1860, Palmerston commented succinctly in a letter to Queen Victoria that 'however great a loss to the Government by the retirement of Mr Gladstone, it would be better to lose Mr Gladstone than to run the risk of losing Portsmouth or Plymouth'.*

In 1870, however, the French, previously thought of as the leading military power on the Continent, were rapidly and comprehensively defeated by the Prussians in the Franco-Prussian War. In 1871, William I, King of Prussia, was proclaimed German Emperor in the Hall of Mirrors at Versailles. From this point on, until war actually broke out against Germany on 4 August 1914, it was the Germans and not the French who were the main imagined enemies.

This shift was confirmed emphatically in 1871, when a professional soldier, Colonel Sir George Tomkyns Chesney, published *The Battle of Dorking*.[23] In his book, the destruction by mines of the Royal Navy leads to a successful German invasion of Britain, with the key German victory being won against a poorly led and inadequately armed British defence force by exploiting the Dorking Gap. The success of Chesney's book, translated into many European languages, spawned a new genre of imagined invasions.

---

*   Both Queen Victoria and Palmerston found Gladstone very trying. Palmerston complained that he received so many letters from Gladstone threatening resignation that he could light a fire with them. Philip Guedalla, *Palmerston* (London, 1950), p. 370. I am most grateful to David Brown, the author of *Palmerston: A Biography* (London and New Haven, 2010), for providing me with this reference.

As well as being a compelling adventure story, *The War of the Worlds* not only reflects the British invasion fears of the day but adds in a number of highly original ingredients. The Martians, by landing directly from space, avoid Britain's main defensive force, the Royal Navy, although later in the book they destroy elements of it with consummate ease. Landing in Surrey and on Primrose Hill itself, they use overwhelming force, in the shape of their war-machines and other advanced technology, to make a mockery of the late Victorian army's attempt to stop their advance. They have no understanding of and no respect for the humans they encounter. In their attitude to the British population, the Martians mirror the effortless superiority of European imperialists towards the native populations with whom they came in contact. In the face of the Martians, the British are reduced to the status of the defenceless inhabitants of Tasmania, who, following the arrival of the British, became extinct in 1876. Even more humiliatingly, it is suggested that the Martians will keep a tame colony of human beings to provide themselves with a pool of food ready for ingestion. To an extra-terrestrial race of higher intelligence, human beings have no more rights than 'the transient creatures that swarm and multiply in a drop of water' seen by a scientist.[24]

The War of the Worlds is simultaneously a biting satire on colonialism, the most memorable of all invasion fantasies and the father of a major genre of Science Fiction, eclipsing the engaging but comforting adventures of Jules Verne. The book also reflects the impact of advances in science in the nineteenth century, not only in imagining the technical advances of rocketry and weaponry displayed by the Martians, but also in creating a race which, in Darwinian terms, had reached a far greater level of sophistication than human beings. More unnervingly, in its depiction of the use of poison gas and of overwhelming force being used against a helpless civilian population, Wells predicted features of the gruesome wars of the twentieth century. Wells himself lived on until after the Second World War in Hanover Terrace, Regent's Park. He not only experienced for himself the destruction that the Luftwaffe brought on London from the sky but also saw the even more horrific destruction of Hiroshima and Nagasaki by atomic bomb, a word that he himself had invented in his novel, *The World Set Free*, begun in 1913 and published the following year. The physicist Leó Szilárd read the novel in 1932, the year when the neutron was discovered, and filed for patents on the neutron chain reaction, using the term 'atomic bomb', in 1934.[25]

As Wells himself wrote in *The World Set Free*:

Certainly it seems now that nothing could have been more obvious to the people of the earlier twentieth century than the rapidity with which the war was becoming impossible. And as certainly they did not see it. They did not see it until the atomic bombs burst in their fumbling hands. Yet the broad facts must have glared upon any intelligent mind. All through the nineteenth and twentieth centuries the amount of energy that men were able to command was continually increasing. Applied to warfare that meant that the power to inflict a blow, the power to destroy, was continually increasing. There was no increase whatever in the ability to escape.[26]

He continued with a prophecy of the threat of terrorism:

Destruction was becoming so facile that any little body of malcontents could use it. ... Before the last war began it was a matter of common knowledge that a man could carry about in a handbag an amount of latent energy sufficient to wreck half a city.[27]

12

The Impact of War

A LTHOUGH regular troops, and Volunteers, destined for South Africa passed through the barracks in Albany Street and St John's Wood on their way to the Boer War between 1899 and 1902, the war itself left little trace on Primrose Hill. In November 1899 F.E. Thompson, the editor of the *Marlborough College Register*, wrote from 16 Primrose Hill Road, overlooking the hill, expressing a not-untypical early reaction to the news from South Africa:

> Will you allow me to state with pardonable pride that Lieutenant H.A.C. Wilson, whose name Mr Winston Churchill stated at Bradford last night that he had discovered as that of 'the young officer who died in the endeavour to establish confidence in his men at Spion Kop' … was a Marlburian? … He was a worthy schoolfellow of Captain de Montmorency and thirty others who have given their lives for their country.[1]

The congregation of St Mary the Virgin Primrose Hill contributed £35 13s. 8d. to the Lord Mayor's war relief fund in December 1899 and another eight shillings to a fund for the wives and families of officers in January 1900.[2] As the war dragged on and brought further casualties, however, the mood of the nation and around the hill darkened. Many began to doubt the effectiveness of the British Empire's army, whatever the contribution of public school men to the war effort.

The First World War, declared in August 1914, while it had a shattering impact on Britain and its empire as a whole, also had few direct repercussions on the hill. None of the German Zeppelin and bomber raids targeted the area immediately around it, though bombs fell not far away on Avenue Road.* Lord's, which was also hit, was handed over by the MCC to the Army Council for training purposes in 1914, though still also used for cricket matches. Apart from a constraint on funds to be spent on

---

* As in the Second World War, the local Tube stations were used as bomb shelters. The mile-long tunnel of the London and North-Western Railway, between Chalk Farm and Loudoun Road, which had recently been completed but was not yet operational, also came under official control. *The Times*, 27 October 1917.

the park, and a loss of park-keepers to the armed forces, the park remained much as it had been throughout the war.* It was not until March 1917 that any of it was taken over to further the war effort. The initiative seems to have been a local one:

> The Hampstead Joint War Production Committee has been informed that the Board [of the Office of Works] are prepared, subject to the consent of the General Officer Commanding London District (as to which no difficulty is expected) to allot about six acres in Primrose Hill to be cultivated as allotments. A rent of £2 per acre; all cost to be met by the committee; resumption on two months' notice at the end of any year; tenancy in any case to expire at the same time as the order in respect of waste lands issued by the Board of Agriculture.[3]

The allotments were in existence until February 1920, their holders having been allowed an extension to 'secure their winter crops'.[4] The allotments had inconvenienced children: 'The only suitable ground for cricket having been devoted to allotments, children are of course driven on to other parts of the hill for their games.'[5]

During the war British forces suffered around 700,000 deaths, a lower portion of the male population than Germany, Russia, France or Serbia, but still a devastating number. Those who lived around Primrose Hill contributed to these casualties. Few families were exempt from a casualty in either their immediate or extended families.

Twenty-three men from the parish of St Mark's Regent's Park had been killed by August 1916.[6] The eight of these for whom dates of death are known were all killed in France or Belgium. Only one, Second Lieutenant Gerard Elrington, killed aged twenty at Ypres on 31 October 1914, was an officer. He had been born in Belgium. Lance Corporal Andrew Woolley, of the London Regiment, who had lived at 64 St George's Road (the then name for Chalcot Road) and who was killed on 30 May 1915, was the son of a park-keeper. Of the thirty-five men and two women on the war memorial of St Mary's Primrose Hill whose graves can be traced, ten were

---

* The fear of invasion was, however, expressed by the arrest of a German, suspected of communicating with Germany, in the first month of the war. 'On an August evening the wife of a first-grade civil servant believed that she saw a man let loose a carrier pigeon on Primrose Hill. She went into the witness box at Marylebone and gave clear evidence of what she had seen. The defendant was a German. I believed the evidence of the lady and sent the man to prison for six months. He was the servant of a Lutheran pastor, who appealed to the Home Office for his release. The plea was successful and the German was set free. I was informed that the case was too weak for conviction, because the lady's statement had not been supported by other evidence.' H.L. Cancellor, *The Life of a London Beak* (London, 1930), pp. 30–1. Despite its title, the book is about the career of a metropolitan magistrate, not the life of a carrier pigeon. Many other Germans, Austrians and Hungarians were arrested and interned during the war, even when they had lived in England for most of their lives. I am indebted to Jerry White for this reference.

officers and fifteen other ranks. Most were killed serving in the army and are buried in France or Flanders, though one died in Africa and one at Gallipoli.

Lieutenant Maurice Beningfield of the Worcester Regiment, who had been born at 9 Elsworthy Road in 1897, was killed by machine-gun fire on 11 March 1915, the second day of the battle of Neuve Chapelle, when he had put his head above the parapet of a trench in order to direct his men's fire. His elder brother, Philip, of the Royal Field Artillery, died of wounds received at Ypres on 27 April 1915. Their parents, Colonel John and Mrs Phebe Beningfield, received two telegrams beginning 'Deeply regret to inform you'. Unusually, instead of the standard, impersonal 'The Army Council express sympathy', both telegrams end, 'Lord Kitchener expresses his sympathy', possibly reflecting a personal connection with Colonel Beningfield. In May Mrs Beningfield wrote to enquire about Maurice's possessions: 'No effects from his body have been received. They would be of small intrinsic value, but unspeakably precious to me. In particular, a very fine knife slung on his waistband and a new pocket book. Can you tell me if the dead are buried in full uniform?' Among Philip Beningfield's effects, which were returned, were a wrist-watch, a pipe and a torch. Amongst his other possessions were five twenty-franc notes, two five-franc notes and two one-shilling British postal orders.[7]

Late in the war, Frederick and Ada Eiloart, at 17 Elsworthy Road, received a similar telegram, announcing that their son, Second Lieutenant Cyril Eiloart of the Irish Guards, had been killed in action in France on 27 September 1918. Eiloart had been out in Salonika as a private before coming back to England to be commissioned. Two other Eiloarts, Horace and Oswald, are on the war memorial, but it is unclear where and when they died.[8]

Maurice and Philip Beningfield, and Cyril Eiloart, were unmarried. The news of the death of Lieutenant Henry Betts, of the Royal Fusiliers, missing believed killed in France on 20 September 1917, was sent to his widow, Elsie, at 30 Elsworthy Road. Betts had begun the war in Iquiqui, Chile, but had hurried home on the RMS *Orita*, via the Straits of Magellan, the Falkland Isles and Montevideo, to join up early in 1915. In 1919, after considerable correspondence with the War Office, Elsie, now living at 12 Eton Road, was reimbursed for the £30 the voyage home had cost her husband.[9]

Not all of those listed on the war memorial died from wounds received on the battlefield. Cecil Duncan Jones, an actor and writer who was travelling for his health at the outbreak of war, was interned by the Germans at Ruhleben, on the outskirts of Berlin. The brother of a vicar of St Mary's, he had published a society novel, *The Everlasting Search*, in which the hero is killed in an air crash, in 1913; and he wrote poetry in the camp. As well as playing a leading part in the religious life of the camp, as president of its YMCA, Duncan Jones produced and directed a memorable performance of Shakespeare's *Twelfth Night*. His health, however, declined in the camp and he was repatriated by ambulance ship in 1918, only to die a few hours before the Armistice. His contribution to camp life was recognised by his fellow-prisoners, who after the war collected over £200 to pay for a headstone for his grave and for a striking statuette of St Christopher, deposited in the Victoria and Albert Museum and still on display there.[10]

The Reverend Percy Dearmer, the Vicar of St Mary's at the outbreak of war, was an exceptional priest. His *The Parson's Handbook*, which first appeared in 1899, and which set out ideals for Anglican services that would be acceptable to a wide range of church-goers, went through thirteen editions. He also had a major effect on the repertoire of hymns sung in twentieth-century churches. His *English Hymnal*, of which the musical editor was Ralph Vaughan Williams, originated at St Mary's, with many of the best known Anglican hymns being sung there for the first time, including 'For all the Saints, who from their labours rest'. Dearmer himself wrote several memorable hymns, among them 'Jesus, good above all other' and 'A brighter day is dawning'. A socialist and sometimes an irritant to the church hierarchy, Dearmer was a well loved and successful vicar at St Mary's, where he was responsible for whitewashing the original red brick of the interior. From 1907, when a house opposite was bequeathed to the church, Dearmer, his wife Mabel and their two young sons, Geoffrey and Christopher, lived immediately next to the hill at 7 Elsworthy Road.[11]

After the outbreak of war, Geoffrey and Christopher Dearmer were commissioned as officers. Percy, determined to do his bit, resigned his living at St Mary's in 1915 and volunteered as chaplain to the British forces in Serbia, the first entrant into the war and a British ally. Mabel Dearmer, a well-known author of children's books, novels and plays, went with him to help nurse in a field hospital in Kragujevac. After only three months in Serbia, on 11 July 1915, Mabel died of enteric fever. Dearmer returned to England just in time to accompany Christopher, a pilot in the Royal Naval Air Service, to Plymouth on his way to Gallipoli. After landing at Suvla Bay, Christopher was killed by a shell on 6 October 1915.[12]

On his way east, Christopher had met up in Malta with his brother, Geoffrey, also bound for Gallipoli. Geoffrey, who was wounded at Gallipoli but survived, then served in the Royal Army Service Corps in France and Flanders, taking part in the Somme campaign. In 1918, he published his *Poems* on the war to widespread acclaim in Britain and America. A second collection, *A Day's Delight*, was published in 1923. Born three days after Wilfred Owen, on 21 March 1893, Geoffrey Dearmer saw as much fighting as Owen or Siegfried Sassoon, but his poetry, informed by his own religious belief, lacks their bitterness.* A typical poem, 'Resurrection' acknowledges the horror of war yet combines it with hope for the future:

---

* Dearmer was instrumental in bringing about the first performance of R.C. Sherriff's play

> Five million men are dead! How can the worth
> Of all the world redeem such waste as this?
>
> …
>
> Shall we then
> Mourn for the dead unduly, and forget
> The resurrection in the hearts of men?
> Even the poppy on the parapet
> Shall blossom as before when Summer blows again.[13]

Although recognised as a leading war poet in the 1920s, Dearmer's poetry slipped from public consciousness and remained forgotten for seventy years. His work and reputation were then revived in 1993, when he reached his hundredth birthday, with general astonishment meeting the realisation that a notable poet of the First World War was still alive in the last decade of the twentieth century. To mark the event, John Murray published a collection of his poems, *A Pilgrim's Song*, and the Imperial War Museum gave a party to celebrate its publication.* He died on 18 August 1996, the oldest member of the Society of Authors and of the Poetry Society, as well as of the Gallipoli Society.[14]

Not everyone had supported the Britain war effort during the First World War. The philosopher and pacifist Bertrand Russell and his mistress, the flamboyant Lady Ottoline Morrell, climbed the hill in March 1915. According to the latter:

> There are a few impressions left in my memory – one of a walk I took with Bertie Russell through Regent's Park, up Primrose Hill. I think it must have been in March, for the sheep and lambs were there, and somehow I had a vivid invasion of Blake into my consciousness. … When we were on top of the hill we looked out over London, stretching far away beneath, right over to St Paul's on the horizon, and a great anguish overtook both Bertie and myself at the sight. The vision we both had, that all this might possibly be swept away and destroyed by enemy bombs.

The walk and the vision, which were even more prophetic of the destruction caused in the Second World War, were recalled by Russell in a letter written immediately afterwards:

> It was extraordinarily happy today – and on the hill it was terribly moving. The children playing, and St Paul's and the thought of all the destruction of war. If

---

Journey's End in 1928. He was also a well-known broadcaster, as Uncle Geoffrey, on *Children's Hour* in the 1940s. 'Geoffrey Dearmer (1893–1996)', *Oxford Dictionary of National Biography*.
* The publication of *A Pilgrim's Song* and the party at the Imperial War Museum were supported by a generous donation from the author Catherine Cookson.

I could really believe that the world will be less warlike after the war, it would half reconcile one, but I don't believe it. I don't believe peace can be inculcated by bayonets. ... St Paul's seemed wonderfully strong and eternal – as if what it stands for would survive all our madness – yet all the time I was thinking of Germans battering it down with their guns. But it can't batter down love – it will spring up again through everything – it has lived and given hope in the darkest ages of the world.*

Between the wars, there was one occasion when large numbers of troops occupied both Regent's Park and Primrose Hill. This was for the coronation of George VI on 12 May 1937. The route from Buckingham Palace to Westminster Abbey was lined with 32,500 men and women from all around what was still the British Empire. The two parks were turned into tented camps for men from the Royal Navy and three of the Guards battalions, as well as for contingents from the Dominions and Boy Scouts from across the Empire.[15]

Even before the outbreak of the Second World War, Primrose Hill was affected by the German threat to peace. The first sign was the felling of trees on the top of the hill. This was observed by the poet Louis Macneice, who in 1938 was living at 16a Primrose Hill Road while teaching Classics at Bedford College. During the Munich crisis of that year, 'I found the Territorials hastily, inefficiently, cutting down the grove on the top of Primrose Hill. ... The next day Primrose Hill looked so forlorn that I took the train to Birmingham ...' Coming back to London, 'Primrose Hill was embarrassingly naked, as if one's grandfather had shaved his beard off. Propped on tree trunks on the top of it were two or three little museum-piece guns, ingenuously gaping at the sky.'[16] In a poem published that year, he wrote:

---

* Both the walk and Russell's letter about it are in Ottoline Morrell, *The Early Memoirs of Lady Ottoline Morrell*, edited by Robert Gathorne Hardy (London, 1963), pp. 280–1. The likely date is March 1915. Bertrand's attraction to Ottoline was spiritual, as, unlike Bertrand, she had little enthusiasm for sex and did not find him physically attractive. He also suffered from pyorrhoea, a discharge of pus from the gums and tooth sockets. On Primrose Hill, however, she was happy: 'It was these passionate moments in him that always held me to him, these moments when he became liberated from himself, when he had power to soar into visions beyond most men's.' For more about the affair, see Miranda Seymour, *Ottoline Morrell: Life on the Grand Scale* (London, 1992), pp. 166–7, 177–8, 206–7, 215–16, 255 and 258–9. Russell (1872–1970) was deprived of his fellowship of Trinity College, Cambridge, in 1916 following a conviction under the Defence of the Realm Act. He was imprisoned in for six months in 1918 for writing what was judged to be a libellous article about the British government and the American army. I am indebted to Alan Bennett for telling me about this wartime visit to Primrose Hill and for pointing me towards Lady Ottoline's memoirs.

> I hear dull blows on wood outside my window;
> They are cutting down the trees on Primrose Hill.
> The wood is white like the roast flesh of chicken,
> Each tree falling like a closing fan;
> No more looking at the view from seats beneath its branches,
> Everything is going to plan;
> They want the crest of this hill for anti-aircraft …[17]

A less poetic but well-observed account of the changes brought by the war to Primrose Hill is to be found in the diary of the local civil servant Anthony Heap. On 22 October 1938 Heap recorded:

> Went over to Primrose Hill to find not only unsightly air-raid trenches dug all around the lower part but the entire summit fenced off and all the trees cut down. Asked a policeman the why and wherefore of it. He told me that anti-aircraft guns had been placed up there during the crisis week and since removed. Meanwhile the public are deprived of a splendid viewpoint and the beauty of the hill marred by ugly tree stumps.[18]

Revisiting the hill on 6 November, Heap found

> more ground at the top of Primrose Hill being fenced off, provisionally for ARP purposes. Apparently this enclosure, which is higher and more elaborate, will when complete supersede the present one. Thus leaving the south fringe of actual summit with its sundial and fine view over London open to the public again. Well thank heavens for small mercies anyway![19]

The trenches in the parks were part of a wider campaign. At a rate of twelve hundred people per acre, Primrose Hill's trenches provided shelter for two thousand people, as against Regent's Park's six thousand. In all, the borough of St Pancras constructed 17,200 places. These were built by the public works contractor, Percy Trentham Ltd, after a government requirement was issued on 24 September 1938 for building places of protection for citizens caught out in the open in a raid.[20] Using four hundred men and two mechanical diggers, plus another four hundred men recruited from the local Labour Exchange, Trentham excavated revetted trenches 5 feet wide and 7 feet deep in the parks. The trenches served the additional function of stopping enemy gliders or other aircraft landing. In November 1939, Heap noted that the trenches on Primrose Hill had 'been reinforced with concrete, covered over and made to look much less unsightly. Can it be that the authorities have at last tumbled to the fact that open trenches with piles of earth alongside are not only not particularly safe but also something in the way of the nature of an eyesore? Incredible!'[21]

The trenches dug on Primrose Hill, itself famous for the difficulty of draining its clay soil, at least provided some sporting entertainment. *The Times* reported in February 1939:

> Carrying fishing rods, between twenty and thirty unemployed men met beside some ARP trenches on Primrose Hill, Regent's Park, on Saturday and fished in the water in the bottom of the trench. They carried posters and streamers demanding 'Give Us Work on ARP' and 'Bring Anderson to 'eel'. Someone had placed a number of eels in the trenches, which had about two inches of water in them, and these were quickly caught. When some police officers arrived the men went away.[22]

Even after the outbreak of war, Air Raid Precautions remained a subject for humour. On 19 September of the same year, it was announced that the Unity Theatre, St Pancras, was putting a new review entitled *Sandbag Follies*, two of whose numbers were 'An Air Raid Shelter for Two' and 'Primrose Hill'.[23]

Living near to the hill, at 54 Fitzroy Road, was one of the main contributors to the pre-war debate on Air Raid Precautions, Professor J.B.S. Haldane, whose wife Charlotte was a St Pancras councillor and a member of its ARP committee.[*] Both were Communists. Haldane, the Professor of Biometry at University College, who had been wounded from the air in the trenches in 1917, was an expert on war gases and had designed an early gas mask. He had also written a popular handbook, *ARP*, on Air Raid Precautions, published in 1938. At the time of Munich, he championed a network of 780 miles of seven-foot tunnels dug sixty feet under London and capable of sheltering 4,400,000 people. Although rejected by Sir John Anderson, Lord Privy Seal and then Home Secretary, on the grounds of cost, the deep shelters won limited backing in 1940, after the first month of the Blitz, from Herbert Morrison, who had replaced Anderson as Home Secretary in October 1940. Three of eight deep shelters to be dug in London, under Tube stations, were at Belsize Park, Camden Town and Goodge Street, each providing room for eight thousand people. They were not completed, however, until late 1942 or opened to the public until 1944.[24]

What would happen to London Zoo during bombing raids, and the threat of animals escaping, attracted considerable attention. As a result, some of the animals, including the elephants and giant pandas, were moved to Whipsnade. The poisonous and constricting snakes, and the black widow spiders, were chloroformed.[†] The

---

[*] Haldane was a Communist despite having been a member of Pop at Eton, where he had been teased for his short temper and intellectual arrogance. 'J.B.S. Haldane (1892–1964)', *Oxford Dictionary of National Biography*.

[†] One young bull African elephant was, however, destroyed, while the big pythons 'have been saved and are at the moment in enormous, strong wooden boxes in the centre space of the

aquarium was drained and some its fish were eaten. The manatees were shot. The carnivores remained, but provisions were made to deal with them if they escaped:

> The mathematical possibilities of the escape of large, dangerous carnivores after an air raid are so remote as to be infinitesimal; but supposing all the laws of probability are broken and a lion, for instance, manages to escape, the animal will be dealt with by one of the six special riflemen stationed in shelters in the Gardens, who (with the wardens) will be the only men to leave the shelters when the 'raiders passed' signal is given.[25]

After a brief closure on the outbreak of war, the Zoo was open again by mid-September and was a popular attraction throughout the war. Exhibits even included an addition in the form of Polly Anna, a reindeer brought back by submarine from Russia as a gift from Britain's war-time ally.[26] By the time the Gardens reopened, air-raid shelters to house a thousand people had already been constructed.

In the event, the Zoo was hit in six raids during the war, causing damage to a number of its buildings. In a raid which destroyed the Zebra and Wild Horse House, in late 1940, a giraffe 'died of a dilated heart due to over-exertion caused by fright'. A zebra stallion also escaped along the Outer Circle, pursued by the distinguished scientist and Secretary of the Zoo, Julian Huxley, who succeeded in shepherding the animal back into the Zoo. 'He was a Grevy zebra stallion, almost as large as a horse, and his nerves were naturally on edge. Every time the AA guns went off on Primrose Hill he backed violently. I was frankly alarmed that he would kick me.' Huxley was told by the zebra keeper the next day, 'Cor, bless you, sir, you needn't have been frightened, 'e's a biter, not a kicker'.[27]

Primrose Hill was used for training, and many of the blocks of flats near the park were taken over by the armed forces.[28] One of those who experienced military life on the hill was the biographer and historian Richard Hough. He recalled that he and his fellow RAF recruits lived in 'requisitioned luxury flats overlooking the tree-lined canal and the hundreds of acres of Regent's Park. ... The windows were bricked up and we could only glimpse the park through a vent. There was no heating or lighting and the lifts were inoperative.'[29]

> We marched a good deal to kill time, we did PT in the park and on Primrose Hill, we lined up for indescribably ghastly food at the Zoo, for ninety minutes or more, and there were always several who fainted from revulsion or hunger. ...

---

house', *The Times*, 9 September 1939. The writer of this article also considered that some of 'the sea-lions, pelicans and penguins will have to learn to eat meat smeared with cod-liver oil or go'. Ming, a giant panda and the Zoo's greatest draw, later returned to London. J. Barrington-Johnson, *The Zoo: The Story of London Zoo* (London, 2005), p. 127.

I shall remember it for the cry of the baboons and wolves, the eerie call of the hoopoe birds, the smell of greasy food and unclean blankets, and the murderous crash of the 4.5 guns on Primrose Hill a quarter-mile away when raiders came over during the short summer nights.[30]

As in the First World War, parts of Primrose Hill were taken over for allotments. These do not seem, however, to have been established as early as the anti-aircraft guns, as they were not yet in place in February 1940. Later on, however, they covered half the hill, as can be seen from aerial photographs taken during the war and shortly afterwards. As Gwyneth Williams, an allotment holder on the hill, recalled: 'No form of storage on the site was allowed, so bicycles were essential, and we rode or walked them along Primrose Hill Road, draped in forks, spades and trowels, returning laden with produce.' The soil proved very fertile and produced potatoes, sprouts, onions, marrows, herbs and lettuces, 'everything helping to enliven the sound but boring diet we were enduring'.[31] A barrage balloon was tethered near the playground.[32]

As might have been expected, the area controlled by the military increased as the war went on. Anthony Heap inspected both Regent's Park and Primrose Hill on Sunday 11 February 1940:

> Then to Regents Park. Found the greater part of it (the whole extent west of the Broad Walk) fenced off with iron railings which at regular intervals bear the cryptic inscription 'Closed to the public – Danger'. As for any reason, there is no indication what. Possibly it is to be used for the disposal of unexploded bombs.
>
> Neither is there much of Primrose Hill left to the public now, what with the trench shelter and the anti-aircraft base, which has extended its areas of ground even further round the slopes. Huge red-brick barracks are now being built to replace the wooden huts put there a year ago. So presumably the war can be guaranteed to last several more years yet if only to justify the erection of these sort of places on Primrose Hill.[33]

The following summer Heap reported: 'As for Primrose Hill, what with the anti-aircraft base and the extensive area taken up by allotments, there's scarcely any part of that erstwhile delightful place left to walk over at all.'[34]

Primrose Hill had a half-battery of 4.5 inch anti-aircraft guns, in a compound covering 13.5 acres, from 1939.[35] This consisted of four guns, with a command post, instrument pits, a slit-trench air-raid shelter, and other buildings and barracks. The militarised area was surrounded by fencing. Because the compound needed access roads, which interrupted the established paths across the hill, the installation also led to tarmac tracks and to new paths skirting the compound fences and allotments. A number of houses in Elsworthy Road were requisitioned to provide accommodation for the gunners. (Later in the war, some of the houses in the road were given over to Americans in the run-up to D-Day. No. 35 housed an American Air Force general, whose thirty-foot high flagstaff remained in the garden until the 1970s.)[36]

Remarkably, the diary of one of the men who manned the anti-aircraft guns on the hill has survived.[37] Gunner Harold Danks arrived on the hill in May 1940 and was on duty there for most of the time until February 1941. Born in 1919, Danks had joined the Territorial Army at the end of 1936.* Included in his diary are two of his sketch maps, showing the installation at two separate dates, drawn in contravention to king's regulations. Both have the four guns surrounding a central command post and protected by slit trenches and by three light-machine gun posts (number 2 was manned by Gunner Danks). The last are only shown in the second sketch, which also marks the position of a searchlight. Underneath the command post was a dugout. A series of tents and huts to the north and south of the main path from Elsworthy Terrace were used for cooking, eating, washing and storage. By the time of the second drawing, dated 3 February 1941, an additional eight brick huts were being built, the mess tents were being used for storage, and a new combined canteen and mess hall was in the process of being completed.[38]

The first three months of Danks's time on Primrose Hill were mostly filled with military routine interspersed by occasional incidents. Two days after his arrival, Danks spent the evening 'in admiring the numerous girls walking round the gun-park fence', but on 22 May 'two girls and a man were arrested and later handed over to the police for taking photos near the gun-positions'. More seriously, on 16 July, 'A man was challenged and fired upon on the side of the hill nearest the Zoo. Six shots were fired by the two pickets and by one of the guard. Later on a trail of blood was reported between Elsworthy and King Henry's Roads.' Two days later, Danks reported that 'the fellow we fired at the other night might have some connection with two fellows who attempted to burgle some flats nearby and who were, I believe, chased by the police'.[39]

---

* From the diary, which gives a good impression of life in the ranks, it is possible to piece together a good deal about Danks's background, character and service career. While he was growing up, his family had lived in Chile and then Vancouver. He had, however, boarded at Kingswood, Bath, the leading Methodist public school. Before his call up, on 24 August 1938, he had been working in a junior capacity for a broking firm at Lloyd's. After leaving Primrose Hill, he spent fifteen months as a gunner in Essex, mainly on Foulness Island and at Shoeburyness. During this time, he attended an OCTU course at Shrivenham but failed to gain a commission. He was told 'that my work in lectures and exams was extremely good but that my PT was not good and also that I did not show personality or leadership', Diary, 27 October 1941. He was also short-sighted. Subsequently Danks transferred to DEMS (Defensively Equipped Merchant Ships), which took him across the Atlantic and to the Mediterranean, before he was sent out to India in May 1945.

As well as having occasional leave, with visits to 'the flicks' and to a club in the West End, the men were entertained by two BBC stars, Josephine Driver and Patrick Waddington. On 11 July, 'The guard turned out and was inspected by Jo. She then came into the canteen and sang us some of Uncle Currie's songs, then some popular songs and lastly dirty songs.' This was followed by some of the men taking part in a BBC programme. On 24 August, 'the BBC had a broadcasting van here and they were able to broadcast our stand-to to the States. Our share of the programme, *London After Dark*, took four minutes.' An important visitor, General Władysław Sikorski, accompanied by other Polish officers, inspected the post in October.[40]

On Sunday 3 November, Danks celebrated his twenty-first birthday in style:

> There were about nine of us at the meal, which was held in the Spotters' Hut. The meal was all tinned stuff except for the hors d'oeuvres and the chicken. It consisted of hors d'oeuvres with a large choice of dishes, asparagus, soup, chicken, potatoes, peas and mixed vegetables, then fruit salad, both tinned and fresh, and biscuits and cheese and cigars. To drink we had a bottle of sherry, one of Château Graves and two of port wine. We then had a little sing-song and then we adjourned to the bar where we drank more port, etc, and then we joined a pontoon school. ... At 11 p.m. I had to go on duty on the Command Post.[41]

While the first months of the war were spent with few enemy aircraft being seen, this was replaced in September 1940 by two months of almost constant action. On 4 November, Danks reported, 'No alarm at all last night. This is the second night that we have not stood-to since the barrage started on the night of 11 September.'[42]

As Macneice had predicted in June 1939:

> And the wind gets up and blows
> The lamps between the trees
> And all the leaves are waves
> And the top of Primrose Hill
> A raft on stormy seas.
>
> Some day the raft will lift
> Upon a larger swell
> And the evil sirens call
> And the searchlights quest and shift
> And out of the Milky Way
> The impartial bombs will fall.[43]

It would be pleasant to think that the guns on Primrose Hill posed an effective deterrent to the Luftwaffe. They were, however, of little use during the early days

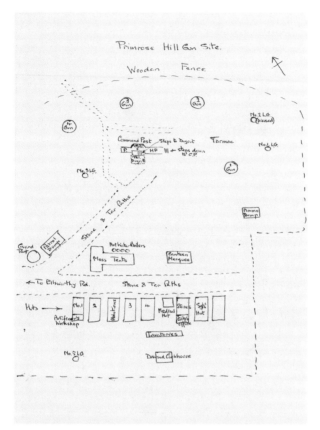

Harold Danks, of 164 HAA Battery, kept a diary during his time as a gunner on Primrose Hill between May 1940 and February 1941. He drew two sketches showing the gun emplacements, stores, tents and other features. These increased considerably and became more permanent during his time on the hill. (*Royal Artillery Museum Library*)

of the Blitz, from 4 to 18 September 1940, when the German daylight raids were concentrated on the commercial and industrial areas of the East End and on the City, Westminster and Kensington. After 18 September, when the Germans turned to night-time bombing, the Luftwaffe suffered far fewer losses, as the British fighters were mostly ineffective at night. Nor did the anti-aircraft batteries do much better. Because of the difficulty of firing accurately at largely unseen targets, General Pile, the head of Anti-Aircraft Command, ordered up a blanket barrage. While this may have been good for the morale, it is likely that shrapnel killed more Londoners than Germans, when it fell to earth.[44] At least collecting pieces of it provided boys with a new hobby.[45] The entire anti-aircraft defence force is credited with bringing down only fifty-seven German aircraft in the critical last three months of 1940. Primrose Hill, nevertheless, did capture one trophy, whether or not it was brought down by its own guns. This was a Junkers 88 which crashed, relatively intact, on the south side of the hill in October 1940.[46]

In 1943 the original single-barrelled guns were replaced by twin-barrelled,

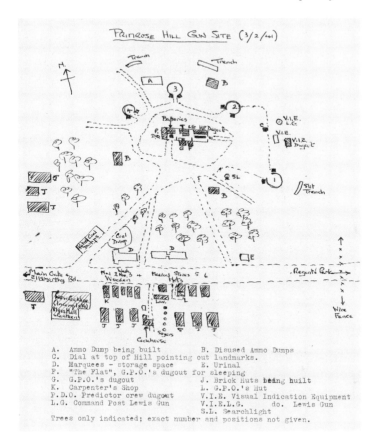

PRIMROSE HILL GUN SITE (3/2/44)

A. Ammo Dump being built   B. Disused Ammo Dumps
C. Dial at top of Hill pointing out landmarks.
D. Marquees - storage space   E. Urinal
F. "The Flat", G.P.O.'s dugout for sleeping
G. G.P.O.'s dugout   J. Brick Huts being built
K. Carpenter's Shop   L. G.P.O.'s Hut
P.D.O. Predictor crew dugout   V.I.E. Visual Indication Equipment
L.G. Command Post Lewis Gun   V.I.E.L.G.   do. Lewis Gun
                               S.L. Searchlight
Trees only indicated; exact number and positions not given.

5.25 inch guns. These were the same as those used as secondary armament on battleships and had a ceiling higher than any other anti-aircraft guns available. They were backed up by a range-finding radar net, with a diameter of 140 yards, on the north-west side of the hill. Unfortunately, this improved capability came too late to be of major use, although the guns may have been of some help during the Little Blitz of early 1944 and against the V1s, when they began to arrive in June 1944, though these were mostly targeted further south. They were of course useless against the V2s, dropping from a height of sixty miles.

The guns, nevertheless, gave psychological comfort to local inhabitants, some of whom preferred to sleep on the hill, 'under the guns', rather than in the uncomfortable local air-raid shelters during attacks. Andrew Sachs, a German Jewish immigrant who later found fame as the Barcelonan waiter, Manuel, in the television comedy *Fawlty Towers*, lived for a time in a house in Oppidans Road belonging to Bronisław Malinowski, the author of *The Sexual Life of Savages*. He remembers the reverberation of the guns which made sleeping almost impossible and broke the window-panes of the houses.[47] Charles Pay, who was staying at 11 Rothwell Street in the second half of 1940, saw the glow of burning across London from the top of the hill during bombing raids, most strikingly after the bombing of the Surrey Docks;[48] an experience shared by Joan Bouverie-Brine, serving in the WAAF, who remembered 'going up to Primrose Hill and watching this red glow in the sky. The whole of the East End was on fire.'[49]

A number of local people have described their memories of being bombed. According to Maureen Hawes:

> A large water tank was erected just inside the gate at the bottom of Primrose Hill Road for use by the ARP's fire fighters – though I never saw it used. An underground air-raid shelter was tunnelled into the lower part of the hill facing what I believe in those days was called Regent's Park Gardens, a terrace of lovely houses. ... Some houses lost their railings too, and the public was asked to donate any old pots and pans or other scrap metal for the war effort.
>
> Sheltering from the air-raids was a grisly business though the sense of community and good cheer – stiff upper lip etc. was tremendous and there were plenty of laughs. A basement room ... had been reinforced with iron posts and at first we spent air-raid nights down there. Two or three neighbours joined us and we played children's card and board games to take our minds off the bombardment. It was rather like camping: flasks of hot drinks, sandwiches, and makeshift beds. But it was freezing and very damp.
>
> Then we started going to the underground shelter on Primrose Hill, a labyrinth of passages, wooden duckboards on the floor. There were some bunks but many people, us included, had to spend the night on the narrow benches which lined the walls. It was wonderful to hear the all-clear siren and we'd emerge in the early morning blinking like animals coming out of hibernation. News came down to us one night that some nearby stables had been hit and horses were running wild through the streets. The raid that night had been horrendous.[50]

Sylvia Ballerini gave another account.

> At the base of the Hill, near the drinking fountain, some public air-raid shelters were built. They were made of bricks, with electricity, but no running water. The shelters looked like long corridors with benches around the walls.
>
> We reckoned the sirens would go off about 5.30 to 6.00 p.m. After that people would choose whether to remain all night at home or go to one of the Tube stations (either Chalk Farm or Camden Town). People took their own food and met up with friends they knew every night.
>
> I knew of several people who went to the Underground. On the whole, people didn't go to the public shelter on Primrose Hill at night. It was a grim place

to go into, especially at night. There was a lot of noise from the guns and the Underground shelter was a warmer and friendlier place.[51]

During the war, a series of bombs fell on the hill, one of which, in September 1940, injured some of those sheltering in one of the park trenches. Professor J.B.S. Haldane usually sheltered in the basement of 54 Fitzroy Road. His wife, Charlotte, in contrast,

> played the piano in the drawing-room above (when I was at home) in order to drown the noise of the guns and to distract my mind during the raids. On this occasion my husband insisted that I should accompany him to the shelter on the hill. No sooner had we arrived there than a small bomb fell on a section of it, which collapsed, injuring several people, and one old lady died of heart failure from the shock.[52]

After this Haldane changed his preference to a Zoo shelter run by his friend Julian Huxley, but Charlotte preferred to stay in Fitzroy Road.[53] An 1850 map of Regent's Park and Primrose Hill was annotated by the park authorities to show where and what type of bombs had fallen on them.[54] In all four high-explosive bombs and two oil bombs fell on the hill itself, while V1s fell on the canal, the Zoo and King Henry's Road.

As a spectacular finale to the war, on Wednesday 21 March 1945, at 11.40 in the morning, a V2 landed near to west gate of Primrose Hill, next to the reservoir, creating a deep crater and destroying the tea rooms and the nearby men's lavatories.[*] No one was killed, although three minor casualties were taken by ambulance to the first-aid post in Bayham Street. The following day Mr M.E. Lefevre, of 37 Ormonde Terrace, reported to the post with pain in his ears and was sent for treatment to the Hospital of St John and St Elizabeth.[55]

---

[*] The V2 landed only six days before the rockets' launching sites were overrun. The last V2 landed in Kent on the evening of 27 March 1945.

13

Shakespeare's Oak

T H E bicentenary of Shakespeare's birth, in April 1764, had been marked by a festival in London and Stratford promoted by the great actor David Garrick.[1] To the success of the festival can be attributed the beginning of the Bard's inexorable rise to literary supremacy as the greatest English poet and dramatist, and as perhaps the world's greatest writer. The question as to how the tercentenary, on 23 April 1864, should be celebrated was therefore widely debated in an England which had become the dominant power in the world, spreading its language and literature to its empire.*

Unfortunately, as opposed to having a single driving force, as Garrick had been in 1764, the right to celebrate Shakespeare's birth was contested by a variety of people and places. The most successful celebration was again in Stratford, but London refused to be left out, despite the failure of its National Shakespeare Committee to attract royal patronage. In the end, the most active London body involved was the Working Men's Shakespeare Committee. As well as putting on a concert at the Royal Agricultural Hall in Islington, the committee decided to celebrate the birthday by the ceremonial planting of an oak, the tree symbolising England, on Primrose Hill.[2] Through the good offices of William Cowper, the First Commissioner of Works, Queen Victoria agreed to give 'a fine young oak', which had been in the plantation for sixteen years at Windsor. Samuel Phelps, the one-time manager of Sadler's Wells Theatre, was chosen to plant the tree, with a reading of an ode to Shakespeare written by the actress Eliza Cook.

A procession, which left Russell Square at 1 p.m., was led by George Cruikshank,

---

* All those who are interested in Regent's Park and Primrose Hill are greatly indebted to John Black, who from 1992 until his death in 2010 collected literary and musical references on both parks. These references, which he regularly updated, are to be found on his indispensable website, 'Regents Park and Primrose Hill in Literature and Music: A Bibliography', www. regentsparklit.org.uk. Although there are many more references to Regent's Park than to Primrose Hill, the latter are helpfully identified by the letter (P). The genesis of John Black's association with, and interest in, the parks is explained in 'A Tour Through the Literature', accessible under 'Tour' on his website.

The Working Man's Shakespeare Committee organised the planting of an oak on Primrose Hill, on 23 April 1864, to commemorate the Bard's tercentenary. The occasion was also marked by a huge turn-out on the hill to protest against the curtailment of a visit to England of the popular Italian patriot, Giuseppe Garibaldi. In the background can been the West Middlesex Water Company's pumping works. (*Private Collection*)

the illustrator and a keen Volunteer officer. It included a band; Cruikshank's own Volunteers, known as 'Havelock's Own' because of their commitment to temperance and in honour of the abstemious hero of the Indian Mutiny, Henry Havelock; and children from two charity schools. It made its way to Primrose Hill via Bedford Square, Tottenham Court Road and Camden Town. Although the procession itself was of modest size, it was met on Primrose Hill by a crowd nervously estimated by the police at one hundred thousand. As Eliza Cook herself was unable to come, due to ill health, the ode was read out by Henry Marston, and the tree was planted and then christened with Avon water. It had, however, become clear to all those there that the meeting had a double agenda. Under the banner of celebrating Shakespeare's birth, the Working Men's Shakespeare Committee had organised a massed meeting in support of the immensely popular Italian hero, Garibaldi, whose visit to England had recently been ended to the intense disappointment of his many admirers.[3]

It cannot be claimed that the ode, composed and due to have been read by Eliza Cook but in the event read by Henry Marston, was good poetry:

> Joyous, yet solemn, is our purpose here
> Claiming, alike, glad smile and tender tear.
> The smile – to know our Jubilee is given
> To him who left on earth some rays from Heaven.[4]

Nor were the verses composed by V.C. Clinton-Baddeley to be read by Dame Edith Evans, who planted a replacement oak in 1964, better:

> Recklessly once you said your words would last –
> 'So long as men can breathe or eyes can see' –
> Lend us a little of your humour, sir,
> That just so long may last this English oak.[5]

These verses, nevertheless, continued a literary tradition: amongst a few good poems, Primrose Hill has attracted a considerable number of bad ones. It would be hard to class a florid *tour d'horizon*, 'The Prospect from Primrose Hill' (1749), amongst the latter. As well as a poetical survey of all the villages visible from the summit, it includes an early recognition of the view south towards London:

> To Primrose Hill lead on the flow'ry way,
> And then the matchless scenes around survey.
> Mean while the Muse shall sing, with fond surprise,
> The various prospects, as by turns they rise:
> Beyond those fields of variegated dye,
> Proud London lifts her glitt'ring spires on high.[6]

There is less of a doubt about the work of Hannah Wallis, a 'poor Methodist' from a village near Chelmsford. In 1787 she published a collection of her poetry in *The Female's Meditations: or Common Occurrences Spiritualized in Verse*. One meditation included:

> I do remember on our way
> We through a field did pass,
> Where quantities of grasshoppers
> Were jumping in the grass …

We soon ascended Primrose Hill,
And did those buildings view,
Which sure have stood in ancient times,
And many that were new ...[7]

A prophetic, but hardly visionary, approach was expressed in 'Primrose Hill', published in 1825:

After a long and dusty round,
A panting upward climb,
'Tis pleasant to attain the mound
Of antiquated Time;
To feel the wind's awakening thrill,
And freshness breathe on Primrose Hill.

Rome was magnificent to view!
London looks powerful here!
Hallowed in smoke the spires point through,
Glittering like many a spear;
And structures, by the mason's skill,
Ere long will compass Primrose Hill.[8]

Thirteen years later, in 1838, in a collection called *Primrose Hill*, Jane Gwilliam welcomed the new queen's reign:

Primrose Hill! There was a time
When thy scen'ry look'd sublime,
Ere they marr'd thy verdant ridges
With their ugly locks and bridges,
Or the dull canal became
Honor'd with the Regent's name ...[9]

The torch was picked up by Olive Douglas in 1908, the first verse of whose poem 'Primrose Hill' reads:

Wild heart in me that frets and grieves,
Imprisoned here against your will.
Sad heart that dreams of rainbow wings.
See! I have found some golden things!
The poplar trees on Primrose Hill

> With all their shining play of leaves,
> And London like a silver bride,
> That will not put her veil aside!*

It is not difficult to find later effusions on Primrose Hill. These include both modern poems on the hill and the lyrics of songs on the hill by pop singers and groups. In 'Emit Remmus' in 1999, the Red Hot Chili Peppers sang:

> Hesitate but don't refuse
> The choice was yours but you said choose
> The look she used was green and sharp
> Stabbed that boy all in the heart
> Come what may the cosmos will
> Take me up and down on Primrose Hill
> What could be wetter than
> An English girl American man ...†

Primrose Hill can, at least, claim links with both the Beatles and the Rolling Stones. Paul McCartney wrote 'The Fool on the Hill' after climbing Primrose Hill at dawn with his Old English Sheepdog, Martha, and encountering an uncommunicative 'middle-aged gentleman, very respectably dressed in a belted raincoat', who appeared and vanished mysteriously:

> Day after day, alone on the hill,
> The man with the foolish grin is keeping perfectly still
> But nobody wants to know him,
> They can see he's just a fool
> And he never gives an answer.
> But the fool on the hill sees the sun going down
> And the eyes in his head see the world spinning round ...[10]

Without their visit leading to any musical composition, the Stones drove up Primrose Hill, following an all-night recording and photo shoot in Barnes, in 1966. After a 5 a.m. breakfast of 'fried eggs, fried bread and hot, strong tea and smoke', they drove in two cars to the hill: 'We made the drive in just under twenty minutes. To keep the group alert (and, hopefully, amused) I had my driver ease

---

* The bride's veil was presumably London's fog. Olive Douglas, 'Primrose Hill', *The Academy*, 17 October 1908.
† The title of the song is intelligible when read backwards. Red Hot Chili Peppers, 'Emit Remmus', *Californication* (1999).

the Phantom V into the park and as far up to the top of Primrose Hill as he could go.'[11] The result was a cover shot for their album *Between the Buttons*.[12]

The group Madness released a song called 'Primrose Hill' in their 1982 album *Rise and Fall:*

> A man opened his window and stared up Primrose Hill
> Out there enjoying themselves I've seen them from this sill.
> Green splashed with white and red going brown
> Children baiting animals running up and down.

The album had a photograph of Primrose Hill on its cover. As the group's frontman Suggs (Graham Macpherson) explained: 'Primrose Hill was somewhere that had featured in most of the band's lives. We all came from the surrounding area so we'd always had good memories of the place. Primrose Hill was somewhere you could play football or, in the winter, go tobogganing, so it's always been a place of fun and frolics.'[13]

In 1993 the group Blur published their second album, *Modern Life is Rubbish*. In it the lead track was 'For Tomorrow (Visit to Primrose Hill Extended)', a longer version of a number first released as a single. The prospects of the 'twentieth-century boy' in it, who is 'trying not to be sick again', improve when he goes up Primrose Hill with Susan:

> Then Susan came into the room,
> She's a naughty girl with a lovely smile,
> Says let's take a drive to Primrose Hill,
> It's windy there and the view's so nice ...

Part of the video promoting the album was also filmed on Primrose Hill.

Popular music indeed has a long history on Primrose Hill. The words and music of 'A Sweete and Courtly Songe of the Flowers that Grow on Prymrose Hill', registered with the Stationers Company in 1586–87, are sadly lost. We know, however, that a seventeenth-century ballad, from the Pepys Collection, 'The Sweet Salutation on Primrose Hill: or I Know You Not', was to be sung to the tune of 'Though Father Be Angry' (a very suitable choice of tune given the outcome of the story told by the song).[14] Another ballad, 'The Maid of Primrose Hill', was published in 1785 in a collection called *An Excellent Garland Containing Four Choice Songs*.[15] The entertainment provided by the Chalk Farm Tavern invariably included popular songs.

In the 1850s music, often provided by military bands, became popular in parks across Britain. Because the concerts were mainly on Sundays, they were opposed by Sabbatarians, who also wished to stop Sunday travel. The attitude of the Lord's Day Observance Society was that it was better 'that a man should be feeble and sickly ... than that he should be strong and healthy through disobeying God'. It was successful in getting concerts in the parks by military bands stopped.[16] That many people enjoyed the music is clear from a protest organised on Primrose Hill in May 1856. The defenders of Sunday music in the parks turned out a large number of their supporters:

> The demonstration, such as it was, accordingly took place in that locality, which ordinarily on a Sunday in fine weather is a favourite suburban rendezvous. Between 2 and 4 o'clock numbers of people continued to wend their way up the hill from all directions, and by the hour appointed for the meeting at least a thousand persons had assembled on its summit.[17]

At 5 o'clock a hearty and almost unanimous cheer, accompanied by a show of hands, greeted the raising of a union jack and signified approval of the committee's motion: 'That the people now in public meeting assembled, considering the music in the parks, established by Sir Benjamin Hall, to be an innocent and healthful recreation, regret its sudden discontinuance, and hope it may be speedily renewed.'* Despite having no bandstand, Primrose Hill therefore played its part in defending the performance of bands in the parks on the one day of rest of most of the working population. The Sabbatarian ban lasted for only a few months, with private bands supported by the Society for Securing the Performance of Sunday Music in the Parks replacing military ones.[18]

Two buildings near the hill have strong associations with popular music. Cecil Sharp House, at the junction of Regent's Park Road and Gloucester Avenue, is the headquarters of the English Folk Dance and Song Society. Named after Cecil Sharp, who recorded traditional songs and dances in England and America, and who once lived in Adelaide Road to the north of the hill, it provides a national focus for the performance and study of folk music. It holds a major folk music archive in the Vaughan Williams Memorial Library, which itself commemorates a great composer who drew much of his inspiration from folk music.[19] On the other side of the hill, St Mary's Church has a long association with sacred and classical music.[20] It was here, with Percy Dearmer as its vicar, that *The English Hymnal* (1906), of which Vaughan Williams was the musical editor, was planned.† According to

---

* *The Times*, 26 May 1856. Sir Benjamin Hall, after whom Big Ben was named, had a long-term connection with Regent's Park and Primrose Hill, first as a vestryman for St Marylebone and then as Liberal MP for Marylebone. He was Chief Commissioner of Works from 1855 to 1858, during which time he made considerable efforts to improve London's parks. 'Benjamin Hall, Baron Llanover (1802–67)', *Oxford Dictionary of National Biography*.

† The Vicar of St Mark's Regent's Park from 1904 to 1912, Maurice Bell, a notable writer

the prolific composer Martin Shaw, organist at the church from 1910 to 1920, and recommended to Dearmer by Vaughan Williams: 'Dearmer and Vaughan Williams were the two men in all England who were best fitted for the work, and it is not too much to say that not merely the rebirth of English hymnody but in a great measure the revival of English church music is due to them.'[21] Next door to the church, at 4 Elsworthy Road, lived Sir Henry Wood, the founder of the massively popular Promenade concerts. He was often visited there by Richard Strauss and he once lent the house to Delius.[*]

Apart from the poems of Louis Macneice on Primrose Hill in the war, the most resonant modern poem about the hill is a very early work by W.H. Auden, 'Evening and Night on Primrose Hill', written in 1922:

> Splendid to be on Primrose Hill
> At evening when the world is still!
> And City men, in bowler hats, return now day is done,
> Rejoicing in embers of the sun.
>
> The City men they come, they go,
> Some quick, some slow.
> Then silence; the twinkling lights are lit upon the hill,
> The moon stands over Primrose Hill.[†]

More poets, however, have lived around Primrose Hill than have written about it. Arthur Hugh Clough, the wittiest of Victorian poets, lived in St Mark's Crescent between 1854 and 1859. Christina Rossetti and her brother, Dante Gabriel, were brought up in Albany Street. W.B. Yeats arrived at 23 Fitzroy Road in 1867 at the age of two and stayed there until 1874. In his *Reveries over Childhood and Youth*, Yeats recalled his earliest memory:

---

on church music, was also involved in the gestation of *The English Hymnal*. His predecessor, William Sparrow Simpson, vicar from 1888 to 1904, was the author of the words set by John Stainer as *The Crucifixion* (1887).

[*]   Two famous singers also lived nearby: Adelina Patti, at 4 Primrose Hill Road; and Clara Butt, at 7 Harley Road. *Streets of Belsize*, edited by F. Peter Woodford (revised edition, London, 2009), pp. 33, 36 and 37.

[†]   This poem was published in the school magazine of Auden's school, Gresham's in Holt, Norfolk, in December 1922. Although the poem is unsigned, it was known that Auden had written a poem about Primrose Hill. This was thought to have been lost until it was rediscovered by John Smart, an ex-master at Gresham's.

> I am looking out of a window in London. It is in Fitzroy Road. Some boys are playing in the road and among them a boy in uniform, a telegraph boy perhaps. When I ask who the boy is, a servant tells me that he is going to blow the town up, and I go to sleep in terror.[22]

The famous poetic duo of Ted Hughes and Sylvia Plath lived together at 9 Chalcot Square and enjoyed walking on the hill:

> Ted and I took a lovely, quiet walk this evening under the thin new moon, over the magic landscape of Primrose Hill and Regent's Park; all blue and misty, the buds a kind of nimbus of green on the thorn trees, daffodils and blue squills out on the lawns and the silhouettes of wood pigeons roosting in the trees.[23]

Two years later, after moving away to Devon and then separating from Hughes, and with two small children, Frieda and Nicholas, to look after, Sylvia moved back to near the hill in November 1962:

> By an absolute *fluke* I walked by *the* street and *the* house (with Primrose Hill at the end) where I've always wanted to live. The house had builders in it and a sign, 'Flats to Let'; I flew upstairs. *Just* right (unfurnished), on two floors with three bedrooms upstairs, lounge, kitchen and bath downstairs *and* a balcony garden! Flew to the agents – hundreds of people ahead of me, I thought, as always. It seems I have a *chance*! And guess what, it is *W.B. Yeats' house* – with a blue plaque over the door, saying he lived there![24]

Unfortunately, she suffered chronic depression during what was an exceptionally cold winter and killed herself in the flat on 11 February 1963.

What is true of poets is also true of novelists, with the shining exception of H.G. Wells. The novelists who have lived near the hill have mostly written little about it. Dickens lived as a boy in Bayham Street in Camden Town, and later to the south of Regent's Park, but there are no descriptions of Primrose Hill in his novels. The same is true of George Eliot, who wrote *Middlemarch* at her house in St John's Wood; and of Wilkie Collins, who lived in Avenue Road as a boy and in Hanover Terrace in the 1850s.* Of more modern novelists, Elizabeth Bowen, a number of whose novels feature Regent's Park, scarcely mentions Primrose Hill. Kingsley Amis's novel *The Folks Who Live on the Hill* (1990) is set in Primrose Hill Village. The characters in it, partly so as to keep up a prodigious drinking schedule, never once stray onto the hill. This is also nearly the case with the characters in Fay Weldon's sub-Orwellian novel *Chalcot Crescent* (2009). Although

---

* George Eliot frequently visited the Zoo, however, describing it as 'my one outdoor pleasure now and we can take it several times a week, for Mr Lewes has become a fellow'. *George Eliot's Life as Related in her Letters and Journals*, ed. J.W. Cross (London, 1885), ii, p. 288.

the book takes its title from one of the roads leading directly towards it, the only comment on the hill is that 'the grass of Primrose Hill is thick and green'; while one character, Polly, comes 'back from Primrose Hill where she had been taking part in a protest' against caning.[25] Douglas Adams sets a scene on the hill in *The Long Dark Tea-Time of the Soul* (1988), but describes the park inaccurately as being closed at night, requiring Thor to leap unnecessarily over the railings before lifting Kate over them.[26]

One of the few novels to use the hill to advantage is Helen Falconer's *Primrose Hill* (1999). The teenage characters in the novel have difficult family backgrounds, and become easily involved in violence, but to them Primrose Hill is a place of community, pleasure and refuge, though the downward spiral of the plot, leading to a plot to kill a drug-dealer and his subsequent bloody revenge, means that the hill is mostly remembered as a land of lost delight. On the hill:

> It wasn't like being in London at all – not down in London where you couldn't see shit, but up here, closer to the sky, like we'd been living down a manhole and climbed up and pushed off the cover. You could imagine you were right out of it, maybe on a mountain top somewhere, real air and a sky you could see. Down in the hot, sweaty, concrete valleys hunted the short-haired packs, with their knives and YSL jeans, but up here we old pony-tailed long-hairs were well out of it.[27]

Another novel from around the millennium, Amanda Craig's *In a Dark Wood* (2000), addresses the threat of psychosis, rather than that of street gangs, but finds a calm ending on top of the hill.[28]

There is no record of Sherlock Holmes climbing Primrose Hill, despite the proximity of his lodgings at number 221b Baker Street. The nearest he gets to it is in 'The Yellow Face', when he walks with Dr Watson in Regent's Park in the spring: 'For two hours we rambled about together, in silence for the most part, as befits two men who know each other intimately.'[29] Ruth Rendell, however, sets scenes in *The Keys to the Street* in and around Regent's Park, and on Primrose Hill.[30] A series of tramps, and then a dog-walker, are murdered in the two parks, with their bodies invariably impaled afterwards on the park railings. The victim on Primrose Hill, a tramp known as Pharaoh with an obsession with collecting keys, is found on the railings on the north side of the hill fronting Primrose Hill Road. 'Where in other places fences might be hedges or walls, here were iron railings, straight, plain, usually painted black, crossed with two horizontal bars at foot and top, crowned with spikes.'[31]

Another modern writer of detective fiction, Paul Charles, has set a number of his books in the area around Primrose Hill, where his hero, Detective Inspector Christy Kennedy, lives. In *Last Boat to Camden Town* (1998), the victim found in the Regent's Canal is called Edmund Berry (echoing the murder of Sir Edmund Berry Godfrey in 1678). In it Charles takes a swipe at Primrose Hill's dogs. Sergeant Irvine reports:

> Sorry to be a bit late. I've been otherwise engaged up on Primrose Hill this morning ... some nutter was sniping at dogs from the high-rise flats. He killed four of the pets before we managed to disarm him ... Apparently, he was fed up going out for a walk on the hill every morning and ending up with dog-shit on his shoes.[32]

A famous children's book gives both Primrose Hill and dogs an important place in its plot. Dodie Smith, a highly successful playwright, published *The Hundred and One Dalmatians* in 1956.[*] With illustrations by Janet and Anne Grahame Johnstone, it tells the harrowing story of fifteen Dalmatian puppies stolen from a house in Regent's Park to make fur coats for the demonic, and diabolically named, Cruella de Vil. Their rescue (with an additional eighty-three other kidnapped puppies), by Pongo, Missis and Perdita, three Dalmatians belonging to Mr and Mrs Dearly, is made possible by information gleaned from a network of dogs across England, activated by the Twilight Barking on Primrose Hill. Once they realise that the puppies have gone, Pongo and Missis have no hesitation:

> From the first, it was quite clear the dogs knew just where they wanted to go. Very firmly, they led the way right across the park, across the road, and to the open space which is called Primrose Hill. This did not surprise the Dearlys as it had always been a favourite walk. What did surprise them was the way Pongo and Missis behaved when they got to the top of the hill. They stood side by side and barked.[33]

Pongo knows that Primrose Hill is the best place to send and receive information, as the reception in the rest of Regent's Park is poor.

Sending the barked message, 'Help! Help! Help! Fifteen Dalmatian puppies stolen. Send news to Pongo and Missis Pongo, of Regent's Park, London. End of Message', they at first receive no news, despite the encouragement from a Great Dane, 'over towards Hampstead'. '"I have a chain of friends all over England", he

---

[*]   Dodie Smith, *The Hundred and One Dalmatians* (London, 1956). It was made into a film as *101 Dalmatians* by Warner Brothers in 1963. The plot and characters in the film vary from those in the book. Dodie Smith was for a long time the mistress of Ambrose Heal, the owner of Heal's store in Tottenham Court Road and the accumulator of the invaluable Heal Collection in the Camden Local Studies and Archives Centre. For Dodie Smith's life, and the writing of the book, see Valerie Grove, *Dear Dodie: The Life of Dodie Smith* (London, 1996), pp. 232–68; for her relationship with Heal, ibid., pp. 63–86. See also 'Sir Ambrose Heal (1872–1959)', *Oxford Dictionary of National Biography*.

said in his great booming bark. "And I will be on duty day and night. Courage, courage, O Dogs of Regent's Park".'[34] At last news comes from an elderly English Sheepdog in Suffolk (or 'Wuffolk') and the dogs travel to pull off a spectacular rescue of the puppies from Hell Hall, a house staffed by Jasper and Saul Baddun and belonging to Cruella de Vil. Back safely in London for Christmas Day,

> at twilight, Pongo and Missis firmly led the Dearlys up to the top of Primrose Hill and barked over a Dogdom-wide network. They even managed to get a message through to the gallant old Spaniel, for two dogs from a village five miles from him made a special trip in order to bark at him. (He sent back a message that he and his dear old pet were very well.) Of course the Dogdom-wide barking *was* relayed. The furthest away dog Pongo and Missis spoke to direct was the Brigadier-General Great Dane over towards Hampstead, who was on great barking form.[35]

What is true of novelists and poets is also true of painters. A number of notable painters have lived in St John's Wood, near the hill, but did not draw or paint it. These included Sir Lawrence Alma-Tadema, Sir Edwin Landseer and James Tissot. William Powell Frith lived for a number of years in Park Village West. William Roberts lived from 1946 until his death in 1980 in St Mark's Crescent. John Waterhouse lived in St John's Wood and painted in Primrose Hill Studios, off Fitzroy Road. Arthur Rackham, who also worked in the studios, lived in England's Lane. Stanley Spencer lived briefly in Adelaide Road before moving to Hampstead. The Camden Town Group, based around Mornington Crescent and true to its name, did not paint Primrose Hill. The Austrian Expressionist Oskar Kokoschka lived in King Henry's Road briefly at the beginning of the Second World War.

There are, however, a number of attractive drawings and other illustrations of the hill from the first half of the nineteenth century.[36] While none of these engravings, lithographs, sketches and water-colours can be categorised as great art, they give a good idea of what Primrose Hill and its surrounding area looked like from a distance and from closer at hand at the time. As well as numerous views of the hill and the Chalk Farm Tavern, there are views of families enjoying Chalk Farm Fair and satirical views of duelling, soldiering and climbing the hill.[37] A charming picture of Primrose Hill in 1875, seen from Regent's Park, is one of a series of water colours by Charles Anderson of the latter park.[38]

The one major modern artist to have painted Primrose Hill on more than one occasion is Frank Auerbach, much of whose work draws on a defined area between Mornington Crescent and Primrose Hill, the subject of a series of drawings and paintings. Born in Berlin in 1931 and, like Lucian Freud, a Jewish childhood refugee from Nazi Germany, Auerbach has lived and worked almost exclusively in London. A latter-day member of the Camden Town Group, he is also the successor of Sickert in the darkness of his work. His portraits are clearly also influenced by Francis Bacon. No other painter has reacted so intensely to Primrose Hill.

> Auerbach's paintings are expressions of love and attachment to their subjects, and yet there is always something slightly threatening about the atmosphere they convey. There are the forever bent trees on Primrose Hill, the strokes that define the pathways, or the white highlights that define the lamp-posts, and above all the unpredictability of the elements that seem to hang in the painted skies with their wild colours that somehow dissolve into black vortexes, forever changing and thus endlessly interesting.[39]

On 19 July 1938, an extraordinary encounter took place at 39 Elsworthy Road, immediately next to the hill. The Catalan surrealist Salvador Dalí had been heavily influenced by Sigmund Freud's *The Interpretation of Dreams*, but his attempts to meet his hero in Vienna had failed. Following the Nazi *Anschluss*, Freud had fled to London via Paris and was living in Elsworthy Road before making his final move to Maresfield Gardens.* A meeting between the two very different geniuses finally came about through the mediation of the art patron Edward James and the Austrian novelist Stefan Zweig, both of whom were present at it. Zweig had previously told Freud that Dalí 'says he owes to you more in his art than to anybody else'. There was little conversation between the two men, as Freud was deaf and Dalí was unable to speak either German or English. Dalí showed Freud his *Metamorphosis of Narcissus*, with a stone hand holding an egg. (The next day Freud told Zweig, 'it would be very interesting to explore analytically the growth of a picture like this'.) While the others talked, Dalí drew Freud's head, making it resemble simultaneously Freud and a snail. Dalí later claimed that the meeting was the most important of his life and that he had persuaded Freud to reconsider art. While Dalí was drawing him, however, Freud had whispered to Edward James in German, 'That boy looks like a fanatic. Small wonder that they have civil war in Spain if they look like that.'[40]

Almost everyone's ideas of the Crimean War are due to the activities of a man with strong claims to have been the world's first war photographer. Roger Fenton (1819–69) was born in Lancashire but lived much of his life in London, owning a house at 2 Albert Terrace, facing onto the hill, for twenty years.[41] Having previously travelled to Russia to bring back some of the first photographs of that

---

* Freud, who was an Anglophile and widely read in English literature, lived at 39 Elsworthy Road between early June and 27 September 1938, greatly enjoying its garden and its proximity to Primrose Hill. H.G. Wells visited him at the house on 19 June. Ernest Jones, *Sigmund Freud: Life and Work*, iii, *The Last Phase, 1919–1939* (London, 1957), pp. 242–7.

country seen in England, Fenton was sent to the Crimea in 1855 to cover the war, which had proved far harder to win than had at first been imagined. Because he had been asked to present a positive image of the war, and as he planned to sell his photographs on his return to London, his images exclude fighting and even more so omit the dead. Sadly for Fenton, once peace had been made, the war ceased to be a major subject of interest, meaning that he had little success in selling his photographs. Indeed, discouraged by his lack of financial reward and worried about threats of litigation, Fenton gave up photography only eleven years after he had taken it up.

Frustratingly, for a prolific photographer who specialised in landscapes, Fenton left no photographs of the hill, despite living opposite it for so long. How near he came to taking pictures of it can be seen in two of his earliest photographs, dated 18 February 1852, before he went on his first trip to Russia. These show the scaffolding erected around a half-built St Mark's Church and the advertising hoardings surrounding the building site.[42] Fenton also took a series of notable photographs of public buildings and spaces in London. The subjects of these photographs include the giant equestrian statue of Wellington on Decimus Burton's Victory Arch at Hyde Park Corner and the same architect's Colosseum in Regent's Park.

Besides photographs of war and of landscapes, Fenton left a remarkable set of photographs with an eastern flavour, showing pashas and odalisques, hookahs and eastern musical instruments. It might well be thought that these were another result of his trips to Russia, or somewhere even more exotic. In fact, they were almost certainly all taken in his studio in the mews at the back of his house in Albert Terrace.[43]

Fenton's modern successor as a photographer living in the area is David Bailey, who lived at 171 Gloucester Avenue for thirty years from the early 1960s. Although more famous for his pictures of glamorous women, Bailey's photographs in *London NW1: Urban Landscapes* (1963) show how run down the area was at the time he came to live there. They include two wintry landscapes of the hill. These, however, are easily trumped by a superb photograph, taken by Bill Brandt in 1963, of the artist Francis Bacon walking down the hill.[44] Although there are very many modern photographs of the hill, there is a surprising dearth of photographs before 1960. Although these must exist somewhere, there are very few in public collections. This is only partially supplied by photographs of the anti-aircraft guns on the hill during the Second World War and by picture postcards of the early twentieth century.

An incident mixing celebrity, photography, Pop Art, misdemeanour and an incipient tragedy occurred in late September 1966. Patrolling Primrose Hill, one of the park-keepers, Margaret Blackman, came across two cars, a Cobra and a Buick, painted in red, green, blue, yellow and purple, which had been driven up the hill for a photographic session. The cars belonged to the Honourable Tara Browne, a member of Swinging London's counterculture. The photographer, unrecognised by WPK 28 Blackman, was Lord Snowdon. When reprimanded, Snowdon claimed, 'As a member of the public, I can take pictures wherever I want. All you can do is to tell the cars to move.' To which WPK Blackman quite rightly responded, 'You can be sure I'm going to report you for this.' According to William Hickey, 'Lord Snowdon kept quite calm, but the woman officer was very annoyed indeed. The people in the cars laughed.'* Less than three months later, Tara Browne was killed in a car crash in South Kensington, an incident celebrated in John Lennon's 'A Day in the Life', later released as part of *Sergeant Pepper's Lonely Hearts Club Band* (1967): 'He blew his mind out in a car. He didn't notice that the lights had changed. A crowd of people stood and stared.'

Despite its use for multiple promotional shots, and occasional use for scenes in feature films, the ultimate film on Primrose Hill has never been made. No director has brought H.G. Wells's Martians to perish upon the hill. The 1953 film version of *The War of the Worlds*, starring Gene Barry and Ann Robinson, was set in southern California. Steven Spielberg's version, *War of the Worlds*, released in 2005, is filmed in five different locations, all of them in America. Of a number of films with scenes shot on Primrose Hill, two examples, both romantic comedies, are *Jack and Sarah*, starring Richard E. Grant and Imogen Stubbs (1995); and *The Wedding Date*, starring Debra Messing (2005). In the latter, the appeal to an American audience is enhanced by a game of baseball. The opening scene of *Bridget Jones: The Edge of Reason*, starring Renée Zellweger, Colin Firth and Hugh Grant (2004), is set on the hill.[45]

If no permanent monument has ever been erected on the top of Primrose Hill, one of the largest of Britain's monuments was constructed at its foot, even if the finished work was destined for elsewhere. The Victoria Memorial, which now stands in front of Buckingham Palace, was created, under the supervision of its designer and principal sculptor, Thomas Brock, in an enclosure near the lodge in the south-west of the park, much to local annoyance, a 'large temporary wooden erection by the side of the gymnasium having been put up for that purpose'.[46] Weighing a total of 2,300 tons, its nautical features, including mermaids, mermen and a hippogriff, reflected Britain's mastery of the waves. Victoria's grandson, George V, was so delighted when he saw the finished memorial that he knighted Brock at the opening ceremony in 1911.

---

* William Hickey column, *Daily Express*, 30 September 1966. Tara Browne was the son of the fourth Lord Oranmore and Browne, who held his peerage for seventy-five years and thirty-eight days, and the heiress Oonagh Guinness, a member of the doomed Guinness family.

14

The Sacred Mount

A FTER 1945, in common with much of Britain and most of London, Primrose Hill took a number of years to recover from war damage and from a lack of upkeep during the war. In late September 1947, the diarist Anthony Heap was able to resume his walks over the top of the hill: 'Delighted to discover that the summit of Primrose Hill has at last been thrown open again to the public, even though it is still disfigured by several unsightly concrete anti-aircraft gun and searchlight emplacements.'[1] It was 1948, however, before all the huts to do with the battery were removed and 1950 before the concrete footings on which they had stood were covered up, after the cost of removing these and replacing an estimated million cubic feet of soil on top of the hill had been judged unaffordable. (The remains of the dug-outs provided 'little rooms' for children playing on the hill.)* With rationing lasting in Britain until 1954, it was several years before the allotments disappeared. Most of the trees planted in the 1880s, especially those on the top and south side of the hill, had also been destroyed.[2] In common with other parks, Primrose Hill had rubble from bombed houses spread on it. This made a noticeable change to the shape of the north-west of the hill. According to one long-term local inhabitant of Elsworthy Road, 'I remember scores of lorries every day bringing this rubble to dump after our house was derequisitioned in 1946. We got our house back sooner than most, because it was deemed uninhabitable, owing to several of the workmen having died due to an unswept flue.'† As Britain as a whole, and London in particular, faced huge problems of housing shortage and pressing demands for urban renewal, it is not surprising that there was little money available to spend

---

* So desperate was the housing shortage after the war that a suggestion was made, but rejected, that these should be used for housing. *The Times*, 27 September 1946. As recalled by Irene Demetriou, 'Buried Treasures', in *Primrose Hill Remembered* (London, 2001), p. 40.
† Where rubble was spread can be clearly seen at the edge of the area to the right of the Elsworthy Terrace gate. Enough rubble was spread on Hackney Marshes to raise their level by ten feet and to provide space for eighty-eight football pitches. Information on Primrose Hill from Louisa Service.

on the improvement of parks, even if their full reopening to the public constituted a welcome re-establishment of a traditional pleasure.

On 8 October 1940 Winston Churchill had said in the House of Commons:

> The papers are full of pictures of demolished houses, but naturally they do not fill their restricted space with the numbers that are left standing. If you go, I am told, to the top of Primrose Hill or any of the other eminences of London and look round, you would not know that any harm had been done to our city.[3]

He had, however, spoken before the main impact of the Blitz. Many familiar landmarks had disappeared by the end of the war, although St Paul's Cathedral still provided its traditional focus. On the hill itself, the war had left a heavy mark. Immediately around it the damage was obvious, even if this was far less severe than to many areas in the east and centre of London. St Mark's Church had been gutted in September 1940, when it was hit twice. Two of the villas on Primrose Hill Road, south of the junction with Ainger Road were badly damaged, as were the nearest houses in St George's Terrace. The other houses in Primrose Hill Road, although they escaped bomb damage, were badly shaken by the vibration caused by the anti-aircraft battery on the hill. Nearly all the houses along Regent's Park Road facing the park were also affected by blast damage, most of it minor. On other sides of the park, one house in Elsworthy Road had been destroyed and a number of others around it badly damaged, as were two of the blocks of flats bordering onto Barrow Hill Reservoir. Despite severe damage to Charlbert Street and St John's Wood Terrace, the parts of St John's Wood nearest Primrose Hill, including Avenue Road, escaped relatively lightly. A V1 destroyed a substantial section of King Henry's Road and of Oppidans Road, while others fell on the Zoo, the canal and Wells Street. The V2 that fell in March 1945 on the tea rooms near the reservoir also damaged the houses in Ormonde Terrace.[4]

The priorities of war, which had led to little work being done to maintain housing, also left what had once been highly desirable houses bordering Primrose Hill in a state of decay, their stucco peeling and structural repairs left undone. In Regent's Park, the Nash terraces themselves were threatened. St Marylebone Council proposed that they should all be demolished to make way for affordable housing, while the Royal Institute of British Architects, more moderately, advocated pulling down half of them to make way for a range of buildings reflecting modern architectural design. The decision to restore the terraces hung in the balance until 1957, when the government finally found the money necessary to restore them. Two of the villas in Regent's Park, Holford House and St Katharine's Lodge, had been so badly damaged by bombing that they were demolished after the war, while other villas were used to provide teaching accommodation for the University of London, in particular for Bedford College, whose main building (used in the war by the

Dutch Government in exile) had been badly hit.[5] Less fortunate was Nash's service area of Regent's Park, to the east of Albany Street, much of which was rebuilt by St Pancras in the 1950s as unsightly blocks of flats with little or no overall cohesion.[6]

The whole area around the hill had a general run-down appearance; something that lasted until the 1970s. Some of the housing taken over by the army, including Stockleigh Hall in Prince Albert Road and a number of houses in Elsworthy Road, was only slowly derequisitioned and renovated. At one point many of the houses in Elsworthy Road were occupied by Irish navvies employed in clearing bomb damage. The cumulative effects of the grime generated by the engines fuelling near the Round House, and of the smoke that hung over a London still without central heating and reliant on coal fires, also blackened the outsides of the houses and rotted the curtains almost as soon as they were hung. The physical decline of the housing all around Primrose Hill was abetted by the Landlord and Tenant Act of 1954, which gave sitting tenants almost complete security of tenure. With their houses split up into multiple units, unable to get rid of tenants and often with several different families living in a single house, there was little incentive for householders to repair their property, let alone improve it. Owners even stood to lose their property if it was condemned as 'Unfit for Human Habitation', when only the value of the site, not of the house on it, was paid out. This was a diagnosis housing inspectors might have little hesitation in reaching when examining damp, overcrowded houses with inadequate lavatories and elementary washing facilities. No bank or building society at the time would lend money on houses built in the 1920s or before, or on those with a basement.

The Ministry of Works nevertheless had plans for reviving the hill, commissioning a report by the celebrated landscape architect Geoffrey Jellicoe.[7] Jellicoe's report, submitted in 1950, had three recommendations. The first was to clear the hill of the remains of the anti-aircraft battery and to restore the hill to its pre-war condition, laying new soil on the affected areas. The second was to reroute the paths on the hill, so that those to the summit from the south approached it from the sides rather than directly. The third, harking back in a minor key to the nineteenth-century ambition of crowning the hill with a building, suggested a belvedere. Only the second of these was implemented, the first being ruled out on the grounds of cost. The third was left hanging for years before being dropped.*

---

* There was even uncertainty as to what had been on Primrose Hill before the war. After a meeting of senior park staff, on 2 February 1956, it was reported: 'Enquiries have been made from the long service men working at Regent's Park and they are of the opinion that twenty years ago the top of the hill was enclosed by unclimbable fencing which formed a circle of approximately 25 feet diameter. Within this area a sundial and telescope were located, together with a small shrubbery surrounded by a pathway and six plane trees. Just prior to this time I am told that several poplars were removed ...' National Archives, Work 16/1886.

As a park official recalled: 'The top of the hill was covered with heavy gun emplacements during the war. Afterwards it was found impossible to persuade the War Office to clear away concrete foundations, shelters etc., and in 1950 this department carried out a scheme at its own expense, whereby the erections were in part demolished and in part buried.' That there was some improvement was confirmed by the diarist Anthony Heap, now a father, who wrote in March 1951:

> Take A to Regent's Park and Primrose Hill, on the summit of which the grass is at last beginning to grow again as it did of yore. The paths leading up to it have also been repaired since we were last there three or four months ago. But the allotment sites on the southern slopes and the broken-down fencing around them remain to be cleared and if the hill is to be made really presentable for the Festival [of Britain], it's high time something was done about it.[8]

As late as 1955, however, the inadequacies of what had been done were still blighting the hill. Park officials explained that

> the ground at the top of the hill and immediately north of it had never been properly cleaned since its wartime occupation … there was no more than a deceptively shallow layer of top soil on which scrubby grass sprouted; moreover there were many lumps of stone and concrete so that mechanical mowing was impossible. Schemes had been propounded from time to time for cleaning the ground, surfacing with good quality top soil and grassing properly, but this had never been thoroughly done.[9]

A suggestion that would have linked Primrose Hill with London's sufferings during the Blitz was, however, promptly rejected. This was by the sculptress Clare Winsten, a friend and neighbour of George Bernard Shaw, who had carved a statue of St Joan for Shaw's Corner in Hertfordshire: 'I might be able to do a similar piece of work for Primrose Hill in memory of the women, and men, who behaved like many St Joans during the last war. I know because I was there when the first bombs were dropped and we saw the flames of London from the Hill.'[10]

The one installation on top of the hill to be approved caused an unexpected amount of trouble. On 24 June 1952, the artist Arthur Kenyon had written to the Minister of Works, David Eccles, to offer the gift of a solid aluminium viewfinder, a guide to the identity of the buildings visible from the top of Primrose Hill: 'Before the war there was a bronze plaque on top of Primrose Hill indicating the buildings which could be seen from that position.'[11] Kenyon's work would replace the indexed dial that had been placed on the hill in 1904. The offer was accepted and the viewfinder unveiled at a ceremony on 24 April 1953.

Unfortunately, the viewfinder proved a magnet to vandals, who had already damaged it by early May 1953. This was only the first of a series of attacks by 'hooligans', which culminated in severe damage to the viewfinder on the night of 5 October 1953, when it was 'prised from its base, carried some eight feet and dropped on the ground'. Additional damage by early 1956 included a Republican message, incised an eighth of inch deep in the metal, 'DOWN BLACK TANS HPIRA SLICO'. Neither a perspex cover, added in 1957, nor special armour-plated glass by Pilkington Brothers, fitted in 1960, provided adequate defence. Finally, the park admitted defeat and the viewfinder was removed in March 1962.[12]

Its disappearance was not regretted by everyone, as, apart from anything else, it contained a number of inaccuracies, including identifying a non-existent Wells Street church.* The viewfinder had also been placed, for its protection but to little avail, inside railings. As Muriel Holland, a neighbouring resident, complained in October 1953, 'The top of the hill is disfigured by a large square of hideous tall iron railings. ... The effect is of a tombstone on top of the hill.' She returned to the attack in 1955: 'It is with the greatest regret that I – and many of my friends living in this vicinity – notice the planned ruin of Primrose Hill. The very unnecessary monument stuck up on top of the hill to show people what they can well see with their own eyes ... is perched on the uneven and dangerous and hideous stone stand.'[13] Another local resident, John Willis, complained in October 1956: 'During the summer it has caused some embarrassment to hear visiting foreigners puzzling over the attitude of the English who allow a summit of a unique and breathtaking viewpoint to be crowned with a shabby paling adorned with a pair of litter bins.'[14]

The damage to the viewfinder had another, wider repercussion. Threatened by repeated hooliganism, the Ministry of Works decided to replace the fencing around the park, which had been open since 1929. Chain-link fencing was accordingly put round the park in 1954, but it was noted that 'the Minister has agreed not to close the gates at night pending a review of the behaviour of the public at night under the new conditions'.[15]

Some of the changes in the years following the end of the war were benign, notably the Clean Air Act of 1956 and the switch from steam to diesel and electric on the railways. The pea-soupers and the grime, from London's coal fires and from the nearby railway depot, slowly gave way to an atmosphere that was cleaner and

---

* Oddly enough, the identification would have been accurate if it had been made between 1847 and 1934. St Andrew's, Wells Street, had been a stronghold of Anglo-Catholicism under Benjamin Webb, its vicar from 1862 to 1885. Webb was a co-founder of the Cambridge Camden Society and the editor of the *Ecclesiologist*. The whole church had, however, been moved to Kingsbury in Middlesex in 1934 and re-erected there. It contains work by A.W.N. Pugin, William Burges and William Butterfield. The Buildings of England, *London*, iii, *North-West*, edited by Bridget Cherry and Nikolaus Pevsner (revised edn, London and New Haven, 2002), pp. 135–7.

healthier. Buildings around Primrose Hill destroyed in the war were replaced. Between King Henry's Road and Oppidans Road, the site of the houses destroyed by a V1 in 1944 became Primrose Hill Court, completed in 1951 under a Compulsory Purchase Order. A restored St Mark's was reconsecrated in 1957. In Regent's Park Road and Gloucester Avenue individual houses destroyed by a stick of bombs were replaced by modern blocks by Ernö Goldfinger and James Stirling respectively.[16] Cecil Sharp House, wrecked in the same incident, was itself rebuilt.

This rebuilding was very understandable, even if little of it was for the better in visual terms. By the beginning of the 1960s, however, a boom in property prices had fuelled large-scale development schemes throughout central London.[17] The inadequate planning controls of the time, and the absence of Capital Gains Tax, brought huge profits to the leading developers, who mainly concentrated on creating office space. At a time when Victorian was a term of abuse to planners, and when conservation was still in its infancy, most schemes went through with remarkably few protests. The higher the buildings, the more profitable, so developers constantly pushed to increase the size and height of their blocks, often located in strategic central locations where the sites and existing buildings had already been bought.

While office blocks were their initial targets, the developers also put in proposals for wholesale new housing projects, often in collaboration with the local authorities, who themselves undertook schemes. Eton's plans, with a developer, to erect one fourteen-storey and two twelve-storey blocks on the corner of King Henry's Road and Primrose Hill Road were rejected by London County Council.[18] Nevertheless, the villas lining Primrose Hill, shaken in the war but structurally sound, were demolished and replaced by a block of flats, Whitton; and by Meadowbank, a mixture of flats and houses.[19] A small but obtrusively tall block of flats, Hill View, was built at a point near to the summit of Primrose Hill on Primrose Hill Road. A much-needed purpose-built school was built on the corner of Primrose Hill Road and Elsworthy Road, at the cost of the demolition of Victorian houses, with substantial gardens, in both roads. The school itself, St Paul's, had previously been in Winchester Road, but its site was needed for the large-scale redevelopment of Swiss Cottage as a leisure centre with a swimming pool and library. On the corner of Prince Albert Road and Albert Terrace, a Victorian villa was replaced by an obtrusive redbrick block of flats.

The worst loss, seen from the summit of Primrose Hill, was the elegant but battered Regent's Park Gardens, facing Primrose Hill to the east of Fitzroy Road. Its Achilles heel was its own spaciousness, with an access road at the front and a mews at the back. It cannot have helped that it was also squatted. Purchased by St Pancras in 1963, it was demolished and replaced by the three blocks of Oldfield, the name being that of the purchaser who had bought the site as a lot in Lord Southampton's 1840 auction.[20] The blocks were built by Lord Samuel of Land Securities, one of the most active and successful of post-war developers. Samuel, who lived at 75 Avenue Road, named the blocks after his daughters Carole, Jacqueline and Marion.[21] While the blocks have provided excellent sheltered accommodation for the elderly, the destruction of Regent's Park Gardens reflected the dominant modernist approach typical of local authorities at the time, exemplified by Camden's chief planner, Bruno Schlaffenberg, who, on the eve of conservation and in the face of opposition from the Victorian Society, pushed through a plan that involved the destruction of a number of distinctive villas by Henry Bassett in Gloucester Avenue, but owned by the nearby railways, in the early 1970s.* Fortunately, a subsequent GLC scheme to redevelop the area between Chalcot Road and the park with a tower, or with blocks of six-storey-high flats, was thwarted.[22]

To the north of the park, the wholesale redevelopment of the Chalcots Estate in the mid 1960s led not only to the destruction of well-built Victorian housing but to the erection of high towers, the four main ones being given the names of villages near Eton: Bray, Burnham, Dorney and Taplow.[23] This massive rebuilding of the estate was triggered in September 1964 when the original ninety-nine-year building leases of the houses in the central block of the estate, granted by Eton in the 1860s, fell in. Eton had been well aware of this opportunity, and had been laying plans for the future of its estate, since the late 1940s; its task being complicated by threats of compulsory purchase by the borough of Hampstead and by the LCC, and by the possibility of a motorway spur being built from Swiss Cottage along the line of Adelaide Road. Believing that redevelopment would raise the value of the whole estate, Eton asked for tenders from four developers. Judged informally by Sir William Holford, the leading town planner of the day and Eton's architectural adviser, the contract for redevelopment was awarded to Max Rayne's London Merchant Securities, for a scheme, involving four tower blocks surrounded by patio

---

* Bruno Schlaffenberg (1915–2005) was Camden Council's first head of planning. Born in Austria to Jewish parents, he grew up in Poland and studied architecture in Rome before the Second World War. As a member of the Free Polish Army, he took part in the battle for Monte Cassino. A Hard Modernist, he became a senior planner at the LCC before moving to Camden. In common with most other planners of the day, he had little interest in conservation. According to Roy Shaw, a long-time Labour councillor: 'Bruno had a tremendous impact on members. One of the problems was his Polish accent. Councillors had to listen carefully to what he was saying in order to understand, and there were some people who hated him.' Forceful and emotional, Schlaffenberg was motivated by a genuine belief in the Modern Movement as held by Le Corbusier and Mies van der Rohe between the wars. Unfortunately, this led to the destruction of many houses which would have later been restored rather than demolished. Obituary, *Camden New Journal*, 11 February 2005. Information from Neave Brown.

and town houses, designed by Dennis Lennon.* Rayne, a leading developer with artistic tastes and a reputation for charitable giving, had earlier shown himself adept at dealing with large, conservative institutions.[24] With the Church Commissioners, he had redeveloped Eastbourne Terrace in Paddington, in a scheme in which he took half the profits while investing no capital of his own.

There was little opposition at the time to the decision to pull down Victorian housing or to the proposal for high-rise towers. Instead, the scheme was delayed for several years by the question of how the existing tenants would be rehoused. Hampstead Council's main criticism was that all the new housing was scheduled for what it considered the luxury market. In the end, Eton, Rayne and Camden (which replaced Hampstead in 1965) reached a compromise. Four twenty-three-storey tower blocks, designed by Dennis Lennon and with low ceilings in all of the flats to increase the housing density, were built by Camden itself, while the mostly three-storey terrace houses nearby, also designed by Lennon, were developed by London Merchant Securities and sold off to individual buyers. On the ground, with the loss of local shops and of streets running north to south, the area lost much of its sense of community, while the tower blocks inevitably had a negative impact on the view north from the summit of Primrose Hill. Eton itself raised nearly £1,000,000 through the redevelopment, mostly from the premiums paid by London Merchant Securities and Camden.

To the west of the hill, the northern part of what had once been part of the Eyre Estate, around St John's Wood Park, suffered similar, if slightly less brutal, redevelopment in the 1960s. Three of St John's Wood's Victorian churches also disappeared: St Stephen's, Portland Town (1859), in 1956; S.S. Teulon's St Paul's, Avenue Road (1864), in 1958; and All Saints, Finchley Road (1846), in 1976.[25] Avenue Road, a prime address for the wealthy, also lost architectural cohesion as most of the villas were rebuilt in a variety of modern styles. In the 1960s the St John's Wood Barracks were also rebuilt, retaining almost none of its early features other than its fine Riding School. In 2012, when the lease of the barracks ran out, the Royal Horse Artillery moved to Woolwich, after a two-hundred-year military association with the area, bringing to an end the much-loved sight of the horses being exercised early in the morning in the streets around the hill.

The position in Portland Town was rather different. On the death of the fifth Duke of Portland in 1879, his London estate passed to his sister, the wife of Lord Howard de Walden. The whole of the estate north of the park, forty acres of what

---

* Sir William Holford was responsible for the Paternoster Square redevelopment next to St Paul's. Holford had earned the approval of the Headmaster of Eton, Robert Birley, by replacing rather than patching the Eton Chapel's roof, which had become infested by death-watch beetle. Gordon E. Cherry and Leith Penny, *Holford: A Study in Architecture, Planning and Civil Design* (London, 1986), pp. 222–5.

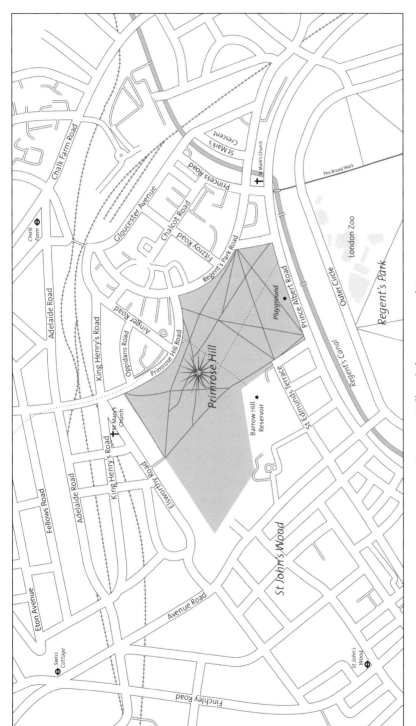

Primrose Hill and the area around it.

had once been Barrow Hill Farm, was sold off for £500,000 in April 1914 to Mr S.P. Derbyshire of Nottingham.[26] As *The Times* reported, 'Although of large area, the property is, for the most part, of a poor description, and it is probably destined for development in the immediate future.'[27] Over the following twenty-five years the estate, notably the area fronting Regent's Park, saw the erection of luxury flats offering views over the park. Three terraces, Lancaster Terrace, Barrow Hill Place and St James's Terrace, facing Regent's Park between Primrose Hill and Titchfield Street, were replaced by flats. Most of the remaining workmen's cottages came down in 1936.[28]

In the Zoo, the new lecture theatre, described 'as a forceful piece of Brutalist architecture' by the Royal Commission on the Historical Monuments of England and very visible from the summit of the hill, was a particularly graceless piece of 1960s architecture.[29] It joined the Snowdon Aviary of 1962–64, an innovative aluminium structure that allowed the public to walk through it and observe the birds directly, in emphasising the divide between Primrose Hill and Regent's Park. The Zoo itself nearly faced closure in 1992, due to a financial crisis stemming from rising costs, falling attendance and a popular perception of zoos as animal prisons. From this low point, aided by various timely gifts, its fortunes revived, with a concentration on education and conservation, and particularly on breeding, paying dividends. Housing fewer animals in more spacious enclosures, the Zoo provides an opportunity to see animals now increasingly threatened in the wild.[30] An additional improvement came from the opening up of the towpath, which passed through the Zoo, along the Regent's Canal.

These nearby changes were echoed by ones further away, with a series of skyscrapers threatening the spirit but not the letter of the legislation protecting the views from the summit of Primrose Hill to St Paul's Cathedral and to the Palace of Westminster.* The end-result of the boom in office-building, some of these towers took a number of years to finish. Of them the most intrusive, because nearest to the hill, was Joe Levy's Euston Tower (1963–70).[31] This joined the idiosyncratic Post Office Tower, later known as the General Post Office and the British Telecom Tower (1961–65), and Centre Point (1962–65).[32] The decisions of the LCC to grant Joe Levy permission to build the Euston Tower and Harry Hyams to build Centre

---

* Thirteen London views in all are protected as a legal requirement within urban planning. Besides the two views from Primrose Hill, the others are from the summit of Parliament Hill to St Paul's and to the Palace of Westminster; from the gazebo at Kenwood to St Paul's; from Alexandra Palace to St Paul's; from Greenwich Park, north-east of the statue to James Wolfe, to St Paul's; from Blackheath Point to St Paul's; from King Henry's Mound, Richmond Park, to St Paul's; from Westminster Pier to St Paul's; from the bridge over the Serpentine to the Palace of Westminster; and from the Queen's Walk at City Hall to the White Tower. *Protecting London's Strategic Views*, Greater London Authority, July 2010.

Point both stemmed from the developers providing adjacent land for road schemes. Making huge profits for their developers, the towers shared a common feature. Their view over London was marketable, and enjoyed by those inside them, but gave nothing back in return to those outside. For a famous viewpoint such as Primrose Hill, the tower blocks and the skyscrapers which have since succeeded them have detracted from the historic landscape. Even worse, these early skyscrapers served as Trojan horses for the future. As opposed to a rational limitation of office towers to areas such as the City and Canary Wharf, their existence in the centre of London encouraged the construction of more tower blocks around them.

From 1960 the area immediately around the hill began to change on all sides. After years of decline in its fabric, inner London began again to be seen as a desirable place to live. With the first improvement grants, and then the growth of mortgage lending, renovating houses became a middle-class pastime and then passion. The advance guard of gentrifiers began to infiltrate what were considered rough, almost derelict, areas, such as Chalk Farm. This led to private money being spent on restoring houses to a high level of outside decoration and to the installation of modern comfort inside. Victorian architecture, previously taken for granted or looked down upon, came back into fashion. Individuals lavished time and money on restoring houses which councils had previously looked at as, and sometimes declared to be, slums. In a relatively short period, conservation replaced automatic redevelopment.* Primrose Hill Village was made a conservation area in 1972, followed by Belsize, Elsworthy Road and St John's Wood. The process also led, inevitably, to richer owners replacing poorer lodgers, and to houses being reunited as single dwellings, maisonettes or flats rather than being split up into numerous bed-sits, though all the neighbourhoods around Primrose Hill continued to be remarkably mixed in social terms. Many houses which had been bought up by the local boroughs in the twenty years after the war remained council property.

While the huge changes of the twenty years after 1945 had often gone unopposed, local campaigners now became increasingly organised and vocal. In 1965 Camden Council erected motorway-style lamp-posts in Chalcot Road, Chalcot Square and Berkley Road. These were put up to light the way for the lorries which, at this time, used these streets as a rat run at night, before going over the bridge at Chalk Farm. When they sent in a petition, the opponents of the lamp-posts were told by the council that it could not deal with individuals. This

---

* An early example of this was the conversion of a piano factory machine room in Hopkinsons' Place, off Fitzroy Road, into the Primrose Hill Community Centre. The factory had been bought by the GLC for demolition but was rehabilitated by a housing association.

led to the birth of one of the first local protest associations and to a campaign which took six months to win.[33]

This initial campaign was followed by another, when Bruno Schlaffenberg floated an imaginative proposal for grassing over Regent's Park Road.[34] This would have allowed local inhabitants direct access to the hill on foot. All the traffic coming over Chalk Farm Bridge would have been redirected down Gloucester Avenue. Although the idea appealed to residents in Chalcot Square, Chalcot Road, Chalcot Crescent and part of Regent's Park Road, it was strongly disliked by those in King Henry's Road and Gloucester Avenue. The latter, the last road in the neighbourhood to revive, was viewed by Schlaffenberg as a mean and shabby street, but it had already attracted a number of buyers who could see its potential. Also opposed to the scheme were the shopkeepers in Regent's Park Road, who thought it would reduce their custom. The row became heated, with the residents' committee unable to give a clear reaction due to the split. 'Hang Schlaffenberg' signs appeared, a sign of the strength of feeling aroused. In the end, the selflessness of some Regent's Park Road inhabitants, who were unwilling to inflict on Gloucester Avenue the traffic they themselves already suffered, decided the issue against the grassing over plan by splitting those in favour of it. The plan never advanced beyond being an initial suggestion and no detailed planning for it was done.[35]

The perception that the traffic through the area was a problem, something that had been thrown up by both the lamp-post and the grassing over campaigns, led to Camden itself carrying out a number of experiments. A variety of roads were closed, in turn, for experimental periods of a couple of months. This was accompanied by local opinion polls about the advantages and disadvantages of these closures. One experiment, that of paving over the top of Chalcot Road, was a definite success. Another, that of closing Chalk Farm Bridge to motorised traffic, caused some initial confusion (with lorries hoping to cross the bridge having to back and turn round), but in the end drew overwhelming support. This change, which was again initially opposed by the retailers in Regent's Park Road, has been a success, even if it has increased the flow of traffic over the hill and along Regent's Park Road.

Inevitably, road use and parking have both been major issues over the last forty years, which have seen a huge increase in car ownership. Adelaide Road, without its once distinctive villas, has become a bleak traffic artery. Avenue Road sees an endless flow of commuters' cars in the morning and evening, even if tranquil in comparison with Finchley Road, a major route into central London. In an area mostly without garages, cars first came to fill spaces by the roadside and then to choke the streets, with the inevitable introduction of parking schemes in the 1990s.

It could, however, have been much worse. The North Cross Route, part of a London Motorway Box scheme, might have seen a motorway similar to the

Westway branching from an enlarged six-lane Finchley Road along Adelaide Road before sweeping round to Camden Town. Stemming from pre-war plans, and from Sir Patrick Abercrombie's *County of London Plan, 1943* and *Greater London Plan, 1944*, the North Cross Route, championed by London County Council, was a serious threat between 1966 and 1972, provoking widespread opposition and a year-long public enquiry. In the end, the expense of the scheme ensured that it was not implemented.*

Reflecting the growth of local activism, and their sense of ownership of the hill, local people strongly opposed an attempt by the Royal Parks Agency, justified by an alleged need to reduce vandalism, to close the gates of Primrose Hill at night in June 1976. This led to a sit-in on the hill from 7 to 18 June and to all the gates being manned to prevent their being shut. Padlocks were smashed and gates, and replacement gates, mysteriously disappeared. Finally, the parks police decided to go home, leaving the protesters in possession. Subsequent negotiations, with Baroness Birk at the Department of the Environment, ended with the views of local inhabitants being taken into account and led to an agreement to leave the entrances to the hill open day and night.[36]

An association dedicated to the protection of Regent's Park was set up in 1991. Rectifying an initial oversight, the Friends of Regent's Park quickly became the Friends of Regent's Park and Primrose Hill. Over the years the Friends have fought a number of inappropriate development plans, including those supported by the Royal Parks Agency, but their aim, wherever possible, has been and is to work together with the park authorities to promote whatever is best for the parks. Other local conservation groups, including the Primrose Hill and Elsworthy Road Conservation Area Advisory Committees, and the Camden Civic Society, which originated as the St Pancras Civic Society, have added their support, with ad hoc activists mobilising for particular campaigns.

In many aspects, Primrose Hill is a local park, though one that attracts many more non-local, non-London and foreign visitors than most local parks. The park is heavily used throughout the year, though particularly in summer, by a wide range of people of different ages and interests. Commuters walk over the hill on their way into London in the morning. A few cyclists speed across it illegally. Early and late, people walk, run and exercise themselves and their dogs. The apparatus in the playground, which has been upgraded several times, is well used and a focal

---

* Local opposition to the scheme can be traced in the minutes of the Camden Civic Society, Camden Local Studies and Archives Centre. A modern echo of this scheme can be heard in plans for the high-speed rail link Birmingham and the North, HS2, which will lead to the wholesale destruction of the area around Euston and to twin tunnels being bored beneath Gloucester Avenue and Adelaide Road. See the Gloucester Avenue Association Submission to HS2 on the website of the Camden Railway Heritage Trust, www.crht1837.com.

point for all families with young children. The gymnasium, or rather a modernised version of it, is still in use, but has been joined since the late 1970s by a dedicated boules pitch.* When it is wet, the bottom of the hill still becomes boggy. Because of this, sporting activities are limited, though many informal games of cricket and football are played near the playground and, slightly more formally, at the back of the hill. The top of the hill, which is an obvious place for kite-flying, quickly turns itself into an impromptu winter sports centre on the rare occasions that snow falls on London. On summer evenings, particularly in hot weather at weekends, the park is covered by picnickers and sunbathers.

The changing make-up of the people to be found on the hill of course reflects changes in the population in the areas around the hill. In common with all of London and most of Britain, Primrose Hill now attracts a far more cosmopolitan and multi-cultural range of visitors than it once did. Unlike in the past, languages other than English are often to be heard on and around the hill. Fortunately, as the pleasures offered by the park are widely appreciated by people with very different backgrounds, colours, languages, creeds and cultures, Primrose Hill can claim to exemplify successful integration in the melting-pot of a great modern city.

Although the thought of being met by the modern equivalent of footpads may deter those of a nervous disposition from walking on Primrose Hill at night, the crime rate upon the hill is in fact remarkably low, as it has been for many years. In the year from mid-October 2010 to mid-October 2011, fewer than forty offences were recorded on the hill. There was one case of minor assault, one of indecent exposure and one of racial abuse. Possession of cannabis, with eighteen cases, was the most common offence. There were twelve cases of robbery, eight of which led to arrests. These robberies nearly all involved gangs of older teenagers snatching mobile phones or other gadgets from younger ones. Almost none targeted an adult. Although this crime rate is higher than that in Regent's Park, where the gates are closed at night, it is so low that Primrose Hill is one of the safest places in London, despite being close to areas with much higher crime rates.[37]

For most of the history of Primrose Hill as a park it was patrolled by park-keepers in distinctive uniforms, often riding bicycles, supported by the police only in the case of necessity. The park-keepers became police, under the Department of the Environment, in 1974. In 2006, the force became part of the Metropolitan Police.[38] Police boxes used to stand near to the children's playground and to the Elsworthy Terrace entrance, but both have now disappeared.[39] There is, nevertheless, a continued police presence on the hill, as the lodge, empty at one point for twelve

---

* An attempt in the 1980s by the park authorities to close the gymnasium, which at that point only had a trampoline, a swing, four rings and a vaulting horse, was abandoned after widespread protest against the idea. Information from Francis Duncan.

years and allowed to deteriorate, is now used again for police housing. The occupants of the lodge benefit from the only two permanent parking spaces on the hill.

A one-time policing problem has also disappeared: the use of the hill as a Gay meeting place. In the 1970s, a prime area for this was near the Elsworthy Terrace entrance. The then-existing shrubberies at the main entrances to the park provided shelter for sexual encounters.[40] Local abhorrence, combined with an opportunity for the park authorities to reduce their own costs, led to the shrubberies being cut down in the early 1980s, while the onset of AIDS in 1982 sharply reduced Gay cruising.

There were, however, also additions.* A park campaign in 1976 saw non-flowering chestnuts planted on the west of the hill, between the summit and the playground, and plane trees on its east. These added to the existing hawthorns, limes, poplars and oaks. A number of older trees were lost in the great storm of 1987, and to Dutch Elm Disease, but considerable efforts by the park authorities, supported by private sponsorship of individual trees, have been made to replace them.†

Primrose Hill's bird life is less rich than that of Regent's Park, reflecting not only its limited size but also the less varied range of habitats it offers. A sharp decline in the migrating species to be seen has taken place over the last fifty years. Whereas in 1960 a team of forty observers saw seventy-one chaffinches and fifty-four redwings in an hour during the day, a team of equal number in 2010 saw only twenty-nine chaffinches and three redwings. Numerous other birds spotted in 1960, including bramblings, house martins, linnets, redpolls, skylarks and song thrushes, were completely absent in 2010.[41] This was undoubtedly mainly due to modern intensive farming methods outside of London, but the large number of dogs exercising on the hill means that it is not a safe place for birds to nest or to rest during migration. Only the undisturbed area around Barrow Hill Reservoir remains attractive to them. A pair of kestrels, however, has occupied a nesting-box on the hill in recent years.[42]

Sylvia Ballerini recalls a time in the 1930s when her dog, Bonzo, used to roll on the hill and bring back sheep's droppings.[43] Now it is the mess left by dogs themselves that causes a problem, partly the result of a national increase in the keeping of dogs as pets.‡ There is certainly no shortage of dogs on the hill,

---

* A less attractive addition was narrowly avoided in 1976, when only swift action by a member of the Camden Civic Society, encountering workmen about to start digging, prevented the erection of public lavatories near to the entrance to the park at the bottom of Primrose Hill Road. Information from Valerie St Johnston.

† The park managers invited people to buy and plant a tree on the hill for £100. Jean Rossiter, 'A Sense of Community', in *Primrose Hill Remembered*, p. 89.

‡ Toxocariasis, spread by roundworms in the faeces of dogs, can cause a variety of unpleasant symptoms in humans, particularly children. Dog urine causes grass burns.

particularly in the morning. Dedicated bins, and a campaign to ensure owners clean up after their dogs have done what their owners have brought them to the hill to do, have made dog mess less of a problem in recent years, when dog-walkers have also been limited to four dogs each. Dogs and their owners provide a distinctive community on the hill and nearby, with human and canine friendships formed over repeated meetings.

While a local park, Primrose Hill is also more than that. For many people, it has come to have a presence of its own. In a city where formal religion is in decline, the summit of the hill, elevated above London and a green outpost in a materialistic world, has a strong spiritual attraction. The differing qualities of light, by day and night, by season and according to the weather, give each visit a distinctive feeling. It is not surprising that numbers of people gather on the hill to greet the dawn at the Summer Solstice and to celebrate the beginning of a new year, or that it is a place well suited to marriage proposals.*

This identification of Primrose Hill as a sacred site has a long history, going back to the Romantic distrust of Civilisation and passion for Nature. Eighteenth-century Londoners, living in the largest city in the world, were well aware of its grime, noise and danger as well as its riches and opportunities. It was easy for them to ignore the grinding hardship of rural life and to reinvent the countryside as a place of innocence and pleasure. This was reflected in the poetry of William Cowper, retreating from London to Olney in Buckinghamshire. Wordsworth and Byron, drawing on Rousseau, added a veneration of mountains, previously seen as barren strongholds of ignorance and superstition.[44] It is not surprising that something of this veneration rubbed off on Primrose Hill, which made up in accessibility what it lacked in grandeur.

The Londoner William Blake's most famous lines celebrate England's fields and hills:

> And did those feet in ancient time walk upon England's mountains green?
> And was the holy Lamb of God on England's pleasant pastures seen?
> And did the countenance divine shine forth upon our clouded hills?
> And was Jerusalem builded here among these dark satanic mills?[45]

It is not difficult to associate the verse with Primrose Hill. According to the

---

* On 15 December 2011, on climbing the hill at about 9 p.m., I came across a young man sitting inside a ring of fairy lights. He was waiting for his girlfriend to arrive, when he was going to propose to her. He seemed confident of a positive response.

archaeologist Stuart Piggott, Blake made 'the revolutionary discovery that Britain was the Holy Land, and Jerusalem not so far from Primrose Hill'.[46]

Another Romantic urge, to give the hill a history even more dramatic than its real one, has added to Primrose Hill's allure. The journalist George Emerson, writing in 1862, reflected this in his invention of a hyper-Romantic past for Primrose Hill's neighbour: 'We do not allude to that square Barrow Hill, close at hand, now crowned by an engine-house, but which tradition avers marks the spot where, at some remote period, a great battle was fought, between whom none can tell, and the bones of the slain were buried beneath the huge mound.'[47] According to a local historian, writing just before the First World War, 'Barrow Hill, on the western side of Primrose Hill, has been beyond the memory of man bare of all vegetable substance. The popular tradition was that there were two brothers, enamoured of the same lady, who met to decide by arms to whom she should belong. Both died at the same time, each by the weapon of his adversary!'[48] Gael O'Farrell expressed a modern version of this urge in 2001:

> Crowning all is our mother, Primrose Hill, said to lie on the same energetic line as that other pregnant mound, Silbury Hill at Avebury. The hill's spiritual significance has been acknowledged for a very long time and as early as the first century, in the days of Boadicea, it was called the 'Temple of Heads', because legendary leaders had prescribed that their heads be buried there after death.[49]

Many prehistoric sites of worship have been shown to have extraordinarily complicated alignments, allowing them to function as solar or lunar observatories. Primrose Hill, without ancient stones upon it, has to make do with being a more modern observatory. It is of course a good place for seeing the stars, as far as anywhere inside the fumes and bright lights of London can make such a claim. A number of UFOs have been reported from its summit. In May 2002 'an object with green flashing lights' was spotted in the sky above St John's Wood, while in April 2004 there was a report of 'a rectangle shape with a white light', both sightings revealed in files released by the Ministry of Defence in response to requests under the Freedom of Information Act. More recently, in February 2012, a witness, named only as Andy G, 'having a break at work in the early hours on Primrose Hill', reported 'no sighting but a deep resonating humming sound coming from the near distance but unable to place the source as it came from all directions at once, but strangely from no specific direction'.[50] As an observatory for such phenomena, the hill has a remarkable, if fictional, pedigree as the leading site of Martian occupation in H.G. Wells's *The War of the Worlds*.[51] The photographer David Bailey contracted psittacosis when he shared his house in Primrose Hill with his girlfriend Penelope Tree, a UFO detecting machine left by Rolling Stone Brian Jones, and around sixty parrots.[52]

Ley lines link places of spiritual significance together, providing an alternative or additional map to the Ordnance Survey. Many of the most significant ley lines, or leys as they are known to their believers, link sites of great antiquity. They reinforce and mirror the lines that have been shown to exist inside Britain's oldest monument sites, including Stonehenge and Avebury. Places standing conspicuously out of the landscape are strong candidates as ley line markers. Ley lines may have been in existence for many thousands of years, yet their discovery is a relatively recent one. It dates back to a single source, published in 1925, *The Old Straight Track*, by a Herefordshire photographer and amateur archaeologist, Alfred Watkins. Deriving the word 'ley', from the traditional word for meadow, a lea or lee, Watkins believed that in prehistoric times it was also used for clearings in the wood made for a track. His leys joined together historic markers of many dates, including neolithic monuments, Iron Age hill forts, medieval castles, churches, hills, crosses, roads and fords.[53] The significance of leys was strongly reinforced by John Michell's book, *The View over Atlantis*, published in 1969, which revealed that ley markers were points of spiritual energy emanating from the Earth.[54]

In these schemes of ley lines and spiritual energy, Primrose Hill is a favourite site. Christopher Street, in *London's Ley Lines*, testifies to the hill's spiritual importance:

> Even with crowds of people on the summit, Primrose Hill is a magical place. I always feel it is more of a goddess site than Parliament Hill and have had several unusual experiences here. The first was to find that as I walked up the hill, I could sense each chakra from the base to the crown, energising one by one as I walked to the crown of the hill. The second was a vision of Primrose Hill as a hill of light.[55]

One of Street's leys connects Primrose Hill with Highgate Hill, Muswell Hill and Southgate.[56] He also supports a theory about the paths on the hill: 'One final thing to look out for on Primrose Hill is in the London A-Z Streetfinder. It shows clearly that the footpaths of the park form a pentagram pointing to the top of the hill.'*

A passage in one of Ben Elton's novels, *Inconceivable*, reinforces the significance of the hill's leys. Sam believes that his wife, Lucy, can only conceive on the top of Primrose Hill, with candles and primrose oil as aids: 'the most positively powerful ley line within this, our ancient and magical land of Albany, runs right across Primrose Hill'.[57] Unfortunately, the aftermath of the occasion is marred by a squirrel which has found its way into Sam's discarded trousers. Perhaps confusion was caused by Sam and Lucy's use of oil made from the North American evening

---

* Christopher Street, *London's Ley Lines: Pathways of Enlightenment* (London, 2010), p. 129. If it has deliberately created a magical pentagram or pentangle, the Royal Parks Agency may have powers which are unusual, and almost certainly undesirable, in a government agency.

primrose (from the unrelated *Onagracea* family), not the English primrose, *Primula vulgaris*. The hill's aphrodisiac properties are also to the fore in *Baggage*, a play by John Muirhead and Mike Charlesworth, premiered at the Arts Theatre on 6 September 2012. Set in the Lansdowne, a gastropub in Gloucester Avenue, it establishes an evening's drinking in the pub followed by an excursion to the top of Primrose Hill as an almost infallible recipe for seduction.

Even if few can now be found on the hill, the primrose itself has a positive resonance for groups as diverse as Conservatives and Druids. The flower was closely associated with Benjamin Disraeli. Queen Victoria, crowned Empress of India by Disraeli in 1877, sent a wreath of primroses to his funeral in April 1883, with the handwritten message: 'His favourite flowers: from Osborne: a tribute of affectionate regard from Queen Victoria.'* (Disraeli had refused Victoria's offer to visit him on his death-bed on the grounds that 'No, it is better not. She would only ask me to take a message to Albert.')[58] Making the most of this royal endorsement, the Primrose League, founded in the same year to commemorate Disraeli and to promote Tory principles, had as its aims: 'To uphold and support God, Queen and Country, and the Conservative cause'; and 'To fight for free enterprise'. Under grand masters including the Marquess of Salisbury the league had over a million paid up members in the 1890s, who wore primroses each year on 19 April. It remained an active force until the Second World War and was only finally wound up, after 121 years, in 2004.

The Druid interest in primroses is a spiritual rather than political one. According to Philip and Stephanie Carr-Gomm, the leaders of the Order of Bards, Ovates and Druids, primroses have always been associated with romantic love and new beginnings, as well as creativity. 'The primrose is the flower of the Bard, and each of us has a Bard within us who longs to sing the song of their soul.' Primrose-flower tea drunk in May was recommended by ancient herbalists to 'cure the phrensie', or as good for the nerves; and the flowers can also be eaten beneficially as the main ingredient of 'primrose pottage'.[59] Primrose flower wine is calming and delicious. The roots of the primrose can also be used as an expectorant. In the 1960s and 1970s, during the heyday of Hippiedom, young people could often be seen with their heads bent, searching the hill for magic mushrooms, *Psilocybe semilanceata*, which are usually associated with sheep pasture.†

---

* W.E. Gladstone expressed doubts as to whether it was, in fact, Disraeli's favourite flower. A.J.P. Taylor once suggested, mischievously, that Victoria was thinking of Prince Albert's favourite flowers, not Disraeli's. Primrose Day was celebrated each year on 19 April, the anniversary of Disraeli's death. The league's motto was 'Imperium et Libertas'. Alistair Cooke, *A Gift from the Churchills: The Primrose League, 1883–2004* (London, 2010), pp. 7–16, 41–74.
† Improved drainage has led to the disappearance of the mushrooms. Other botanical rarities on the hill include the bracket fungus *Ganoderma resinaceum*. More recently, wild carrot has

As the scene of Iolo Morganwg's proclamation of the Gorsedd of the Bards in September 1792, Primrose Hill is a natural site for Druid meetings. Latter-day Druids can be split into two principal branches: those claiming to be the direct heirs of the ancient Druids of Wales, who form a well-established part of the Welsh cultural establishment; and alternative Druids, not restricted to any geographical territory and adherents of paganism.[*] Pagan Druidism draws on magical and mystical learning, distilled from the teachings of Christianity, Cabbala, Buddhism and Zoroastrianism. Its early leader was a Scot, George Watson Reid, who founded the Universal Bond of the Sons of Men in Clapham in 1907, claiming unbroken descent from the Druids. From 1912 Reid performed Druidic rituals at Stonehenge, challenging the Ancient Order of Druids, which had been holding ceremonies there since the turn of the twentieth century. On his death in 1946, the Universal Bond split between followers of Reid's son, Robert MacGregor-Reid, and the elder Reid's chosen successor, G.W. Smith. In the nature of sects, the Druids have since then split into many groups, of which the Order of Bards, Ovates and Druids is currently the most prominent.[60]

There were no Druids on Primrose Hill in September 1892, the centenary of Iolo's proclamation, but in September 1952 they reappeared:

> The occasion was a meeting of members of the British Circle of the Universal Bond of the Order of Druids to mark the autumnal equinox of the sun. Garbed in their white robes, the Druids, during the fifteen-minute ceremony, made a call from the four points of the compass to all united in the order, and displayed fruit and vegetables symbolic of God's gifts to humanity.[61]

They were there again in 1954 and in most subsequent years.[62] A grand celebration, reuniting many of the different types of Druid, was held on the hill at the Summer Solstice in 1992.

The Established Church has not, however, entirely ceded possession of Primrose Hill, which is still divided between three parishes. The church with the most obvious connection to the hill is St Mary's Primrose Hill, which has the advantage

---

thrived in the long grass, left unmown to promote biodiversity: good for arthritis and gout, it has a traditional, but unreliable, reputation as a contraceptive. (I am grateful for this information to Christopher Hedley, a herbalist living close to Primrose Hill.)

[*] Conservative and ecumenical enough to count both the Queen and Prince Philip, as well as Rowan Williams, Archbishop of Canterbury, as honorary Druids, Welsh Druidism has mainly been expressed at *eisteddfodau*, festivals of poetry and singing in Wales. These incorporate the ceremonies of the Gorsedd, including the construction of rings of stones and the wearing of Druidic robes. A highpoint is the crowning of the winning Bard. Dillwyn Miles, *The Secret of the Bards of the Isle of Britain* (Llandybie, 1992), pp. 75–214, gives an account of the history of the Welsh *eisteddfod*.

of having the summit within its parochial boundaries. Its congregation now begins its ceremony of blessing palms for Palm Sunday on the top of the hill before processing down to the church.[63] The vicar also takes the children of St Paul's School up to the top of the hill on Ascension Day, and members of the choir and congregation have sung carols there in recent years on Christmas Eve.[*]

As a place of celebration and ritual, Primrose Hill's fame certainly grew with its annual display of fireworks. This was reviving an ancient tradition, as the hill had been used for celebrations from at least the time of George IV's coronation in 1821, as well as for the spectacular display to celebrate the end of the Crimean War. Most years have seen more modest celebrations of Guy Fawkes Night, though these were banned during the Second World War, when bombs and real rockets threatened London. As an organised neighbourhood celebration, firework displays, with a large bonfire, began to be held on the hill from 1981. From modest beginnings, the fireworks, run by the Primrose Hill Community Centre until 1996, grew to a point where they were taken over by Camden Council. In 2001, the year before they were cancelled on the grounds of cost and safety, almost 50,000 people watched, with spectators drawn not just locally but from across north London.[64] Following the end of the official displays, many people still celebrated Guy Fawkes by letting off their own fireworks on the hill. Due, however, to rowdy and dangerous behaviour on 5 November 2011, the police decided to close the hill from 9 p.m. on 3, 4 and 5 November 2012; and to refuse earlier entry to anyone carrying fireworks.[65]

Primrose Hill's name and fame have also spread, due to the successful rebranding of what was previously known as Chalk Farm as Primrose Hill Village. While mainly an estate agent's marketing device, the name has been accepted by most local residents. It even shows signs of spreading to the north of the hill, though not to its west. This identity has in turn been reinforced by an influx of celebrities into the roads around the hill. Adding to the earlier literary and artistic celebrity of Ted Hughes, Sylvia Plath, Kingsley Amis and David Bailey, Alan Bennett now lives near the hill. Joan Bakewell, a long-term resident in Chalcot Square, was an early arrival in the area in the 1960s. Both Liam and Noel Gallagher lived nearby in the 1990s, complementing Paul McCartney in St John's Wood. Jamie and Jools Oliver have two houses facing the hill. The area has also proved itself a breeding

---

[*]   For a time, the vicars of St Mary's had an unusual advantage over their rivals. After the garden wall of the vicarage, at 7 Elsworthy Road, fell over in January 1955, the Reverend G.B. Timms was allowed, on licence, to have a self-locking wooden door opening onto the hill. 'Mr Timms is basing his claim on the ancient privilege of clergy whereby the lawful incumbent of a parish is permitted the easiest access to all parts of his parish, which includes the major portion of Primrose Hill.' National Archives, Work 16/1604. The vicarage, which was acquired in 1907, was sold off by the Church Commissioners in the early 1980s.

ground of politicians. Boris Johnson, Ed and David Miliband all attended the same primary school, Primrose Hill Primary in Princess Road, before moving on, in Boris's case to Eton and in the Milibands' to Haverstock School.[*]

To the west of Primrose Hill, the West Middlesex Water Works reservoir, now owned by Thames Water, is about to be deepened and restored. When completed, Barrow Hill's current summit, an unsightly roof of concrete, will be replaced and topped by grass for the first time in almost two hundred years. Perhaps it will be covered by a carpet of primroses in the spring, even if they will have to be enjoyed from a distance, as there will be no public access. Changes are still also being made to the summit of Primrose Hill. The most recent reworking, by the park authorities, despite the repeatedly expressed misgivings of the Friends of Regent's Park and Primrose Hill, provides a viewing platform. Unfortunately, in the disastrous tradition of the previous viewfinder, the new viewfinder unveiled by the Royal Parks Agency on 21 June 2012 contained numerous mistakes. As well as wrong dates for St Mark's Church and the Houses of Parliament, it misidentified a free-standing tower near Caledonian Road, with a block of flats behind it, as Holloway Prison. Finally, taking its information from Wikipedia, it gave a wrong height of 256 feet for the hill. The earlier installation at the centre of the viewing platform of a plaque with Iolo Morganwg's motto, 'Y Gwir yn Erbyn y Byd', 'The Truth against the World', is an odd tribute to a habitual forger.[†]

Primrose Hill today faces a number of challenges, including the rational use of the park to the greatest advantage without the loss of its particular character. A sign of the hill's popularity, but one that also causes problems, is the overuse of the top of the hill, which has led to scarring. Wear and tear to the park has been countered recently by allowing the grass to grow considerably longer than had previously been the case. Stopping more high-rise building around it is a particular priority, yet one that seems to have little hope of success. The future of the Royal Parks is also unclear, with a transfer announced by the Coalition Government to the control of the Greater London Authority later diluted, leaving

[*] Other celebrities associated with Primrose Hill include Helena Bonham Carter, Gurinder Chadha, Daniel Craig, Nicholas Crane, Harry Enfield, Matthew Freud, Sir Nicholas Hytner, Sir Derek Jacobi, Stanley Johnson, India Knight, Jude Law, John McCririck, Stephen Mangan, Julian Manyon, Sir Jonathan Miller, Elisabeth Murdoch, Mary Portas, Fiona Shaw, Jon Snow, Gwen Stefani, Rachel Stevens, Sam Taylor-Johnson, David Walliams, Deborah Warner and Fay Weldon. To these must be added numerous authors and reviewers, including Michael Arditti, Selina Hastings, Andrew Lycett, Caroline Moorehead and A.N. Wilson.

[†] The date given on the plaque is 22 June 1792 is in itself controversial. There is no evidence for a Druidic meeting on this day, other than the unreliable word of Iolo himself. In contrast, the meeting on 22 September 1792 is well attested. Ronald Hutton, *Blood and Mistletoe: The History of the Druids in Britain* (New Haven and London, 2009), pp. 155–6, for Iolo's adoption of this motto.

Whitehall with final control.* The importance of Primrose Hill as part of London was at least recognised in Sir Terry Farrell's Ramblas plan for a pedestrian route linking the hill with St James's Park, in doing so harking back in part to the vision of John Nash.† Primrose Hill cannot claim to have escaped formally from Mother Shipton's prophecy, 'When London surrounds Primrose Hill the streets of the Metropolis will run with blood'. If, however, it retains its place as a place of spiritual refreshment until this long awaited bloodbath takes place, it will perhaps remain so afterwards.

No doubt Primrose Hill and its surroundings will continue to change and to attract visitors, drawn by its superb view. A proposal was recently put forward for a striking display on its summit. On 26 January 2012 the *New Camden Journal* unveiled a plan, to be funded by the Brazilian government, for a thirty-foot-high replica of the Rio de Janeiro statue of Christ the Redeemer to be placed on the top of the hill to celebrate the end of London's Olympic Games and mark the transition to Rio, the site of the games in 2016.[66] Although it has been suggested that the installation of Christ on the summit would only be a temporary one, for four years, the hurdles of planning permission, and of avoiding accusations of sectarian bias in a multi-cultural society, made the statue's chances of success little better than those of Andrew Robertson's proposal to erect a full-scale replica of the Parthenon on the same site in 1816.

In the end, Primrose Hill does not need to rely on magical practices or alternative theories to explain its attraction. As James Leigh Hunt described it in 1837, the hill was a place of delight: somewhere where even the poor could gain a respite from their life of toil. There they could enjoy an escape from London to the countryside, looking over the city in tranquillity:

> Pleasant indeed it was … to feel that in this green altitude of Primrose Hill, higher than Ludgate, they can enjoy, as it were, home and country together – the sight of their great hive, full of action at least, if not of greater sweets – and at the same time the consciousness of the Sabbath flower, from which they may bear back to it a little sweeter sweet, something like the honey of health, or the

---

* The Mayor of London now chooses an advisory board from existing members and other candidates, including a member of the royal household. He also chooses its chairman. This gives the GLA and the London boroughs more influence over the parks. Whitehall, however, retains the purse strings. Information from Judy Hillman.

† Announced at the Institute of Contemporary Art in June 2004, the 'Nash Ramblas' is a scheme for a pedestrian boulevard stretching from Primrose Hill to Buckingham Palace and Westminster. Under the Localism Act of 2011, a draft plan for a Primrose Hill Neighbourhood Forum, made up from the areas surrounding the hill, including to its west, was drawn up in 2013.

notion of it; or at least a passing breath of it; a glimpse of the country, if they can go no further; a hovering on the borders of a sensation of ease and retirement.[67]

In less rarefied terms, a line from Blur's 1993 album, *Modern Life is Rubbish*, painted on one of the paths leading to the summit of the hill, expressed a drastically shortened version of the same thought: 'the view's so nice'.[68] This graffito was, however, removed by the Royal Parks Agency in July 2012.

Nowadays, both rich and poor still need to escape from the pressures of life in a great city, away from the cars which crowd the streets. The view from the top of Primrose Hill offers an open perspective close to the heart of London. For those who look carefully, St Paul's and the towers of the Houses of Parliament can still be seen amidst the skyscrapers. Even if they cannot share the intensity and idiosyncrasy of William Blake's vision, they can understand something of what Blake meant when he said: 'I have conversed with the spiritual Sun: I saw him on Primrose Hill.'[69]

Notes

Notes to Chapter 1: A Hill without Primroses

1 Edmund Gosse, *Father and Son* (London, 1907), pp. 48–9. For a far more positive account of Philip Gosse, see Ann Thwaite, *Glimpses of the Wonderful: The Life of Philip Henry Gosse, 1810–1888* (London, 2002). For doubts on the accuracy of Edmund Gosse's account of his father, see ibid., pp. 352, 354, 357, 360, 363, 365, 366, 368.

2 J. Cryer, 136 Taplow, Adelaide Road, London NW3, to editor, *Hampstead and Highgate Express*, 29 September 1972.

3 *Observer*, 10 May 1981.

4 See below, p. 5.

5 Giuseppe Maria Campanella, *An Italian on Primrose Hill: A Narrative* (London, 1875), pp. 6, 7.

Notes to Chapter 2: Above the City

1 For the early history of London, see Stephen Inwood, *A History of London* (London, 1998), pp. 13–50; Roy Porter, *A London: A Social History* (London, 1994), pp. 11–33; and Francis Sheppard, *London: A History* (1998), pp. 7–122.

2 Mellitus is the third London notable in Boris Johnson, *Johnson's Life of London: The People Who Made the City That Made the World* (London, 2011), pp. 17–23. The first St Paul's may have been built on the site of a temple to Diana. The original church was destroyed by fire in 1087. For the history of Old St Paul's see Ann Saunders, *St Paul's: The Story of the Cathedral* (London, 2001), pp. 9–27, 39–51; and Nikolaus Pevsner, The Buildings of England, *London*, i, *The Cities of London and Westminster*, revised by Bridget Cherry (3rd edn, Harmondsworth, 1973), pp. 123–6. Saunders gives the height of Wren's St Paul's as 365 feet; Pevsner adds one foot.

3 The hill may have lost height during the Second World War due to the installation of gun emplacements. The Ordnance Survey map of 1871 gives its summit as 219.5 feet high.

4 Stationers Company Register, 1586–87; H.B. Wheatley and P. Cunningham, *London Past and Present: Its History, Associations and Traditions* (1891), iii, p. 120. It is impossible to be sure which 'Prymrose Hill' is referred to.

5 *Roxburghe Ballads*, ed. J.W. Ebsworth, viii–ix (1897), pp. 86–7. The original was

from the Pepys Collection, 3.53, printed before 1685. The theme of the song, *mutatis mutandis*, is reprised in Charlie Chester's 'Primrose Hill' of 1948.

6 Greenberry Hill contains the name of three men, Green, Berry and Hill, executed for their alleged involvement in the Popish Plot of 1678. See below, pp. 13–15.

7 For the geology of London see Eric Robinson, 'Geology and Building Material', in Bridget Cherry and Nikolaus Pevsner, The Buildings of England, *London*, iii, *North West* (London, 1991), pp. 91–3; and iv, *North* (London, 1998), pp. 87–9. See also *The Geology of London*, compiled by Diana Clements (London, 2010), pp. 1–14, 39–55. I am extremely grateful to Eric Robinson and Diana Clements for explaining the geological history of Primrose Hill to me.

8 While no borehole has been sunk directly from the top of Primrose Hill itself, boreholes were sunk during Robert Stephenson's construction of the London and Birmingham Railway in the 1830s, when excavating clay from the Primrose Hill Tunnel caused him many problems. Other boreholes have been sunk from the Zoo, from the canal junction and, more recently, near Barrow Hill, when work was being done there to renew the reservoir. Eric Robinson, letter to the author, 10 November 2011.

9 According to David Sullivan, *The Westminster Corridor: The Anglo-Saxon Story of Westminster Abbey and its Lands in Middlesex* (London, 1994), p. 127, the Chalcots Estate contained eighty acres of woodland in 1312. See also Colin Bowlt, 'Commons and Woodlands in the London Area', *Transactions of the London and Middlesex Archaeological Society*, 60 (2009), pp. 286–91.

10 Sullivan, *The Westminster Corridor*, pp. 29–36, provides an account of the numbers of pigs in Middlesex at the time of Domesday Book and what this meant in terms of woodland in the areas north of the Thames.

11 There was no road or even path where the Finchley Road now runs until the early nineteenth century. For its genesis, see F.M.L. Thompson, *Hampstead: Building a Borough, 1650–1964* (London, 1974), pp. 110–24; and Simon Morris, 'The Marylebone and Finchley Road Turnpike, 1820–1850', *Camden History Review*, 22 (1998), pp. 24–32.

12 St Pancras has often claimed great antiquity and even continuity from the days of Roman Christianity. For doubts about these claims, see Jeremy Harte, 'St Pancras Church', *Times Literary Supplement*, 4 March 2011, p. 6.

13 Barrow Hill has a longer recorded history than its neighbour, appearing as a landmark in the boundary charter of Hampstead in 986. John Richardson, *Hampstead One Thousand, AD 986–1086* (London, 1985), pp. 9, 12.

14 The other subsidiary manors were Cantelowes; St Pancras, which was itself divided into two manors; and Tottenhale (also known as Tothele and Tottenhall; and, later, as Tottenham). John Richardson, *Kentish Town Past* (London, 1997), pp. 14–16.

15 For these transfers, see David Sullivan, *The Westminster Circle: The People Who Lived and Worked in the Early Town of Westminster, 1066–1307* (London, 2006), pp. 115, 369, 372, 375. In 1258 the hospital paid a rent of £2 to the abbey. John Stow incorrectly credited the gift of Chalcots, or 'Calcote', to St James's Hospital to 'sundry devout men of London'. *A Survey of London by John Stow: Reprinted from the Text of 1603 with Introduction and Notes*, ed. Charles Kingsford, 2 vols (Oxford, 1908), ii, p. 101.

16 Survey of London, xvii, *The Village of Highgate* (London, 1936), p. 1.

17 Survey of London, xix, *Old St Pancras and Kentish Town* (London, 1938), p. 3.

18 *A Survey of London by John Stow*, ed. Kingsford, i, p. 105. Stow also describes the hospital as having been founded by the citizens of London 'before the time of any man's memory, for fourteen sisters, maidens, that were leprouse, living chastly and honestly in divine service', Alan Farmer, *Hampstead Heath* (London, 1984), p. 135.

19 The best account of the hospital is in Gervase Rosser, *Medieval Westminster, 1200–1540* (Oxford, 1989), pp. 300–10. See also, 'The Hospital of St James, Westminster', Victoria County History, *London*, i (1909), pp. 542–6.

20 Rosser, *Medieval Westminster*, pp. 307–9.

21 For Henry's acquisition of the hospital and its lands, Victoria County History, *Middlesex*, xiii (Woodbridge, 2009), p. 72. See also, H.C. Maxwell Lyte, *A History of Eton College, 1440–1898* (London, 1899), p. 108. Four women residents of the hospital were granted annuities in 1536.

22 *A Survey of London by John Stow*, ed. Kingsford, ii, p. 101. Henry had confiscated Cardinal Wolsey's York Place, which became the palace of White Hall, after the latter's fall in 1529. Victoria County History, *Middlesex*, xiii, pp. 64–5.

23 For the history of Marylebone Park, see Ann Saunders, *Regent's Park: From 1086 to the Present* (2nd edn, London, 1981), pp. 15–39.

24 In 1708 John Holles, Duke of Newcastle, had bought the manor of Tyburn for £17,500. The duke's daughter and heir, Henrietta, married Edward Cavendish, second Earl of Oxford, the developer of St Marylebone. Saunders, *Regent's Park*, pp. 41, 47.

25 The Duke of Portland's estate, split to the south and north of Marylebone Park, consisted of the ancient manor of Tyburn minus the land taken by Henry VIII to make his park in the 1530s. For the farmers who worked the land before development, see Saunders, *Regent's Park*, pp. 41–2.

26 N.T. [Nathaniel Thompson], *A True and Perfect Narrative of the Late Terrible and Bloody Murder of Sir Edmund Berry Godfrey* (London, 1678), p. 4. This is the clearest contemporary account. Sir Roger L'Estrange, *A Brief History of the Times: Treating of the Death of Sir E.B. Godfrey* (London, 1688), contains a great deal of evidence, though it is by no means impartial. For modern accounts of Sir Edmund Berry Godfrey's death, see Alan Marshall, *The Strange Death of Edmund Godfrey: Plots and Politics in Restoration London* (Thrupp, 1999); and John Kenyon, *The Popish Plot* (London, 1974). See also 'Sir Roger L'Estrange (1616–1704)' and 'Nathaniel Thompson (d. 1687)', *Oxford Dictionary of National Biography*.

27 N.T., *A True and Perfect Narrative*, p. 4.

28 Ibid., p. 5.

29 *A Letter to Mr Miles Prance in Relation to the Murder of Sir Edmund Bury Godfrey* (London, 1681), folio, half sheet.

30 This account of Godfrey's movements follows Nathaniel Thompson's *A True and Perfect Narrative*, p. 2. Other witnesses reported sightings of him elsewhere, including near Primrose Hill.

31 Ibid., p. 7.

32 Ibid., p. 6.

33   Ibid., p. 6; Edward Walford, *Old and New London: A Narrative of its History, its People and its Places*, v, *The Western and Northern Suburbs* (London, *c.* 1880), chapter 22, 'Primrose Hill and Chalk Farm', pp. 287–300.

34   N.T., *A True and Perfect Narrative*, p. 7.

35   National Archives, SP 29/366, folio 305; Marshall, *The Strange Death of Edmund Godfrey*, p. 99.

36   L'Estrange, *A Brief History of the Times*, p. 340; Marshall, *The Strange Death of Edmund Godfrey*, p. 99.

37   *A Letter to Mr Miles Prance in Relation to the Murder of Sir Edmund Bury Godfrey*.

38   Marshall, *The Strange Death of Edmund Godfrey*, pp. 74–115; Kenyon, *The Popish Plot*, pp. 70–96, 302–9.

39   'Miles Prance (fl. 1678–88)', *Oxford Dictionary of National Biography*.

40   The name was said by Narcissus Luttrell to predate their execution. 'It is remarkable that the place where Sir Edmondbury Godfrey's corpse was found is in the old leases called Green Bury Hill, being the names of the three persons condemned for the murther', Narcissus Luttrell, *A Brief Historical Relation of State Affairs from September 1678 to April 1741*, six vols (Oxford, 1857), i, p. 8. Luttrell's evidence about the name of the hill would carry more weight if it had been written before the trial of Green, Berry and Hill.

41   Kenyon, *The Popish Plot*, pp. 281–94.

42   Marshall, *The Strange Death of Edmund Godfrey*, pp. 160–3. See Alan Marshall, *Intelligence and Espionage in the Reign of Charles II, 1660–1685* (Cambridge, 1994), pp. 185–243, for the murky world of government espionage at this time.

43   National Archives, MPE 1/576. The map must be before 1710, when Thomas Baker died.

44   The earliest map of St John's Wood, dating from 1679, the year after Godfrey's murder, shows 'White Lodge' to the north-west of a roughly drawn Primrose Hill, Camden Local Studies and Archives Centre, ST2 1A/5 (formerly Hampstead Deeds, 136). The earliest map of the Eyre Estate, dating from 1733, has a building at the bottom corner of 'The Blewhouse formerly called the Whitehouse Field', Westminster City Archives, EE 2652/1. Both maps are reproduced in Mireille Galinou, *Cottages and Villas: The Birth of the Garden Suburb* (London and New Haven, 2010), pp. 25, 32.

45   N.T., *A True and Perfect Narrative*, p. 5.

46   This would tally with the site suggested by A.D. Webster: 'Until quite recently a stone in the ditch by the northern iron fence of the reservoir marked the spot where the body was found.' A.D. Webster, *The Regent's Park and Primrose Hill: History and Antiquities* (London, 1911), p. 87.

47   John Richardson, *Camden Town and Primrose Hill Past* (London, 1991), p. 93. It had, however, a cellar.

48   Gilbert Burnet, *History of My Own Time* (London, 1725), ii, p. 757.

49   Keith Thomas, *Man and the Natural World: Changing Attitudes in England, 1500–1800* (London, 1984), pp. 55, 74, 274.

50   Saunders, *Regent's Park*, pp. 46, 51 and 55. London's long-term boundary also marked the northernmost extent of the Taplow terraces, upon which building was much easier than upon clay.

51 Alan Faulkner, *The Regent's Canal: London's Hidden Waterway* (Burton-on-Trent, 2005), pp. 1–15.

52 Saunders, *Regent's Park*, pp. 40–60. Willan's Farm had previously been called Daggett's Farm or Marylebone Farm.

53 Malcolm Brown, '"The Fields of Cows by Willan's Farm": Thomas Willan of Marylebone (1755–1828)', *Westminster History Review*, 4 (2001), pp. 1–5. The other teahouse was the Queen's Head and Artichoke.

54 William Blake, *Jerusalem*, 'To the Jews', lines 13–16, *The Complete Writings of William Blake*, ed. Geoffrey Keynes (London, 1957), p. 431. The Green Man was a tavern on the New Road.

55 Brown, 'The Fields of Cows by Willan's Farm', p. 3.

56 For the history of Chalcots before development, Victoria County History, *Middlesex*, ix (London, 1989), pp. 63–6. The site of Rhodes's farm can be clearly seen on the Tompson map of St Pancras (1804). The Rhodes family rented many of the fields in St Pancras between the New Road and Primrose Hill.

57 For the early history of Belsize, see Thompson, *Hampstead*, pp. 33–7, 90–3.

58 The Ashbridge Collection, Westminster City Archives, contains a number of early images of Primrose Hill. Simon Jenkins and Jonathan Ditchburn, *Images of Hampstead* (Richmond-upon-Thames, 1982), is a comprehensive collection of images for a wider area, which includes the hill.

59 *Mother Goose Rhymes* (London, 1780). Given in the form 'As I was going up Pippen Hill', in *The Oxford Dictionary of Nursery Rhymes*, edited by Iona and Peter Opie (Oxford, 1952), p. 352.

60 See above, frontispiece, p. ii. Jenkins and Ditchburn, *Images of Hampstead*, pp. 128 and 252, image no. 422. Reproduced in George Clinch, *Marylebone and St Pancras: Their History, Celebrities, Buildings and Institutions* (London, 1890), opposite p. 76.

61 'The Pastimes of Primrose Hill', by Isaac Cruikshank, in Jenkins and Ditchburn, *Images of Hampstead*, no. 422.

62 Anthony Cooper, 'Old Chalk Farm Tavern', *Camden History Review*, 6 (1978), pp. 2–5.

63 *General Evening Post*, 1 November 1748. See also *London Evening Post*, 29 October 1748.

64 *The Proceedings of the Old Bailey, 1674–1913*, t17490113–28; OA17490220.

65 Cooper, 'Old Chalk Farm Tavern', p. 2. For advertisements of the freehold of 122 acres, including the Stag and Hounds, *Morning Chronicle*, 28 April 1785, and *Morning Post*, 3 June 1786. For the lease of what was now the 'Chalk Farm Tavern and Tea Gardens', *Morning Post*, 14 February 1789.

66 Advertisement, 1787, cutting in Hampstead Collection, Camden Local Studies and Archives Centre. An 'ordinary' meant the standard provision of a fixed menu.

67 Ibid.

68 The best account of the background to the meeting, and of the events that followed it, is Alan Wharam, *The Treason Trials, 1794* (London, 1992). For the Chalk Farm meeting, ibid., pp. 79–82.

69 Boyd Hilton, *A Mad, Bad and Dangerous People? England, 1783–1846* (Oxford, 2006), pp. 65–74; Clive Emsley, *Britain and the French Revolution* (Harlow, 2000), pp. 29–40; 'John Frost (1750–1842)' and 'Thomas Hardy (1752–1832)', *Oxford*

Dictionary of National Biography. Frost should not be confused with his namesake, John Frost (1784–1877), a Chartist martyr.

70   Wharam, *The Treason Trials, 1794*, pp. 51–8.

71   *Oracle and Public Advertiser*, 16 April 1794.

72   *Morning Post*, 15 April 1794.

73   'John Thelwall (1764–1834)', *Oxford Dictionary of National Biography*.

74   *World*, 16 June 1794.

75   *World*, 16 June 1794.

76   *Morning Post*, 15 April 1794.

77   Besides the London Corresponding Society meeting, there were large Radical meetings in Sheffield and Halifax, and news of a conspiracy in Ireland. There were also numerous reports about weapons being collected. Wharam, *The Treason Trials, 1794*, pp. 68–90.

78   The arrest warrant needed to be signed by one of the secretaries of state or any six members of the Privy Council. Emsley, *Britain and the French Revolution*, p. 32.

79   Wharam, *The Treason Trials, 1794*, pp. 137–42.

80   Ibid., pp. 143–93.

81   *Sun*, 1 November 1794; *Oracle*, 1 November 1794; see also, *True Briton*, 1 November 1794. Emsley, *Britain and the French Revolution*, p. 33.

82   Preamble to the Act suspending Habeas Corpus, 34 George III, c. 54 (1794).

83   Wharam, *The Treason Trials*, p. 192.

84   'John Horne Tooke (1736–1812)', *Oxford Dictionary of National Biography*. For the trials of Horne Tooke and Thelwall, see Wharam, *The Treason Trials, 1794*, pp. 194–228.

85   Emsley, *Britain and the French Revolution*, pp. 34–9.

Notes to Chapter 3: A Question of Honour

1   *Caledonian Mercury*, 16 August 1806.

2   For duels in the sixteenth and seventeenth centuries, see Markku Peltonen, *The Duel in Early Modern England: Civility, Politeness and Honour* (Cambridge, 2003).

3   For an account of the importance of honour, see Keith Thomas, *The Ends of Life: Roads to Fulfilment in Early Modern England* (Oxford, 2009), pp. 147–86.

4   For English duelling in the eighteenth and nineteenth centuries, see Robert Shoemaker, *The London Mob: Violence and Disorder in Eighteenth-Century England* (London and New York, 2004), pp. 16–214; Donna T. Andrew, 'The Code of Honour and its Critics: The Opposition to Duelling in England, 1700–1850', *Social History*, 5 (1980), pp. 409–34; and Antony Simpson, 'Dandelions on the Field of Honour: Duelling, the Middle Classes and the Law in Nineteenth-Century England', *Criminal Justice History*, 5 (1988), pp. 99–155. For general accounts of duelling, see Robert Baldick, *The Duel: A History of Duelling* (London, 1965); Richard Hopton, *Pistols at Dawn: A History of Duelling* (London, 2007); and V.G. Kiernan, *The Duel in European History: Honour and the Reign of Aristocracy* (Oxford, 1988). For older works, including lists of duels, see James Gilchrist, *A Brief Display of the Origin and History of Ordeals: Trials by Battle, Courts of Chivalry or Honour, and the Decision of Private Quarrels by Single Combat. Also a Chronological Register of the Principal Duels*

Fought from the Accession of His Late Majesty to the Present Time (London, 1821); J.G. Millingen, *The History of Duelling*, 2 vols (London, 1841); Lorenzo Sabine, *Notes on Duels and Duelling, Alphabetically Arranged: With a Preliminary Historical Essay* (3rd edn, Boston, 1859); Andrew Steinmetz, *The Romance of Duelling in All Times and Countries*, 2 vols (London, 1868); and Ben C. Truman, *The Field of Honor: Being a Complete and Comprehensive History of Duelling in All Countries* (New York, 1884), pp. 226, 497. See Table, above pp. 27–30, for a full list of duels at or near Primrose Hill, including those aborted before an exchange of fire.

5   The binding over of intending duellists seems to have been remarkably successful in preventing duels. Stephen Banks, *A Polite Exchange of Bullets: The Duel and the English Gentleman, 1750–1850* (Woodbridge, 2010), pp. 154–60, shows that recourse to the law by prosecuting challengers for a breach of the king's peace could also be successful.

6   Camden Local Studies and Archives Centre, Heal Collection, A IX, 14. The Heal Collection has many newspaper cuttings dated by their collector, Ambrose Heal, by year but not day. The name of the newspaper is usually not cited.

7   Heal Collection, A IX, 16.

8   Heal Collection, A IX, 16.

9   'Lieutenant of the Coast Blockade versus veteran army captain on half pay', *Standard*, 7 April 1830; *Morning Chronicle*, 8 April 1830.

10 For Irish duels and duellists, see James Kelly, *'That Damn'd Thing Called Honour': Duelling in Ireland, 1570–1860* (Cork, 1995).

11 It has been claimed that less than one in ten duels ended with a death, though one in three may have brought about a more or less serious injury, Shoemaker, *The London Mob*, p. 182. The general casualty rate calculated by Antony Simpson, 'Dandelions on the Field of Honour', pp. 106–7, 110, for duels between 1785 and 1850, matches more closely the experience of duellists on Primrose Hill.

12 An account of the duel between Humphry Hobart and Thomas O'Reilly in 1804, however, describes the protagonists, at one point before the duel, as standing back to back but fifteen or sixteen paces apart. Heal Collection, A IX, 14. See below, pp. 44–5.

13 See Hopton, *Pistols at Dawn*, pp. 80, 84–8, 352, 368, 371, for barrier duels.

14 Charles James Perry, in 'Poetic Reflections on Viewing Blood Hill', in *The House of Mornington: A Pastoral Drama* (London, 1826), included Barrow Hill as the site of a fictional duel, renaming it Blood Hill, 'so designated from the circumstance of two brothers who fought thereon, one of whom, was killed by the hand of the other'. See also A.M. Eyre, *Saint John's Wood: Its History, its Houses, its Haunts and its Celebrities* (London, 1913), pp. 250–1.

15 *Morning Post*, 8 April 2012.

16 'Colonel M. versus Mr W.', *Morning Post*, 29 April 1813; 'Mr C-y versus Mr S-y', *Morning Post*, 5 December 1806; 'Littleton versus Rogers', *Caledonian Mercury*, 14 October 1824; 'Sandoz versus Dubois', *Morning Chronicle*, 30 July 1808.

17 'Colonel Montgomery versus Captain Macnamara, 6 April 1803', *Proceedings of the Old Bailey*, t18030420–2; 'John Scott versus Jonathan Christie, 16 February 1821', *Proceedings of the Old Bailey*, t18210411–29.

18 *Public Advertiser*, 29 June 1790.

19 *Memoirs of George Elers: Captain in the 12th Regiment of Foot, 1777–1842*, edited by Lord Monson and George Leveson-Gower (London, 1903), pp. 168–9.

20 *Report of the Trial on an Inquisition, upon a Verdict of Manslaughter against Captain Macnamara for Killing and Slaying Colonel Robert Montgomery* (London, n.d.), pp. 5–22; Steinmetz, *The Romance of Duelling*, ii, pp. 185–8; 'James Macnamara (1768–1826)', *Oxford Dictionary of National Biography*; Charles Nottidge Macnamara, *The Story of an Irish Sept* (London, 1896), p. 297. The duel was widely reported in contemporary newspapers. See *Aberdeen Journal*, 27 April 1803; *British Gazette*, 10 April 1803; *Bury and Norwich Post*, 13, 20 and 27 April 1803; *Derby Mercury*, 14 April 1803; *Hampshire Telegraph and Portsmouth Gazette*, 18 April 1803; *Hull Packet*, 26 April 1803; *Ipswich Journal*, 16, 23 April 1803; *Jackson's Oxford Journal*, 16, 23 April 1803; *Morning Chronicle*, 9, 16, 21, 22, 23 April 1803; *Morning Post*, 8, 9, 16, 22 and 23 April 1803; *Newcastle Courant*, 16, 23 April 1803. The fullest reports of the trial are in the *Morning Chronicle*, 23 April 1803, and the *Morning Post*, 23 April 1803.

21 *Morning Post*, 8 April 1803; 'James Macnamara (1768–1826)', *Oxford Dictionary of National Biography*.

22 *Bury and Norwich Post*, 13 April 1803.

23 *British Gazette*, 10 April 1803. Sir William Keir, an officer in the Dragoons, had only one arm, having lost the other in a duel with Sir Marcus Somerville, *Morning Post*, 8 April 1803.

24 *Report of the Trial on an Inquisition, upon a Verdict of Manslaughter against Captain Macnamara for Killing and Slaying Colonel Robert Montgomery*, p. 14.

25 'John Heaviside (baptised 1748, died 1828)', *Oxford Dictionary of National Biography*; *Morning Post*, 8 April 1803.

26 The coroner stated that 'where two persons met to fight without having sufficient time to cool upon their quarrel, in the event of the death of one, the crime of murder could not be charged against the other'. *Newcastle Courant*, 16 April 1803.

27 *Report of the Trial on an Inquisition, upon a Verdict of Manslaughter against Captain Macnamara for Killing and Slaying Colonel Robert Montgomery*, p. 22.

28 See above, pp. 19–22.

29 Banks, *A Polite Exchange of Bullets*, pp. 140, 150, 163–4, 166.

30 *Report of the Trial on an Inquisition, upon a Verdict of Manslaughter against Captain Macnamara for Killing and Slaying Colonel Robert Montgomery*, pp. 15–17; Millingen, *The History of Duelling*, ii, p. 169.

31 *Report of the Trial on an Inquisition, upon a Verdict of Manslaughter against Captain Macnamara for Killing and Slaying Colonel Robert Montgomery*, p. 18.

32 *Morning Post*, 8 April 1803.

33 The newspaper sources for the duel differ in detail but agree on its main elements. See *Aberdeen Journal*, 8 March 1809; *Bury and Norwich Post*, 8 March 1809; *Caledonian Mercury*, 4 March 1809; *Derby Mercury*, 9 March 1809; *Examiner*, 5 March 1809; *Gentleman's Magazine*, 79, part 1 (1809), p. 273; *Hull Packet*, 14 March 1809; *Ipswich Journal*, 4 and 11 March 1809; *Jackson's Oxford Journal*, 11 March 1809; *Morning Chronicle*, 6 March 1809; *Morning Post*, 2, 3, 6 and 14 March 1809; *Observer*, 5 March 1809; *The Times*, 6 March 1809; and *Trewman's Exeter Flying Post*, 9 March 1809. Although many of the papers give Powell's Christian name as Alexander, he was Arthur Annesley Powell (1772–1813). There are no descriptions of the exact location

of the duel, though nearly all give Chalk Farm as the place of encounter. Two accounts place it at Golders Green.

34 *Examiner*, 5 March 1809.

35 *Morning Chronicle*, 2 March 1809; *Trewman's Exeter Flying Post*, 9 March 1809.

36 *Ipswich Journal*, 11 March 1809.

37 *Ipswich Journal*, 11 March 1809; *Jackson's Oxford Journal*, 11 March 1809.

38 *Ipswich Journal*, 4 March 1809; *Examiner*, 5 March 1809; *Bury and Norwich Post*, 8 March 1809.

39 G.E.C., *The Complete Peerage*, v (London, 1926), pp. 243–4.

40 *Morning Post*, 7 February 1809; *Aberdeen Journal*, 8 March 1809.

41 *The Farington Diary*, ed. J. Greig, 8 vols (London, 1922–28), iii, p. 112; F.M.L. Thompson, *English Landed Society in the Nineteenth Century* (London, 1963), p. 50.

42 *Caledonian Mercury*, 2 February 1809.

43 *Caledonian Mercury*, 4 March 1809; *Trewman's Exeter Flying Post*, 9 March 1809.

44 *Examiner*, 5 March 1809.

45 *Morning Chronicle*, 6 March 1809.

46 *Morning Post*, 2 March 1809; *Ipswich Journal*, 4 March 1809; *Morning Chronicle*, 6 March 1809.

47 *Morning Chronicle*, 6 March 1809.

48 *Ipswich Journal*, 4 March 1809.

49 *The Times*, 6 March 1809.

50 *The Times*, 6 March 1809.

51 *Observer*, 5 March 1809; *Jackson's Oxford Journal*, 11 March 1809; *Hull Packet*, 14 March 1809.

52 'Lucius Bentinck Cary, Tenth Viscount Falkland (1803–84)', *Oxford Dictionary of National Biography*; *Byron's Letters and Journals*, i, *In My Hot Youth, 1798–1810*, ed. Leslie A. Marchand (London, 1973), p. 195; Leslie A. Marchand, *Byron: A Biography*, 3 vols (London, 1957), i, 169–70. For Lady Falkland's letters to Byron, ibid., i, pp. 346–7.

53 *Morning Chronicle*, 10 July 1807.

54 'Captain E-n versus Mr J-n', Heal Collection, A IX, 16; 'Captain M-n versus Mr P-e', *Johnson's*, 11 September 1808; 'Lt Br-ke versus Lt Sh-rd-n', Heal Collection, A IX, 16; 'Two military gentlemen', Heal Collection, A IX, 16; 'Lieutenant of the Coastal Blockade versus veteran army captain on half pay', *Standard*, 7 April 1830.

55 Ronan Kelly, *Bard of Erin: The Life of Thomas Moore* (Dublin, 2008), p. 139; *Edinburgh Review*, July 1806.

56 *Edinburgh Review*, July 1806.

57 Steinmetz, *The Romance of Duelling*, ii, pp. 196–203.

58 Thomas Moore, *Memoirs, Journal and Correspondence of Thomas Moore*, ed. Lord John Russell, 8 vols (London, 1853–56), i, pp. 199ff. Moore bought the powder and bullets in a shop in Bond Street.

59 Ibid., i, p. 201.

60 Kelly, *Bard of Erin*, pp. 139–47; Baldick, *The Duel*, pp. 185–7.

61 Baldick, *The Duel*, p. 187; Kiernan, *The Duel in European History*, pp. 210, 239–40.

62 *The Times*, 12 August 1806. For Moore's claim that the pistols *had* been properly loaded, see *Morning Chronicle*, 18 August 1809, and *Morning Post*, 18 August 1809.

63 *Morning Post*, 13 August 1806.

64 Marchand, *Byron*, i, pp. 299–306.

65 The best account of the circumstances which led up to the duel is by Andrew Lang, *The Life and Letters of John Gibson Lockhart*, 2 vols (London, 1897), i, pp. 268–77. Lockhart was Sir Walter Scott's son-in-law and later his biographer.

66 *Proceedings of the Old Bailey*, t18210411–29; *Jackson's Oxford Journal*, 24 February 1821; Kiernan, *The Duel in European History*, p. 227.

67 Edmund Gosse, *Coventry Patmore* (London, 1905), pp. 2–3.

68 E.R. Vincent, *Ugo Foscolo: An Italian in Regency England* (Cambridge, 1953), pp. 154–6, 175. Edward Walford, *Old and New London*, v, p. 290, states that the duel was fought on Barrow Hill, but gives no source for this.

69 *Examiner*, 19 and 26 March 1826; 'Robert Lyall (1789–1831)', *Oxford Dictionary of National Biography*.

70 *Lloyd's Evening Post*, 16 July 1792.

71 Heal Collection, A IX, 14.

72 *Proceedings of the Old Bailey*, t18040516.

73 *Morning Post*, 12 October 1824; *Caledonian Mercury*, 14 October 1824.

74 Heal Collection, A IX, 14.

75 *Bell's Weekly Messenger*, 18 January 1818; Heal Collection, A IX 18, 19.

76 Heal Collection, A IX, 14.

77 Heal Collection, A IX, 14.

78 *John Bull*, 20 August 1832.

79 *Jackson's Oxford Journal*, 25 August 1832; *John Bull*, 20 August 1832.

80 *Examiner*, 28 May 1837.

81 For a balanced account of the personalities and issues involved in this extraordinary case, Saul David, *The Homicidal Earl: The Life of Lord Cardigan* (London, 1997), pp. 108–70.

82 Ibid., p. 120.

83 Ibid., pp. 156–70. See also, Hopton, *Pistols at Dawn*, pp. 264–7; and Kiernan, *The Duel in European History*, pp. 215–16.

84 David, *The Homicidal Earl*, pp. 156–70. Unlike previous duellists, Cardigan was charged under the Ellenborough Act of 1803, which made to 'shoot at, stab or cut' a capital offence, Banks, *A Polite Exchange of Bullets*, pp. 135–6, 217–20, 241, 285–6.

85 Kiernan, *The Duel in European History*, p. 217; 'Sir Charles Napier (1786–1860)', *Oxford Dictionary of National Biography*.

86 National Archives, PRO 30/29/6/11; Treasury 29/116, p. 747; PRO, Treasury 29/117, p. 73.

87 'Granville Leveson Gower, First Earl Granville (1773–1846)', *Oxford Dictionary of National Biography*.

88 *A Full Report of the Trial of John Bellingham for the Murder of the Right Hon. Spencer Perceval* (Hull, 1812), p. 5; *Caledonian Mercury*, 21 May 1812. The gunsmith, W.A. Beckwith, was at 58 Skinner Street, Snow Hill, near the Old Bailey. Bellingham probably tried out his pistols at the target near the Chalk Farm Tavern.

Notes to Chapter 4: The Gorsedd of the Bards

1 *Gentleman's Magazine*, 62 (1792), pp. 956–7; Ronald Hutton, *Blood and Mistletoe: The History of the Druids in Britain* (New Haven and London, 2009), pp. 158–9; Ronald Hutton, *The Druids* (London, 2007), p. 160.

2 The study of the Druids, in all their manifestations, has been transformed by Ronald Hutton, whose books combine scholarship, readability and originality in equal measure. Hutton's *Blood and Mistletoe* is a long and detailed account of the Druids from prehistory to the modern day. His *The Druids* is a succinct and thematic treatment of their history. My account of the Druids in this chapter relies heavily on these books.

3 For a short biography of Williams, see Prys Morgan, *Iolo Morganwg* (Cardiff, 1975). For recent scholarship on him, see Hutton, *Blood and Mistletoe*, p. 443, nn. 13–16. Elijah Waring, *Recollections and Anecdotes of Edward Williams* (London, 1850), contains two portraits of, and many anecdotes about, Williams.

4 Hutton, *Blood and Mistletoe*, pp. 150–5; Hutton, *The Druids*, pp. 22–4, 29 and 160.

5 Hutton, *Blood and Mistletoe*, p. 148; Hutton, *The Druids*, p. 21.

6 Morgan, *Iolo Morganwg*, pp. 1–5.

7 Ibid., p. 7. The Society of Ancient Britons was no longer in existence by this date.

8 Hutton, *Blood and Mistletoe*, pp. 162–5.

9 Ibid., p. 153, for Dafydd ap Gwylym, and p. 160, for Llywelyn Sion.

10 Dillwyn Miles, *The Secret of the Bards of the Island of Britain* (Llandybie, 1992), p. 59; Hutton, *Blood and Mistletoe*, pp. 125–8, 158.

11 *Gentleman's Magazine*, 62 (1792), pp. 956–7; *Evening Mail*, 24 September 1792; Hutton, *Blood and Mistletoe*, pp. 158–60.

12 *Gentleman's Magazine*, 62 (1792), pp. 956–7.

13 *Gentleman's Magazine*, 62 (1792), pp. 956–7; *Evening Mail*, 24 September 1792.

14 *The Times*, 1 January 1793. This was the first of three loyal verses.

15 Hutton, *Blood and Mistletoe*, p. 154.

16 *The Times*, 1 January 1793. Miss Harper was almost certainly Sarah Owen's sister.

17 Hutton, *Blood and Mistletoe*, pp. 162–72.

18 Ibid., pp. 2–6, 12–14, 16–17, 23–30. With the exception of Ireland, for which see ibid., pp. 30–46, and Hutton, *The Druids*, p. 6.

19 Hutton, *Blood and Mistletoe*, pp. 23–30. For the Druids' relations with modern archaeologists, ibid., pp. 374–417.

20 Ibid., pp. 49–53, 57; Hutton, *The Druids*, pp. 7–16.

21 Hutton, *Blood and Mistletoe*, pp. 69, 70; Hutton, *The Druids*, p. 121; Richard Hayman, *Riddles in Stone: Myths, Archaeology and the Ancient Britons* (London, 1997), p. 63. The wicker man first appeared in Aylett Sammes, *Britannia antiqua illustrata* (London, 1676), p. 105.

22 Stuart Piggott, *William Stukeley: An Eighteenth-Century Antiquary* (Oxford, 1950), pp. 92–131.

23 John Richardson, *Kentish Town Past* (London, 1997), pp. 33–4; Piggott, *William Stukeley*, p. 179; Hutton, *Blood and Mistletoe*, pp. 98–102, 128–9.

24 Hutton, *Blood and Mistletoe*, pp. 132–45. Togodubline seems to be a mixture of the historic Togodumnus and his son Cunobelinus or Cymbeline, ibid., p. 137.

25 Iolo's work had not, however, appeared in a vacuum. In the years before his proclamation of the Gorsedd on Primrose Hill, or perhaps Plynlimon, a number of other writers, mostly members of the London Welsh societies, had suggested a connection between Wales and the Druids. Hutton, *Blood and Mistletoe*, pp. 146–50.

26 The Tudors themselves made little or nothing of their Welsh origins, C.S.L. Davies, 'A Rose by Any Other Name', *Times Literary Supplement*, 13 June 2008; and C.S.L. Davies, 'The Tudors or Not', *Oxford Historian*, 9 (2011), pp. 6–10.

27 Hutton, *Blood and Mistletoe*, pp. 146–7; Hutton, *The Druids*, p. 20.

28 Hutton, *Blood and Mistletoe*, pp. 146–7, 177–8; Hutton, *The Druids*, pp. 57–8.

29 Hutton, *The Druids*, pp. 57–8. A third expert, in 1918, rejected both translations.

30 Hutton, *Blood and Mistletoe*, pp. 313–14; Hutton, *The Druids*, pp. 25–8.

31 Hutton, *Blood and Mistletoe*, p. 168.

32 Ibid., p. 181.

33 Morgan, *Iolo Morganwg*, p. 14.

34 Hutton, *Blood and Mistletoe*, p. 151; Hutton, *The Druids*, p. 23.

35 Macpherson announced his discoveries in 1761. 'James MacPherson (1736–96)', *Oxford Dictionary of National Biography*; Hutton, *Blood and Mistletoe*, pp. 115–17, 185–7.

36 Hutton, *Blood and Mistletoe*, pp. 155–6, for Iolo's adoption of this motto.

37 For a full list of *eisteddfodau* and Gorsedds, see Miles, *The Secret of the Bards*, pp. 220–37.

38 Ibid., pp. 263–71.

39 Henry Crabb Robinson, *Diaries, Reminiscences and Correspondence*, ed. T. Sadler, 2 vols (London 1872), ii, p. 8.

40 Jack Lindsay, *William Blake: His Life and Work* (London, 1978), 157–65.

41 William Blake, 'Auguries of Innocence', lines 1–4, *The Complete Writings of William Blake*, ed. Geoffrey Keynes (London, 1957), p. 431.

42 Stuart Pigott, *The Druids* (London, 1968), p. 173.

43 Robinson, *Diaries, Reminiscences and Correspondence*, ii, p. 9.

44 Hutton, *Blood and Mistletoe*, pp. 193–8.

45 *The Letters of William and Dorothy Wordsworth*, viii, *A Supplement of New Letters*, ed. Alan G. Hill (Oxford, 1993), p. 113. The walk was on 24 May 1812.

46 Robinson, *Diaries, Reminiscences and Correspondence*, i, pp. 385–6.

47 Hutton, *Blood and Mistletoe*, pp. 204–9.

48 Thomas Love Peacock, *Memoirs of Shelley*, ed. Howard Mills (London, 1970), p. 58.

49 Lord Byron, *Don Juan* (London, 1823), canto 11, stanza 25.

Notes to Chapter 5: Regent's Park

1 Keith Thomas, *Man and the Natural World: Changing Attitudes in England, 1500–1800* (Cambridge, 1984), pp. 243–68.

2 Eton College Records, 51, no. 8; see also nos 6 and 7.

3 Eton College Records, 49, no. 19; 51, nos 7 and 9.

4 Eton College Records, 49, no. 19.

5 Ibid. A fine in this context was not a punishment but a sum paid on the renewal of a lease.

6 Ibid.

7 *From Primrose Hill to Euston Road*, ed. F. Peter Woodford (2nd edn, London, 1995), is an excellent guide to the individual buildings of the area.

8 For the history of Camden Town's name, see John Winter-Lotimer, 'The Chislehurst Connection: Camden Place and Camden Town', *Camden History Review*, 23 (1999), pp. 5–8.

9 John Summerson, *The Life and Work of John Nash, Architect* (London, 1980), pp. 114–29; Ann Saunders, *Regent's Park: A Study of the Development of the Area from 1086 to the Present* (2nd edn, London, 1981), pp. 61–74. See also, Martin Sheppard, *Regent's Park and Primrose Hill* (London, 2010), p. 11.

10 Saunders, *Regent's Park*, pp. 69–75; Sheppard, *Regent's Park and Primrose Hill*, pp. 13–17. See also J. Mordaunt Crook, *London's Arcadia: John Nash and the Planning of Regent's Park*, Soane Lecture, 2000 (London, 2001), pp. 1–13.

11 Michael Mansbridge, *John Nash: A Complete Catalogue* (London, 2004), pp. 158–61.

12 Summerson, *The Life and Works of John Nash*, pp. 100–45, 156–74.

13 For the construction of the canal from Paddington to Camden Town, see Alan Faulkner, *The Regent's Canal: London's Hidden Waterway* (Burton-on-Trent, 2005), pp. 16–25.

14 See, for instance, the 1826 map of Regent's Park in Sheppard, *Regent's Park and Primrose Hill*, p. 16.

15 Saunders, *Regent's Park*, pp. 108, 158.

16 Saunders, *Regent's Park*, pp. 70, 86; Mansbridge, *John Nash*, p. 160.

17 Saunders, *Regent's Park*, pp. 86–7.

18 Sheppard, *Regent's Park and Primrose Hill*, pp. 40–7.

19 For correspondence on the barracks, see National Archives, Cres 35/3288; *Morning Chronicle*, 28 November 1811.

20 National Archives, MPHH 1/554, dating from 1812, shows Nash's plan for the barracks, with twenty-seven acres for the cavalry to the west and thirteen acres for the artillery to the east. Roads are shown both to the north and south of the barracks, with the canal to the south.

21 John Nash to Commissioners of Woods and Forests, 10 March 1810, National Archives, Cres 35/3288.

22 John Nash to Commissioners of Woods and Forests, 3 November 1811, National Archives, Cres 35/3288.

23 Commissioners of Woods and Forests to John Nash, 9 November 1811, National Archives, Cres 35/3288.

24 Crook, *London's Arcadia*, p. 8.

25 *Parliamentary Debates*, 1 May 1812, columns 1137–51. For Burdett's speech, see columns 1145–8. See *Morning Chronicle*, 14 April 1812, for an earlier debate on barrack estimates.

26 *Parliamentary Debates*, 1 May 1812, column 1138.

27 James Anderson, 'Marylebone Park and the New Street: A Study in the Development of Regent's Park and the Building of Regent Street, London, in the First Quarter of the Nineteenth Century', unpublished Ph.D. thesis, University of London (1998), pp. 257–62.

28 Catherine Jamison, *The History of the Royal Hospital of St Katharine by the Tower*

of London (Oxford, 1952), pp. 161–71; M.H. Port, 'St Katharine's Royal Hospital, London', *The History of the King's Works*, vi, *1782–1851* (London, 1973), pp. 479–80.

29 Saunders, *Regent's Park*, p. 105; Richard D. Altick, *The Shows of London* (Cambridge, Massachusetts, 1978), pp. 132–48.

30 Geoffrey Tyack, *Sir James Pennethorne and the Making of Victorian London* (Cambridge, 1992), pp. 24–7 and 29.

31 For Raffles and the Zoo, Victoria Glendinning, *Raffles and the Golden Opportunity, 1781–1826* (London, 2012), pp. 285–6, 289, 295 and 299.

32 Wilfred Blunt, *The Ark in the Park: The Zoo in the Nineteenth Century* (London, 1976), pp. 23–41; Peter Guillery, *The Buildings of London Zoo* (London, 1993), pp. 2, 3 and 11; J. Barrington-Johnson, *The Zoo: The Story of London Zoo* (London, 2005), pp. 13–39.

33 Guillery, *The Buildings of London Zoo*, pp. 10–12.

34 Guy Meynell, 'The Royal Botanic Society's Garden, Regent's Park', *London Journal*, 6 (1980), pp. 135–46.

35 F.M.L. Thompson, *Hampstead: Building a Borough, 1650–1964* (1974), pp. 110–24; and Simon Morris, 'The Marylebone and Finchley Road Turnpike, 1820–1850', *Camden History Review*, 22 (1998), pp. 24–32.

36 William Babington and others to Samuel Ware, 10 April 1810, National Archives, Cres 26/166. See also the letters from Samuel Ware to Alexander Milne, 9 February 1820, and from John Nash to Alexander Milne, 14 June 1820, on the rights of the duke to connect to the sewer running across Regent's Park.

37 Samuel Ware to Alexander Milne, 7 March 1827, National Archives, Cres 26/166.

38 Case of Sir T.M. Wilson against the Finchley Road Bill, London Metropolitan Archives, E/MW/H/III/38/15, quoted in Thompson, *Hampstead*, p. 119. St Giles, to the north of Covent Garden, was a notorious rookery of thieves.

39 Walpole Eyre to Colonel Rowan, 27 May 1830, Eyre Estate, letter book M, Westminster City Archives; quoted in Mireille Galinou, *Cottages and Villas: The Birth of the Garden Suburb* (New Haven and London, 2010), p. 141.

40 Samuel Ware to M.K. Knight, 21 May 1821, London Metropolitan Archives, ACC/2558/WM/A/23/020.

41 Ibid.

42 *The Times*, 26 August 1825.

43 Sir Francis Bolton, *London Water Supply*, revised by Philip Scratchley (London, 1888), pp. 98–110. Bolton provides an excellent account of the West Middlesex Water Works, founded in 1806, and the different pumping engines used at Barrow Hill, a reservoir with a capacity of 4,750,000 gallons, in the years up to 1888. The company had acquired Barrow Hill in 1822. Ibid., pp. 100–7, 110.

44 Galinou, *Cottages and Villas*, pp. 61–137.

45 Stephen Green, *Lord's: The Cathedral of Cricket* (London, 2003), pp. 17–46.

46 Anonymous, in E.L. Tarbuck, *Handbook of House Property* (5th edn, London, 1875), p. 161; quoted in Thompson, *Hampstead*, p. 215.

Notes to Chapter 6: London's Crowning Glory

1   *The Times*, 23 August 1791.

2   *World*, 23 September 1791. In the 1820s, Titchfield House, a substantial villa facing Regent's Park, was built on the corner of Wells Road. It can be seen on Greenwood's map of 1827.

3   For a wider range of grand, grandiose and megalomaniac buildings proposed for London, see Felix Barker and Ralph Hyde, *London as it Might Have Been* (London, 1982). This includes a number of the schemes suggested for Primrose Hill, ibid., pp. 62–3, 75, 141–6 and 168–9.

4   Ibid., pp. 76 and 168–9.

5   Thomas Moore, 24 October 1811, *Memoirs, Journal and Correspondence of Thomas Moore*, ed. Lord John Russell, 8 vols (London, 1853–56), viii, p. 97.

6   John Summerson, *The Life and Work of John Nash, Architect* (London, 1980), pp. 130–42; Ann Saunders, *Regent's Park: A Story of the Development of the Area from 1086 to the Present Day* (2nd edn, London, 1981), pp. 65, 71 and 77.

7   Michael Mansbridge, *John Nash: A Complete Catalogue* (London, 2004), pp. 160, 282.

8   Martin Sheppard, *Regent's Park and Primrose Hill* (London, 2010), p. 17. The Prince Regent was notorious for his profligate spending. His need to pay off debts of £630,000 had earlier led to his disastrous marriage to Caroline of Brunswick in 1795. Saul David, *Prince of Pleasure: The Prince of Wales and the Making of the Regency* (London, 1998), pp. 150–74.

9   *Standard*, 15 May 1829.

10   Holger Hoock, *Empires of the Imagination: Politics, War and the Arts in the British World, 1750–1850* (London, 2010), pp. 361–3; *Parliamentary Debates*, xxxi, columns 1049–53 (29 June 1815); *House of Commons Journals*, 70, pp. 446, 448; 71, pp. 11–12; National Archives, Treasury 27/74, p. 74.

11   Barker and Hyde, *London as it Might Have Been*, pp. 71–2; Hoock, *Empires of the Imagination*, p. 362.

12   'James Elmes (1782–1862)', *Oxford Dictionary of National Biography*.

13   Ibid., pp. 3, 5. Elmes may have had the Duke of Portland's Barrow Hill estate in mind as the site of his proposed development.

14   Ibid., p. 6.

15   Ibid., pp. 12–13.

16   Ibid., pp. 11–12.

17   Ibid., pp. 11–12.

18   Ibid., p. 13.

19   *Letters and Papers of Andrew Robertson, A.M., Miniature Painter to his Late Royal Highness the Duke of Suffolk* (2nd edn, London, 1897), pp. 281–3; letter, 22 May 1816, to John Ewen, Aberdeen, ibid., pp. 280–1; 'Andrew Robertson (1777–1845)', *Oxford Dictionary of National Biography*.

20   Ibid., p. 281.

21   *The Times*, 8 April 1817. The letter is signed 'N', a 'person who literally did not know the author of it by name, before he accidentally saw the model'.

22   *The Times*, 8 April 1817.

23 *The Times*, 8 April 1817. See Hoock, *Empires of the Imagination*, p. 362.

24 *Bell's Life*, 29 November 1846.

25 *Punch*, 28 November 1846.

26 *Magazine of Science*, 5 (1845), p. 162. The casino is illustrated, ibid., plate 281, p. 261. See also, Simon Jenkins and Jonathan Ditchburn, *Images of Hampstead* (Richmond-upon-Thames, 1982), nos 453 and 454.

27 *Magazine of Science*, 5 (1845), p. 162.

28 'John Harrison Curtis (1778–1860)', *Oxford Dictionary of National Biography*.

29 John Harrison Curtis, *Observations on the Preservation of Health in Infancy, Youth, Manhood and Age* (London, 1837), p. 69.

30 Recounted in 'John Harrison Curtis (1778–1860)', *Oxford Dictionary of National Biography*. This must have been before 1830, when Peel inherited his father's baronetcy.

31 F.H.W. Sheppard, *Local Government in St Marylebone, 1688–1835* (London, 1958), pp. 21–3, 28, 32–3, 46–7, 178, 248–9 and 251.

32 Following an earlier extension in 1726, more land for burials was acquired in 1792. *Survey of London*, xix, *St Pancras and Kentish Town* (1938), pp. 72–95. See also Roger Samuel Draper, 'Democracy in St Pancras: Politics in a Metropolitan Parish, 1779–1849', unpublished Ph.D. thesis, Harvard University (1979), p. 63.

33 For one of the first modern cremations in Britain, on 13 January 1884, see Ronald Hutton, *Blood and Mistletoe: The History of the Druids in Britain* (New Haven and London, 2009), pp. 283–4. This was predated by Captain Hanham's cremation of his wife and mother in an outbuilding of his house at Manston, near Sturminster Newton, Dorset, in October 1882. Brian Parsons, *Committed to the Cleansing Flame: The Development of Cremation in Nineteenth-Century England* (Reading, 2005).

34 Owen Dudley Edwards, *Burke and Hare* (2nd edn, Edinburgh, 1993).

35 James Stevens Curl, *The Victorian Celebration of Death* (Thrupp, 2000), pp. 1–36.

36 Saunders, *Regent's Park*, p. 64. See St Marylebone Vestry Minutes, Westminster City Archives, 26 March, 9 April 1791; 11 February, 20 and 27 October 1792; 23 April and 18 May 1793; 5, 19, 26 March, 2 April, 7 and 28 May, 18 June, 26 November, 17 December 1796; 18 March 1797; 10 April, 15 May and 29 May 1802.

37 John Oliver and Peter Bradshaw, *Saint John's Wood Church, 1814–1955* (London, 1955), p. 19. Five acres of the burial ground, taken from the Great Garden Field and Willow Tree Field, were bought from the Eyre Estate and one acre from the Duke of Portland, both at £600 an acre. Sheppard, *Local Government in St Marylebone, 1688–1835*, p. 252.

38 Charles E. Lee, *St Pancras Church and Parish* (London, 1955), p. 45. In 1854 St Pancras opened a new cemetery in East Finchley.

39 Oliver and Bradshaw, *Saint John's Wood Church*, pp. 36–7.

40 'George Carden (1798–1874)', *Oxford Dictionary of National Biography*; *General Cemetery Company for Providing Places of Interment, Secure from Violation, Inoffensive to Public Health and Decency, and Ornamental to the Metropolis*, prospectus, 21 May 1830, appendix of 1825 proposals, p. 22.

41 General Cemetery Company, prospectus, appendix, p. 6; Barker and Hyde, *London as it Might Have Been* (London, 1982), p. 142.

42 *General Cemetery Company*, prospectus, appendix, pp. 41–3.

43 Curl, *The Victorian Celebration of Death*, p. 44. The A.C. Pugin plan for a Primrose Hill cemetery seems not to have survived. Pugin was presumably inspired by Père Lachaise, of which he had previously published a series of prints, showing its monuments. James Stevens Curl, *A Celebration of Death: An Introduction to Some of the Buildings, Monuments and Settings of Funerary Architecture in the Western European Tradition* (London, 1980), p. 163.

44 James Stevens Curl, *Kensal Green Cemetery* (Chichester, 2001), p. 35.

45 *Derby Mercury*, 14 April 1830; Curl, *The Victorian Celebration of Death*, p. 49; 'Francis Goodwin (1784–1835)', *Oxford Dictionary of National Biography*; 'Francis Goodwin', in Howard Colvin, *Biographical Dictionary of British Architects, 1600–1840* (4th edn, London, 2008), pp. 435–7.

46 'Thomas Willson', in Colvin, *Biographical Dictionary of British Architects*, p. 1129.

47 Thomas Willson, *The Pyramid: A General Metropolitan Cemetery to be Erected in the Vicinity of Primrose Hill* (London, 1830), p. 4. There are copies in the Camden Local Studies and Archives Centre, the London Metropolitan Archives, the Royal Institute of British Architects Library and the Royal Library at Windsor, but not the British Library.

48 Willson, *The Pyramid*, p. 2.

49 Ibid., pp. 2, 3.

50 Ibid., p. 6.

51 Ibid., p. 4.

52 Ibid., p. 2.

53 Ibid., p. 2.

54 Ibid., p. 6.

55 Ibid., p. 7.

56 Ibid., p. 7.

57 Curl, *The Victorian Celebration of Death*, pp. 48–67. Cholera was thought incorrectly to be spread by miasma.

58 *Streets of Highgate*, edited by Steven Denford and David A. Hayes (London, 2007), pp. 14–18, for the genesis and history of the cemetery.

59 Secretary of the West Middlesex Water Works Company to the Department of Woods and Forests, 26 May 1841, National Archives, Work 16/180. While no observatory was built on the top of Primrose Hill, the West Middlesex Water Works built a series of engine houses at the reservoir. One of these can be seen in illustrations of the fireworks on Primrose Hill celebrating the end of the Crimean War in 1856. The engine house's chimney, to a modest height, was rebuilt in 1870. See Sir Francis Bolton, *London Water Supply*, revised by Philip Scratchley (London, 1888), pp. 98–110.

60 Geoffrey Tyack, *Sir James Pennethorne and the Making of Victorian England* (Cambridge, 1992), pp. 89–114.

61 Alan Faulkner, *The Regent's Canal: London's Hidden Waterway* (Burton-on-Trent, 2005), pp. 79–81 and 93.

62 Barker and Hyde, *London as it Might Have Been*, p. 168; Jenkins and Ditchburn, *Images of Hampstead*, p. 137.

63 *Builder*, 2 July 1853.

64 For Telegraph Hill, see Alan Farmer, *Hampstead Heath* (London, 1984), pp. 53–4.

65 Mireille Galinou, *Cottages and Villas: The Birth of the Garden Suburb* (London and New Haven, 2010), pp. 182–3.
66 Richard Foulkes, 'Shakespeare and Garibaldi on Primrose Hill', *Camden History Review*, 9 (1981), pp. 13–16.
67 Ibid.
68 Jenkins and Ditchburn, *Images of Hampstead*, p. 137.
69 *Observer*, 3 September 1854.
70 *Observer*, 24 July 1854.
71 *Art Journal*, September 1854, p. 260.

Note to Chapter 7: Public Walks

1 Thomas Dale, *Five Years of Church Extension in St Pancras* (London, 1852), pp. 3–4.
2 Clive Emsley, *Britain and the French Revolution* (Harlow, 2000); Simon Schama, *Citizens: A Chronicle of the French Revolution* (London, 1989); 'Thomas Robert Malthus (1766–1834)', *Oxford Dictionary of National Biography*.
3 Donald Read, *Peterloo: The 'Massacre' and its Background* (Manchester, 1958), pp. 106–54; Robert Reid, *The Peterloo Massacre* (London, 1989), pp. 165–95.
4 Robert Shaw, *Cato Street* (London, 1972).
5 For a perceptive and highly entertaining account of Whig attitudes and priorities, see Leslie Mitchell, *The Whig World* (London, 2005).
6 Todd Longstaffe-Gowan, *The London Square: Gardens in the Midst of Town* (London and New Haven, 2012), pp. 24, 55, 63, 76–9, 97, 136, 140, 155, 160, 164, 166 and 186. For later campaigns to open squares, ibid., pp. 175–7, 183.
7 Hazel Conway, *People's Parks: The Design and Development of Victorian Parks in Britain* (Cambridge, 1991), pp. 1–38; Hazel Conway, *Public Parks* (Princes Risborough, 1996), p. 1.
8 *Report from the Select Committee on Public Walks with the Minutes of Evidence Taken before Them*, 27 June 1833, p. 3. See also, Conway, *People's Parks*, p. 26.
9 *Report from the Select Committee on Public Walks*, 23 June 1833. Slaney was later responsible for promoting the Recreation Grounds Act of 1859, Conway, *People's Parks*, p. 21. 'Robert Aglionby Slaney (1792–1862)', *Oxford Dictionary of National Biography*.
10 *Report from the Select Committee on Public Walks*, pp. 14–15, questions 29–34.
11 Ibid., p. 6.
12 Survey by Abraham and William Driver, 30 November 1796, Eton College Records, 49, no. 19.
13 Eton College Records, 49, no. 12.
14 Survey by John Jenkins, 20 December 1824, Eton College Records, 51, no. 13. For the development of the estate, see Donald J. Olsen, 'House upon House: Estate Development in London and Sheffield', *The Victorian City: Images and Reality* (London, 1973), ii, pp. 333–57.
15 Eton College Records, 49, no. 27. The college made slow progress in finding builders willing to take on its leases. In the fifteen years after 1826 new housing was restricted mostly to the plots offered on the west of Haverstock Hill, between Chalk Farm and

England's Lane. See F.M.L. Thompson, *Hampstead: Building a Borough, 1650–1964* (London, 1974), pp. 210–29.

16 Edward Driver to Alexander Milne, 10 August 1840, National Archives, Work 16/180.

17 John Shaw junior to George Bethell, 2 August 1831, Eton College Records, 49, no. 28; John Shaw junior to William Clarke, 1 September 1831, 49, no. 28.

18 Ibid.

19 John Shaw junior to George Batcheldor, 2 August 1831, Eton College Records, 49, no. 28.

20 Outline of botanical garden, Eton College Records, 51, no. 22. Clarke's plans were exhibited at the Royal Academy in 1832, 'William Bernard Clarke', in H.M. Colvin, *Biographical Dictionary of British Architects, 1600–1840* (4th edn, London, 2008). The Rugmoor field, on the southern slopes of the hill, was eighteen acres in area.

21 Prospectus, London Metropolitan Archives, SC/GL/PR/PER –P3.

22 Guy Meynell, 'The Royal Botanic Society's Garden, Regent's Park', *London Journal*, 6 (1980), pp. 135–46.

23 *Morning Chronicle*, 22 February 1834.

24 6 & 7 William IV, c. 136 (1836).

25 John Shaw to Thomas Batcheldor, 7 May 1836, Eton College Records, 49, no. 77.

26 Ibid.

27 Hugh Meller, *London Cemeteries* (3rd edn, 1994, Aldershot), pp. 153–71. The company bought the park of Ashurst House for £3,500. In 1840 the company opened Nunhead Cemetery in south London, also on a hilltop and on the site of what had been the Nun's Head Tavern, ibid., pp. 232–6.

28 *Observer*, 14 May 1837.

29 *The Times*, 15 May 1837. As a charity, Eton had no power to dispose of its land without an Act of Parliament. See also letter from 'R.C.' to the editor, 17 May 1837. In another letter, Blaquiere Talbot, the secretary of the London Necropolis and National Cemetery Company, distanced himself from the Portland Cemetery Company, *The Times*, 27 May 1837.

30 'An Act to Enable the Provost and College of Eton, in the County of Bucks, to Grant Building Leases of Lands in the Parishes of Hampstead and Marylebone, in the County of Middlesex, and for Other Purposes', 7 George IV, c. 25. This Act does *not* mention 'public squares, streets, crescents (or any form of building)' but does refer to 'public streets, squares, paths and passages'.

31 *Observer*, 22 May 1837.

32 St Marylebone Vestry Minutes, 24 May 1837, Westminster City Archives.

33 *Bell's Life*, 21 May 1837.

34 *Observer*, 5 June 1837.

35 *Observer*, 11 June 1837.

36 Sir Samuel Whalley (1800–83) was MP for Marylebone from 1833 to 1838, when he lost his seat after being unable to prove that his property qualification was sufficient in the general election of 1837. Obituary, *The Times*, 8 February 1883.

37 *Minutes of Evidence Taken at the Bar of the House of Commons in the Matter of an Alteration Not Authorized by the Committee, Having Been Made in the Commons Bill, by Sir Samuel Whalley, a Member of the House, 8 and 13 July 1837.*

38 'Thomas Wakley (1795–1862)', *Oxford Dictionary of National Biography*.
39 Hansard, *House of Commons*, 8 June 1837.
40 'Thomas Slingsby Duncombe (1796–1861)', *Oxford Dictionary of National Biography*.
41 *Standard*, 16 June 1837.
42 *Observer*, 11 June 1837.
43 St Marylebone Vestry Minutes, 10 June 1837, Westminster City Archives.
44 Lord Melbourne to Lord Duncannon, 12 June 1837, National Archives, Work 16/180. The Department of Woods of Forests was under the control of the Treasury, whose approval was required for purchases.
45 *Report from the Select Committee on Public Walks*, p. 8.
46 *Satirist*, 27 February 1848.
47 *Morning Chronicle*, 18 July 1821.
48 Survey by Abraham and William Driver, 30 November 1796, Eton College Records, 49, no. 19.
49 F.M.L. Thompson, *Hampstead*, pp. 220–2.
50 See, for instance, Eton College Records, 49, no. 110.
51 Memorial, February 1840, Eton College Records, 49, no. 86.
52 Edward Driver to John Shaw, 9 April 1838, National Archives, Cres 2/793.
53 John Shaw to George Bethell, 15 March 1839, Eton College Records, 49, no. 80.
54 *The Times*, 18 March 1841.

Notes to Chapter 8: Lord Southampton

1 For a general history of the Fitzroy family, Bernard Falk, *The Royal Fitzroys: Dukes of Grafton through Four Centuries* (London, 1950). The lease of the manor of Tottenhale was inherited by Charles, second Duke of Grafton, from his mother, Isabella, Countess of Arlington. He renewed the lease for three lives in 1723.
2 Ibid., pp. 98–102.
3 London Metropolitan Archives, M/90/283. Although the survey shows the fields as they were in 1771, Lord Southampton did not acquire his freehold of the Rugmere fields until 1786. It is likely therefore that this terrier dates from the time of his acquisition of the freehold from the executors of John Badcock in 1786.
4 To the north of Chalk House Lane is a small piece of meadow, shown as 'The Slip by Chalk House Lane', whose existence influenced the later development of the streets and houses to the north of Regent's Park Road. The 'Slip', abutting onto Eton College land, provided a cramped area for development. The boundary between the estates, which was also the boundary between Hampstead and St Pancras, explains why St George's Mews and Chamberlain Street are both cul-de-sacs. See *From Primrose Hill to Euston Road*, ed. F. Peter Woodford (revised edn, London, 1995), p. 76.
5 Tompson's map should be examined with John Tompson, *The Terrier Book: Referring in Alphabetical Order to the Accurate Engraved Map of the Parish of St Pancras in the County of Middlesex from a Minute and Correct Survey, Taken for the Purpose, by John Tompson, Land Surveyor, Grafton Street, Fitzroy Road* (London, 1804). This shows all the St Pancras fields between the Chalk Farm Tavern and the New Road. Rutherford's holding, including 'The Pikel' (the 'Slip by Chalk House Lane' in the 1771 survey), came to 11 acres 3 perches and 37 roods.

6   Frank Cole, 'Charles Fitzroy at the Wars: The Military Career of the First Baron Southampton', *Camden History Review*, 16 (1989), pp. 14–16; 'Charles Fitzroy, First Baron Southampton (1737–97)', *Oxford Dictionary of National Biography*.

7   G.E.C., *The Complete Peerage*, xii, part 1 (London, 1953), 'Southampton, Barony', pp. 135–8.

8   The canal company bought two acres from the Southampton Estate for the canal itself and agreed to lease another twelve acres for ninety-nine years for buildings and wharfs. This was an agreement along the lines the company had already reached with the Eyre Estate. National Archives, Rail 860/1, p. 172; see also Rail 860/5, pp. 224–5, and Rail 860/8, pp. 9–45.

9   The Regent's Canal Act, 42 George III, c. 195, clause 127. The Act was passed on 13 July 1812.

10   Robert Henrey, *A Century Between* (London, 1937), p. 11.

11   J.M.K. Elliott, *Fifty Years' Foxhunting with the Grafton and Other Packs of Hounds* (London, 1900), p. 79.

12   Ibid., p. 205.

13   Ibid., p. 63.

14   In London, he was a governor of Highgate School from 1836 to 1859, Survey of London, xvii, *The Village of Highgate* (London, 1936), p. 143.

15   G.E.C., *The Complete Peerage*, xi (London, 1949), pp. 746–7; xii, part 1, pp. 137–8.

16   'Henry Fitzroy (1807–59)', *Oxford Dictionary of National Biography*.

17   Henrey, *A Century Between*, pp. 11–72.

18   Ibid., pp. 23–63, for Henry Fitzroy's diary of this trip.

19   Ibid., pp. 69–173.

20   Charlotte to Lionel Rothschild, 10 December 1864, Niall Ferguson, *The World's Banker: A History of the House of Rothschild* (London, 1998), p. 346.

21   'Edward Algernon Fitzroy (1869–1943)', *Oxford Dictionary of National Biography*.

22   F.M.L. Thompson, *Hampstead: Building a Borough, 1650–1964* (London, 1974), pp. 67–8. Short building leases discouraged builders from investing more than a minimum in the houses they erected.

23   'An Act to Extend a Power of Leasing Contained in the Marriage Settlement of Charles Lord Southampton and Harriet Lady Southampton his Wife', 5 and 6 Victoria, c. 31 (1842).

24   L.T.C. Rolt, *George and Robert Stephenson: The Railway Revolution* (London, 2009), pp. 168–211.

25   Thompson, *Hampstead*, pp. 218–20. The railway crossed part of the Bedford Estate, Figs Mead, to the north of Euston. Donald J. Olsen, *Town Planning in London: The Eighteenth and Nineteenth Centuries* (New Haven and London, 1982), pp. 65–7 and plate 51. The huge disruption caused by the construction of the line near Euston is vividly described in chapter 6 of Charles Dickens, *Dombey and Son*, written in 1846–48.

26   For the date of the tunnel's completion, *Bell's Life*, 29 January 1837.

27   John Richardson, *Camden Town and Primrose Hill* (London, 1991), p. 47.

28   'George Henry Robins (1777–1847)', *Oxford Dictionary of National Biography*.

29   *Morning Chronicle*, 6 August 1840.

30   London Metropolitan Archives, M/90/274.

31 London Metropolitan Archives, M/90/274, 277–80. M/90/272 has all the prices in guineas rather than pounds.

32 *Standard*, 6 August 1840.

33 *Morning Chronicle*, 22 August 1840. The sale was, in fact, made to Lord Mansfield's trustees, as the third Earl of Mansfield had died earlier in the year.

34 *Age*, 16 August 1840. Twenty acres was, in fact, over twice as much as the crown actually bought.

35 *Freeman's Journal*, 26 August 1840.

36 *Age*, 16 August 1840.

37 The seven lots came to eight acres, one rood and thirty-seven perches. Of this seven acres, three roods and thirty-one perches became part of the park, while the two roods and six perches of Lot 237 became St Mark's Church. National Archives, Cres 60, *Nineteenth Report of the Office of Woods and Forests*, 12 August 1842, p. 36.

38 These two lots, amounting together to two acres, one rood and thirty perches, were bought by the Reverend Dr Edward Thompson for £2,541.

39 Edward Driver to Alexander Milne, 13 August 1840, National Archives, Work 16/180.

40 Ibid.

41 Dr Edward Thompson to the Earl of Lincoln, 7 November 1842, National Archives, Cres 2/794.

42 Guerrier and Pearse to the Commissioners of Woods and Forests, 15 September 1843, National Archives, Cres 2/794.

43 The lot was also eyed, in the years after Lord Southampton's auction, by the projectors of the Regent's Canal railway as the site for a station.

44 Joseph Tringham, presumably a relative, held a £3,000 mortgage on the main public house in St John's Wood, the Eyre Arms, in 1826. A member of a later generation, the artist Holland Tringham, drew illustrations of Sir Edwin Landseer's house, at 18 St John's Wood Road, in 1894, shortly before it was pulled down. Mireille Galinou, *Cottages and Villas: The Birth of the Garden Suburb* (New Haven and London, 2010), pp. 208 and 277; *Illustrated London News*, 1 September 1894.

45 There are three copies of the 1841 auction catalogue in the London Metropolitan Archives, M90/273, 275 and 276. Of these, M90/273 contains hand-written details of prices and purchasers for the odd-numbered lots.

46 1841 auction catalogue, London Metropolitan Archive, description of Lot 61.

47 London Metropolitan Archives, 4241/A/02/004, 4241/A/02/008 and 4241/A/02/009, contain detailed calculations by George Bassett, the surveyor of the Southampton Estate, on the sales to the railway company. The figure of £50,000 is based on these figures but is an informed guess rather than an exact one. The figures for the 1840 and 1841 sales do not include a deduction for the auctioneer's commission. For the earlier sale of land to the Regent's Canal Company, see above, p. 263, n. 8.

48 Falk, *The Royal Fitzroys*, p. 88n.

49 Charles E. Lee, *St Pancras Church and Parish* (London, 1955), p. 38.

50 There is substantial material about Southampton's country estate in Warwickshire Record Office, CR 1661/1220–30. For transfers of money, CR 1661/1222. For a list of purchases, London Metropolitan Archives, 4241/A/01/008, pp. 421–2.

51   Warwickshire Record Office, CR 1661/1221.

52   A graphic account of the sales can be found in Jacob Birt's itemised description of his meetings between 1871 and 1876, London Metropolitan Archives 4241/A/01/008.

53   Elliott, *Fifty Years' Foxhunting*, p. 69.

54   F.M.L. Thompson, *English Landed Society in the Nineteenth Century* (London, 1963), p. 97.

55   William C.A. Blew, *The Quorn Hunt and its Masters* (London, 1899), pp. 122–3.

56   Elliott, *Fifty Years' Foxhunting*, p. 79.

57   Henrey, *A Century Between*, p. 11.

58   Elliott, *Fifty Years' Foxhunting*, p. 37.

59   Thompson, *English Landed Society in the Nineteenth Century*, pp. 144–5.

60   'An Act to Extend a Power of Leasing Contained in the Marriage Settlement of Charles Lord Southampton and Harriet Lady Southampton his Wife', 5 and 6 Victoria, c. 31 (1842), mentions an agreement with the estate's trustees whereby Lord Southampton bought the freehold of lands inside the estate from the trustees for £2,977 in January 1839. This may have been the prelude to the auctions.

61   For the Bill's passage through Parliament, see *Journals of the House of Commons*, 97 (1842), pp. 303, 304, 352, 356, 370, 398, 402, 449, 454, 455, 459, 463, 571, 577 and 586.

Notes to Chapter 9: The New Park

1   Hazel Conway, *People's Parks: The Development of Victorian Parks in Britain* (Cambridge, 1991), pp. 228–34.

2   Geoffrey Tyack, *Sir James Pennethorne and the Making of Victorian England* (Cambridge, 1992), pp. 88–9. See above p. 92.

3   *Age*, 16 August 1840.

4   National Archives, Works 16/184.

5   Camden Local Studies and Archives Centre, Heal Collection, A IX, 151. Opened in 1848 but visible on Sayer's map of 1847.

6   National Archives, Work 16/1670, February 1929.

7   In the 1850s the other sporting facility associated with Primrose Hill, the 'target' or rifle range, was filled in, A.D. Webster, *The Regent's Park and Primrose Hill: History and Antiquities* (London, 1911), p. 85. Later maps of Victoria Park show the provision of a gymnasium there.

8   Edward Kemp, *The Parks, Gardens etc of London and its Suburbs Described and Illustrated, for the Guidance of Strangers* (London, 1851), p. 15.

9   *Bell's Life*, 9 April 1843.

10   *English Gentleman*, 2 August 1845.

11   *Bell's Life*, 23 May 1847.

12   Ibid. See also Sayer's map of 1847, which shows that all internal boundaries had been removed.

13   *London Dispatch and People's Political and Social Reformer*, 28 October 1838.

14   *Observer*, 9 May 1841.

15   Hampstead Vestry Minutes, committee report, 13 December 1835, Camden Local Studies and Archives Centre.

16   Ibid., vote on committee report, 7 January 1836.

17 *Observer*, 13 July 1846.
18 *Observer*, 13 July 1846.
19 *Observer*, 13 July 1846.
20 The latter tea rooms also contained a ladies' lavatory. There was a separate lavatory for men nearby. National Archives, Work 16/927.
21 John Phipps to Office of Works, 11 January 1861, National Archives, Work 16/924.
22 *Economist*, 30 August 1851.
23 National Archives, Work 6/525.
24 *The Times*, 22 November 1866.
25 Cutting, 29 February 1868, Heal Collection, Camden Local Studies and Archives Centre, A IX, 146.
26 For the history of this fountain, National Archives, Work 16/704.
27 The fountain, which cost £200, was paid for by the Band of Hope of Okehampton. National Archives, Works 16/704.
28 Letter from 'A Pedestrian' to the editor, *The Times*, 26 April 1845.
29 *Economist*, 30 August 1851.
30 Webster, *The Regent's Park and Primrose Hill*, p. 86.
31 William Ray Smee to editor, *The Times*, 23 July 1860.
32 Webster, *The Regent's Park and Primrose Hill*, p. 86.
33 *The Times*, 13 August 1863.
34 See, above, p. 124. See also, *Bell's Life*, 19 May 1850.
35 *Lloyd's*, 4 October 1846.
36 *Lloyd's*, 4 October 1846.
37 W.R. Smee to W.E. Gladstone, 5 April 1873, W.R. Smee, *Primrose Hill Park, Regent's Park and Hampstead Heath* (London, 1873), pp. 5–6. The cricket ground comprised over eleven acres. There was another plot of five acres adjoining it.
38 Ibid., p. 6.
39 Ibid., p. 12.
40 'William Willett senior (1837–1913) and William Willett junior (1856–1915)', joint article, *Oxford Dictionary of National Biography*.
41 F.M.L. Thompson, *Hampstead: Building a Borough, 1650–1964* (London, 1974), p. 347.
42 *The Times*, 2 July 1890.
43 *The Times*, 2 November and 9 December 1892.
44 Thompson, *Hampstead*, p. 346.
45 Ibid., pp. 344–51; the quotation is from p. 347. In accordance with William Willett junior's commitment to the use of natural light, the houses have no basements.
46 Charles Booth, Descriptive Maps of London Poverty, 1889. These maps, which were colour-coded to show levels of wealth and poverty, were issued to go with Booth's large-scale survey of London wealth, *Life and Labour of the People of London*, 9 vols (London, 1892–97).
47 K.A. Scholey, *The Railways of Camden* (London, 2002), pp. 24, 28 and 29. There was also a service between Chalk Farm and Euston until 1915. I am uncertain when this began.
48 National Archives, Work 16/174.
49 E.W. Streeter to editor, *The Times*, 8 December 1880.

50   National Archives, Work 16/174, bill from James Gridwood for £470 3s. 1d., 5 May 1882; A.D. Webster, *The Regent's Park and Primrose Hill* (London, 1911), p. 86.

51   Louis Macneice, *Autumn Journal* (1938), canto 7, p. 113.

52   *Pall Mall Gazette*, 1 October 1883. The 'umbrageous plane trees' were in fact poplars.

53   *Jackson's Oxford Journal*, 30 August 1851.

54   National Archives, Work 16/698.

55   For an extensive correspondence on fencing, National Archives, Work 16/1667.

56   B.J. Dale to George Lansbury, 5 February 1930, National Archives, Work 16/1667.

57   Correspondence on playground and clock, National Archives, Work 16/1670.

58   For instance, 'The Commissioners of Works are prepared to receive tenders for the exclusive privilege of depasturing sheep in Regent's Park and Primrose Hill', *The Times*, 10 December 1920.

59   See the exchanges about the problems of keeping sheep on Primrose Hill in National Archives, Work 16/1667.

Notes to Chapter 10: Across the Hill

1   George Rose Emerson, *London: How the Great City Grew* (London, 1862), pp. 254–5.

2   'A Magistrate for Middlesex' to editor, *The Times*, 11 March 1830.

3   *The Times*, 11 March 1830.

4   *The Times*, 11 March 1830.

5   *Morning Post*, 1 July 1808.

6   *Penny Satirist*, 5 July 1845. The history of Hampstead Heath, which attracted large numbers of visitors, including those belonging to the working class, provides many parallels to that of Primrose Hill.

7   'Character of a Cockney', *Hull Packet*, 1 September 1832.

8   *Morning Chronicle*, 18 July 1821.

9   *Illustrated London News*, 7 June 1856. There were also fireworks in Green Park, Hyde Park and Victoria Park.

10   Camden Local Studies and Archives Centre, Heal Collection, A IX, 149.

11   *Morning Chronicle*, 2 May 1810.

12   Clive Emsley, *Britain and the French Revolution* (Harlow, 2000), pp. 29–40.

13   *Morning Post*, 6 November 1819.

14   *John Bull*, 11 April 1836.

15   *The Times*, 5 April 1836. See also, *Figaro in London*, 16 April 1836.

16   'Joseph Rayner Stephens (1805–79)', *Oxford Dictionary of National Biography*.

17   *John Bull*, 13 May 1839.

18   David Goodway, *London Chartism, 1838–1848* (Cambridge, 1982), pp. 21–96, 99–149.

19   'John Frost (1784–1877)', not to be confused with 'John Frost (1750–1842)', one of the founders of the London Corresponding Society, *Oxford Dictionary of National Biography*. Van Dieman's Land was later renamed Tasmania.

20   *The Times*, 16 September 1856.

21   Derek Beales, 'Gladstone and Garibaldi', *Gladstone*, edited by Peter Jagger (London, 1998), pp. 137–56, 264–6.

22   *Reynolds's Newspaper*, 1 May 1864.

23   *Scotsman*, 12 April 1864.

24   Beales, 'Gladstone and Garibaldi', pp. 144–53; *The Times*, 6 May 1846. For the Shakespeare tercentenary, see below, pp. 204–6.

25   *The Times*, 6 May 1864.

26   *The Times*, 19 May 1853.

27   *The Times*, 19 May 1853.

28   *The Times*, 19 May 1853.

29   *Observer*, 20 April and 25 May 1835; 27 March, 22 and 30 May 1837; 6 May 1839.

30   *Observer*, 1 July 1844.

31   Poster, 1850, Heal Collection, A IX, 25.

32   Ibid.

33   Ibid.

34   Poster, 2 September 1851, Heal Collection, A IX, 27.

35   Poster, Whit Monday, Tuesday and Wednesday, 1850, Heal Collection, A IX, 26.

36   Petition of John Morgan of 8 St George's Square, Primrose Hill, in the parish of St Pancras in the county of Middlesex, London Metropolitan Archives, MR/L/MD/0856; MR/L/MD/0857, 20 September 1860.

37   *From Primrose Hill to Euston Road*, edited by F. Peter Woodford (revised edn, London, 1995), pp. 71–3.

38   Guiseppe Campanella, *An Italian on Primrose Hill: A Narrative* (London, 1875), p. 11. *Gendarme* is spelt *gen d'arme* in the original.

39   Frederick Miller, *Saint Pancras Past and Present: Being Historical, Traditional and General Notes of the Parish Including Biographical Notices of Inhabitants Associated with its Topographical and General History* (London, 1874), p. 199.

40   W.R. Smee to W.E. Gladstone, 5 April 1873, W.R. Smee, *Primrose Hill Park, Regent's Park and Hampstead Heath* (London, 1873), p. 5.

41   W.R. Smee to W.E. Gladstone, 26 April 1873, ibid., p. 7.

42   *John Bull*, 3 August 1850.

43   *The Times*, 2 August 1866.

44   *The Times*, 2 August 1866.

45   *The Times*, 2 August 1866. Their likely refuge was the Queens public house, opened in 1864.

46   W.C. Galloway to editor, *The Times*, 7 November 1868. For another violent incident on Guy Fawkes Day in the 1830s, when a mob tore down fencing to make a bonfire, see Heal Collection, A IX, 29.

47   *The Times*, 24 May 1877.

48   16 November 1764, Heal Collection, A IX, 149.

49   October 1802, Heal Collection, A IX, 22. In the same month, the artist and writer James Northcote (1746–1831) was robbed, 'at ten o'clock in the day', on Primrose Hill. *Morning Post*, 14 October 1802.

50   *The Proceedings of the Old Bailey, 1674–1913*, t18210912–2. He was recommended by the prosecution to mercy.

51   *Bell's Life*, 31 October 1847.

52   *Morning Post*, 13 July 1810.

53   *Morning Chronicle*, 25 October 1825.

54   For an earlier case, where a respectably dressed man, William Thompson, robbed

two small boys, who had been playing on Primrose Hill, of their clothes, *The Times*, 1 April 1853.

55 *The Times*, 21 August 1900. The article incorrectly gives Amy Hobart's Christian name as May.

56 *The Times*, 21 August 1900.

57 *The Times*, 21 August 1900.

58 *R. v. Hope*, 11 September 1900, *Proceedings of the Old Bailey*, T19000911–573.

59 *Morning Post*, 29 August 1795. The large amount of money found in his pockets echoes the case of Sir Edmund Berry Godfrey in 1678.

60 Heal Collection, A IX, 149.

61 *The Times*, 23 June 1828.

62 *The Times*, 23 June 1828. For arsenic poisoning, see Katherine Watson, *Poisoned Lives: English Poisoners and their Victims* (London, 2004), pp. xi–xii, 2–52.

63 *Observer*, 5 May 1861; *York Herald*, 11 May 1861.

64 *Morning Post*, 18 September 1805.

65 *John Bull*, 14 July 1849.

66 National Archives, Work 16/1604, 7 October 1936.

67 National Archives, Work 16/1604, 28 and 30 September 1937.

68 National Archives, Work 16/1604, undated but 1937.

69 Ibid., i, p. 5.

70 Gordon Mackenzie, *Marylebone: Great City North of Oxford Street* (London, 1972), p. 265.

71 William Michael Rossetti, *Some Reminiscences of William Michael Rossetti* (2 vols, London, 1906), ii, p. 440.

72 Juliet M. Soskice, *Chapters from Childhood* (London, 1921), pp. 43–4.

73 Asa Briggs and John Callow, *Marx in London* (London, 2008), p. 58.

74 Ibid., p. 65.

Notes to Chapter 11: The Martian Invasion

1 Austin Gee, *The British Volunteer Movement, 1794–1814* (Oxford, 2003); Boyd Hilton, *A Mad, Bad and Dangerous People? England, 1783–1846* (Oxford, 2006), pp. 70–1, 100–3.

2 1804 cutting, Heal Collection, Camden Local Studies and Archives Centre, A IX, 13.

3 Ibid.

4 Roy Allen, 'Napoleon's First Invasion Threat: The Proposed Northern Line of Defence round the Capital', *Camden History Review*, 12 (1984), pp. 24–6.

5 Hilton, *A Mad, Bad and Dangerous People?*, p. 102.

6 Roy Allen, 'The Hampstead and Highgate Citadel: Defence Plans against Napoleon', *Camden History Review*, 10 (1982), p. 9. The medal was to have been 'frappée à Londres'.

7 *Illustrated London News*, 7 June 1856. See above, pp. 156–8.

8 See *Roger Fenton: Photographer of the 1850s*, exhibition catalogue (London, 1988). For more on Fenton, see below, pp. 216–17.

9 John Richardson, *Camden Town and Primrose Hill Past* (London, 1991), pp. 28–9.

10   *Illustrated London News*, 10 October 1874; Alan Faulkner, *The Regent's Canal: London's Hidden Waterway* (Burton-on-Trent, 2005), pp. 125–6.

11   H.G. Wells, *Experiment in Autobiography: Discoveries and Conclusions of a Very Ordinary Brain (since 1866)* (London, 1984), pp. 317–33; Ann Thwaite, *A.A. Milne: A Biography* (London, 1991), pp. 32–9.

12   Thwaite, *A.A. Milne*, p. 34.

13   Michael Sherborne, *H.G. Wells: Another Kind of Life* (London, 2010), pp. 21–85.

14   H.G. Wells, *The Invisible Man* (London, 1987), p. 96.

15   The best known of Wells's other science fiction books is *The First Men on the Moon* (1901).

16   H.G. Wells, *The War of the Worlds* (London, 2005), pp. 11, 37, 45, 89, 105, 106, 121. Wells spells Bushy Park, near Hampton Court, as Bushey Park, ibid., p. 89.

17   Wells, *The War of the Worlds*, pp. 13–26.

18   Ibid., p. 7.

19   Ibid., pp. 124–30.

20   Ibid., p. 88.

21   Ibid., p. 125.

22   Ibid., pp. 167–8.

23   For a survey of invasion threats and the British reaction to them, see I.F. Clarke, *Voices Prophesying War, 1763–1984* (Oxford, 1966). On Chesney and his imitators, ibid., pp. 30–63.

24   Wells, *The War of the Worlds*, p. 7.

25   Richard Rhodes, *The Making of the Atomic Bomb* (New York, 1986), pp. 14, 21, 24, 44, 107, 266, 637 and 754.

26   H.G. Wells, *The World Set Free* (London, 1914), pp. 117–18.

27   Ibid., p. 118.

Notes to Chapter 12: The Impact of War

1   *The Times*, 15 November 1900.

2   *The Times*, 19 December 1899 and 6 January 1900.

3   National Archives, Cab 27/7, 10 March 1917.

4   National Archives, Cab 24/89.

5   National Archives, Work 16/1667, 3 July 1917.

6   St Mark's Regent's Park, magazine, August 1916.

7   Maurice Beningfield, National Archives, WO 339/25904; Philip Beningfield, WO 339/22130.

8   Cyril Eiloart, National Archives, WO 339/99852. Horace and Oswald Eiloart are not listed in the Commonwealth War Graves Commission's online database.

9   Henry Betts, National Archives, WO 339/2191.

10   Cecil Duncan Jones was the younger brother of Arthur Duncan Jones, who was the vicar of St Mary's Primrose Hill from 1915. For Ruhleben, see *The Ruhleben Story: The Prisoners of Ruhleben Civilian Internment Camp, 1914–1918*, www.ruhleben.tripod.com, which contains a database of camp prisoners. I am grateful to Professor Katherine Duncan-Jones for information on her great uncle.

11   Donald Gray, *Percy Dearmer: A Parson's Pilgrimage* (Norwich, 2000), pp. 56–92.

12   Ibid., pp. 93–109. After leaving Serbia, Percy Dearmer worked during the war for the YMCA in France and India, ibid., pp. 115–23.

13   'Resurrection', Geoffrey Dearmer, *A Pilgrim's Song: Selected Poems to Mark the Poet's 100th Birthday* (London, 1993), p. 14.

14   'Geoffrey Dearmer', obituary by Lawrence Cotterell, *Independent*, 20 August 1996.

15   *The Times*, 17 March, 8, 14 May 1937; *Observer*, 21 March 1937. The Scouts camped in the north-west corner of the hill; information from Louisa Service.

16   Louis Macneice, *The Strings Are False*, pp. 174–5; 'Louis Macneice (1907–63)', *Oxford Dictionary of National Biography*.

17   Louis Macneice, *Autumn Journal* (1938), canto 7, p. 113.

18   Anthony Heap, Diary, London Metropolitan Archives, accession no. 2243, 22 October 1938. I am most grateful to Dr Robin Woolven to drawing this source to my attention.

19   Heap, Diary, 6 November 1938.

20   C. Allen Newbery, *Wartime St Pancras*, Camden History Society (London, 2006), p. 7; Robin Woolven, 'Air Raid Precautions in St Pancras, 1935–1945', *Camden History Review*, 16 (1989), pp. 20–5.

21   Heap, Diary, Sunday, 5 November 1939.

22   *The Times*, 13 February 1939.

23   *The Times*, 19 September 1939.

24   Woolven, 'Air Raid Precautions in St Pancras, 1939–45', pp. 20–5; Robin Woolven, 'Playing Hitler's Game from Fitzroy Road NW1: J.B.S. Haldane, the St Pancras Branch of the Communist Party, and Deep-Shelter Agitation', *Camden History Review*, 23 (1999), pp. 22–5; Robin Woolven, 'The Belsize Deep Shelter', *Camden History Society Newsletter*, 121 (September 1990), p. 3.

25   *The Times*, 26 August 1939.

26   *The Times*, 9 September 1939; J. Barrington-Johnson, *The Zoo: The Story of London Zoo* (London, 2005), pp. 121–8. Philip Ziegler, *London at War, 1939–1945* (London, 1995), pp. 43–4; Stephen Inwood, *A History of London* (London, 1998), p. 781.

27   Julian Huxley, *Memories*, i (Harmondsworth, 1978), pp. 243–4; Barrington-Johnson, *The Zoo*, pp. 126–7. The flying bombs of 1944–45 greatly depressed visitor numbers.

28   Another block nearby was filled with Maltese children evacuated from the besieged island. Gerald Eve, 'Rabbit Stew and Brylcreem', in *Primrose Hill Remembered* (London, 2001), p. 33. In 1940 Eve used 'to watch the dog-fights between fighter planes over the City and East London' from the attic of 41 Ainger Road. Ibid.

29   Richard Hough, *Other Days Around Me: A Memoir* (London, 1992), p. 41.

30   Ibid., pp. 42–3.

31   Gwyneth Williams, 'Allotments on the Hill', in *Primrose Hill Remembered*, p. 55. See also pp. 33 and 47.

32   Maureen Hawes, 'A Journey into the Past', in *Primrose Hill Remembered*, p. 47.

33   Heap, Diary, 1 December 1940.

34   Heap, Diary, 23 July 1941.

35   Royal Parks Agency, *Regent's Park: An Archival Review of the Nash Landscape and its Development, 1811–1945: Including the Addition of Primrose Hill and its Early History* (Colvin and Moggridge, Lechlade, 1998), pp. 100–1. There are photographs of the gun emplacements in the Imperial War Museum Collection, H 847–845; and H 868–875.

36 Information from Louisa Service.

37 A typescript transcription of entries from the diary of Harold Ernest Danks between 5 December 1936 and 6 March 1945 is in the Royal Artillery Museum Library, Woolwich, MD/596, accession 1894. The diary is continued, in the form of letters mainly written from India, between April and October 1945. With the diary and letters are notebooks with handwritten notes by Danks on a wide range of military matters but primarily on the technical side of gunnery. Photographs given by Danks to the Imperial War Museum are in the Imperial War Museum Collection, HU 17593–17601.

38 Danks, Diary, 'Primrose Hill Gunsite', two maps: one undated; one dated 3 February 1941.

39 Danks, Diary, 16 May, 16 July 1940.

40 Danks, Diary, 11 July, 26 August and 10 October 1940.

41 Danks, Diary, 3 November 1940. Hors d'oeuvres is spelt 'hors d'ouvres' in the original and Château is spelt 'Chateaux'.

42 Danks, Diary, 4 November 1940.

43 Louis Macneice, 'Primrose Hill', *The Last Ditch* (Dublin, 1940), pp. 18–19.

44 Inwood, *A History of London*, p. 788.

45 Hawes, 'A Jouney into the Past', *Primrose Hill Remembered*, p. 47.

46 See the series of photographs, taken on 10 October 1940, of the Junkers. Imperial War Museum Collection, HU 69556, HU 73453, HU 73444 and HU 81586.

47 Imperial War Museum, Sound Archive, no. 28893.

48 Imperial War Museum, Sound Archive, no. 27248.

49 Imperial War Museum, Sound Archive, no. 28596.

50 Hawes, 'A Journey into the Past', in *Primrose Hill Remembered*, p. 47.

51 Sylvia Ballerini, 'World War II', in *Primrose Hill Remembered*, pp. 49–50.

52 Charlotte Haldane, *Truth Will Out* (London, 1949), pp. 187–8. The old lady may well have been Reg Pleeth's maternal aunt Cecily, Reg Pleeth, 'The Primrose Hill Connection', in *Primrose Hill Remembered*, p. 23, although Pleeth describes her as being killed outright.

53 Woolven, 'Playing Hitler's Game', p. 25. The Haldanes divorced after the war.

54 *Regent's Park: An Archival Review*, illustration 149; *The London County Council Bomb Damage Maps, 1939–1945*, edited by Ann Saunders, with an Introduction by Robin Woolven, London Topographical Society Publication, 164 (London, 2005), does not show bombs which fell on parkland, as the maps were restricted to showing damage to buildings.

55 Heap, Diary, 21 March 1945; Westminster City Archives, Civil Defence Records, report of V2 incident.

Notes to Chapter 13: Shakespeare's Oak

1 Alan Kendall, *David Garrick: A Biography* (London, 1985), pp. 129–42; Christian Deeling, *The Great Shakespeare Jubilee* (London, 1964).

2 *The Times*, 25 April 1864; Richard Foulkes, 'Shakespeare and Garibaldi on Primrose Hill', *Camden History Review*, 9 (1981), pp. 13–16.

3 Derek Beales, 'Gladstone and Garibaldi', in *Gladstone*, ed. Peter Jagger (London, 1998), pp. 137–56, 264–6. See above, pp. 161–2.

4   Camden Local Studies and Archives Centre, H 712/5, Eliza Cook, 'Tercentenary Ode', lines 1–4.

5   Camden Local Studies and Archives Centre, H 712/5, V.C. Clinton-Baddeley, 'Lines Written to be Spoken at the Planting of an Oak by Dame Edith Evans DBE on Primrose Hill, April 23rd 1964', lines 21–4.

6   'The Prospect from Primrose Hill', *Gentleman's Magazine*, June 1749, lines 9–14.

7   'To Mrs. ?, on the Death of her Husband', *The Female's Meditations: or Common Occurrences Spiritualized in Verse* (1787); reprinted in *Eighteenth-Century Women Poets*, ed. Roger Lonsdale (Oxford, 1989), p. 408. For more information on Wallis, and two other poems by her, ibid., pp. 407–12.

8   Anon., 'Primrose Hill', *Literary Chronicle*, 7 May 1825.

9   Jane Gwilliam, *Primrose Hill, a Poem: To Which Are Added 'The Queen's Jubilee' and Other Metrical Effusions* (printed for the author, London, 1838). Jane Gwilliam may have been a pseudonym for John Gwilliam.

10 Paul Macartney, 'The Fool on the Hill', from the Beatles album *Magical Mystery Tour* (1967). See Alistair Taylor, *Yesterday: The Beatles Remembered* (London, 1967), pp. 167–8.

11 Andrew Loog Oldham, foreword to Gered Mankowitz, *The Stones, 65–67* (London, 2002), pp. 2–3.

12 *Primrose Hill Remembered* (London, 2001), plate 4.

13 'Primrose Hill' (McPherson/Forman), from Madness, *The Rise and Fall* (1982); interview with Graham McPherson, *Q Magazine*, April 2001.

14 Pepys Collection, 3.53, printed before 1685. Reprinted in *The Roxburghe Ballads*, ix, ed. J.W. Ebsworth (1897), pp. lxxxvi–vii.

15 *An Excellent Garland Containing Four Choice Songs* (Manchester, *c.* 1785).

16 Hazel Conway, *People's Parks: The Design and Development of Victorian Parks in Britain* (Cambridge, 1991), pp. 200–3.

17 *The Times*, 26 May 1856.

18 Conway, *People's Parks*, p. 202.

19 Vaughan Williams lived at 10 Hanover Terrace, in Regent's Park, from 1953 to 1958.

20 Donald Gray, *Percy Dearmer: A Parson's Pilgrimage* (Norwich, 2000), pp. 62–8.

21 Martin Shaw, *Up to Now* (Oxford, 1929), p. 102. For his time at St Mary's, ibid., pp. 98–103, 114, 116–19, 130. With Percy Dearmer, Shaw produced *The English Carol Book* (1913). He also wrote music for Mabel Dearmer's *The Soul of the World*, *The Dreamer*, *The Cockolly Bird* and *Brer Rabbit*. 'Martin Shaw (1875–1958)', *Oxford Dictionary of National Biography*. See also, Gray, *Percy Dearmer*, pp. 69–71, 86, 135–6, 140, 142, 152 and 187.

22 W.B. Yeats, *Reveries over Childhood and Youth* (London, 1936), p. 5.

23 Sylvia Plath to Aurelia and Warren Plath, 31 March 1960, Sylvia Plath, *Letters Home: Correspondence, 1950–1963*, edited by Aurelia Schober Plath (London, 1975), p. 373.

24 Sylvia Plath to Aurelia Plath, 7 November 1962, ibid., pp. 477–8.

25 Fay Weldon, *Chalcot Crescent* (London, 2009), pp. 27 and 245.

26 Douglas Adams, *The Long Dark Tea-Time of the Soul* (London, 1988), pp. 188–9; see also pp. 66–7.

27   Helen Falconer, *Primrose Hill* (London, 1999), p. 5.

28   Amanda Craig, *In a Dark Wood* (paperback edn, London, 2001), pp. 267–72. See also Amanda Craig's contribution, 'The Seasons in Primrose Hill', in *Primrose Hill Remembered*, pp. 73–5, about growing up in Primrose Hill Village.

29   Arthur Conan Doyle, 'The Yellow Face' (1893).

30   Ruth Rendell, *The Keys to the Street* (London, 1996). For Primrose Hill, see pp. 126, 153, 157–8, 164 and 184–5.

31   Ibid., p. 158.

32   Paul Charles, *Last Boat to Camden Town* (London, 1998), p. 13. Other Charles novels mentioning Primrose Hill are *Fountain of Sorrow* (London, 1998), *The Ballad of Sean and Wilko* (London, 2000), *I've Heard the Banshee Sing* (London, 2002), *The Hissing of the Silent Lonely Room* (London, 2001), *Sweetwater* (Brandon, 2006) and *The Beautiful Sound of Silence* (Brandon, 2008). In the last, the victim is drugged and then burned to death in the Primrose Hill Guy Fawkes bonfire.

33   Dodie Smith, *The Hundred and One Dalmatians* (London, 1956), pp. 48, 172.

34   Ibid., p. 49.

35   Ibid., p. 184.

36   Simon Jenkins and Jonathan Ditchburn, *Images of Hampstead* (Richmond-upon-Thames, 1982), 'Primrose Hill', pp. 127–41, 252–6, and illustrations numbers 416–74.

37   Ibid.

38   Westminster City Archives, T136, 1–18. No. 12 is a fine view of Primrose Hill from near Hertford Villa (now Winfield House) in Regent's Park.

39   Catherine Lampert, Norman Rosenthal and Isabel Carlisle, *Frank Auerbach: Paintings and Drawings, 1954–2001* (London, 2001), p. 12. For Primrose Hill, see ibid., pp. 12, 13, 17, 42–3, 101–7, 149.

40   Craig Brown, *One on One* (London, 2011), pp. 294–6, on which this paragraph depends, gives an elegant account of the meeting.

41   *Roger Fenton: Photographer of the 1850s*, exhibition catalogue, Hayward Gallery, 4 February to 17 April 1988 (London, 1988); John Hannavy, *Roger Fenton of Crimble Hall* (London, 1975).

42   They are in the collection of the Société Française de Photographie. Fenton was a member of the committee formed to promote the building of St Mark's. Marian Kamlish, 'Claudet, Fenton and the Photographic Society', *History of Photographie*, 26 (2002), pp. 296–306, gives an account of Fenton's friendship with the distinguished French photographer Antoine Claudet, who lived at 11 Gloucester Road (later 21 Gloucester Avenue) in the early 1850s.

43   Gordon Baldwin, *Roger Fenton: Pasha and Bayadère* (Malibu, California, 1996). I am grateful to Marian Kamlish for drawing this book to my attention.

44   David Bailey, *London NW1: Urban Landscapes* (London, 1963), plates 46 and 59; Bill Brandt, *Portraits* (London, 1982).

45   I am grateful to Polly Kemp for these references.

46   A.D. Webster, *The Regent's Park and Primrose Hill: History and Antiquities* (London, 1911), p. 90; 'Sir Thomas Brock (1847–1922)', *Oxford Dictionary of National Biography*. Occasionally, in modern times, sculptures have been displayed on the hill for a limited period.

Notes to Chapter 14: The Sacred Mount

1 Anthony Heap, Diary, London Metropolitan Archives, accession no. 2243, 27 September 1947.
2 See, for instance, National Monuments Record, 241/AC16692, frame 61.
3 Winston Churchill, Commons debate on the War Situation, 8 October 1940, *House of Commons Debates*, ccclxv, columns 261–2.
4 *The London County Council Bomb Damage Maps, 1939–1945*, edited by Ann Saunders, with an Introduction by Robin Woolven, London Topographical Society Publication, 164 (London, 2005), shows clearly what was damaged by wartime bombing, and the degree of severity experienced, across London.
5 Ann Saunders, *The Regent's Park Villas* (London, 1981), pp. 10, 15, 18, 22 and 30.
6 Bridget Cherry and Nikolaus Pevsner, The Buildings of England, *London*, iv, *North* (London, 1998), pp. 382–3.
7 'Sir Geoffrey Jellicoe (1900–96)', *Oxford Dictionary of National Biography*.
8 F.E.J. Gillard to G.J. Spence, 29 April 1954, National Archives, Work 16/1886. Heap, Diary, March 1951. The footings of the anti-aircraft installations are still there and can be detected in dry weather. They were recorded by English Heritage during alterations to the summit of Primrose Hill in 2011.
9 Report of a meeting between K. Newis, Major Hobkirk and Mr Austin, 21 February 1955, National Archives, Work 16/1886.
10 National Archives, Work 16/1886, letter from Clare Winsten, 20 June 1956.
11 National Archives, Work 16/1886, Arthur Kenyon to David Eccles, 24 June 1952.
12 National Archives, Work 16/1886. Its battered remains were moved to Highgate Library, but I have been unable to discover whether they still survive.
13 National Archives, Work 16/1886, letters from Muriel Holland, 10 Elsworthy Terrace, 20 October 1953 and 4 December 1955.
14 National Archives, Work 16/1886, letter from John Willis, 10 St George's Terrace, 14 October 1956.
15 National Archives, Work 16/1886. This were later replaced by iron fencing with spiked heads. The hedge bordering Prince Albert Road was expertly cut back and relayed by a master hedge-layer, Mr Tunk, in 1994. Valerie St Johnston, 'The Friends of Regent's Park and Primrose Hill', in *Primrose Hill Remembered* (London, 2001), p. 149. The hedge has suffered from its proximity to the heavy volume of traffic on the road and needs relaying again. While no attempt to close the park was made during these years, the cost of doing so, and then of having one man with a dog patrolling the hill at night, was calculated by the park authorities at £600 a year.
16 For the Hungarian-born Goldfinger, see 'Ernö Goldfinger (1902–87)', *Oxford Dictionary of National Biography*; at the time he designed his block, Stirling was part of the architectural practice Stirling and Gowan. 'Sir James Stirling (1924–92)', *Oxford Dictionary of National Biography*.
17 Oliver Marriott, *The Property Boom* (London, 1969), pp. 11–23, 82–144, 181–95; Simon Jenkins, *Landlords to London: The Story of a Capital and its Growth* (London, 1975), pp. 209–47.
18 Bruno Schlaffenberg, Camden's Planning Officer, commented, 'These high blocks would make development at the rear difficult and not so advantageous'.

19   The villas which disappeared included Myra Lodge, where Frances Buss, the founder of Camden School for Girls and North London Collegiate, lived from 1868 to 1894. *Streets of Belsize*, edited by F. Peter Woodford (2nd edn, London, 2009), p. 33.

20   Mary Wylie, 'The Siege and the Oldfield Plot', in *Primrose Hill Remembered*, pp. 103–4. Charles Oldfield had bought Lot 258 in the Southampton auction of 1840 for £630.

21   Information from Françoise Findlay. 'Harold Samuel, Baron Samuel of Wych Cross (1912–87)', *Oxford Dictionary of National Biography*.

22   Jean Rossiter, 'A Sense of Community', in *Primrose Hill Remembered*, pp. 86–7. This was the site of the Railway Cottages, which were demolished to make way for Auden Place. The Primrose Hill Conservation Area Advisory Committee saved the west side of Chalcot Road, between Fitzroy Road and Princess Road, during its campaign against the planned redevelopment. *Hampstead and Highgate Express*, 23 July 1965.

23   There is a wealth of detail at Eton concerning the college's plans, in gestation since the war, for the future of the Chalcots Estate. See Eton College Records, 4/1, Central Red; *Streets of Belsize*, ed. Woodford, p. 32; 'William Graham Holford, Baron Holford (1907–75)', *Oxford Dictionary of National Biography*. The outlying tower block, Blashford, built at the same time, may be named after the Blashford lakes in Dorset.

24   'Max Rayne, Baron Rayne (1918–2003)', *Oxford Dictionary of National Biography*.

25   Mireille Galinou, *Cottages and Villas: The Birth of the Garden Suburb* (London and New Haven, 2010), pp. 328–37; London Metropolitan Archives, P81/PAU/023.

26   *The Times*, 8 April 1914.

27   *The Times*, 7 April 1914.

28   *The Times*, 24 July, 19 September and 31 October 1936.

29   Peter Guillery, *The Buildings of London Zoo* (London, 1993), pp. 115–17.

30   Martin Sheppard, *Regent's Park and Primrose Hill* (London, 2010), pp. 88–90.

31   Marriott, *The Property Boom*, pp. 181–95; Jenkins, *Landlords to London*, pp. 21–2. A second tower, next to the original Euston Tower, was built in 2012.

32   Herbert Wright, *London High* (London, 2006), pp. 67–74, 121–2.

33   David Secker Walker was the chairman, Sarah, Lady Redesdale, was secretary, and Colin and Valerie St Johnston were active members.

34   Jean Rossiter, 'A Sense of Community', in *Primrose Hill Revisited*, p. 87.

35   Information from David and Lorna Secker Walker.

36   Hervey Blake, 'Primrose Hill Sit-In', in *Primrose Hill Remembered*, pp. 112–13; Mary Wylie, 'The Siege and the Oldfield Plot', ibid., p. 103. See also newspaper cuttings in Camden Local Studies and Archives Centre.

37   I am most grateful to Inspector John Archell, of the Royal Parks Constabulary, for this information. The record of Regent's Park was sadly tarnished by the early-morning rape of a jogger near the Avenue Garden on 30 May 2012.

38   Information from Mark Watson. The force also came briefly under the Department of Transport.

39   Information from Francis Duncan.

40   Information from Diana Athill and Francis Duncan.

41   Both counts were organised by Ian Wallace: www.open.edu/openlearn/body-mind/across-the-skyline.

42 I am grateful to Tony Duckett for this information. Developments on and near Barrow Hill are scheduled to disturb the birds' refuge.

43 Sylvia Ballerini, 'World War II', in *Primrose Hill Remembered*, pp. 49–50.

44 Keith Thomas, *Man and the Natural World* (Harmondsworth, 1983), pp. 243–69.

45 William Blake, *Milton* (1804–8), preface, *Blake: Complete Writings*, edited by Geoffrey Keynes (Oxford. 1972), p. 480.

46 Stuart Pigott, *The Druids* (London, 1968), p. 173.

47 George Rose Emerson, *London: How the Great City Grew* (London, 1862), pp. 256.

48 A.M. Eyre, *Saint John's Wood: Its History, its Houses, its Haunts and its Celebrities* (London, 1913), pp. 250–1.

49 Gael O'Farrell, 'Home', in *Primrose Hill Remembered*, p. 108. Others think that it may be the burial mound of Boadicea herself.

50 *Hampstead and Highgate Express*, 9 February 2012. There were three other witnesses. In H.G. Wells, *The War of the Worlds* (London, 2005), p. 26, the Martians make a hissing noise, which 'passed into a humming, into a long, loud, droning noise'.

51 Ibid., pp. 167–9.

52 *See Like Me*, 30 August 2011.

53 Richard Hayman, *Riddles in Stone: Myths, Archaeology and the Ancient Britons* (London, 1997), pp. 206–13.

54 John Michell, *The View over Atlantis* (London, 1969), pp. 13–75.

55 Christopher E. Street, *London's Ley Lines: Pathways of Enlightenment* (London, 2010), p. 124.

56 Ibid., pp. 123–32.

57 Ben Elton, *Inconceivable* (London, 1999), p. 119.

58 Robert Blake, *Disraeli* (London, 1966), p. 747.

59 The quotation and other information in the first half of this paragraph are from Philip and Stephanie Carr-Gomm's *Plant Oracle*. I am grateful to Philip Carr-Gomm for sending this to me.

60 Ronald Hutton is the best guide to modern as well as to historic Druids. See Ronald Hutton, *Witches, Druids and King Arthur* (London, 2003), pp. 239–58; Ronald Hutton, *Blood and Mistletoe: The History of the Druids in Britain* (New Haven and London, 2009), pp. 313–417; and Ronald Hutton, *The Druids* (London, 2007), pp. 157–204.

61 *St Pancras Chronicle*, 26 September 1952.

62 *St Pancras Chronicle*, 1 October 1954.

63 Information from the Reverend Marjorie Brown, vicar of St Mary the Virgin Primrose Hill, 29 January 2012.

64 Keith and Betty Bird, 'Fireworks on the Hill', in *Primrose Hill Remembered*, pp. 105–6.

65 Circular letter from Inspector John Archell, 18 October 2012.

66 'Brazil Nuts?', *Camden New Journal*, 26 January 2012.

67 Leigh Hunt, 'Primrose Hill', *The Idler and Breakfast-Table Companion*, 27 May 1837, p. 23.

68 See above, p. 209.

69 See above, p. 62 and n.

Bibliography

General

This bibliography makes no attempt at being exhaustive. There are chapters on Primrose Hill in Martin Sheppard, *Regent's Park and Primrose Hill* (London, 2010); and A.D. Webster, *The Regent's Park and Primrose Hill: History and Antiquities* (London, 1911). See also, Royal Parks Agency, *Regent's Park: An Archival Review of the Nash Landscape and its Development, 1811–1945: Including the Addition of Primrose Hill and its Early History* (Colvin and Moggridge, Lechlade, 1998). *Primrose Hill Remembered* (London, 2001) contains many short personal reminiscences of Primrose Hill and Primrose Hill Village. Two guides published by the Camden History Society, *From Primrose Hill to Euston Road* (London, 1995); and *Streets of Belsize* (London, 2009), are excellent street by street guides to areas near the hill.

The best history of London is Stephen Inwood, *A History of London* (London, 1998). See also, Stephen Inwood, *Historic London: An Explorer's Companion* (London, 2008). Roy Porter, *A London: A Social History* (London, 1994); and Francis Sheppard, *London: A History* (1998), are also excellent. Jerry White has recently completed a scintillating trilogy. *London in the Eighteenth Century: A Great and Monstrous Thing* (London, 2012), has followed *London in the Nineteenth Century: A Human Awful Wonder of God* (2007), and *London in the Twentieth Century: A City and its People* (2001). For a spirited canter through London notables, see Boris Johnson, *Johnson's Life of London: The People Who Made the City That Made the World* (London, 2011). Simon Jenkins, *Landlords to London: The Story of a Capital and its Growth* (London, 1975), is a readable guide to the history of many of the major London estates. For an older compilation, Edward Walford, *Old and New London: A Narrative of its History, its People and its Places*, v, *The Western and Northern Suburbs* (London, c. 1880), chapter 22, 'Primrose Hill and Chalk Farm', pp. 287–300.

For areas around Primrose Hill, see John Richardson, *Camden Town and Primrose Hill Past* (London, 1991), which has little on the hill itself; John Richardson, *Hampstead One Thousand, AD 986–1086* (London, 1985); John Richardson, *Kentish Town Past* (London, 1997); *Belsize 2000: A Living Suburb* (London, 2000); Gordon Mackenzie, *Marylebone: Great City North of Oxford Street* (London, 1972); and, for the Eyre Estate, Mireille Galinou, *Cottages and Villas: The Birth of the Garden Suburb* (New Haven and London, 2010). F.M.L. Thompson, *Hampstead: Building a Borough, 1650–1964* (London, 1974), is an outstanding history of the development of Hampstead, Belsize and the Eton Estate. On Regent's Park, see Ann Saunders, *Regent's Park: From 1086 to the Present* (2nd edn,

London, 1981). Simon Jenkins and Jonathan Ditchburn, *Images of Hampstead* (Richmond-upon-Thames, 1982), reproduces historical illustrations of a wide area around Hampstead, including Primrose Hill. See also Camden History Society's wider series of street guides, including *Streets of Camden Town* (2003); *Streets of Gospel Oak* (2006); *Streets of Hampstead* (2000); *Streets of Highgate* (2007); and *Streets of St Pancras* (2002). The annual *Camden History Review* (1973–) provides a wealth of knowledge on all things to do with the history of Camden (which was formed in 1965 from the older boroughs of Hampstead, Holburn and St Pancras). See also the society's newsletters.

The most relevant volume of the Victoria County History, *A History of the County of Middlesex*, is ix (London, 1989); see also xiii (Woodbridge, 2009), for the early history of Westminster. For the history of St Pancras, see Survey of London, xvii, *The Village of Highgate* (London, 1936); xix, *Old St Pancras and Kentish Town* (1938); *Tottenham Court Road and Neighbourhood* (London, 1949); and xxiv, *King's Cross and Neighbourhood* (London, 1952).

Databases and Dictionaries

The *Oxford Dictionary of National Biography*, which is available online in major libraries, as well as in a printed edition, is a superb resource, giving authoritative but very readable lives and sources for a great number of remarkable characters. For architects, see Howard Colvin, *Biographical Dictionary of British Architects, 1600–1840* (4th edn, London, 2008). The task of finding relevant references in contemporary newspapers has been transformed by the availability of searchable databases in major libraries. As well as *The Times*, *Guardian* and *Observer*, which have their own databases, a wide range of eighteenth- and nineteenth-century newspapers can be searched online in the *Seventeenth- and Eighteenth-Century Burney Collection*; *Nineteenth-Century British Library Newspapers*; and *Nineteenth-Century UK Periodicals*. John Black's literary database, *Regent's Park and Primrose Hill in Literature and Music: A Bibliography*, is the first stop for all literary and musical references to Primrose Hill. *The Proceedings of the Old Bailey, 1674–1913* is a searchable database for major crimes. *House of Commons: Parliamentary Papers, 1688–* is a searchable database of parliamentary legislation, including debates and reports.

Archives

The following archives contain substantial original material on the history of Primrose Hill. For detailed references, see the notes to this book or consult their catalogues.

Camden Local Archives and Study Centre
Heal Collection of historical cuttings and illustrations
Vestry minutes of Hampstead and St Pancras
Copies of local papers

Eton College Archives
Early history of the Chalcots Estate
Exchange of Primrose Hill with the crown
Modern history of the Chalcots Estate

Imperial War Museum
Photographs of Anti-Aircraft Battery
Sound Archive interviews

London Metropolitan Archives
Southampton Estate Archive
West Middlesex Water Works
Licensing records
Parochial records

National Archives
Marylebone Park
Regent's Park, including the Regent's Canal
Acquisition and administration of Primrose Hill
London and Birmingham Railway

Warwickshire County Record Office
Lord Southampton's country estate

Westminster City Archives
Vestry minutes for St Marylebone

Individual Chapters

1. The Hill without Primroses
For two very different views of Philip Gosse, see Edmund Gosse, *Father and Son* (London, 1907); and Ann Thwaite, *Glimpses of the Wonderful: The Life of Philip Henry Gosse, 1810–1888* (London, 2002). For an early literary response to Primrose Hill, James Leigh Hunt, 'Primrose Hill', *The Idler and Breakfast-Table Companion*, 27 May 1837.

2. Above the City
For the geology of London, see Eric Robinson, 'Geology and Building Material', in Bridget Cherry and Nikolaus Pevsner, The Buildings of England, *London*, iii, *North West* (London, 1991), pp. 91–3; and iv, *North* (London, 1998), pp. 87–9; and *The Geology of London*, compiled by Diana Clements (London, 2010). For the medieval history of Westminster, including the Hospital of St James, and for the wider area around it, Gervase Rosser, *Medieval Westminster, 1200–1540* (Oxford, 1989); David Sullivan, *The Westminster Corridor: The Anglo-Saxon Story of Westminster Abbey and its Lands in Middlesex* (London, 1994); and David Sullivan, *The Westminster Circle: The People Who Lived and Worked in the Early Town of Westminster, 1066–1307* (London, 2006). See also Colin Bowlt, 'Commons and Woodlands in the London Area', *Transactions of the London and Middlesex Archaeological Society*, 60 (2009), pp. 286–91. For the first history of London, *A Survey of London by John Stow: Reprinted from the Text of 1603 with Introduction and Notes*, ed. Charles Kingsford, 2 vols (Oxford, 1908). See also, Ann Saunders, *St Paul's: The Story of the Cathedral* (London, 2001).
    For the Popish Plot and the death of Sir Edmund Berry Godfrey, see Alan Marshall, *The

Strange Death of Edmund Godfrey: Plots and Politics in Restoration London (Thrupp, 1999); and John Kenyon, *The Popish Plot* (London, 1974). For contemporary accounts, see N.T. [Nathaniel Thompson], *A True and Perfect Narrative of the Late Terrible and Bloody Murder of Sir Edmund Berry Godfrey* (London, 1678); and Sir Roger L'Estrange, *A Brief History of the Times: Treating of the Death of Sir E.B.* Godfrey (London, 1688). See also, *A Letter to Mr Miles Prance in Relation to the Murder of Sir Edmund Bury Godfrey* (London, 1681).

Anthony Cooper, 'Old Chalk Farm Tavern', *Camden History Review*, 6 (1978), pp. 2–5, gives details of the first building to the east of Primrose Hill. For Radical activities there, Clive Emsley, *Britain and the French Revolution* (Harlow, 2000); and Alan Wharam, *The Treason Trials, 1794* (London, 1992). John Winter-Lotimer, 'The Chislehurst Connection: Camden Place and Camden Town', *Camden History Review*, 23 (1999), pp. 5–8, explains the origins of Camden Town's name; and Malcolm Brown, '"The Fields of Cows by Willan's Farm": Thomas Willan of Marylebone (1755–1828)', *Westminster History Review*, 4 (2001), pp. 1–5, gives an account of the life of a leading eighteenth-century dairy farmer near the hill. For the early history of St John's Wood, see Mireille Galinou, *Cottages and Villas: The Birth of the Garden Suburb* (New Haven and London, 2010).

3. A Question of Honour

Modern books on duelling include Robert Baldick, *The Duel: A History of Duelling* (London, 1965); Stephen Banks, *A Polite Exchange of Bullets: The Duel and the English Gentleman, 1750–1850* (Woodbridge, 2010); Richard Hopton, *Pistols at Dawn: A History of Duelling* (London, 2007); James Kelly, *'That Damn'd Thing Called Honour': Duelling in Ireland, 1570–1860* (Cork, 1995); V.G. Kiernan, *The Duel in European History: Honour and the Reign of Aristocracy* (Oxford, 1988); and Markku Peltonen, *The Duel in Early Modern England: Civility, Politeness and Honour* (Cambridge, 2003). See also Robert Shoemaker, *The London Mob: Violence and Disorder in Eighteenth-Century England* (London and New York, 2004). On specific aspects of duelling, see Donna T. Andrew, 'The Code of Honour and its Critics: The Opposition to Duelling in England, 1700–1850', *Social History*, 5 (1980), pp. 409–34; and Antony Simpson, 'Dandelions on the Field of Honour: Dueling, the Middle Classes and the Law in Nineteenth-Century England', *Criminal Justice History*, 9 (1988), pp. 99–155. Among older works are J.G. Millingen, *The History of Duelling*, 2 vols (London, 1841); Lorenzo Sabine, *Notes on Duels and Duelling, Alphabetically Arranged: With a Preliminary Historical Essay* (3rd edn, Boston, Massachusetts, 1859); Andrew Steinmetz, *The Romance of Duelling in All Times and Countries*, 2 vols (London, 1868); and Ben C. Truman, *The Field of Honor: Being a Complete and Comprehensive History of Duelling in All Countries* (London, 1884).

On individual duellists, see, for Hervey Aston, *Memoirs of George Elers: Captain in the 12th Regiment of foot, 1777–1842*, edited by Lord Monson and George Leveson-Gower (London, 1903); for James Macnamara and Robert Montgomery, see *Report of the Trial on an Inquisition, upon a Verdict of Manslaughter against Captain Macnamara for Killing and Slaying Colonel Robert Montgomery* (London, n.d); for Thomas Moore and Francis Jeffrey, see Ronan Kelly, *Bard of Erin: The Life of Thomas Moore* (Dublin, 2008), and Thomas Moore, *Memoirs, Journal and Correspondence of Thomas Moore*, ed. Lord John Russell, 8 vols (London, 1853–56); for Ugo Foscolo, E.R. Vincent, *Ugo Foscolo: An Italian in Regency England* (Cambridge, 1953); and for John Scott and Jonathan Christie, see Andrew Lang, *The Life and Letters of John Gibson Lockhart*, 2 vols (London, 1897). For Lord Byron's involvement with several of the duellists, Leslie A. Marchand, *Byron: A Biography*, 3 vols (London, 1957). Later editions of Byron's *English Bards and Scotch Reviewers* (first published 1809) contain notes on Lord Falkland and Thomas Moore.

See also the Heal Collection of historical cuttings and illustrations, Camden Local Studies and Archives Centre; contemporary newspapers; and *The Proceedings of the Old Bailey, 1674–1913*.

4. The Gorsedd of the Bards

Three excellent books by Ronald Hutton are the basis of all modern study of the Druids: Ronald Hutton, *Blood and Mistletoe: The History of the Druids in Britain* (New Haven and London, 2009); Ronald Hutton, *The Druids* (London, 2007); and Ronald Hutton, *Witches, Druids and King Arthur* (London, 2003). Earlier works on the Druids, T.D. Kendrick, *The Druids: A Study in Keltic Prehistory* (London, 1927), and Stuart Piggott, *The Druids* (London, 1968), are now dated. Richard Hayman, *Riddles in Stone: Myths, Archaeology and the Ancient Britons* (London, 1997), shows how often people have changed their minds about Britain's prehistoric remains. Stuart Piggott, *William Stukeley: An Eighteenth-Century Antiquary* (Oxford, 1950), is a good biography of Kentish Town's most famous archaeologist.

Elijah Waring, *Recollections and Anecdotes of Edward Williams* (London, 1850), is an early account of Iolo Morganwg's life and character; Prys Morgan, *Iolo Morganwg* (Cardiff, 1975), is a short but readable modern biography. Although not published under Iolo's own name, much of William Owen, *The Heroic Elegies and Other Pieces of Llywarç Hen, Prince of the Cumbrian Britons, with a Literal Translation* (London, 1792), is by him. When Iolo published his *Poems, Lyric and Pastoral, in Two Volumes* (London, 1794), he hoped for recognition as the Welsh Robert Burns. Dillwyn Miles, *The Secret of the Bards of the Island of Britain* (Llandybie, 1992) is a history of the Welsh *eisteddfod*. The standard edition of Blake is *William Blake, The Complete Writings of William Blake*, ed. Geoffrey Keynes (London, 1957).

5. Regent's Park

For the history of Regent's Park, see Ann Saunders, *Regent's Park: From 1086 to the Present* (2nd edn, London, 1981); Martin Sheppard, *Regent's Park and Primrose Hill* (London, 2010); and A.D. Webster, *The Regent's Park and Primrose Hill: History and Antiquities* (London, 1911). For John Nash and the genesis of the park, see John Summerson, *The Life and Work of John Nash, Architect* (2nd edn, London, 1980); J. Mordaunt Crook, *London's Arcadia: John Nash and the Planning of Regent's Park*, Soane Lecture, 2000 (London, 2001); and Michael Mansbridge, *John Nash: A Complete Catalogue* (London, 2004). Alan Faulkner, *The Regent's Canal: London's Hidden Waterway* (Burton-on-Trent, 2005), includes the early history of another Nash project. See also James Anderson, 'Marylebone Park and the New Street: A Study in the Development of Regent's Park and the Building of Regent Street, London, in the First Quarter of the Nineteenth Century', unpublished Ph.D. thesis, University of London (1998); and F.H.W. Sheppard, *Local Government in St Marylebone, 1688–1835* (London, 1958).

For specific buildings and areas, see Ann Saunders, *The Regent's Park Villas* (London, 1981); Catherine Jamison, *The History of the Royal Hospital of St Katharine by the Tower of London* (Oxford, 1952), pp. 161–71, and M.H. Port, 'St Katharine's Royal Hospital, London', *The History of the King's Works*, vi, *1782–1851* (London, 1973), pp. 479–80; Guy Meynell, 'The Royal Botanic Society's Garden, Regent's Park', *London Journal*, 6 (1980), pp. 135–46;

and John Oliver and Peter Bradshaw, *Saint John's Wood Church, 1814–1955* (London, 1955). For the origins of the Zoo, Wilfred Blunt *The Ark in the Park: The Zoo in the Nineteenth Century* (London, 1976).

6. *London's Crowning Glory*

Felix Barker and Ralph Hyde, *London as it Might Have Been* (London, 1982), contains a range of megalomaniac but unbuilt plans, including some of those proposed for Primrose Hill. Official patronage of the arts is explored in Holger Hoock, *Empires of the Imagination: Politics, War and the Arts in the British World, 1750–1850* (London, 2010). James Stevens Curl, *The Victorian Celebration of Death* (Thrupp, 2000), is the best general account of nineteenth-century attitudes to death and burial.

Specific schemes are to be found in [James Elmes], *Description of the New Village of Waterloo: Formed into a Limited Number of Allotments for Building, on a Most Enchanting and Salubrious Spot Contiguous to the Regent's Park, near Primrose Hill, in the County of Middlesex* (London, 1816); *Letters and Papers of Andrew Robertson, A.M., Miniature Painter to his Late Royal Highness the Duke of Suffolk* (2nd edn, London, 1897); M.H. Port, 'The Wellington Statue', *The History of the King's Works*, vi, *1782–1851* (London, 1973), and John Martin Robinson, *The Wyatts: An Architectural Dynasty* (Oxford, 1979); *General Cemetery Company for Providing Places of Interment, Secure from Violation, Inoffensive to Public Health and Decency, and Ornamental to the Metropolis*, prospectus, 21 May 1830; and Thomas Willson, *The Pyramid: A General Metropolitan Cemetery to be Erected in the Vicinity of Primrose Hill* (London, 1830). See also, Geoffrey Tyack, *Sir James Pennethorne and the Making of Victorian London* (Cambridge, 1992).

7. *Public Walks*

The *Report from the Select Committee on Public Walks with the Minutes of Evidence Taken before Them* (1833) is the key document on the campaign for parks in the first half of the nineteenth century. For Whig attitudes to life and politics, see Leslie Mitchell, *The Whig World* (London, 2005). The collapse of the parliamentary passage of the North Metropolitan Cemetery Bill can be found in the *Minutes of Evidence Taken at the Bar of the House of Commons in the Matter of an Alteration Not Authorized by the Committee, Having Been Made in the Commons Bill, by Sir Samuel Whalley, a Member of the House, 8 and 13 July 1837*. On another matter of public concern, see Sir Francis Bolton, *London Water Supply*, revised by Philip Scratchley (London, 1888).

For building activities near Primrose Hill, F.M.L. Thompson, *Hampstead: Building a Borough, 1650–1964* (London, 1974); Wilfred Blunt *The Ark in the Park: The Zoo in the Nineteenth Century* (London, 1976); Donald J. Olsen, 'House upon House: Estate Development in London and Sheffield', *The Victorian City: Images and Reality* (London, 1973), ii, pp. 333–57; and Donald J. Olsen, *Town Planning in London: The Eighteenth and Nineteenth Centuries* (New Haven and London, 1982). For a gallant attempt to get Gladstone to buy the Eton and Middlesex Cricket Ground, W.R. Smee, *Primrose Hill Park, Regent's Park and Hampstead Heath* (London, 1873). The maps (1889) produced to go with Charles Booth, *Life and Labour of the People of London*, 9 vols (London, 1892–97), give a snapshot of the social standing of the area around the hill.

See also the Heal Collection of historical cuttings and illustrations, Camden Local Studies and Archives Centre, and contemporary newspapers.

8. Lord Southampton

For the Fitzroy family in general, see Bernard Falk, *The Royal Fitzroys: Dukes of Grafton through Four Centuries* (London, 1950). See also, G.E.C., *The Complete Peerage*, v (London, 1926), 'Southampton, Barony'. Part of the first Lord Southampton's career is traced in Frank Cole, 'Charles Fitzroy at the Wars: The Military Career of the First Baron Southampton', *Camden History Review*, 16 (1989), pp. 14–16. For the third Lord Southampton, see Robert Henrey, *A Century Between* (London, 1937), which focuses on the marriage of Henry Fitzroy and Hannah Rothschild. Niall Ferguson, *The World's Banker: A History of the House of Rothschild* (London, 1998), provides more facts and figures on the relationship. For the third lord's hunting activities, see William C.A. Blew, *The Quorn Hunt and its Masters* (London, 1899); and J.M.K. Elliott, *Fifty Years' Foxhunting with the Grafton and Other Packs of Hounds* (London, 1900). For hunting and aristocratic attitudes in general, F.M.L. Thompson, *English Landed Society in the Nineteenth Century* (London, 1963), is an excellent guide. L.T.C. Rolt, *George and Robert Stephenson: The Railway Revolution* (London, 2009), outlines the arrival of the London and Birmingham Railway in London.

9. The New Park

On nineteenth-century parks in general, see Hazel Conway, *People's Parks: The Design and Development of Victorian Parks in Britain* (Cambridge, 1991); and Hazel Conway, *Public Parks* (Princes Risborough, 1996). For Primrose Hill, see Martin Sheppard, *Regent's Park and Primrose Hill* (London, 2010); Geoffrey Tyack, *Sir James Pennethorne and the Making of Victorian London* (Cambridge, 1992); and A.D. Webster, *The Regent's Park and Primrose Hill: History and Antiquities* (London, 1911). See also Edward Kemp, *The Parks, Gardens etc of London and its Suburbs Described and Illustrated, for the Guidance of Strangers* (London, 1851). For a major new road, see Simon Morris, 'The Marylebone and Finchley Road Turnpike, 1820–1850', *Camden History Review*, 22 (1998), pp. 24–32; for railways, see K.A. Scholey, *The Railways of Camden* (London, 2002).

See also the Heal Collection of historical cuttings and illustrations, Camden Local Studies and Archives Centre, and contemporary newspapers.

10. Across the Hill

For general views from the hill, George Rose Emerson, *London: How the Great City Grew* (London, 1862); Giuseppe Maria Campanella, *An Italian on Primrose Hill: A Narrative* (London, 1875). See also, Frederick Miller, *Saint Pancras Past and Present: Being Historical, Traditional and General Notes of the Parish Including Biographical Notices of Inhabitants Associated with its Topographical and General History* (London, 1874).

For political meetings and activists, Derek Beales, 'Gladstone and Garibaldi', in *Gladstone*, edited by Peter Jagger (London, 1998), pp. 137–56, 264–6; Asa Briggs and John Callow, *Marx in London* (London, 2008); Richard Foulkes, 'Shakespeare and Garibaldi on Primrose Hill', *Camden History Review*, 9 (1981), pp. 13–16; and Nadezhda Krupskaya, *Memories of Lenin* (London, 1970). See also, David Goodway, *London Chartism, 1838–1848* (Cambridge, 1982).

Household Words: A Weekly Journal Conducted by Charles Dickens, Saturday 8 May 1852, has the best description of Chalk Farm Fair. For other visits and visitors, Eleanor Farjeon, *A Nursery in the Nineties* (Oxford, 1935); Charles Lamb, 'Detached Thoughts on Books and Reading', *The Last Essays of Elia* (London, 1833); William Michael Rossetti, *Some*

Reminiscences of William Michael Rossetti (2 vols, London, 1906); and Harriette Wilson, *The Memoirs of Harriette Wilson Written by Herself*, 2 vols (London, 1924).

See also the Heal Collection of historical cuttings and illustrations, Camden Local Studies and Archives Centre; contemporary newspapers; and *The Proceedings of the Old Bailey, 1674–1913*.

11. The Martian Invasion

I.F. Clarke, *Voices Prophesying War, 1763–1984* (Oxford, 1966), is an elegant account of British paranoia over two hundred years. Austin Gee, *The British Volunteer Movement, 1794–1814* (Oxford, 2003), shows how vigorously the British reacted to the threat of French invasion. Roy Allen, 'Napoleon's First Invasion Threat: The Proposed Northern Line of Defence round the Capital', *Camden History Review*, 12 (1984), pp. 24–26; and Roy Allen, 'The Hampstead and Highgate Citadel: Defence Plans against Napoleon', *Camden History Review*, 10 (1982), pp. 7–9, give specific local defence plans. George Tomkyns Chesney, *The Battle of Dorking* (London, 1871), is the most famous conventional invasion fantasy. See also, Keith Wilson, *Channel Tunnel Visions, 1850–1914* (London, 1994). *Roger Fenton: Photographer of the 1850s* (London, 1988), reproduces a selection of Fenton's photographs of the Crimean War.

For H.G. Wells, see Michael Sherborne, *H.G. Wells: Another Kind of Life* (London, 2010); and H.G. Wells, *Experiment in Autobiography: Discoveries and Conclusions of a Very Ordinary Brain (since 1866)* (London, 1984). Wells's teaching career is described in Ann Thwaite, *A.A. Milne: A Biography* (London, 1991). Apart from *The War of Worlds* (1898), Wells's main other scientific fantasies are *The Time Machine* (1895); *The Island of Doctor Moreau* (1896); *The Invisible Man* (1897), *The First Men on the Moon* (1901); and *The World Set Free* (London, 1914). On the invention of the atomic bomb, see Richard Rhodes, *The Making of the Atomic Bomb* (New York, 1986).

12. The Impact of War

Donald Gray, *Percy Dearmer: A Parson's Pilgrimage* (Norwich, 2000), and Geoffrey Dearmer, *A Pilgrim's Song: Selected Poems to Mark the Poet's 100th Birthday* (London, 1993), provide two angles on one family's experience of the First World War. Five personal files of local officers killed in the First World War are in the National Archives.

Philip Ziegler, *London at War, 1939–1945* (London, 1995), is a good general account. See also C. Allen Newbery, *Wartime St Pancras*, Camden History Society (London, 2006). *The London County Council Bomb Damage Maps, 1939–1945*, edited by Ann Saunders, with an Introduction by Robin Woolven, London Topographical Society Publication, 164 (London, 2005), is a superb resource: its maps show the precise impact of bombing across London. Three articles on local preparations before the war are Robin Woolven, 'Air Raid Precautions in St Pancras, 1935–1945', *Camden History Review*, 16 (1989), pp. 20–5; Robin Woolven, 'Playing Hitler's Game from Fitzroy Road NW1: J.B.S. Haldane, the St Pancras Branch of the Communist Party, and Deep-Shelter Agitation', *Camden History Review*, 23 (1999), pp. 22–5; and Robin Woolven, 'The Belsize Deep Shelter', *Camden History Society Newsletter*, 121 (September 1990), p. 3. J. Barrington-Johnson, *The Zoo: The Story of London Zoo* (London, 2005), recounts the Zoo's experiences in both world wars. Two diaries with excellent accounts of Primrose Hill in the war are Anthony Heap, Diary, London Metropolitan Archives, accession no. 2243; and Harold Danks, Diary, typescript, Royal

Artillery Museum Library, Woolwich, MD/596, accession 1894. Richard Hough, *Other Days Around Me: A Memoir* (London, 1992), has memories of training on and nearby the hill. For his war poetry on Primrose Hill, see Louis Macneice, *Autumn Journal* (1938); and *The Last Ditch* (Dublin, 1940). *Primrose Hill Remembered* (London, 2001) contains memories of the war by Sylvia Ballerini, pp. 49–50; Maureen Hawes, pp. 45–7; and Gwyneth Williams, p. 55. In the Imperial War Museum's Sound Archive are three interviews with those with memories of Primrose Hill during the war: Joan Bouverie-Brine (no. 28596); Charles Pay (no. 27248); and Andrew Sachs (no. 28893).

13. Shakespeare's Oak

For literature and music, consult in the first place John Black's online database, *Regent's Park and Primrose Hill in Literature and Music: A Bibliography*. For images of the hill, Simon Jenkins and Jonathan Ditchburn, *Images of Hampstead* (Richmond-upon-Thames, 1982). For Frank Auerbach, see Catherine Lampert, Norman Rosenthal and Isabel Carlisle, *Frank Auerbach: Paintings and Drawings, 1954–2001* (London, 2001). For photographers, *Roger Fenton: Photographer of the 1850s*, exhibition catalogue (London, 1988); John Hannavy, *Roger Fenton of Crimble Hall* (London, 1975); Gordon Baldwin, *Roger Fenton: Pasha and Bayadère* (Malibu, California, 1996); David Bailey, *London NW1: Urban Landscapes* (London, 1963); and Bill Brandt, *Portraits* (London, 1982).

Novels set around Primrose Hill include Kingsley Amis, *The Folks Who Live on the Hill* (London, 1990); Amanda Craig, *In a Dark Wood* (paperback edn, London, 2001); Ben Elton, *Inconceivable* (London, 1999); Paul Charles, *Last Boat to Camden Town* (London, 1998); Helen Falconer, *Primrose Hill* (London, 1999); Ruth Rendell, *The Keys to the Street* (London, 1996); Dodie Smith, *The Hundred and One Dalmatians* (London, 1956); and Fay Weldon, *Chalcot Crescent* (London, 2009).

14. The Sacred Mount

Primrose Hill Remembered (London, 2001) contains many post-war memories. Amongst them, see Keith and Betty Bird, 'Fireworks on the Hill', pp. 105–6; Hervey Blake, 'Primrose Hill Sit-In', pp. 112–13; Irene Demetriou, 'Buried Treasures', pp. 39–42; Gael O'Farrell, 'Home', pp. 108–9; Jean Rossiter, 'A Sense of Community', pp. 86–9; Valerie St Johnston, 'The Friends of Regent's Park and Primrose Hill', pp. 148–4; and Mary Wylie, 'The Siege and the Oldfield Plot', pp. 103–4. The reports of the Friends of Regent's Park and Primrose Hill are a valuable source for both parks. For accounts of new building since the war, Simon Jenkins, *Landlords to London: The Story of a Capital and its Growth* (London, 1975); Oliver Marriott, *The Property Boom* (London, 1969); and Herbert Wright, *London High* (London, 2006). Keith Thomas, *Man and the Natural World: Changing Attitudes in England, 1500–1800* (London, 1984), accounts for the Romantic enjoyment of hills. The Camden Local Studies and Archives Centre has runs of newspapers for this period and a host of other relevant material.

Index

Burke and Hare, murderers 86

Burkett, John 18

Burnet, Gilbert, bishop 15

Burns, Robert 60

Burton, Decimus 72, 83, 153n., plate 10; Colosseum 72, 153 and n., 217, colour plate 6; Victory Arch, Hyde Park Corner 83, 217, plate 10

Bury, Lancashire 99

Buses 148; General Omnibus Company 148

Bush Inn, Staines 32

Bushy Park 132, 182

Buss, Frances 276

Butt, Clara 211n.

Butterfield, William 223n.

Byron, lady, Anne Isabella (Annabella), née Milbanke 65 and n., plate 8

Byron, George Gordon Noel Byron, sixth lord 37, 38, 40, 42, 43, 63, 65, 138, 234, plate 8; his death 65; his marriage 65; on Druids 65

—, *Childe Harold's Pilgrimage* 40; *Don Juan* 65; *English Bards and Scotch Reviewers* 37, 38n., 42 and n.; 63, 65

Cabbala 238

Caen Wood, *see* Kenwood

Caledonian Asylum 81

Calvert, Felix and Co., brewers 124, 125, 126

Cambrian Society for Dyfed 61

Cambridge, Nicholas, surgeon 12

Cambridge Camden Society 223n.

Cambridge University 116; Trinity College 193n.

Camden, Charles Pratt, first earl of 67

Camden, William 68

Camden Civic Society 231, 233

Camden Council 225 and n., 226, 229, 239

Camden House, Chislehurst, Kent 68

Camden New Journal 241

Camden Town 34, 48, 66, 67, 70, 112, 119, 120, 124, 127, 140, 143, 148, 172, 173, 205, 231; Bayham Street 212; Camden High Street 113; Hamilton Street 173; *see also* Charles, Paul

Camden Town Group 215

Camden Town Underground Station 195

Campanella, Giuseppe Maria 3, 167 and n.; *An Italian on Primrose Hill* 167 and n.; *My Life and What I Learnt in It* 167n.; *Life in the Cloister, in the Papal Court and in Exile* 167n.

Campbell, John, first lord 35n.

Canada 198n.; Vancouver 198n.

Canals, *see* Grand Junction Canal; Grand Union Canal; Regent's Canal

Cancellor, H..L., *The Life of a London Beak* 189n.

Canning, Charles Canning, viscount 145

Canning, George 23n.

Cantelowes, manor 244

Cape St Vincent, battle 33

Carden, George 87, 88, 89, 91; and Francis Goodwin 88; and Kensal Green Cemetery 91; and Thomas Willson 88, 91; General Burial Grounds Association 87, 88

Cardigan, James Brudenell, seventh earl of 47–48

Cardington Cross, Bedfordshire, plate 29

Carey, Henry, *Chrononhotonthologos* 35n.

Carleton, Henrietta 36n.

Carleton, Lieutenant Colonel George 36n.

Carlton House 79

Caroline of Brunswick, queen, wife of George IV 257

Carriages 26, 129, 148, 157

Cars 217, 218, 230, plate 20

Casino, proposed on Primrose Hill 84–5

Castlereagh, Robert Stewart, viscount 23n.

Catherine of Braganza, queen, wife of Charles II 13

Cato Street Conspiracy 98

Cats 35n., 169; Foss 35n.

Cattle 9, 13, 15, 16, 17, 67 and n., 109, 115, 141, 142

Catullus, poet 38n.

Cavendish Rooms, St Marylebone 41

Cecil Sharp 210

Cecil Sharp House 210, 224

Celebrities, modern, in Primrose Hill 239, 240 and n.

Wellington, Arthur Wellesley, first duke
    of 23n., 32n., 71, 79, 80, 81, 82, 83
    and n., 179n., plate 10; Apsley House
    82n.; giant equestrian statue of 82 and
    n., 83 and n., 217, plate 10
Wells, H.G., 181–6, 212, 216n., 218;
    The First Men on the Moon 270; *The
    Invisible Man* 182; *The Island of Dr
    Moreau* 182; *The Time Machine* 182;
    The War of the Worlds 182–6, 218, 235,
    277; *The World Set Free* 186–7
Wells, Isabel 181
Wells, Mary 181
Wells Street, Portland Town 220
Wells Street, St Marylebone 223
Wells Street Church, *see* St Andrew's
Wesleyans 159
West End 17, 23, colour plate 1
West Indies 33, 38, 180; St Domingo 33n.
West London Central Anti-Enclosure
    Association 139 and n.
West Middlesex Water Works 75, 76, 78,
    136, 240, 259; plan for tower of a
    great elevation 91–2; pumping works
    205, 259
Westbourne, river 4
Westminster 8, 9, 10, 50, 66, 78, 127, 140,
    200, 241; King's Mews 89n.; Orchard
    Street 171; palace of 228 and n.;
    Spring Gardens 127; Thorney Island
    8; York Street 140; *see also* Parliament;
    Whitehall
Westminster Abbey 5, 8, 9, 193
Westminster Pier 228n.
Westmorland wrestling, *see* Cumberland
Westway 231
Whalley, Sir Samuel 103; accused of
    altering bill 106–7; unable to prove
    property qualification 261
Wheat Field 14
Whigs 98, 102, 105, 107, 116
Whipsnade Zoo 195
White, John, junior 99
White Hall 245
White House, tavern 11, 12, 14, 15, 18
White House Field 14
White House Mead, field 14

Whitehall 10, 240, 241, 245
Whitsun 109, 156, 164, 165
Whittlebury Lodge, Northamptonshire
    116, 128, 129; fire 130
Whitton 224
Wilberforce, William 60n.
Wildlife and Countryside Act (1981) 3
Wikipedia, wrong about height of
    Primrose Hill 240
Wilkins, William 79
Willan, John 16, 17
Willan's Farm 16
Willesden 118
Willett, William, junior 147; *The Waste
    of Daylight* 147
Willett, William, senior 146, 147
Willett houses 147
William I, king of Prussia 185
William IV, king 85n., 132n.
Williams, Edward, *see* Morganwg
Williams, Gwyneth 197
Williams, Dr John 60
Williams, Rowan, archbishop of
    Canterbury 238n.
Willson, Thomas, 88, 89–91; *The
    Pyramid: A General Metropolitan
    Cemetery to be Erected in the Vicinity
    of Primrose Hill* 89–91
Wilson, Harriette 174 and n., 175; *The
    Memoirs of Harriette Wilson Written by
    Herself* 174n.
Wilson, Lieutenant H.A.C. 188
Wimbledon Common 23n., 48
Winchester Road 224
Winchilsea, George Finch-Hatton, tenth
    earl of 23n.
Windsor 62n., 103, 149, 204; Windsor
    Castle 110
Winsten, Clare 222
Wolfe, General James, statue of 228n.
Wollstonecraft, Mary, 64; *A Vindication
    of the Rights of Women* 64
Wolsey, Thomas, cardinal 245
Wolves 197
Women's Auxiliary Air Force (WAAF)
    202
Wood, Sir Henry 211